FROM BIG BANG TO BAGHDAD

A BRIEF STORY OF THE ORIGIN AND EVOLUTION OF RELIGION

Qazi Ashraf

INDIA • SINGAPORE • MALAYSIA

ISBN 979-8-89067-981-9

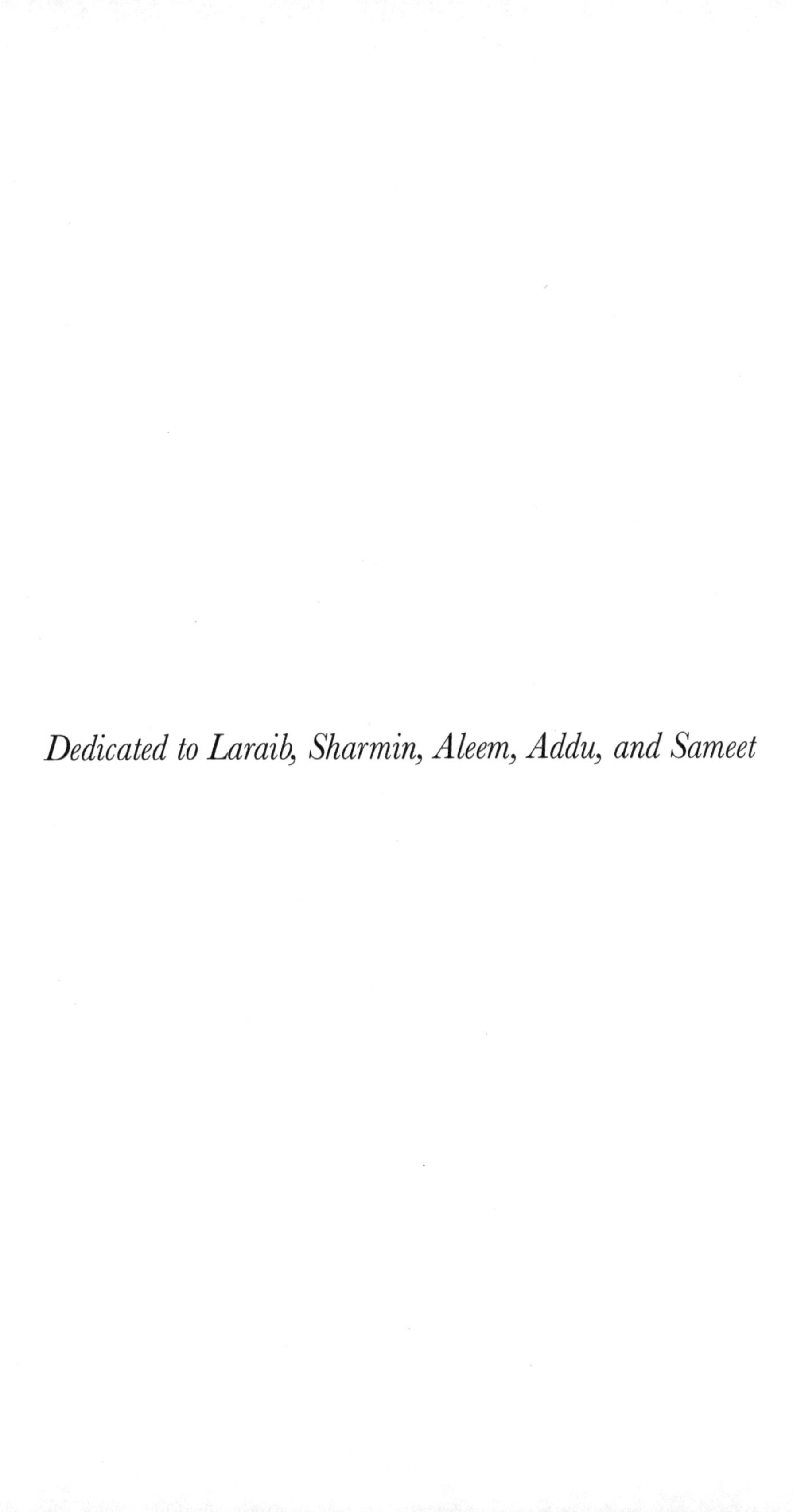

Dedicated to Laraib, Sharmin, Aleem, Addu, and Sameet

Contents

Preface 7

Acknowledgments 9

Part One

The Origin of the Universe and Sacred History

1. The Collision That Birthed Religion 13
2. Fear, Word, and the Sword.......................... 50
3. Mesopotamia - Salt, Marsh, Water, and God.......................... 77

Part 2

India Violence, Sacrifice, and Throes of Ahimsa

4. From Cattle Rustling Aryans to Cow Revering Community 103
5. Buddha or Bhagavad Gita.......................... 143

Part 3

Greek Hegemony and the Birth Pangs of Israel

6. The Mediterranean 175
7. Moses to Midrash 212
8. The End Time and Jesus Christ.......................... 248
9. The Eastern Rome 267

Part 4

The Sands of Arabia – From Caravans to Kingdom

10. The Most Improbable Figure 299
11. The Unanswered Question 321
12. A Flood of Blood 349

Bibliography 399

Preface

There are plenty of books written by scholars of religion and history for scholars. This book is for the lay public. It has taken more than twelve years of research to come up with this book, yet I feel reluctant to call it a piece of scholarship. Simply because I have not followed the standard technical protocol of inserting references in the text. In the end, there is a list of books in the bibliography. These are the sources on which I have heavily relied all along, in addition to articles downloaded from the internet. I have spared the readers from the trouble of sifting through references from journals and magazines and listed only books for further reading for curious readers.

The book is written in simple language. It takes the reader on an intellectual journey through the unbelievable tapestry of the Sacred history. It is a magisterial account of the pains, struggles, humiliations, wars, and bloodbaths that humankind has engaged in during the process of civilization making. From Big Bang to Baghdad is a chronicle of the brutal conflicts that have plagued all the major religions of the world. It is an intricately researched written account of the world and religious history of humankind. The book tries to answer the question that appears at the end of its last chapter: Could human history have been different without religion? It is the answer to this question that takes the reader on a meandering journey through its twelve chapters.

The book doesn't argue in favor of or against any religion. Instead, it brings forth a brief account of the events and circumstances that led, in the first place, to the appearance of Religion. Here the history is traced from the Big Bang to the appearance of the first forms of art and religion (rudimentary) to polytheism and transition to monotheism. Put simply, the book takes the reader on a fascinating journey through the unfolding-over-centuries tapestry of Sacred history and its influence over the civilizational progress of humankind. The story is told in four parts spanning over 12 chapters.

The first three chapters (Part 1) are crucial, though, loaded with technical language. They deal with physical phenomena that led to the formation of the Universe from the Big Bang onward to the evolution and appearance of humans some 13.8 billion years later and 4.5 billion years after the formation of the planet Earth. The second chapter deals directly with the invention of Religion – primarily out of necessity – to handle the Struggle for Survival in an environment red in tooth and claw.

Chapters 4 and 5 (Part 2) examine the formation of religious thought and theocratic polity in ancient Mesopotamia and India simultaneously with the invention of agriculture and, uncomfortable yet necessary, abandonment of the hunter-gatherer lifestyle.

Chapters 6, 7, 8, and 9 (Part 3) briefly bring forth the highlights of the religious-philosophical transformation of the Greeks and the birth of Israel and Judaism – by far the first successful experiment of monotheism – and its continuous refinement under the forces of the genuine history of the ancient Middle East. It was here in ancient Israel that the concept of the Holy War (Jihad) took root and spread out to be institutionalized later by the other two Abrahamic religions – Christianity and Islam. Chapters 8 and 9 deal with the socio-political circumstances that led to the birth of Christianity, its subsequent conquest of the East and West under the auspices of the Roman Empire, and its tussle with Islam.

Chapters 10,11 and 12 (Part 3) trace the historical context in which Islam showed its head in the sands of Arabia and went on to become the dominant creed, wielding immense spiritual and temporal powers over a thousand years. Stunningly Islam touched the zenith of temporal power within only a century after the death of its founder. The most spectacular symbol of its power was the city of Baghdad. Yet the seemingly splendid history of Islam was never so splendid, being overridden by internal schisms and sectoral disharmony, like its two predecessors, leading to a bloodbath on its way to empire formation. Chapter 12 examines the chequered political history of this so-called sophisticated monotheistic creed.

Let's hope the book evokes the interest and curiosity of the readers.

Qazi Ashraf
Srinagar, 29/08/2023

Acknowledgments

For me From Big Bang to Baghdad was a fantastic intellectual journey through the maze of history. And I am confident it will be the same for the readers of this book. During all these years that I spent researching and writing this book, I had tremendously fruitful discussions and deliberations with people from different academic and professional backgrounds. Two persons deserve special acknowledgment: Monica Jeller and Anna Volkin. Monica is an anthropologist who studied in Britain and got especially interested in visual anthropology. She devoted a lot of her time to this book while she was in India and pushed me to the edge to complete the first draft. It was her steadfast nudging that the book got the final shape. Anna Volkin did the editing. She is an erudite editor and doesn't leave a single word unchecked. She would always have queries – queries about everything, dates, names, places, etc., you name it. It was tough to work with her, but in the end, it was rewarding. Thank you, Monica and Anna.

I am grateful to my family and friends, especially Mr M Y Bhat, Adv. Asrar, Dr Saroj and others. Without their encouragement, the book wouldn't have seen the light of the day so soon.

Last but not least I am thankful to the staff at Notion Press for their professionalism and cooperative effort to bring out the book before the readers.

PART ONE

The Origin of the Universe and Sacred History

Chapter – 01

The Collision That Birthed Religion

Religion – the divine origin

The Universe is big. Very big. And old. Roughly 14 billion years old. In comparison, our planet Earth is young. Only 4.5 billion years old. For the best part of more than 4 billion years, Earth was undergoing Evolution. The conditions were harsh. Only rudimentary life forms could exist. The complex Life that Earth is teeming with evolved late, hardly a few million years ago. We humans appeared later, barely some 100-200 thousand years ago. Finally, some 70,000 years ago, the first modern humans started migrating out of Africa, their homeland, to peregrinate far and wide as hunter-gatherers and foragers. It took our ancestors more than 50,000 years of living as hunter-gatherers that they finally stumbled on agriculture. And, only some 12000 years ago, humans began to abandon the hunter-gatherer lifestyle and settle in agricultural communities. That's to say, human civilization, after all, is quite a recent phenomenon when we consider how long Earth has already existed. Civilization is a costly affair and, as such, requires adequate cultural, technological, and societal innovation to get going. By the day modern humans started laying the foundations of civilization; they already possessed the required package of inventions and technologies. One such invention crucial to their success was religion.

Hunter-gatherer communities were comparatively small but well-knit, consisting of extended yet intimately related family groups. Cooperation came easy. In the settled villages, on the contrary, there could well be unrelated strangers living side by side, which was possible only when reasonably high levels of trust and cooperation existed among different groups and individuals. In the book *The Origin of (almost) Everything,* Graham Lawton writes, "In evolutionary biology, trust and cooperation are usually explained in one of the two ways: kin helping each other, and reciprocal altruism, 'you scratch my back, and I'll scratch yours.' But neither of these easily explains cooperation among large groups of unrelated humans. With ever greater chances of encountering strangers, opportunities for cooperation among the kin decline. Reciprocal altruism also stops paying off."

Here religion comes in handy, bonding strangers into shared communities that grow larger with time, surpassing neighboring ones that lack such social glue as religion. The bigger communities expand out and spread, taking their religion to places and obviously, their civilizational tools and technologies. It turns out, contrary to the commonly held notion, religion rather than agriculture created the conditions for village settlements and larger societies, which in turn made the invention of agriculture necessary to feed the people.

When exactly religion appeared or who created religion in the first place is hard to establish with certainty. The most plausible explanation seems that, evolutionarily, humans are "born believers" naturally tipped toward God and religion. The religiously inclined people have no difficulty accepting that God sent religion from time to time to guide the progeny of Adam – the first man created by God. "Evolution," Graham Lawton observes, "has endowed us with a default assumption that everything in our environment is caused by a sentient being." We are more comfortable in assuming that God created everything, religion included. That is a better bet, as the 17th-century French mathematician Blasé Pascal put out in his famous philosophical argument called "Pascal's wager." Most religious people assume that humankind simply couldn't invent religion. Yet, the evidence points more toward religion as one of the countless products of human cognition than of divine origin.

Human cognition was never a fixed thing. It evolved like many other variables as life and life forms attained structural complexity over eons. The evolution and perfection of cognition sparked the invention of religion, like language, art, culture, agriculture, the wheel, etc. Typically when we talk of Evolution, we mean Darwinian Evolution. However, Evolution can be thought of in a broader sense, in which case it has touched everything and put before us the vast Universe with all its diversity and awe-inspiring complexity that fascinates our imagination. How did this all happen? That's a fascinating story in itself.

The Beginning

In the beginning, there was no beginning. In the no-beginning, there was nothing. In the nothing, there became something. That something was small, infinitesimally small, way smaller than the period at the end of this sentence (precisely 1×10^{-33} in size). That is another way of saying: Take 1 gram of a substance. Divide it 10 billion, billion, billion, billion times. Take one part out of this heap of no-things, and that's your Universe – you can call it "Something" - "something out of nothing." It appeared about 13.8 billion years ago, 10^{-43} seconds after Time Zero, in an event we call the "Big Bang," though there was neither a Bang nor anything Big. Rather, Big Bang was a term casually blurted out by Fred Hoyle in a radio talk to ridicule his opponents, particularly George Lemaitre, a Belgian priest and physicist who toyed with the idea of the beginning of the universe. Big Bang simply picked.

Another term often used about the universe is "Singularity." It is the small dense point of distorted gravity, time, space, and energy; all packed together. Because of the ridiculously small size, the Universe of Time Zero is called the "Big Bang singularity." The Big Bang roughly coincides with Time Zero from the point of view of physics. In mathematics speak, though, Time Zero represents a transition point – between real and imaginary times – a moment at which time began flowing. From the Big Bang onward, our "real" time flows forward (arrow of time points ahead), and imaginary time flows backward (arrow of time points back). At Time Zero, everything was held within Singularity. Within a fraction of a second, just 3×10^{-43} seconds, the Universe started expanding at breakneck speed. That was Inflation. Soon inflation ended (at 10^{-33} seconds) leaving the Universe to expand at a much slower rate. That created a universe much smoother than before but far from uniform – with tiny variations and quantum fluctuations. In broad terms, that is to say, specks of matter arose here and there due to the interaction of forces of gravity, quantum state, and thermodynamics. After the expansion of the Universe slowed down, the clumps and specks of matter were stretched further, as if in a matrix of space-time to collide to form blobs. From these clumps, specks, and blobs, stars, planets, and galaxies came into being.

Some blobs came to contain more matter (at that time, it was only hydrogen and helium) and gravity clumped them into bigger objects -

bigger enough that nuclear fusion in their cores made them shining stars. Nuclear fusion happens under extremely high temperatures (10 million degrees Celsius) within the core of the star. Under these temperatures, hydrogen nuclei get crushed to form helium nuclei, releasing energy that is seen as light. The more and faster the fusion happens, the brighter the star, and the hotter its core becomes. In these woefully hot-core stars, further nuclear fusion creates a chain reaction in which helium fuses into carbon, out of which neon, oxygen, silicon, and sulfur are born. Silicon and sulfur fuse and make iron. Here the reaction stops. Iron doesn't fuse further at these temperatures. As a result, the core becomes dense. Gravity squeezes the dense core further, causing tremendous compression of matter. The compression produces heat raising the temperature a bit more - a bit more means a couple of thousand degrees. Eventually, the core collapses under the effect of colossal heat, and the star explodes into space as a Supernova to throw everywhere its debris – practically a flood of neutrons – which condenses under lower temperatures of the surrounding space and forms heavy elements. These flying elements get incorporated into other stars and planets, including Earth. Over billions of years of these Supernova bombardments Earth got all the component matter needed to get things going. But before Earth would be formed, other things needed to happen.

Let me repeat. During the first billion years after the Big Bang, massive concentrations of matter formed. We call them galaxies. There were a hundred billion of them. After nine billion years, our galaxy Milky Way was born and the universe had expanded to a diameter close to 100 billion light years. Hydrogen and helium continued to condense under thermonuclear fusion as clouds of matter in galactic space. Under the gravitational effect, condensed matter collapsed, generating heat and energy, raising the temperature further, and pushing thermonuclear fusion to happen steadily. It was in that brewing confusion, that our Sun, a big and scorching star, shot into existence. The Sun sucked in the surrounding matter leaving behind a part of the matter-cloud - stardust - that gravity shaped into a disc orbiting around this newly born star. The orbiting disc caused the coagulation of the stardust into ever larger clumps and blobs, ultimately shaping them into planets revolving around the Sun. Depending on the distance from the Sun, planets evolved into rocky (for example, Earth), gaseous and icy types.

Which brings us to our Solar System. It began its formal existence 4.56 billion years ago. Earth was nowhere then. Half of Earth only got assembled in the next 10 million years, and in the following 20 million years, it solidified and settled around the Sun. No sooner had it happened than a giant meteorite smashed into Earth, depositing layers upon layers of molten rock on its surface. During the next nearly half a billion years many meteorite bombardments followed. That is to say, in its initial years - the Hadean (hellish) eon - Earth was going through hell. After emerging from this Hellish eon, Earth was no longer a ball of molten rock, yet was nothing like today. It was still in the process of getting shaped into the future Earth. The next half billion years were comparatively better for this yet primitive Earth. There was water interspersed here and there with volcanic eruptions as the first continents were beginning to take shape. They were not the continents that we see today but simply rocky deposits of volcanic granite. Slowly, Earth was stepping into the next eon, the Archean eon. The water on Earth came from different sources across the solar system in bombardments of icy comets and asteroids. As water appeared, Life was bound to start. And, start it did for the first time around 4.1 billion years ago. That is what the chemical signatures of organisms in zircon crystals have revealed recently. However, four billion years ago Earth wasn't still a hospitable place to sustain Life. It didn't even have an atmosphere; leave aside a suitable one for complex life.

Rock, Water, and CO2

How did life, after all, come to occupy every bit of this planet? We don't know each detail, but we know a lot of them. The story of life in the Universe, as, for instance, John Gribbin tells us, is an example of "surface complexity built upon foundations of deep simplicity." We know the four most common reactive elements in the Universe are carbon, hydrogen, oxygen, and nitrogen. The same four elements overwhelmingly contribute to the composition of living things on Earth. Carbon plays a key role in life because of its rich chemistry. It combines with as many as four other atoms at a time, forming rings and chains – organic compounds, for instance.

Recent spectroscopic analysis of the interstellar space material has revealed that it contains many carbon compounds such as methane, carbon dioxide, formaldehyde, ethyl alcohol, and even amino acid Glycine. This eye-opening discovery points to the fact that any or all of this interstellar material is likely to have been present in the matter from which our Solar system was born five billion years ago. The implications of this discovery are humongous for understanding the origin of life. Put simply, amino acids formed over a very long time in the depths of space were brought down to the surface of any young planet like the Earth. And when the Earth is just right, they get the opportunity to organize themselves into living systems.

Long story short, as Graham Lawton concludes in his best-seller book, "the emergence of life is an almost inevitable consequence of the interaction of three essential ingredients of the planetary system: rock, seawater, and carbon dioxide." He explains that rocks in the seabed developed fissures due to underlying pressure forming alkaline hydrothermal vents. Through these vents, CO2 and hydrogen seeped out. They reacted with seawater and minerals, creating complex organic compounds like sugars, amino acids, and even ribonucleic acid (RNA) – the basic building block of life. RNA can act both as protein and self-replicate – the essential prerequisite for qualifying as a living substance. The energy needed by RNA to replicate was supplied by the proton gradient at the mouth of the hydrothermal vent. "One of the best pieces of evidence," Lawton says, "for this crucial step in evolution is that living cells are still powered by the proton gradient across cell membranes." Water, it turns out, occupies the central place in the creation and evolution of life. It may seem like a coincidence, but the truth is that the ancient philosophers rightly intuited that life came from water though they found themselves at a loss to explain how that could happen.

The Greek philosopher Thales of Miletus (today's Turkey), born around 624 BCE, was the first to claim and even try to prove, unsuccessfully though, that all life came from water. His view was upheld by the greats like Aristotle and others who followed him, making it the mainstream Creation Myth. Over time, this Greek myth became the celebrated narrative for more than two thousand years, finding its way into influential religious scriptures like the Bible and the Quran. Aristotle also formalized a model of the Universe based on Anaximander's views, wherein the Earth was the center of the Universe, totally unmoving - also in line with Parmenides, another Greek philosopher who postulated the "static universe" theory that even Einstein feared to transgress - and Sun, the moon, and the stars revolving in the sky along predetermined, fixed paths. According to Aristotle, the Sun, Moon, and stars are nested within invisible crystal spheres and move along trajectories; the Sun is the source of light, and the Moon, the stars, and the planets are lit by reflected light. Gravity pulls everything to Earth and levity acts as a counter force that pulls things away. He surmised that heavy objects would fly off into space if Earth were not the center of the Universe. And, to keep, according to Aristotle, everything in place - that is, spheres within spheres - a greater than levity -and -gravity force powered the whole Universe. He called this force the prime mover. It was this prime mover who gave life to everything there was. In the mind of a religious person, that prime mover is God.

Which brings us back to how Life, after all, began in the first place. For creationists, it is simple – God wanted it. He did it. Period. Religion consistently upholds the infallible view that God created everything. Simultaneously, though, sacred scriptures don't shy away from subscribing to the Thalesian premise that all life came from water – a clear vindication of the influence of Greek thought on the everyday life of ancient and medieval people. Rather than rejecting Thales's views or giving credit to Thales where it belonged to him, the scriptures carried his views as if revealed by God – in a way endorsing Greek thought as an accepted folk wisdom. In Science, contrary to religion, nothing is infallible. Any law, theory, or premise that doesn't corroborate with evidence is mercilessly chopped off and thrown away.

The origin question (of the Universe and life) is fascinating and has given many brilliant minds a headache. Many conjectures, hypotheses, and theories came and went. The question stands where it was despite that many of its details have been untangled conclusively. It is hoped that the creation puzzle will be conclusively cracked in the near future, maybe in the coming decades. Mathematicians, physicists, and astronomers are teaming up with biologists, geologists, paleoanthropologists, and others to do science to solve the riddle of the creation of life. It remains to be seen how religion will face the new challenge posed by 21st-century science. Good luck with it.

To the Big Bang: With it, 13.8 billion years ago, "Deep History" not only happened but also left an imprint. Where did it leave its imprint? Nobody knows where exactly, but it is somewhere here – actually, everywhere – in space, planets, stars, galaxies, black holes, Earth, atmosphere, and so on. We may not be in a position to know, locate, or read every page of the deep history yet, but that doesn't mean it can't be done in the future. The day doesn't seem to be too far when we can perhaps experimentally demonstrate the exact chronology of events that shaped deep history and vice versa. Perhaps it should come as no surprise, then, that the geologists have meticulously pieced together a reasonably magisterial account of the history of Earth from the geological archive – rocks, fossils, water, ice, gases, etc. Even sewer gases have a story to tell the geologist. Given the geological archive comprises practically the tidbits and half-rotten, half-decayed leftovers scattered in the corners and crevices here and there in deeper layers of Earth's crust, it is commendable that the science of geology has been able to connect the dots and put forward a robust body of verifiable data.

Geological Archive and Life

As mentioned a page or two earlier, Earth is a relatively young entrant into the drama of history, formed barely 4.5 billion years ago. In geology speak, Earth's history spans four *Eons* – Hadean, Archean, Proterozoic, and Phanerozoic. This division into Eons is based on a geological principle called the "principle of faunal succession," coined by an eighteenth-century British surveyor and geologist, William Smith. He was the first to note a peculiarly consistent ordering of fossils in the sections of rocks he and others studied. When "something new," say, a fossil, "appears in the geologic archive, it marks a new phase of history," Smith observed. Using faunal succession alongside modern techniques of dating Earth's history can be divided into definite slices: Eons, Eras, Periods, Epochs, and Ages. The Hadean (hellish) was the dark, dead, and burning phase. The next Eon – the Archean – commenced when the first Life appeared some five hundred million years after the formation of Earth (i.e., four billion years ago). The Archean Life was essentially single-celled, from which *Prokaryotes* (the bacteria and the archaea) evolved. The prokaryotes have no separate nucleus and survive on chemical energy derived from the depths of the ocean or sunlight. It is a simple life, recognizable.

The Archean Eon lasted for about a billion years. By that time another new event took place. Cyanobacteria, or the blue-green algae, emerged on the scene through an evolutionary jump heralding the third or Proterozoic Eon. The Proterozoic organisms (cyanobacteria) possessed an improved set of tools for trapping sunlight and converting it into energy for their living. That is to say, they could do *Photosynthesis* to meet their nutrient demands. One billion years of natural selection had pushed these organisms a step ahead of their ancestors, the Prokaryotes. Unfortunately for them, *Photosynthesis* came at a cost. It produced Oxygen as a by-product. Oxygen turned out to be a highly toxic waste and there accumulated so much of this waste product, Oxygen, that the Earth became saturated, the excess flowing into the atmosphere. This is known as the *Great Oxidation Event.* Huge quantities of Oxygen manufactured through cyanobacterial photosynthesis intoxicated the Earth and its primitive atmosphere so much that almost all Life was wiped out.

With Oxygen everywhere and practically no carbon dioxide (CO2) left around to cause a greenhouse effect, the temperature on Earth fell steeply. But that wasn't all. There was more to come. Oxygen combined with methane, rarefying the primitive atmosphere to the extent that no scope for the greenhouse effect was left. The atmospheric temperature plunged further, and the Earth headed into a catastrophe – the Ice Age – that lasted half a billion years. All that simple life that barely survived the initial Great Oxidation Event came to a standstill. Photosynthesis completely stopped. Now, at last, CO2 began accumulating. Slowly. After millions of years, when CO2 gathered in sufficient quantities to cause a greenhouse effect, the atmospheric temperature rose a bit, just enough for the melting of ice. As the ice melted, life rebounded. Once again, the Oxidation Event took place. Thankfully, this time enough ozone had accumulated, which established a protective layer that helped maintain a greenhouse effect mitigating the precipitous fall in the atmospheric temperature. As a result, the second Oxidation Event couldn't prove as catastrophic as the first. The ozone-induced greenhouse effect kept the atmospheric temperature stable enough for Life to continue and evolve. Life gave to the atmosphere capacity, over the next three billion years, to slowly attain the composition of gases we have today.

Had Evolution not invented a mechanism called respiration to utilize Oxygen, the Earth probably would have been left barren and frozen into a snowball. Respiration permanently changed the entire equation of Life on Earth. Life, in turn, created a favorable crust, atmosphere, and ecology of Earth for more Life to follow.

Now with respiration in place and under favorable circumstances, oxygen became an excellent energy source for a new set of life – *Eukaryotes* – that evolved to utilize this toxic gas. That was Proterozoic Eon. Eukaryotes were definitely ahead of prokaryotes. Natural Selection gave them a better tool kit called "Nucleus," which housed chromosomes – the information reservoir of the cell and the organism. Chromosomes carry genetic material or DNA that holds genes and proteins. The information contained in the chromosomes is transmitted to the next generation through a process called cell division. It is a complex energy-requiring process. Eukaryotes had to manufacture enough energy to carry on cell division and passage of information to the next generation. How could they do that? Natural Selection came to their rescue. They had evolved enough to retain through endosymbiosis prokaryotes, their ancestors, as powerhouses called *Mitochondria.* These powerhouses manufacture energy by utilizing Oxygen from the environment. The manufactured energy (stored as adenosine triphosphate, ATP) is used for running life's complex tasks.

While all this Evolution of life was happening, it was impacting Earth which was also changing - its crust was becoming cooler and more rigid in consistency to accommodate more and more new forms of life.

Nearly four billion years into Earth's age, an event called the Cambrian Explosion occurred. With it, the Earth's history transitioned from the Proterozoic into the last Eon called Phanerozoic Eon (we live in this Eon, which is to say, it is barely 500 million years old). In this Eon, multicellular organisms evolved. A remarkably diverse array of life forms like insects, worms, corals, marine and terrestrial animals, and plants successively appeared on the scene, exhibiting a relatively quick transformation in the geological archive. It is a quick transformation of the fossil record that took merely 70 to 80 million years to happen – a bitsy period on a Geologic time scale.

What is Life?

How did complex life-forms evolve from simple one-celled life? It turns out that the *Great Oxidation Event* changed the entire equation by pushing the Oxygen levels across a critical point. That is to say, when an environment with abundant Oxygen became available, Evolution drove the once simple Life to adapt to this toxic gas and utilize it for some good purpose, i.e., energy production. Once that happened, - and given the abundance of Oxygen in the environment -, it was cheaper to manufacture big energy using Oxygen. Big energy could then be easily and efficiently utilized to undertake more complex functions – like processing and passing information to the next generation that requires humongous amounts of energy in the form of ATP. As the information could be passed on to the next and next, and so on, generations, the scope for errors, mutations, and genetic mistakes, as well as improvements, selections, and adaptations, increased. The evolutionary process of Natural Selection facilitated the appearance of new and improved life forms. Slowly, many entirely new life forms and species sprang out following millions of years of reproductive cross-over and hybridization.

After all, what is Life? Two of the world's most influential minds, Simon Lewis and Mark Maslin, answer: Life is simply a collection of entities that undergo Evolution, grow, and reproduce, passing copies of information to the next generation. The colossal energy requirement for information processing, transcribing, and transferring could only be met with adequate amounts of Oxygen.

Which brings me back to the Phanerozoic Eon. We live in the Cenozoic era of this Eon that began some half a million years ago. The Paleozoic (200 million years) and, the Mesozoic (250 million years) eras of the current Eon (Phanerozoic) saw many upheavals and transformations. During the Paleozoic Era, only ancient and simple life forms thrived. Climatic upheavals from volcanic eruptions, tectonic movements, meteorite strikes, methane release, and increased carbon dioxide killed much of life. Whatever survived the relentless and merciless assault of natural phenomena had to adapt to changed conditions.

Life then entered the Mesozoic Era which saw the appearance of dinosaurs and other reptiles – hugely complex and sturdy life forms. That is the era when rifts in the Earth deepened; Continents and smaller land masses began drifting away; and a gigantic meteorite hit modern-day Mexico, causing horrendous volcanic eruptions to eliminate much of the life from the Earth's surface. Dinosaurs became completely extinct.

It took sixty-six million years for Life to creep in again slowly and catch real pace in the third and final era – the current or the Cenozoic, also called the Era of Mammals. The dinosaurs were gone, and life saw unexpected diversity (post the enormous trauma and loss): mammals and flowering plants sprang up from everywhere to fill and feed on the vastness of the Earth.

The geological record of Life now shows the Age of Fish (*Cambrian*), followed by the Age of Reptiles, and then by the Age of Mammals up to its culmination – the Age of Humans or the God species!

Which brings me, meanderingly, back to History. The planet Earth holds within its layers of dust and debris scattered pages of the Book of

Life that keep the secret of how History happened over eons, eras, and ages. Nowadays, History is being revealed as never before. The revelations are happening fast, aided by scientific advances. The accumulating data, which is huge, has the real, *real*, potential of endangering the whole edifice of knowledge and understanding that humans have so far held infallible.

Consider the Genome-wide Ancient DNA Project. Its revelations about human ancestry, racial make-up, and migrations have rattled far-right nationalists and populist groups who hold on tenaciously to their unfounded, mythical, and outrageously supremacist narratives. Turns out, the human species emerged in Africa and spread in all directions thenceforth. DNA study is enabling detailed reconstruction of deep relationships amongst ancient human populations. "Human genome project has surpassed the traditional toolkit of archeology in what it can reveal of changes in human populations in the deep past," writes David Reich, founder of the ancient DNA laboratory at Harvard, in his book *Who We Are and How We Got Here*. The DNA bombshell has upended many myths, half-truths, and pseudoscience, and is expected to uproot many more unfounded yet celebrated narratives in decades to come. Will the revelations of hard science ultimately lead to rethinking, redefining, or even permanently shifting the paradigm for the better? Or, will they lead to ultimate frustration, chaos, and misunderstanding, thus paving the way for unseen violence? It can be both. Perhaps.

The second outcome is not surprising, if it happens, given that violence has been a companion of history ever since life took root. One may disagree with Thomas Hobbes's premise that "violence is deeply ingrained in human nature," nonetheless, he does have a point. How far his conclusions are relevant in our postmodern, post-human world is a matter of debate.

Take Harvard psychologist Steven Pinker. In his book *Enlightenment Now*, he brilliantly demonstrates - elaborating on Hans Rosling's work published in book form titled *Factfulness* - that baring a few unpleasant events happening of late on the world scene, tremendous good has touched human life, especially over the last seven decades. Pinker took the world almost by surprise when he enumerated how much improvement humanity has seen in nearly every aspect, from reason, science, and humanism to progress. The indices for violence, disease, and death have remarkably improved. The violence, though, hasn't wholly vanished (Hobbes can't be trounced). But then that's how our world works. Tides may turn, anytime.

To avoid the unwanted fall outs of escalated violence, humankind has no options other than to shift the paradigm. The truth is that without violence the world is unimaginable. What we can try, though, is to aim at keeping violence at an acceptably low level.

First Humans Arrive on the Scene

With the commencement of the Phanerozoic Eon half a billion years ago, higher-order living organisms – plants and animals – began to appear on the Earth. Their appearance was made possible by the preceding four billion years of Natural Selection, which got elementary chemical molecules slowly and steadily organized along the evolutionary path. The crowning moment of this evolutionary process was the emergence of the hominins. When humans (*Homo sapiens)* exactly appear along this trajectory is hard to say with certainty, but rough estimates fall within 300,000 and 200,000 BCE.

Ten million years ago - i.e., during the Miocene epoch of the *Cenozoic* era in which we currently live - severe climate change hit Africa, Asia, and parts of Europe, almost wiping out ape populations in these regions. Only one African ape lineage survived the catastrophe. Two million later, the gorilla lineage emerged. Another 2 million years down the line (i.e., around 6 million BCE), an ape lineage called the *Last Common Ancestor* (LCA) diverged from the parent ape family. It was this LCA that, according to evolutionary biological evidence, gave rise to modern humans and chimpanzees. Since *Homo sapiens* (modern humans) share biological, genetic, and socio-ecological traits with apes, they are called the "great ape family." Surprisingly, and perhaps ironically, humans are much closer genetically to the chimpanzee than the gorilla or the orangutan.

The biologists call the great ape family, which includes humans, the *hominid* family (its members are called *hominins*).

Around 1.8 million years ago, *Homo erectus,* appeared on the scene and continued to exist until sixty thousand BCE - the longest surviving hominins that dominated the scene. These bipedal apes (they walked on hind legs) spread out of Africa into Eurasia. They possessed bigger brains and used primitive stone tools. Around 60,000 years ago, they vanished. Probably - but not necessarily - Archaic Humans who had emerged in Africa around 1.3 million years after they eliminated them.

The first archaic humans that showed up on the scene are called *Homo hidelbergensis*. They possessed bigger brains than *Homo erectus and* made better tools and thus could easily outmaneuver the latter. H. hidelbergensis didn't stay in Africa for long. They also migrated out of Africa into Europe where they evolved into *Homo neanderthalensis* (or simply the Neanderthals), adapting to living in the cold climate and high-altitude habitats of Europe during the glacial epoch or Ice age (*Pleistocene* or 6th epoch of the Cenozoic era). The Ice Age lasted from 2.6 million BCE to 11,700 BCE. The epoch in which we now live is sometimes called the seventh or *Holocene* epoch of the Cenozoic era. It began 11,700 years ago when the climate became warmer, leading to an "interglacial period."

The Neanderthals were bodily short and stout. Their body habitus helped them minimize heat loss in the cold climates of Europe to the extent that these archaic humans could comfortably roam almost all of Europe and Eurasia hunting and foraging in open lands and the wild. In all, they inhabited Europe for 250,000 years – a pretty good chunk of time on the evolutionary Time Scale – during which no rivals could stand up to their might.

But then, history, as we know, takes no sides. It respects power. The Neanderthals were mighty creatures, but their power and might pale before the brain power of the new entrants into the scene. Somewhere between 300,000 to 200,000 years ago, another transformation took place in the hominid family in the same African landscape where earlier hominins had appeared. This time, archaic humans evolved into *Homo sapiens,* or the anatomically modern humans (AMH). Little did the Neanderthals know that the new entrants, AMH, would not only redefine power but reset the power equation to their liking.

These newcomers had better and bigger brains (especially the Frontal lobes of the brain) but comparatively less robust and hairless bodies than the archaic humans. There were not a lot of them to begin with. Quite a few. The genetic evidence (mitochondrial DNA analysis) tells us that a meager number of females (in all 5,000) have contributed to the origin or the gene pool of the entire human population. The first humans, a few thousand in number, perhaps enjoyed life in the vastness of Northeast Africa, devouring the abundance of nature and increasing their population exponentially. The resulting population explosion ultimately compelled some to seek food sources outside the African jungles and plains.

Finally, 70,000 years ago, around four thousand modern humans (AMH) moved out of Africa and passed along the shore of the Red Sea to find themselves in what is now the Middle East. They couldn't take a northern route to Europe probably because of the fear of the Neanderthals out there. The southern route brought them to the Arabian Peninsula which they made their home. It was from this "second home" along the south coast of Arabia that the subsequent batches of migrants spread out to finally reach India (55000 years ago), Europe (40000 years ago), America (15000 years ago), and Australia. Wave upon wave, the migration continued out of Arabia until the rest of the world was populated. Like it or not, the DNA analysis traces our origin from Africa to Arabia. We are migrants at our core descended from beduins, if you like. The environment shaped out color and phenotype in such a way that we forgot our origins and divided ourselves into proud races and nationalities, perpetually at war with one another.

Walkers, Makers, and Thinkers

If the Israeli historian Yuval Noah Harari is to be believed then it was primarily humans who displaced the Neanderthals, the undisputed masters of Europe, forcibly interbreeding with some, slaughtering others, and pushing the rest eventually to the brink, leading thereby to Neanderthals' extinction - all blame rests on Europeeans' ancestors' shoulders. They are guilty and their progeny, the modern-day Europeans should collectively seek atonement for their ancestors' sins. However, to Harari and his likes' chagrin, there is not a shred of evidence, archeological or otherwise, to support their claim except, of course, the argument made popular by H G Wells in his famous 1922 book, *A Short History of World*. Well's argument picked and refused to die down even though the world of knowledge transformed exponentially since then. The discipline of Geology progressed, and so did Science at breakneck speed. The undeniable truth is that by 28,000 BCE, Neanderthals had become completely extinct. Not a single soul was alive. All they left was traces of their story in archives of Earth that we dug out 30,000 years later in the Neander valley, hence the name Neanderthals. A chunk of their genes also remained well preserved in the gene pool of the immigrant hordes – the modern Europeans – who usurped their habitat. Nature has its way of keeping memories alive.

How did humans, bodily less robust, and at the bottom of the food chain to start with, requiring at least 20 years of protective care to develop into productive adults, jump to the top of the food chain? How could they displace – to believe Harari's story ethnically cleanse – the 250,000-year-old masters of Europe and also control other continents?

The four crucial achievements of Natural Selection that made this bare-bodied, helpless AMH species master of the Earth are *bipedalism, tools, brain size*, and *culture.*

Only humans exhibit strict bipedalism. All other apes are essentially "knuckle-walkers," though they can walk upright for short distances. They climb trees and heights deftly using all four in a coordinated manner but they are not as good long-distance runners as humans are. Knuckle-walking doesn't ensure them access to distant food sources as quickly as bipedalism (walking upright for long distances) does to walkers. Besides making humans efficient runners, bipedalism, by significantly increasing their horizontal and vertical fields of vision, allowed humans to survey larger areas for food and screen wider spaces for the presence of predators. Yet for one, bipedalism alone wasn't enough for AMH to score the decisive victory over hominin and animal competitors.

Tools supplanted bipedalism. Together they helped AMH to fare well in the struggle for survival. Tools no doubt helped modern humans to kill and cut better, but archaic humans also used tools. Even crows and chimpanzees can make primitive tools, but tool-making didn't make the crows kings, at least bird kings. And chimpanzees - they are where they were millions of years ago. Subsisters. Not masters. Arguably humans made better tools than the archaics, primates, and crows. True. But, it raises the question: How could humans make better tools from the same raw material available in abundance to archaic humans and others as well? We will come to this question but first this: *Homo erectus* was adept at long-distance running, hunting, and using good stone tools. They roamed the Earth for 2 million years. Quite a time! They even domesticated fire, obtaining it from wildfires and then maintaining and using it for cooking to get a better caloric supply from the foods. Yet, despite being good toolmakers and food eaters, they never rose to the apex. Eventually, they succumbed to the pressure of natural selection.

The significant evolutionary transformation that tipped the balance in hominins' favor (and ultimately in AMH's) was their progressively increasing brain size over 6 million years since their appearance. First, *Homo habilis* saw a significant (as compared to animals) increase in brain size, followed by the archaic humans. Finally, a rapid size increase occurred in the brains of the AMH (anatomically modern humans). The curious thing about brain growth was that it was not a mere linear growth in the size of the brain; instead, it was differential. Some specific brain areas grew more than others, which made all the difference. In terms of the overall brain size, *Homo erectus* and *Homo neanderthalensis* don't differ strikingly from *Homo sapiens (AMH),* yet when you consider the frontal lobes of the brain - yes. That changes everything.

Neanderthals' occipital lobes (the back portion of the brain), were better developed than humans'. Their skull took a peculiar shape to accommodate the extra-sized lobe. The well-developed occipital lobes of the Neanderthal brain were a terrific evolutionary adaptation to handle the poor visibility due to the low sunlight levels at high altitudes of Europe - a clear advantage in evolutionary terms Yet this advantage came at a price. The Neanderthal frontal brain remained smaller. In comparison, the AMH brain is endowed with a more considerable frontal portion at the cost of other areas. As a consequence eyesight, smell, or hearing are compromised, but "thinking"? You are right, no. Thinking is beyond compromise.

The bigger and better frontal lobes allowed AMH, and still do, to engage in abstract thinking. They could do things within their minds. This power of abstract thought and imagining, called "mentalization," lets the "cumulative culture" (the storage, transmission, and expansion of knowledge) happen.

The historian Yuval Harari emphasizes that since humans could cooperate, they could quickly jump to the top of the food chain and become apex predators. However, that's only half of the story. All animals cooperate, they hunt in groups, they maintain animal communities, and some even play politics, as the primatologist Jane Goodall conclusively documented in chimpanzees and other primates. What these lower animals, primates, apes, and archaic humans couldn't do, though, was establish "cumulative culture." One of the reasons that prevented them from doing so was a less evolved frontal brain coupled with higher levels of circulating testosterone (male sex hormone) in their bodies. The higher circulating level of male sex hormones in their bodies makes them exquisitely prone to "reactive violence."

Humans produce comparatively lower amounts of testosterone, facilitating social tolerance, living in larger groups, and establishing a cumulative culture. The cumulative culture, in turn, permits valuable cooperation. The cumulative culture was possible when humans possessed the requisite evolutionary brain hardware to imagine, simulate, plan, and draw futurist strategies and even assess the possible outcomes – all in their minds. The well-developed frontal brain made that possible. Mentalizing allowed them to view cooperation as a logical necessity, rather than an instinctive reaction, to direct targeted violence on others in a systematic and organized manner. Cooperation alone, devoid of conscious awareness, didn't help animals rise the ladder from subsisters to masters; neither could it have helped humans. Logical cooperation and cumulative culture did. And culture is a remarkable product of "thought."

Cumulative Culture and Sacred History

With cumulative culture already in place, some 70,000 years ago, the first batch of humans set out to emigrate out of the African Rift Valley in search of food and fodder. Eventually, humans came to settle in all corners of the Earth. The first batch would hardly have thought that this small step would prove a giant leap that would take human culture to great heights of complexity. With this small step of great migration, the seeds of the "sacred history"* were sown far and wide.

What exactly led to the making and shaping of Sacred history? Was it the result of a "quantum leap" of consciousness – a cognitive revolution? And if so, was this cognitive quantum leap a sudden occurrence or a protracted process – a consequence of cumulative knowledge gained through successive periods of historical time coupled with a slow process of accumulating beneficial "variations" (as Darwin would have it in Evolution of life) over millions of years?

By the way, "cognitive revolution" is a catchy phrase. It has created a lot of buzz in academia, enthusing Humanities disciplines (e.g. history, archeology, philosophy, anthropology, etc.) to study their fields more or less like biological sciences. With the increased availability of modern research tools, these disciplines are becoming increasingly technology-dependent. Unfortunately, the quick and unexpected proliferation of technology has a shady side. The more the communication technology proliferates, the more the educated class transmogrifies into a purely professional labor class. Glamor and quick wealth acquisition have created a widespread public indifference toward scientific inquiry. Some quarters under the garb of nationalism compel science to conform to their politico-religious agendas. In the age of Google, WhatsApp, and Facebook, pseudoscience is fast spreading, even taking over hard science. That's a matter of concern.

**(The dictionary definition of Sacred History is history that is retold to instill religious faith, which may or may not be founded on the fact. However, throughout this book, the phrase "sacred history" is used to mean history shaped directly or indirectly by religious impulses)*

Back to the cognitive revolution. It has tremendously helped the human species to come out as a winner in the struggle for survival. With well-developed frontal lobes, the human brain is better positioned to register, learn, remember, and accumulate information about the environment and respond to the surrounding environment accordingly. Humans were weaklings in the ruthless world of apes, predators, and other big-bodied animals of Africa. They could either leave things at the mercy of the environment risking losing the battle for survival, or they could use the cunning of their mind and devise ingenious defensive and offensive strategies to hold their ground. They chose the latter. It was a do-or-die situation. Humans, in contrast to other creatures that remained wedded to instinctual behavior - fight or flee, handled innovatively a world filled with ruthless competition and constant danger lurking on all sides. Imagine – by the way, only humans can imagine things – when our ancestors lived in open spaces, deserts, or forests, with a limited defensive arsenal in their possession, perhaps only a primitive set of tools made of wood, flint, or stone, they would be on their toes, perpetually fearful of the surrounding environment full of ruthless, unkind, cruel, and dangerous predators, skulking carnivores, or other humanoids. For a moment, slide back mentally into those "good old" historical times and ask yourself: What kind of life early humans were living?

For them surviving was struggling against the seen and the unseen, and the known and the unknown. It was a struggle against the darkness of the night and the light of the day - a never-ending, perpetual battle against everything and everybody. The nighttime particularly increased manifold the odds of being suddenly charged upon by predators from any corner. It would simply be a matter of luck – tremendous luck to live to see another day of life. The fear of death and the uncertainty of life loomed from all sides. And, it was precisely this perpetual fear coupled with the uncertainty that ultimately led to the invention of religion and the creation of what we call the Sacred history of humankind. Who else could invent abstract things if not a Frontal-brained, thinking species like Homo sapiens?

The invention and subsequent evolution of sacred history has undoubtedly been a long, drawn-out stepwise process. The "which led to what" cascade of steps is often difficult to trace in sacred history precisely because its deep past has left behind an indistinct, nay an imperceptible, wake. Identifying the exact sequence of the events, and reconstructing the whole story, to trace the birth and evolution of the sacred history is hard to do, given how difficult it is to decipher the deep history. If future technology helps overcome the difficulty of probing the deep history deeper than we can at the moment, that will be an ultimate feather in the cap of human intellect – a gratifying moment given the complexity of the task.

With "genuine history," things are comparatively more straightforward than Sacred history though not entirely unproblematic. The leftover evidence of genuine history is more abundant and ubiquitous. That, however, doesn't mean that interpreting this data is easy. The mute remains – rocks, artifacts, and layers of dead tissue and fossils – are a "read-only" script that requires smart deciphering first and accurate corroboration and correlation next. That is hard. There are empty spaces, gaps, and deficiencies in archeological and geological archives. Gaps need to be filled. And it is during this process of filling in the blanks that trouble arises. History becomes infested with bias. It turns out that, to borrow Will Durant, most of history is guessing, and the rest is prejudice.

History-telling is story-telling. Stories replace facts, and fiction becomes faith. Not always. But quite often. Hard history is as good a science as Biology. Yet, as observed by Will Durant in *The Lessons of History*, unfortunately, history usually is "beclouded by ambivalent evidence and biased historians, and perhaps distorted by our own patriotic or religious partisanship." By nature, humans love stories – stories that stir emotion. The more the stories tickle emotion, the more they power the narrative. Eventually, history is transformed into a living philosophy – not a text of biology – that stirs the passions of the human species. In truth, story, emotion, and narrative are extrinsic to history, and should not - ideally - bemire history. Yet, they get laid over the facts. The mute rocks and fossils are – well, mute. When history-makers and history-writers add the above extrinsic characteristics to the fossilized past, history becomes laden with all types of biases, some intentional and some unintentional. Deep history is more problematic than the recorded history of the recent past. The gaps in the sources leave a vast scope for getting overfilled or underfilled depending on which direction the wind is blowing.

Nonetheless, there is no dearth of hard data and evidence on Deep history that can tumble many a myth down to rubble. The same doesn't hold for sacred history. Sacred history is more challenging to handle objectively given the paucity of hard data and fossilized evidence. Sacred history (religion) has mostly survived and propagated in the deep past as oral tradition, leaving no written records. All the same, it is pretty intriguing and, well, exciting to explore sacred history despite the limitations it poses. Proper exploration aids in introspection.

For one thing, Sacred history is cognition-dependent and draws much of its strength from human imagination than from factual evidence. Cognition, as we know, is directly proportional to the size and architectural complexity of the brain (particularly the frontal lobes). Well-developed frontal lobes allow us to engage in abstract thinking or imagining – a unique feature that differentiates *Homo sapiens* from other species - wherein lies the secret of our success as a species. Yet the undeniable scientific fact is that our big frontal lobes bring to the fore a subtle yet significant pitfall, which we almost invariably ignore: at the fundamental level, our brain doesn't distinguish between the real and the imaginary - a fallacy that has cost us dearly in terms of blood and flesh, as we shall talk about later.

Our brain can be thought of as hardware and the mind as software. The brain holds pictures and words as memory files, and the mind, like computer software, plays out these pictures and words on our mental screen as successive movies, kind of. These movies, we call thoughts. We can have thoughts about real things or imaginary ones. It doesn't matter to our brain when it comes to reacting to such thoughts. We look, say, at our favorite food, our mouth waters. Or we think about our favorite dish and our mouth waters. Two types of stimuli bring out an identical result. Fundamentally, our brain ignores the difference between the real and the imaginary. It reacts to thoughts (pictures and word movies). The repetitive playing of thoughts, as we follow and carry them out, creates patterns in us - our habits, beliefs, perspectives, and paradigms. These patterns then play out on autopilot – once set in place, the software automatically generates the same sequences repeatedly. That is how over time beliefs get established and firmly entrenched. In one of my previous books, *Open Secret – A Giant Leap to Success, Prosperity, and Peace,* I dealt with belief formation in detail. Beliefs don't need to be realistic. They can be far removed from reality. Religious beliefs belong to this category. Some religious belief patterns can be outrightly dangerous.

Sense of Safety –A Key to Success

Our story is interesting. We are bodily weak. A newborn is entirely helpless; it needs constant care and protection for years, in contrast to the offspring of other species, which are mostly fully formed and mature at birth. As infants and children, we are powerless creatures. We require a long learning time to become livable and useful adults. And still, in our brute nature, we as a species survived the hardships, calamities, and merciless disasters that made many living species extinct. Life in modern times has become far smoother and easier to live. That was not always the case. We have come a long way and our perspective is so transformed that most of us have a hard time imagining how difficult life was for our ancestors. But that was that.

What we are today is a result of the cumulative legacy of thousands of years of sacrifice and forbearance of our ancestors through the ruthless circumstances of the past. We carry that imprint of struggle - that fear, that uncertainty, that anxiety, etc. in our genes and blood - that our ancestors went through in an environment of "kill or get killed." They perpetually found themselves at the edge of uncertainty. They lived in a state of heightened awareness about their surroundings. A tiger, a cobra, or a pack of hyenas could be creeping in the nearby bushes; any misstep and you end up as lunch for the hungry predator. The nighttime particularly would be horrifying koshmar to live amid dangerous predators.

Living in a precarious situation is a trial for the weak. When it is impossible to fight back the enemy, the weak invent novel methods to ensure their safety or a "sense of safety." The "state of safety" and the "sense of safety" are two different things. The former is a real or temporal phenomenon implying the relative absence of threat. In contrast, the sense of safety is merely a concept with no temporal existence, neither in the brain, mind, body nor in the surrounding environment. It is purely a template, a mental construct, or perhaps even a mental trick, not even a belief. Only the human brain can do such tricks: create "something" out of nothing.

Ironically, the sense of safety, never mind the falsehood, was one of the driving engines of our success. Our brain short-circuits the mental cascade by ignoring many irrelevant or relatively unimportant elements to create a sense of safety. That is not to say that the human mind only seeks out relevant and potentially beneficial things all the time. Not at all. Many seemingly irrelevant and irrational things have served our species well along our historical journey to success. To adapt to the changing circumstances of the struggle for survival, we simply couldn't afford to chase after only strictly relevant and rational things. That would not be very smart. Foolishness pays when circumstances demand.

A hundred millennia ago, surviving in an unkind environment of African forests was quite a deal. In that ruthless world, everything went. There wasn't much room in there for toying with concepts and theories to dissect what was relevant from what was not. The choices were limited. Food was scarce. It would have been hard, if not foolish, to waste time nitpicking. Whatever came in hand was devoured.

What else could the first humans do if not eat plants and roots or devour insects and worms before they learned to hunt for the big game? Or, what better options did these weaklings, humans, have than breaking open the dead animals' bones and eating their marrow? Some researchers believe that breaking animal bones to eat marrow was the original niche skill of humans. That may seem preposterous (and also an extraordinarily irrelevant or foolish thing to do by today's standards), but humans were not always as powerful or sophisticated as today. For thousands of years, humans have struggled to survive in a self-centric, individualistic, and hostile-to-each-other environment. That is not the least surprising. Individualism is the rule rather than the exception in biological systems, and humans belong in that system. Only after early humans learned to live in groups and assemblies was strict individualism overshadowed by collectivism. Groupism imparted them a sense of safety. Belonging to a group became a matter of utmost importance and prestige – the bigger the group, the better the chances of survival and the better the sense of safety.

Big Brain to Big Groups

Some spark ignited the fire of transformation: it dawned on early humans that they could successfully hunt in groups like the predators, for instance, lions, hyenas, and others. Hunting in coordinated groups, it turned out, was more profitable than stalking the big carnivores for their leftovers. A small behavior change returned big dividends. For thousands of years, humans then hunted, first for small and over time for bigger and bigger games. Simultaneously they better learned to defend themselves against stronger predators.

As humans learned to form bigger and bigger groups, the tide turned in their favor. In groups and assemblies, they were a formidable power to reckon with, and big game hunting became their regular affair posing now a threat even to predators. Fairly quickly then, our species jumped from the bottom to the middle of the food chain 100,000 years ago and began moving to the apex 50,000 years ago. Monkeys, gorillas, chimpanzees, buffalos, sheep, and chickens also live in groups and assemblies, and lions, tigers, and hyenas hunt in packs. All of them live in communities or animal societies. But they stayed where they were in the food chain. How could humans (AMH) accomplish a "quantum leap" to the apex of the food chain? The truth is that there has been nothing like a leap or jump. It has been a slow and laborious process stretched over centuries. However, to fathom how this so-called touch fashionably "quantum leap" occurred, we need to look at the structure, formation, and maintenance of animal and human assemblies or communities.

Which brings us back to the brain size for a moment. Brain imaging studies (fMRI, Brain Scan, and PET scan) show that the brain's frontal lobes are directly responsible for how complex a species' behavior can be and how big a species' social group can be. In other words, social behavior puts a limit on social group size. And, social behavior is determined by the frontal brain. That is to say, the bigger the frontal brain of a species, the bigger the groups they maintain. In short, the group size is the index of a species' cognitive capacity, which underpins its relationship and adaptation to the environment.

Imaging studies have demonstrated that the volume of the orbitofrontal cortex (a part of the frontal lobe of the brain just behind the eyes) determines mentation or abstract thinking – a prerequisite for maintaining a big group size. The group size hinges on a species's ability to control impulses, which is directly proportional to frontal lobe size. In our case, it takes twenty to twenty-five years for the brain to become adept at handling the complexities of social behavior.

The primates and apes can maintain an average group size of 55 and 100 members, respectively, beyond which the group becomes unstable. All others falling outside the group are enemies. Compare that with human groups. The smallest closely knit, functional human group size is 150, which can comprise relatives and unrelated friends held together as a community. People outside the 150-member group are regarded as acquaintances, not enemies, contrary to what is seen in primate populations. The cognitive limit placed by the frontal lobe makes it impossible for non-humans to even think of anything like systematic and broader purpose-driven cooperation.

So a big brain is good. But it asks for an equally good price: it demands considerable energy. Energy is costly. How to handle extra costs?

The solution lay in the gut (intestine). Typically, both the gut and the brain consume high energy. To handle energy demands, one of these two organs needs to compromise. To accommodate the big brain, the knife of evolution fell on the gut. It was cut to size to save energy for the big brain to devour. The caveat here was that by reducing gut size, you effectively reduce the nutrient supply; and hence the overall energy supply to the body.

To circumvent the nutrition problem, the *Hominins* needed one of two things: either switch over to a different source of energy supply or come up with a better way to improve nutrient extraction, especially *Niacin* (vitamin B3), from foods. They finally settled on the second option. Social evolution came to their rescue to make the best out of it, albeit over a period stretching over thousands of centuries. Niacin is essential for proper brain development and growth. Meat is a rich source of Niacin, though, but hard to digest raw. It needs to be cooked to extract enough Niacin out of it. AMH (our species) mastered the use of fire and learned cooking. Cooked foods provided better digestible fats, proteins, and Niacin, which obviated the need for a long gut. Cooking made the job easy for Evolution to cut the intestine in favor of the brain.

Archaic humans learned – not mastered, unlike AMH – the use of fire around 1.8 million years ago, much before the AMH (our species) had even evolved. That, however, doesn't mean that the archaics were using fire for cooking. There is not much evidence of cooking as a regular feature before 400,000 ago. Despite being much more evolved and sophisticated than contemporary apes, primates, and other mammals, the archaic humans (*H.ergaster/erectus* and early *Heidelberg*), faced a severe handicap in systematically and purposefully handling the fire. However, in contrast to the early the later *Heidelberg*, it seems, did a lot of cooking and even organized communal eating. Undoubtedly, that might have increased social bonding, group size (approximately 100-110 members, reasonably good size), and cooperation. It seems that *Neanderthal* community sizes were more or less the same as the late *Heidelberg*.

The early AMH also started life with small community sizes, progressively increasing later. The increased group size of AMH significantly impacted the mega-fauna, archaic humans included. In contrast to archaics and primates, AMH relatively easily managed to widen the circle of interaction so that they could organize better and concerted offense and defense strategies against enemies, predators, and competitors.

Fire, food, communal eating, social bonding, kinship within the group, and other activities (big game hunting and ambush-hunting in the Neanderthals) could indeed increase the non-human group size even beyond 110 (from 50 in primates to 110 in *Heidelberg*). But that still couldn't match AMH. Non-humans, despite big groups, couldn't come up with civilization. They couldn't master and control the environment as humans did. What did humans do differently with their bigger brains that archaic humans couldn't? They combined fire with other tools: language, stories, and religion – a deadly combination that catapulted them to the apex of the food chain. They created history, both genuine and sacred. Non-humans couldn't match humans in that arena. The frontal lobes of the human brain changed everything. Thinking. That is that.

Talking out the Thoughts

Language, one of our most sophisticated tools, made us a "God species." In his book *The Unfolding of Language*, Guy Deutscher notes: "Language is mankind's greatest invention – except, of course, it was never invented." What is so remarkable about language that Guy Deutscher lists it at the top of the hierarchy of special tools? At a glance, nothing. But delve a little deeper, and there is a sea of mysteries around this language thing. For instance, how did the human language originate and evolve? Or, why and whence did the faculty of language come from? We don't have all the answers. We have speculations. Which leaves much to be desired.

The fantastic thing about language is its simplicity. There is hardly a score and a half of sounds, noises, mumblings, or splutters. That is all there is to language. And every animal, at least in mammalian species, possesses them. Yet we humans put them in order, and guess what? We only surprise ourselves by watching what these meaningless noises can achieve: from banal signs of dissatisfaction to mind-boggling epic stories about the unseen realms of the Universe. The fantastic thing about human language is that even non-sounds are indispensable. They add to the beauty of the construction when placed in a particular place; otherwise, the bland tapestry of words could never get transformed into a live expression, richly sprinkled with colors of emotion. That is what language does every minute of the day!

We humans, in a sense, are lucky to enjoy nature's generosity. The language faculty that nature endowed us with proved to have tremendously far-reaching consequences on our civilizational development. Language is undoubtedly a marvel of Evolution – if you are like me, raised in a deeply religious society, you may have trouble accepting this. However, the fact is that religion, too, has been quite mystified by this remarkable capacity of us being able to use language. It is surprising, perhaps intriguing, that almost all the Holy scriptures except the Bible have avoided a direct discussion on language.

Only the Bible has gone on record to defend the variations and differences among the spoken languages. Without wasting time explaining the origin of language, the Bible comes straight to the point: "God invented language," yet acknowledges in the same breath that language made people too powerful. It goes on to say God regretted having given men this tool. *He,* in *His* power, did *His* best to punish the people by scattering them all over the face of the Earth. God didn't stop there. *He* confounded their languages. Much to God's chagrin, it turned out that this seemingly simple gossiping tool was a devastatingly powerful thing that even God had to think twice about. After all, isn't God the all-knowing and almighty? What does a human being amount to when facing Him? But no! It turned out humans couldn't be taken for granted; they could even change the Mind of God because of their gossip – at least, that is what the Bible wants us to believe. One may agree or disagree with the biblical narration. Still, the fact remains that the story of the Tower of Babel is a remarkable testimony that language has been an outstandingly powerful weapon in the possession of human beings.

Weapon or not, language, no doubt, is a unique tool. Why could only our species acquire this special tool? How could language come to us with so much ease? When did language reveal itself in History? There is no one-line answer to these questions. It seems that we were not the only ones who possessed language back then. Few other species, too, had language – at least some form of rudimentary language. Scientific estimates are that language appeared around 1.5 million years ago (Homo erectus roamed approximately 1.5 million years ago, and that is how we settle on this time stretch back in history). The exact time of the language's appearance is difficult to pinpoint. Nonetheless, the clue that the researchers and scholars find interesting is that Homo erectus already possessed a primitive form of language.

Did Homo erectus indeed possess a structured language? That is hard to say. However, there are plenty of clues pointing to the same. For example, Homo erectus's large brain size, standardized stone tools, and use of fire all point to the fact that they used advanced communication methods to pass on the information in groups and to their descendants. Only some form of language could have accomplished that.

In general, the learned consensus upholds that language could not have emerged earlier than 150,000 years ago–the time when modern humans arrived on the scene. It is argued that only we possess an appropriately shaped and positioned larynx, and only our brain houses the necessary infrastructure or hardware for mastering the language. So far as the specific language hardware is concerned, nothing even remotely resembling hardware has been identified in any particular area of our brains. The premise that some specific and unique language hardware exists is backed, at the most, by truism. However, certain areas of the brain are closely associated with different aspects of language. That can't be denied. But it doesn't solve the hardware problem.

Noam Chomsky, an influential linguist, subscribes to the view that humans are innately equipped to learn a language. He and his school argue that the elements of the language structure are specified in the genes so that the general grammar rules are biologically predetermined. In other words, a newborn baby possesses all the necessary neuronal circuits to handle the complex grammatical structures of languages. Chomsky argues this: if you take a human baby from one part of the globe and raise them in another part of the globe, within only a few years, they will grow up and speak fluently and flawlessly the native language of that region. The same is not true for other species. In this sense, humans are unique. It is hard to reject this observation of Chomsky, but does this prove that language hardware is innate only to the human brain? No.

We know that chimpanzees don't exhibit the same learning ability for human language as human babies; nonetheless, these poor fellows in captivity have demonstrated remarkable communication skills. In the 1980s, a baby chimp named Kanzi was born at the Language Research Center of Georgia State University, USA. Kanzi was the first ape who learned to communicate with humans without undergoing formal training. He developed cognitive and communicative skills far surpassing any other ape before him. He reportedly understood some simple sentences and more than 500 spoken words. No doubt, Kanzi never came close to anything like human speech, but that doesn't exclude the possibility that chimps are also equipped with a toolkit to learn some tidbits of human language. What about chimp language? Their toolkit seems sufficient for them to master "chimp language."

We tend to look at everything from our human perspective. Just as it is difficult for us to look at life from the chimpanzees' perspective, so is the case with chimps to have a human perspective. Perhaps a chimpanzee won't simply want to learn human skills and language because it may be demeaning to its self-esteem. Just as prisoners don't always follow their captors' orders and behave defiantly at times, maybe Kanzi resented human presence. In any case, the speaking Kanzi has put to rest Chomsky's claim that only humans possess language hardware. Humans are no special.

Long story short: language is a species-specific trait. For chimps, their specific trait works well, and, for us ours. Could human language serve chimps as well as it does humans? Theoretically, yes, if the behavior were a simple arithmetic model. It is not. There are many parameters to it. Possibly, human language can put chimps at a real disadvantage.

Chomsky and others argue that children acquire good linguistic skills even from scanty or insufficient inputs and that, according to them, is sufficient proof of the existence of innate capacity. They argue that children are not taught their mother tongue systematically; nevertheless, they acquire grammatical rules. The only plausible explanation, Chomsky says, for the remarkable success of human babies in developing linguistic skills is that some of the grammar rules are already hardwired in the brain. So humans never had to learn them in the first place. That sounds good, but.

Artificial intelligence-based modern computer-speech technology has destroyed the Chomskian argument. It has reduced language to a bunch of algorithms. And much more will come in the near future. That's how science makes and breaks the edifice of knowledge. Hard science is ruthless.

Well then, it brings us back to why Guy Deutscher called language humankind's greatest invention. Guy Deutscher is not the only one who is fascinated by language. Celebrated historians like Yuval Harari and others have also talked about language and its power. Surprisingly, from a scientific perspective, language is simply a "thing" like many other things; Language per se has nothing special about it; Language is merely one of the components of humans' toolkit—no puns intended here. As can be recalled from a page or two earlier, even Homo erectus possessed language, or even chimps have some coarse linguistic skills. But none of them went any further with it. We did. What made the real difference for us was that we used this simple tool uniquely. Herein lay our genius as a species. It is a fact that every living organism does some" thinking," some more, some less, but what they can't do is talk out their thoughts. We do. And that makes us different from all other creatures.

This is to say, we can translate information: What happens inside our brain is transferred outside to the environment in a way that influences the recipient.

Language is one of the best tools for conveying to others what happens inside our brains. It gives form to imaginations, abstract thoughts, and memories hosted within each of us. Language made it possible for humans to carry knowledge from generation to generation. Stories, epics, myths, poetry, culture, society, history, science, and civilization came into existence because of language. No language, no civilization. Period.

Stories and Story-telling

Language made it possible for our ancestors to weave stories about almost everything about their immediate surroundings or the far-off world of the Sun, the Moon, the stars, and other heavenly bodies. Since the human brain and mind work simultaneously in two worlds – the real and the imaginary – it becomes difficult, at times, to draw a line between them. The real and the imaginary merge at the deeper levels of our subconscious, making us skip the difference. In trance states – which we often get into without being aware – the fuzzy boundary between fact and fiction is obscured, and we are lulled into accepting all sorts of myths and fables as a component of reality.

You can prove that to yourself with a simple experiment: think for a moment about some tasty food or fruit like, say, a lemon. Imagine putting a slice of lemon in your mouth and enjoying its taste. In a moment, your mouth will water. Did you taste the lemon slice physically? No. Why did your mouth water? Simply because your brain responded to a picture you held in your thoughts (mind)! The brain is fooled into believing mere thoughts as a *reality,* with all its temporal dimensions and qualities. At a fundamental level (neuronal level) brain can't differentiate between a physical thing (real) and an imagined thing (thought). That is innate to our brain. It serves good ends, but it can be dangerous also, and if we consider the frustration, violence, oppression, and outright wars fought in the name of stories, then? You are right. D*angerous* is a mild word to qualify that innate property of our brain.

The hunter-gatherer lifestyle brought our ancestors face-to-face with the challenges posed by nature, demonstrating to them that on permanent metrics, the world belonged to none and that violence underpinned the struggle for survival. They had to live with it.

In the wild of the old, early humans couldn't help but watch the daily spectacle of violence playing out in front of them. A giraffe or an elephant could only be brought down by a pride of lions attacking collectively; in the case of a gazelle, the lioness could do the job single-handedly. The survival was directly proportional to the hunter's strength and hunting prowess. The hunting prowess could quickly rise exponentially when more group members cooperated. That was plain common sense. Even to lions, jackals, hyenas, and other predators. Perhaps.

So, cooperation was nothing new for humans. Nor did they invent it. It is an innate trait of the animal kingdom. Humans, like animals, cooperated instinctively. But that wasn't enough to handle the ruthless world of the jungle and the wild, red in tooth and claw. Something more, call it strategy, was needed—some brilliant and remarkable strategy given the comparatively weaker physique of Homo sapiens.

Primatologists tell us that non-humans also plan and devise defense, offense, and survival strategies. But how many non-humans have managed to rise to a higher than their previous level on the food chain? None. Many living species have tremendously outnumbered others. True, but the numbers alone don't matter. The algae and the eukaryotes are still ubiquitous, yet they are in the same place they were billions of years ago. The chicken and the sheep outnumber any known mammalian species at a given time, but they get slaughtered in equally great numbers daily.

The strategy, plan, or scheme is, in other words, an idea. Ideas are nothing but a bunch of thoughts. They are useless unless communicated to others, discussed, and improvised. A species that can do that has the advantage. Lower animals, apes, or archaic humans couldn't do that. Humans could. No wonder they rose on the ladder of the food chain and civilizational success.

It would be impossible for humans without language to translate ideas into words to have succeeded as they did. Without language ideas however brilliant would have remained buried in their womb. Through language, they could effectively be shared with other group members. Thus, what was happening in one mind was transported to many minds. That is to say, ideas in one mind became a collective property, the precursor to a collective consciousness. Once there were ideas and language, it was natural that the story would take birth. The stories stretched the ideas, sprinkling them with spices and thus making them spread quickly and definitively. Stories – the vehicle for carrying the ideas – became the hallmark of our cumulative culture.

Myths, Culture, and Violence

Real and imagined, stories became an indispensable part of human culture. They gave rise to myths. The myths are powerful. They definitively shaped the outlook of humankind. Different groups, communities, and societies identified with their respective myths. People became so possessive about their abstractions, concepts, stories, and legends that they didn't hesitate to write history with each other's blood. The evolutionary struggle for survival transmogrified into a fierce battle for sacred history, pitting human groups against each other.

The history, genuine and sacred, got soaked in blood and written with the blood of the weak. Violence was, is, and will perhaps remain one of the significant hallmarks of human history (more so of sacred history). When viewed from this perspective, it strikes as strange and unbelievable that an all-out nuclear war didn't happen in the twentieth century.

It is wishful thinking to contemplate a world without violence. In the aftermath of the September 2001 terrorist attack on the Twin Towers in Manhattan, New York, the violence got a new role: to establish peace. Violence and peace came to be viewed as interdependent—nothing oxymoronic in that. Ah! What a shameless chameleon you are. You struggle for survival!

That's not to say that I mean we don't have ways and means to substitute violence with peace. We sure have. As, for instance, Steven Pinker observes, we have already brought down the violence to a great extent. The question is how to eliminate it from our everyday life. Is that realistic to even ask that question? As of now, no. Take food procurement. It doesn't take a rocket scientist to see how many sheep, goats, and pigs are slaughtered daily for meat. You kill a human being or a wild animal, especially of endangered species, that is violence. You cull chicken and turkeys in tonnes; that is food. And what about the countless tons of plants devoured daily by a vast population of humans and herbivore animals? After all, plants also are living creatures. You cut them down. That's not violence because plants don't cry and weep from pain! You justify one as violence and the other as lawful food procurement. From a biological point of view, both meat-eating and vegetarianism qualify as violence.

Violence is the law of biology. All animals commit violence, but they kill to eat; humans do both – they kill to eat and eat to kill (quite often). If Yuval Harari is to be believed, then humans are a disaster – they wiped out the Neanderthals and other competitors; they could have been a little kinder to the archaic humans, but they chose not to. That, however, is not entirely true. Neanderthals became extinct because they lost the struggle for survival. They couldn't adapt to the changing circumstances or perhaps succumbed to the infectious diseases spread by peregrinating human populations. For a minute, let's suppose Harari is right; Humans killed Neanderthals. Given the law of biology, you kill or get killed in the struggle for survival. Had humans not killed Neanderthals, they would have killed humans. In that case, there would be no Harari to castigate humans for being brutal toward Neanderthals. Perhaps.

Contrary to Harai's view, the truth is that Neanderthals couldn't view violence through the same prism as humans. That was their problem. We, humans, are remarkably ingenious when it comes to justifying violence against others. Our sleight for logic and rationalization always came in handy. We lived on slaughter, violence, crime, and exploitation of others throughout history, yet we rationalized and justified our acts and moved on. How could we do that – justify the violence?

Again language came in handy. It helped our species create a propaganda machine through word of mouth or gossip. Underlying the drama of violence was a struggle for survival. This survival struggle resulted in nasty things that couldn't probably be averted. Could the magnitude of nastiness have been lessened? That's debatable. It can't be said for sure what might have happened had the humans behaved more mercifully, kindly, or peacefully. Did they have the luxury of being more civil and polite in that ruthless world of the ancient and deep past? Should we project today's perspective onto the past, demanding from our ancestors to fit into it? I, for one, think no.

Back to language. It birthed gossip, and gossip, in turn, perfected language as a tool. With gossip, sophisticated cumulative culture started its life. Both cooperation and conflict became manageable. That is not to ignore that gossip-fueled scandals, power struggles, and outright fights between individuals and groups, sometimes tip the balance toward serious conflicts. Inflamed by gossip reports, opposing confederacies would sometimes inflict unprecedented brutalities on each other.

As can be recalled from a couple of pages earlier on group formation, humans, like birds of the same feather, also flock together. They create cohesive groups and live in an organized society. The mere capacity of a species to create groups, though, doesn't guarantee its dominance over others. The real genius lies in a species' ability to maintain an organized group and set up regulating rules and conventions for everyone in the group to follow. Only humans can do that systematically and methodically. Language makes it possible.

Ringleader and Alpha male

Until recently, it was primarily believed that the concept of a ringleader is a purely human thing. In the second half of the twentieth century, that belief was challenged. It turned out that this ringleader thing is a biological trait rather than a purely cultural one. Primatologists have documented that ringleaders exist in chimp and other ape societies. Chimps, like humans, live in hierarchical organizations, calling them societies, and pivoting on friendships and social bonds. Their group leader is almost always a male, called the *Alpha* male. It seems that male dominance is an innate trait of the animal kingdom inherited by humans through Evolution. Perhaps that is why, historically, male members of society felt discomfort whenever women assumed leadership roles. Even a cursory reading reveals that that discomfort is reflected in bias toward women in religious scriptures.

The *Alpha* male in a chimp community maintains the order and is usually uncontested in his decisions. When two males aspiring for the top job of *Alpha* are in the fray, they go out to form coalitions of supporters within the group. Usually, all types of campaigns intrigues, and mechanizations, we are told by Jane Goodall and others, are seen during such contests. Eventually, the winner isn't the male who is more robust in physique but the one who has a larger and more stable coalition of supporters. That is an ultimate show of chimp-oligarchy that uses violence, coercion, and muscle power.

There's nothing in the human social system that isn't seen, in some or the other form, in ape communities. The tussle for power and dominance can be observed in almost all life forms. Perhaps humans merely took it to a new height with the attendant unnecessary bloodshed of their fellow humans. Here is the point: a typical chimpanzee society consists of fewer than 50 members. When it grows beyond fifty, the order breaks down, and splinter groups are formed. These splinter groups grow, and different groups seldom cooperate; they only compete for territory and food. The primatologists have documented long drawn-out wars between groups. In some cases, chimp wars extend over many years.

Human behavior is almost identical to that of chimps. Despite the language, gossip, and cumulative culture, human groups also reach a threshold number (150 members) that puts a constraint on their proper functioning. It can be observed in organizations, institutions, and corporate companies. They face problems when the group size grows beyond the threshold number. The numbers – 50 in chimps and 150 in humans – are an index of the cognitive capabilities of a species; they don't matter in guaranteeing a species its place in the hierarchical biological pyramid.

No numbers matter. Dinosaurs were terrifyingly numerous. They got wiped out. Similarly, today there are far more farm animals – more than ten times the number of humans on the planet, as Yuval Harari notes – they get slaughtered day in and day out. On average, fifty billion farm animals are put to the knife every year. That is more than seven animals per human being. How do numbers help sheep, chickens, or cattle? A linear or even exponential increase in the population doesn't matter except to save a species from extinction. In a dog-eat-dog world with a cut-throat competition to reach the top, brains matter, not bodies. Like it or not, the plain truth is that Life on Earth sustained itself by violence. Thousands of years ago, when their civilization was struggling against enormous odds, humans needed not only numbers, language, and gossip but something more – if you will, some additional efficient tools to maintain effective cooperation and unity. Gossip alone can't guarantee an index size as big as 150 members.

The Trinity - Gossip, Story, and Religion

Gossip needed to be supplemented with auxiliaries. That was not difficult to do, given that humans possess the wherewithal to invent other uses for language. Deep thinking, imagination, and different abstract contemplative capacities are built into human nature courtesy of the well-developed frontal lobes of the brain. Abstract thinking happens in closely related formats: pictures and words. Words are supplied by language, and pictures are already in abundance. All the five sense organs, particularly the eyes, help record impressions of the environment in the brain as pictures. What remains for the mind to do is to associate words with the pictures. That is pretty easy. Our mind is a master at creating streams of thoughts from words and pictures. Then those thoughts are spoken out as poems, prose, and stories. Stories are a powerful tool of communication. We are inherently hardwired to tell and listen to stories. We gather in groups, gossip, and listen to stories. Good stories can hold bigger groups together. We own our stories, identify with them, celebrate them, and build our identity around stories. In the process, we glue ourselves as a society through our shared stories, myths, and legends. Idle gossip alone can't achieve such a feat. It is the stories, tales, and myths that strengthen and multiply our chains of communication.

Which leads us to this: we create a *story* from an *idea*; one story leads to another, then another, and on and on, still more, giving rise to *myths*; myths create *fiction*; the fiction leads to the creation of more and more new fantasies – call them *concepts*; and concept takes us back to the idea – the building block of everything that we have. The cycle repeats itself *ad infinitum*. That is to say, one mental construct fuses with another, and another, on and on, giving rise to a tapestry of stories, myths, and fiction. In that tapestry, individual images, pictures, and memories get transmogrified – the Sky, Heaven, Earth, and the Sun derive meaning, and beauty, ugliness, love, or hate get a life. That all is a trick of the mind.

This brings me back to gossip and stories: they are potent tools for bonding. Telling stories at the fireside about the day's experiences, deceased relatives or people, nature and spirits, ghosts and demons, or about the past, present, and future creates a sense of community among people who share a common worldview. However, gossip and stories are good bonding tools when the community size is small (50 to 150 members). For establishing and maintaining bigger community groups like clans (150 or more), mega-clans (500), and tribes (1500), individual stories, however powerful, won't help much. It would be best if you have a composite tapestry blending gossip, stories, and myths– all in one and something more.

The search for that "something more" led humankind to lay the foundations of the Sacred History. The sacred history inevitably had to collide with Genuine History, and, as Reza Aslan says in *No god but God*, precisely there, at that moment of collision, religion was born. It was this trinity of "gossip, story, and religion" that altered the entire equation of raw power of numbers, permanently tilting the balance in favor of *Homo sapiens* in that cruel game of nature – the struggle for survival.

Chapter – 02

Fear, Word, and the Sword

One World, Two Histories

Fossils, remains and leftovers of the past buried deep into the belly of our planet hold many secrets and treasures under lock and key. When I say under lock and key, I mean still hidden away from our sight, not yet explored. Those unearthed and deciphered have given rise to many an as-yet unsettled dispute. Identification, decipherment, and study of fossils, remains and artifacts of deep history are not easy things to do. They constitute a laborious, slow, frustrating – and, above all, costly enterprise. It goes without saying how much intellectual and physical labor is spent assessing and studying history's artifacts. A small error in detail can sometimes spoil months' or even years' work, sending you back to square one. In that case, the whole process has to go afresh from zero, which is arduous and often frustrating even when modern scientific tools cull much of yesteryears' drudgery. It is often disappointing, modern technology notwithstanding.

The problem is that artifacts don't tell stories; they only provide us "cues." It is the proper interpretation of these cues that complicates the whole matter.

Genuine deep history builds on cues. Not all but most of it. The onus falls on us to fill the gaps and empty spaces that show up. In doing so, we project our perspective on the past. That's to say, our narrative of history is inherently biased because we are inclined to impose our standards on our ancestors' stories and paint them in colors of our liking. We tend to forget that they lived and behaved in an entirely different world governed by an altogether different, perhaps unique, set of priorities and paradigms of their day.

They lived and died in a world of oral history. Written history is a recent phenomenon, hardly a couple of millennia old. In ancient, word of mouth affected history telling, positively and negatively, but that didn't matter to them much. What mattered to them were the story and its outline. Telling the same story in different versions or fine-tuning it to suit the circumstances was an acceptable, even a favored, practice. A story that couldn't be modified to suit the prevailing circumstances would go into oblivion. The bestselling ones would be those malleable stories that could be twisted, turned, and tossed at will. For hunter-gatherers, gossip, fireside conversation, assemblies, and feasts were matters of importance. Imagine, for a moment, a fireside conversation without a story. You are right. It won't flow. The story brings life to the conversation. What we call culture is primarily spun around stories and not the other way around.

Our mind is a silly monkey. It jumps and constantly hops from one thought to another because thoughts pull our strings. They create restlessness, frustration, curiosity, and – you name it. Curiosity spurs us to touch the unknown or try our hand at novel things. How long could we, or our ancestors, resist the urge to experiment with the unknown? The temptation to explore and experiment drove early humans to caves, forests, and rocky terrains. During their iterations into the wild, they also tried their hand at scribbling, whether intentionally, accidentally, or just as a time-pass activity; we don't know exactly. Initially, their scribblings were vague, sketchy, and chaotic, but over time, well-defined figures and pictures came to life – the art as we call it was born. Art preceded formal writing.

Back to cues: Fossils and artifacts tell a bland story, but primitive art adds quaint punch lines to cues. From cues, we then get to "clues." So, clues take us to the Second phase of genuine history. That is to say, what we are clueless about is the First phase! Not so cool. With the commencement of the second phase, genuine history could no longer stay disconnected from the sacred history (which luxury, in any case, the former couldn't afford earlier, but we are clueless). From then on, what we formally call "history" is, in fact, an intimate interplay of the two histories – the genuine and the sacred history. And, the undercurrents of sacred history formally began to show up in the surface events of genuine history. Time had arrived when religious fantasy could no longer remain confined and buried within the human consciousness as a mental construct merely expressible in oral stories alone. Instead, it started crystallizing, albeit still in primitive shape, as pictures, drawings, sketches, etc. This development can rightly be viewed as a colossal phenomenon in sacred history. With it began the era of religious depiction.

The pictorial depiction captures the "world of the mind with all its fantasies and imaginations" in a two-dimensional mode. The historicity of depicted events is seldom a matter of concern here. That's to say, in pictorial depiction, sacred history transcends the boundaries of time. Reza Aslan, a prominent Iranian-American scholar of religion, agrees that "Sacred history has no concern for the boundaries of time and space." In his unique, penetrative style, he declares in his *No god but God* that "Religion in itself is the story of faith." In other words, Sacred history is a story of a story. And the story may easily defy time and space.

Religion - An impulse and a story

Scholars concur on the premise that religious impulse is inseparable from the human story. Its deep-reaching roots within the collective psyche of the *Paleolithic* or the Old Stone Age civilization should not surprise evolutionary biologists. For starters, the *Paleolithic* age comprises three segments: the Lower segment – between 2.5 million BCE and 200,000 BCE – when humans evolved from related members of the *Homo* family (such as *Homo habilis)* and used simple stone tools; the Middle segment – between 200,000 and 40,000 BCE – when the primitive works of art began appearing; and the Upper segment – 40,000 to 10,000 BCE – when humans began formally engaging in religious behavior, burial, and ritual.

The oldest record – record in the form of cave paintings – that we have of sacred history is not so very old. It comes from the closing centuries of the Middle Paleolithic age. Sadly the old Paleolithic period is, in a sense, bland – clueless, as I said earlier. The middle Paleolithic paintings happen to be remarkably shielded, preserved, and protected in caves, on rocks, etc., away from the ravages of Nature. This pictorial sacred history, the first of its kind, preserved on the walls of the caves and the rocks, takes us back in time, some 40,000 years. Indeed, it must be thrilling for those interested in history to examine this documentary evidence left by the earliest human civilization. I, for one, am not a historian. I am more interested in the psychological underpinning of History, both genuine and sacred. And how religion has shaped the history and thought process of the human species and vice versa. Yet that is only one of the many things this book tries to explore indirectly.

Scholars interpret these "clues" as legitimate evidence to prove the premise that the early human civilizations believed in a three-tiered

Cosmos consisting of the sky, the Earth, and the underground. In that three-tiered cosmology, the Earth was at the center of the hierarchy. That's to say, early humans believed that the universe was geocentric. Moreover, the underground world beneath the crust of the Earth was no less important than the sky. For them, the underground was teeming with some paranormal activity. This belief in the existence of a vibrant underground world must have played a critically important role in the life of early humans – otherwise, why would they bury the dead when there was so much of the vast and empty planet around them? It was far easier and much more commonsensical to throw the deceased over a mountain or into an open space to let them decay or be devoured by scavenger birds or animals. But no, they wouldn't do that! Doing that would amount to cruelty.

A sense of respect towards fellow human beings called for honoring the dead. Not allowing the dead bodies of fellow humans to be devoured by other creatures speaks of a prevailing sense of collective responsibility and moral obligation. Humans have always been good at inventing methods to circumvent distress and creating a systematic and organized body of rituals to handle distressing situations. That's what made humans human. No wonder humans landed up in the lap of religion, or if you may, religion landed in their lap. Either way is correct. The rest is details.

The Caves and the Story of Faith

As can be recalled from the previous page, religion is a story of faith. There are significant clues about the origin of this story in the book of art – well, there are some interesting pages in there, but unfortunately, they don't tell the whole story. These pages, though well preserved, are scattered in the caves across Europe, Asia, and Australia. The Kapova cave in the Ural, Russia; the Cuciulat cave in Romania; the Lena river valley caves in Siberia; El Castillo cave in Spain; Font de Gaume and Le Combarelles caves in Vezere valley and Chauvet, and Lascaux in France, are a few such examples. The Volp caves in the foothills of the Pyrenees have been thoroughly investigated. They possess a wealth of information about humans' quest for the meaning of life and perhaps religion.

Ironically, the "quest for meaning" has troubled humankind throughout all of history. Never content with all the abundance that the planet Earth provided, the "quest for meaning" made them pay a high price in terms of human life and blood. Yet, paying the price, big or small, never stopped them from taking their gaze off this "meaning" thing. They happily paid the price and lugged on with life, never ceasing experimenting. They built the cumulative culture and went on to dominate both animal and plant kingdoms. That is an outstanding achievement. But it pales before our one significant failure as a highly evolved species: we never learned to live at peace with one another. That is, well, sad.

The caves: The first systematic study of the Volp (caves) was performed by archeologist Abbe Breuil. This study sparked mainstream academics' interest in examining cave paintings in greater detail. These caves are difficult, perhaps even hazardous, to traverse for the less familiar people, but that hardly seems to have prevented visitors from engaging in all sorts of activity in these caves thousands of years ago. Some spaces in these caves, like the waiting room (anteroom), bear the evidence that whole groups of people – perhaps worshippers – gathered, ate, performed rituals, drew art, enjoyed being together, and slept there. The early paintings are placed a certain distance from the entrance, suggesting the caves were sacred spaces rather than sheltering places. More importantly, what immediately strikes the eye of the observer in these caves are hearths with piles of animal bones all around them with no evidence of firewood anywhere in their vicinity.

Was it that the bones, because of being combustible, could have been used to set fires in the absence of firewood? Some historians speculate that that could be the case, others like Reza Aslan have some trouble agreeing with it, and still, others reject it outrightly. It is hard to buy this explanation because of the simple question that naturally arises here: Why should they go to such lengths as to get animal bones to start a fire in the hearth when in the surroundings around with thick forests, firewood was in abundance and easy to procure? Perhaps there was more to the story. We know many secret societies and cults of the recent past have been fascinated by bones. Some cults even today believe bones have some "mediating power" to transport the believer from one realm of the universe to another – an experience intensely sought after by the believers in such phenomena. The cave visitors were no different. Possibly.

The interior of these caves is so crooked that traversing the convoluted chambers would have been a ritual in itself, a kind of unique experience. We are told that in one of the caves, the main path forks into two: the left and the right. The left path leads to a long chamber. Here the earliest cave paintings, dated more than 40,000 years ago, adorn the walls. These paintings – if they can be regarded as paintings – are clusters of red and black dots in rows. What these rows of dots signify is hard to say, but the overall pattern of the depiction of dots is hard to miss. Maybe this primitive art, all the same, carried esoteric significance for the early dwellers.

The path on the right leads to chambers with a "handprints" motif on the walls. These motifs date back to 39000 to 40000 years ago. The "handprint" can also be seen in many such caves worldwide – Australia, the USA, Sub-Saharan deserts, Argentina, and other parts of Latin America. In *God: A Human History,* Reza Aslan emphasizes that the peculiar thing about this handprint art is that it is never placed on smooth surfaces. It follows its pattern, which is characteristically similar in all parts of the globe. A fair question in need of an answer, asks Reza, is: Could these artistic imageries have predated the first migration of humans 60,000 years [sic] ago out of the Rift Valley in East Africa to the Middle East along the shores of the Red Sea? In that case, they must have appeared 100,000 years ago. The dating methods, however, haven't established this art as that old.

Some scholars believe that these handprints belong to women. If they are correct, then it means that women were actively involved in creative works of art during the formative years of human civilization and hence deserve more credit than is usually reserved for them. But, here is the complication: if the doctrine of original sin is correct, how can women's role in the early years be reconciled with the original sin? How could Eve's offspring be allowed to play an essential role in the creation and establishment of a secular institution as that of art? Either the theology of Original Sin is a myth, or history folks have got it wrong. The needle of the evidence points more in the direction of original sin being a pure myth than the historians being wrong. For those who hold original sin theology as an infallible one, it is worth paying attention to the role played by women in the civilizational growth of our species.

Furthermore, the commonality of handprints is a solid testimony that although humans may look different, they each share common interests, imaginations, and musings no matter how far removed they are on the geographical or geological timeline. Just like a garland is held in place by a common thread running through the hearts of individual beads, so are humans connected by an invisible bond of a common origin.

Scholars marvel at the weird coincidence that handprints in different caves are similar, which leads them to conjecture that these prints represent some common symbolic language. That, however, seems too farfetched a conclusion. A logical and better explanation is that these handprints point to the pictorial representation of a shared belief system in some form of a god or god-like entity. Equally likely, they may represent a sacred ritual periodically carried out by these early dwellers who trotted far and wide. After all, the human species evolved in one place, Africa, and migrated out to spread all over the planet. They must have carried along their beliefs and faith system everywhere they went.

In the sanctuary of one of the caves, walls bear bright, colorful drawings and engravings of animals and other mysterious creatures that don't fit into any category of life forms. The French anthropologist Claude Levi-Strauss commenting on this art, observes: "primitive humans chose the animals they cast upon the rock not because they were 'good to eat but because they were 'good to think.'" Levi-Strauss's observation makes sense, especially concerning a complex image – of a mysterious creature called the *Sorcerer* – on the ceiling at the far end of the sanctuary. The *Sorcerer* has the legs and feet of a human being, the ear of a deer, the face and eyes of an owl, and antlers on its head. This unique figure is both painted and engraved. It might have been a highly revered figure, held in high esteem by the worshippers or visitors thronging here forty millennia ago. Was this the earliest image of God? Was this how these early dwellers understood and imagined the syncretic essence of God? Perhaps.

Religious Impulse or Simply Art

Most scholars subscribe to the view that "Paleolithic cave art is the expression of a religious impulse." A minority, including some eminent scholars like Sharpe and Van Gelder, strongly differ. They reject the premise that this art is a "religious art," accusing the pioneer of such interpretation, Henri Breuil, of seeing religion in everything. Sharpe points out, a touch sarcastically, that all people, including Breuil, involved in this so-called "discovery" were clergymen and thus had a particular inclination to read religious meaning into these awe-inspiring and majestic pieces of secular art. He accuses Henri Breuil and others of being heavily biased in their analysis of this magnificent legacy from the past. Sharpe observes that these scholars were guided more by the prevailing cultural ethos of the late nineteenth century than by the need to follow methods of scientific inquiry.

Sharpe's criticism wasn't taken lightly by mainstream academia. He, along with Van Gelder and their sympathizers, was ruthlessly attacked. As a result, Sharpe and Van Gelder both mellowed down, fearing ostracism. That is a different matter, but they certainly have a point: nothing absolves scholars and researchers of their duty to carefully interpret historical data. Absent objectivity, the interpretation of sacred history reflects a blind majoritarian perspective. There can be no denying that the religious impulse is rooted in our past, but that everything is colored in a religious hue shouldn't be encouraged. That does no good to the present and future of humanity.

The improvements in dating technology and other tools like DNA fingerprinting during the second half of the twentieth century have allowed us to peek much deeper into our past. Furthermore, in 2016 carbon dating of some rings of an altar discovered in the caves in France revealed that they are more than 176,000 years old. The discovery of cave paintings in Indonesia adds another dimension to this story of ancient art. It seems other members of the *Homo* species, apart from humans, also dabbled in this activity. Some of the articles found in these caves were made more than one hundred thousand years before modern humans began migrating out of Africa (70,000 years ago) and thus could well have been created by the Neanderthals. Recently in the Golden Heights, an idol was excavated that is estimated to be more than 300,000 years old. In China, for instance, *Homo erectus* sites reveal traces of sacred history estimated to be as old as 500,000 years. All these recent finds have further complicated the already complex tapestry of sacred history.

The problem with artifacts of history is that even though they unambiguously point toward humans being engaged in religious behavior, they don't tell the story in full detail. Historians and archeologists have to rely on indirect evidence to construct the narrative of history. True. But that doesn't give a scholar the liberty to substitute evidence with opinion. For instance, in his influential book *God, a Human History,* Reza Aslan boldly asserts that what we see in the Volp (caves) or elsewhere must have resulted from thousands of years of religious thought. That is merely an observation. An observation made even by a reputed scholar – in this case, Reza Aslan – is only an observation, a fair guess, until it's corroborated by evidence.

At the same time, caution also needs to be exercised to not construe the lack of direct and irrefutable proof as evidence that religion or some form of a belief system didn't exist in ancient society at all. It did.

Fear or Fact

Many theories try to explain the origin and emergence of religion. Emile Durkheim, for instance, views religion as a purely social fact. He rejects almost all the theories that hinge primarily on dreams, supernaturalism, or spirits and soul. According to him, the origins of religion *per se* are grounded in the social life and the rites and rituals based on real experiences that help a community form a collective consciousness. Durkheim's thesis builds on a plausible socio-anthropological argument that sees religions as a social glue that helped maintain solidarity among primitive societies. From an evolutionary point of view, this glue argument makes quite sense. This glue helped create and maintain a sense of bonding and collectivity in human society and civilization at large. It follows that religion was the primary and the most dominant source of cohesiveness among the prehistoric communities, except that it never was.

Other theories (they are assumptions more and theories less) seem quite struggling to dissect the human religious impulse. They persistently fail to pay attention to – or maybe they deliberately ignore – an interesting yet ticklish issue: how did religion arise in the first place?

David Hume, a Scottish philosopher, was the first to take the bull by its horns at a time when subjective experience was considered robust scientific evidence to prove or disprove an argument. He tried to tackle the "origin of the religion" question with some measure of genuine objectivity and courageously wrote, "The primary religion of mankind arises chiefly from an anxious fear."

A century later, an Austrian Jewish psychiatrist Sigmund Freud gave a new twist to Hume's idea by getting libido and sex into the picture. His picture of the origin of religion was more vivid than that of Hume's, but his colors were laden with the sediment of the Jewish community's ages-old anger against the Christian West. Freud wasn't oblivious to the suffering, violence, and discrimination that the Jewish community had gone through. No wonder he was dismayed and furious with religion that had given Jews nothing but misery, suffering, subjugation, exploitation, and wretched life throughout history. His German predecessor and co-religionist, a dedicated rebel against laissez-faire, Karl Marx, had long denigrated religion by calling it "nothing but opium for the poor people," and Freud was determined, perhaps, to give psychological mooring to Marx's uttering. He boldly called for breaking free from the shackles of religion.

Others joined the chorus, but Marx and Freud particularly distinguished themselves, the former sparking off a furor and the latter working out to set off a silent revolution in motion. Both these distinguished Jews stood on the shoulders of another giant – Charles Darwin, a student of theology turned naturalist – who took the world by storm with his publication of "*The Origin of Species*" in 1859 on "Evolution by Natural Selection."

Which leads me to digress a little here. Jews, unlike others, consciously and dedicatedly cultivated a love of books and set up community educational institutions. They were quick to seriously turn their attention to scientific inquiry, taking caution and, at the same time, not to ignore the humanities disciplines. In both these branches of modern education, they excelled. Their pragmatic approach toward education ultimately bore the fruit – they could fulfill their dream of returning to Jerusalem, which no Messiah – whom they had anxiously and eagerly waited for 2000 years – could have fulfilled. Marx shrewdly let off the spark that ignited the fire of revolution. Other Jews, in turn, adroitly handled the unfolding events, patiently waiting for the winds and the waves to churn out a pattern in the chaotic waters of history. At the peak of the tempest, the boat of Jewish destiny finally docked at the shores of Jerusalem. There would be no more wildernesses and no more wandering now. The Jews may not give Marx credit for their emancipation, but that doesn't belittle Marx's stature. Without Marx, history would have happened differently, at least for the Jews. Perhaps.

Back to Freud: Everything he postulated about religion has been rejected except that "religion" – echoing Hume's and Marx's musings – "is born from man's need to make his helplessness tolerable." That is that.

Self-deception or Self-defense

The human organism is as complex as the universe itself, and the human society is a collection of individual human universes, each working independently and in unison with the whole. Each of us is unique, yet there are common things, traits, and everyday actions shared by all of us.

Surprisingly the shared commonalities don't undermine the uniqueness of any of us. Since our appearance on this planet, we as a species have faced all kinds of challenging situations, circumstances, events, processes, demands, and whatnot. None of us was born with a tool kit or a user manual that would provide readymade solutions to our problems.

A lot of things were apparently beyond the grasp of our ancestors, given the primitive life they lived. But then there was no escape either. They continued with their everyday life; society continued functioning day in and day out; questions and mysteries that popped up were answered and explained relative to the circumstances of their day to smoothly handle the burden of life. When out of the blue, a lightning bolt would strike, a predator would charge, an earthquake would shake the ground, a flood would create devastation, or some disease would cause mass death and debilitation, it would scare the hell out of them. They would find themselves paralyzed with fear of the known, and awed by the power of the unknown. In a state of helplessness, stricken with fear, not understanding what was happening, what could our forefathers do? They had to explain somehow what was happening in their surrounding environment. And deceive themselves into believing that they fathomed it right unless they stumbled on a better alternative explanation.

The only seemingly plausible explanation that our ancestors could have thought of, given their limited understanding of natural phenomena, was that something unknown and unseen was doing all the merciless drama to intimidate them into acknowledging its existence. H G. Wells put it thus: "Primitive man probably thought very much as a child thinks, that is to say in a series of imaginative pictures. He conjured up images or images that presented themselves to his mind, and he acted per the emotions they aroused. So a child or an uneducated person does today." Throughout the ages, humans would live their lives in perpetual frustration, fear, and awe of the unknown. Who exactly was behind all this strange, funny, and unpredictable "Nature"? They surely would ask of themselves and each other. The more Nature behaved unpredictably and the more they found themselves at the receiving end, the more defenseless they felt. Nothing is more depressing and damaging to the human psyche than the feeling of defenselessness. Fortunately, the well-developed brain came to our species' defense. It makes us brilliant at assuaging psychological burdens by rationalizing and brushing off our defenselessness and powerlessness. The power of imagination came in handy in helping our forefathers trivialize frustrating situations. That's self-defense 101. Or is it a brilliant self-deception?

For ages, we humans have known when you explain a problem, you have solved half of the problem. This understanding has served our species tremendously. Whether "explanation" is based on accurate and sound principles or not doesn't matter much as long as it helps handle the psychological burden or frustration. Such a mindset has prevailed throughout the human existential period, effectively shelving rational thinking. We are humans because we observe, think, and try to understand and rationally explain what is happening around us. Yet we become desperate when we can't put our finger at the right spot, and in those moments of desperation, we tend to latch on to the straw, knowing full well that the straw can't keep us afloat. The straw provides us with a psychological alibi. We are masters at deceiving ourselves and feigning ignorance about it because the neuronal network of our brains is fundamentally structured to do so.

There is so much mystery out there. For our poor forefathers, everything was a mystery. Take this. You are walking in an unknown place when nobody is out there to tell you the way, what will you do? You are right. Make guesses. If your guess turns out correct, out of pure coincidence, you become confident to make more guesses and suppose all of them turn out right. You remember them as your experience. A time comes when you accumulate a body of experiences, which becomes your knowledge about certain things. Over time, that knowledge becomes a property too dear for you to part with. That holds for everybody. Suppose in a community somebody comes up with better guesswork or explanation based on his experience (knowledge) of some inexplicable problem. Soon others tend to gravitate toward that particular "somebody." It will be a matter of time before this "somebody's" opinion is sought on other issues too. And soon, that "somebody" becomes a respectable person. In society, things mostly work that way. The ancient societies were no different in that respect. A respectable person would explain how thunder and lightning happen, why it rains, why winds turn into blizzards etc., and the rest would agree. The crowds would follow in madness.

The deep ancient times, rather mired in ignorance and lack of know-how, made Nature look merciless and mysterious. Take lightning or thunder. What could one expect these ancient "respectables" to know about thunder? The loud sound would scare the hell out of them. The most plausible explanation was that two or more gods were fighting and roaring horribly, and they heard that noise. They didn't understand why and how lightning kills, but they knew it kills. It was good for them to seek shelter in their homes when the gods were fighting. As they quickly ran for cover in their dwellings, they would save many lives from being lost to lightning strikes.

Master storytellers among them came up with the story – thunder god, ghost, spirit, or devil – and it stuck and sold. It didn't matter when and how the story was spun. What mattered was that it scared the people to run for shelter in their dwellings and saved people's lives. Many such stories stuck.

Some people worked hard to create preposterous and hallucinatory stories about gods to get others to pay attention. Mostly, people believed such stuff and would readily worship the imaginary gods. Some performed rituals and sacrifices, while others sought to beseech their respective gods with all seriousness. That helped bargain the anxiety and fear for the hope of a better tomorrow.

Over time the fictional or conjured-up stories would pass on from generation to generation. People would recall, recite, or even re-enact these ancestors' stories to solicit a sense of belonging to the tribe, group, community, or religion. Gradually, the stories and myths became incorporated into the belief patterns of individual communities. With successive generations, a formal and organized belief pattern evolved. It was then a matter of time before some beliefs would become infallible – dangerous to be challenged. In the words of H G Wells, a sort of mental fossilization is found in folklore and the deep-lying irrational superstitions and prejudices that still survive among modern people.

Stories disseminated. Gossip matured. The propaganda machine evolved. That set the tone for gossipers and ballad singers to popularize stories, myths, epics, ballads, and other stuff. In a matter of hours and days, a story would become the talk of the town. Storytellers would recite it to audiences, family gatherings, and community groups; ballad singers would add more color, spice, and drama to the content, making it palatable to wider audiences. A story could quickly become an irrefutable truth and part of cumulative culture.

Furthermore, the real-world phenomena depicted and explained through stories, myths, and fiction set the tone for human civilizational and religious-cultural progress. No wonder different religions – stories of faith imperceptibly born out of the need of the human species to assuage its ignorance, helplessness, and fear of uncertainty – took firm roots. Otherwise, from a strict biological evolutionary perspective, religion doesn't seem to have any specific survival advantage for humankind.

Ethics and Religion

Theologians may insist that religion is essential for moral and ethical behavior; however, scientific data don't support that claim. Neuroscience (or cognitive science) has effectively laid to rest the issue that religion has any moral effect on society. A massive body of scientific literature conclusively rejects the premise that religion, per se, or even faith in God or gods, is essential for morality. In 2012, Yale University psychologist Paul Bloom published his research in the *Annual Review of Psychology*. He convincingly demonstrated that one, "religious belief is an unlikely candidate for a biological adaptation," and two, there is no evidence to support the notion that the "world's religions have an important effect on our moral lives."

As can be recalled from the previous chapter, humans stood out throughout history because of the faculty of the language they used with remarkable efficiency. It is in language that sociologists find the answer to puzzles like how religion evolved in the first place and why humankind trod the path to faith and religion.

Generally, for us, gossip is a waste of time. Not so for the ancients. For them, it served tremendously—gossip in its various forms knit together groups, tribes, and communities. Fireside gossip and dinner-time talk bonded groups together, which shared common stories. That is to say, the identity of groups and tribes depended on shared stories and beliefs. The stories adapted accordingly when the groups, tribes, or communities became larger. It was the shared stories that, over time, metamorphosed into complex tapestries and myths that we call religion. Religion was yet another addition to the human toolkit of gossip. True, religion may not be an efficient evolutionary adaptation, but its advantages were many to fledgling societies and civilizations. It helped facilitate extended cooperation among unrelated tribes and communities to achieve common goals.

Power and Violence

Establishing one's dominance in a group is a recognized animal instinct – an evolutionary trait – and undeniably, this particular instinct is the driving engine for much of the violence in nature. Take the pride of lions. A lion aspiring to become the dominant member of the pride invariably has to resort to violence. The first thing it has to accomplish is to fight the other lion, lay claim to its lioness, copulate with her, and sire its cubs. Getting the lioness to nod is not easy. The aspiring new king must mercilessly kill the cubs sired by the previous lion. That brings the lioness into heat, in which she turns to the new king to impregnate her. In other words, to create his own family, the new king kills the other lion's family and forcibly snatches his wife. Merciless might! Power talks and bullshit walks.

Humans also lust for power, though, unlike animals, they can choose peaceful means to attain power. However, more often than not, power tussle begets violence. Power knows no ethics. It uses ethics, religion, and morality as tentacles to reach farther and more expansive space.

The Third Phase

In his book *Hegemony or Survival,* Noam Chomsky dissects in his characteristically brilliant academic style the "manufacture of consent" in modern history. He observes, "...and that it would be necessary to devise new means to tame the beast [people], primarily through control of opinion and attitude." The means (tools, devices, and mechanisms) humans use to "manufacture consent" are myriad. Religion is only one of them.

Religion has served man excellently throughout history (women had less space in the male-dominated religious hierarchy). As David Hume recognized, religion has been crucial for "containing the opinion," which "is the foundation of government from the most despotic to the most free." Religion and faith have kept people primarily engaged in the quest for the mysterious, but the wise, as is always the case, used religion to embark on the road less traveled to power. The power brokers and power structures used religion to accord divine sanction to their right to dominate others. That is strikingly evident on examination of the "Third phase" of history that started its life on the fertile plains of ancient Mesopotamia (see Chapter 3).

History entered the "Third phase" around 12,000 years ago when the melting of continental glaciers had slowed down. It coincided with when humans began seriously pondering their way of life. After ages of nomadic life, the hunter-gatherer lifestyle had become dull and probably monotonous. New experiments were long overdue. By 10,000 BCE, the tipping point to do away with the millennia-old hunter-gatherer way of life had finally reached. The time had come for humans to reorganize their primitive communities into settlements.

Humankind was up for a huge transformation – a change of behavior and relationship toward the environment. For the first time, humans embarked on a novel experiment on a much grander scale than ever attempted – a scale of an experiment that would prove pivotal to getting us within only 14000 years to where we stand today. Humans began to control Nature rather than be satisfied with what the wild offered. They began tempering with the plants, cross-breeding them, raising for the first time what we call crops, and domesticating animals. Thus began a life of continuous experimentation and toil.

There is no denying the fact that the new lifestyle turned out harder to go with than expected. Initially, the agricultural enterprise seemed lucrative; it promised a considerable advantage compared to foraging in the dangerous wild, but over time it turned out to be costly, burdensome, and highly labor-intensive. The crop yield was low, and manure was unknown. As the family size increased, demand for food rose, and nutrition suffered, leading to bodily weakness and disease over the years. That is to say, the amount of energy expenditure on agricultural labor increased dramatically, but the output remained too meager to handle the demand. It was a trap.

Consider the hunter-gatherer lifestyle. Hunting is a game full of uncertainty. There is no guarantee of success. You leave for a kill in the wee hours of the morning. You return with your bag full or empty; you provide a meal or leave your family to starve. In case you are unlucky, you can, at the most, pick some fruit, berry, or roots if you stumble onto them on your way back home. In the hunting gamble, you could win; you could lose. The chances of losing were always more.

Many yearned to get rid of this perpetual gambling game. Settling for agriculture looked promising, and some put their bet on it. Little did they know they were pushing for a silent revolution that would bring, in centuries ahead, all to the edge of uncertainty greater in magnitude than foraging and hunting.

The agricultural enterprise turned out no less dangerous, unpredictable, and unreliable than hunting-gathering. The agriculturists found themselves at the receiving end from all sides – climate, weather, water, agricultural yield, crop failure, famines, disease epidemics, you name it. The whole universe, it seemed, was conspiring against them. There seemed to be no end to the vagaries of Nature and the appalling miseries it brought upon farming communities. With no remedy in sight, no escape route out of the trap, and the woes multiplying with each passing season, it was but natural that farming communities ended up anxious, fearful, and frustrated. In the difficult-to-deal situation, some way out was desperately needed; not necessarily a permanent solution, yet something that could at least help assuage the increasing uncertainty, helplessness, anxiety, and fear; some hope, even if false, in the face of a doubtless annihilation; or something even irrational or preposterous with a promise of light at the end of the dark tunnel of despair and dismay. Something needed to be done. Handling the loss of crops and life after investing their blood and sweat posed a formidable challenge for the newly settled communities. They had taken up a tricky enterprise.

It wasn't easy for the fledgling farming communities to handle the challenges created by their new lifestyle. Under pressure, the parvenu settlers could easily slide back to the traditional hunter-gatherer lifestyle. That was problematic for the leader class and the tribal elite. Sliding back to foraging would mean abandoning the settlement, depriving the newly established tribal power structure of easy income. Motivated by self-interest, power brokers had to prevent these fledgling farming communities from falling apart. That necessitated putting in place some robust mechanism. Here, religion came in handy. In that superstitious society, a religion built on vague and imagined ideas and concepts inspired by fear could be adroitly used by the power brokers to " manufacture the consent." Otherwise, how else could the ancient man be convinced to tolerate his helplessness?

The essentially systematic dissemination of esoteric stories constructed around an element of fear put religion on a firm footing. Fear has a hypnotizing effect. It paralyzes the thought process. In a state of thought paralysis, the mind registers unfounded, irrational, and preposterous stories without questioning their veracity and integrity. The mind takes them as a suggestion and reprograms itself to accept fiction as fact. The programmed mind facilitates the manufacture of consent. When fear is juxtaposed with hope for a better tomorrow, people could be motivated better to suffer with patience. In the case of those terrified parvenu farming communities, "belief in a better tomorrow" worked like a soothing balm in the face of calamities striking them from all sides. That is to say, religion provided farming communities hope – an escape route, if you may – and, to believe Freud, encouraged them to endure their helplessness before Nature patiently. This "belief in tomorrow" or simply "religion" worked like glue to hold the sprouting civilization together.

Religion could, well… Actually, it could have ended up as any other story merely getting transmitted from mouth to mouth hadn't society put pressure on it to adapt, transform, and update itself to meet its demands. As the ancients adopted a settled lifestyle – voluntarily or otherwise – the need for redressal of emerging fault lines in the societal architecture and dangerous psychological void in the collective consciousness compelled religion to undergo evolution to better adapt to and express different facets of faith. Religion sorely needed the requisite organizational framework to serve the interests of the smart. Inevitably religious networks sprang up in the communities, and in the centuries ahead, the religious networks would become an essential ingredient of the cultural scaffolding for the developing human civilization.

The Mental and Physical

Religion was never a luxury. It was a need. Without religion, would human civilization have seen the light of the day? Well, it is a hard-to-answer question. Hunter-gatherers could do well without organized religion. They still do, as in the case of some nomadic tribes living in the jungles. They practice some or the other form of primitive religious belief and are happy. Perhaps. Settled agrarian societies and civilization was a different matter. They had to invent an organized religion. Kinship alone couldn't create a robust cultural scaffolding on which "identity" could rest. Organized religion did.

Religion could easily extend the sphere of influence beyond a single group to outside tribal groups and units. Different tribes could come together to form a community and adopt some common and preferred religious practices and conventions. Communities then practiced their preferred rituals to identify with one or the other communal units. Over time the communities came to be recognized for the particular religious practices they had adopted. It was then a matter of time before identity politics would be born – the settlements would become excessively possessive about their religious identity and defend it as their cultural identity. The identity had to be protected, nourished and fought for with blood and sweat. There could be no turning back. To that end, religion provided the stories and myths – a necessary warp for the cultural weft – to keep society connected and glued. The so to say cultural weft was strengthened further with the warp of shared beliefs, values, and customs.

This whole process was not as straightforward as it seems in the above description. Here we assume, for the sake of simplicity, that the human religious evolution and cognitive transformation happened in discrete steps and stages. Not exactly. It was indeed a complex process with everything overlapping where the "mental" was integrated with the "physical." The "mental" component was harder to put through; the "physical" element shaped itself on the mental template, and the rest was a matter of detail. Down the timeline, the two – the Mental (ideation) and the Physical (physical expression) – paved the way for the religious narrative, representation, imagery, art, etc., each merging so smoothly with the other that an imperceptible boundary is all that was left between the imagined and the real. It couldn't be otherwise. "Religions," after all, "are the greatest of all collectively created works of art of humanity." Who said that? Whoever said that said it well.

The Garden of Eden

Setting up groups, communities, and then composite villages was a revolutionary undertaking backed by equally revolutionary ideas. Having ideas is no big deal but succeeding in the battle of ideas is a gigantic achievement. The fierce battle of ideas fought to replace the then-existing hunter-gatherer way of life ultimately won the day. Yet, a thousand Religions couldn't have achieved anything had there not existed a laboratory – not an ordinary one but a natural laboratory of fertile lands and plenty of water – where the ideas could be put into practice. Where was that laboratory?

The low alluvial lands of Mesopotamia fed by the great rivers, Tigris and Euphrates – the Garden of Eden – were the most significant and vital piece of land in the famously known "Fertile Crescent" (natural laboratory) that stretches from the Persian Gulf to the Mediterranean coast. It was here that the first farming villages took shape. Down the line, the first towns and city centers of ancient antiquity arose in and around the "Garden of Eden." It was here, many believed until recently, that the first man, Adam, was created. As mentioned in the Biblical book Genesis (2: 8-9): in the Garden of Eden, "planted by the Lord God" with "every tree that is pleasant to the sight and good for food," and "he (Adam) found himself amidst the plentitude." It was here that the civilization started out its life – in and around the Garden of Eden – on the rich fields of the "Promised Land" between the two rivers. Fertile Crescent is also called the "Cradle of Civilization."

Agriculture was the pioneering technological revolution that happened in the Garden of Eden. It created new vistas of opportunity. But it also put human resilience to the test. The yield of grains was initially relatively plentiful. As the years passed and the population grew, the crop yield didn't increase proportionately because more and more lands lay fallow. To overcome overall food scarcity, more land needed to be cleared to cultivate crops. The overall investment in terms of labor soared. As the years passed, this business of clearing, cultivating, and leaving the lands fallow became a burdensome industry. Add to that floods, droughts, pests, and locusts almost perennially destroying the crops. That was a miserable ordeal for the early agrarian society. With no means to handle the merciless vagaries of Nature and no efficient methods to increase crop output, whole populations could get wiped out. It was resilience that kept early societies going when going got tough.

Resilience comes from the mind: when faced with an imminent threat, the mind responds by dolling out mental tricks that keep us motivated to face the danger. One consequence of the mental trickery is myths and stories suited to the time and circumstances to distract us from everyday life's woes and hardships and goad our attention toward abstract themes like gods, heaven, hell, and a sense of collectiveness, a sense of belonging, sense of motherland and fatherland, and so on. In the Mesopotamian cradle, the civilization survived because of human resilience. The people were roped in to cultivate a sense of belonging in that developing civilization. Old stories and myths were recast and retold in a new frame to hypnotize people into hallucinating that agriculture was the holiest enterprise, a panacea for all their miseries despite being labor-intensive and low-yield.

Stories work wonders. Some historians like Yuval Harari maintain that the farmers were forced into accepting the agriculture story despite seeing and knowing perfectly well that agriculture was unpredictable and not everybody's piece of cake. Farming demanded physical prowess and endurance far more significant than that for hunting-gathering. Humans were tricked, Harari thinks, through all kinds of stories and fiction to go for a backbreaking occupation in the hope of a better tomorrow. That's not wholly true. The stories did play a role in spreading framing enterprise, no one can deny that, but farming was doable, too. Otherwise, how could it spread from place to place? How could it be that this southern Mesopotamian agricultural enterprise had spread over some 400 hectares towards the end of the fourth millennium BCE; Villages had given rise to towns, and urbanization was gaining speed; Migration to urban centers and cities was taking place at a fast pace? How come humans had already embarked on an unending journey to improve their way of life? How could that all happen?

Vere Gordon Childe, an archeologist, coined the term "Neolithic revolution" and popularized the view that agriculture kick-started the "settled way" of life, paving the way for the building of village societies over time, towns, and urban centers. Yuval Harari, the Israeli historian, disagrees. He calls the Neolithic agricultural revolution "history's biggest fraud" because ancient agricultural societies were not cost-effective enterprises at all. Harari notes that the farming enterprise has exuberantly enormous demands on human resources, "proving" in his words, "a terribly burdensome yet the least profitable institution for the investment of human labor and time."

Childe and Harari seem to be off the mark here. Both Childe's thesis that the "settled way" of life led to the Neolithic agricultural revolution and thus indirectly gave birth to organized religion, and Harari's provocative argument that the agrarian revolution was the biggest fraud, don't stand up to scrutiny in the light of recent evidence. Take, for instance, the recent excavation of Gobekli Tepe in southeastern Turkey, led by Klaus Schmidt. These archeological findings leave no doubt as to what spurred what. That is to say, it was religion that goaded the existence of permanent settlements first, and agriculture followed, not vice versa. The respectable French archeologist Jacques Cauvin also agrees that studying Gobekli Tepe and other devotional sites or temples strongly suggests that organized religion has spurred the "Neolithic revolution." He further clarifies that for the Neolithic revolution to happen, it would have required not only the technological revolution such as farming, the invention of the wheel, and the domestication of animals but also, sort of, a *revolution of symbols*.

The *revolution of symbols* was underpinned by a revolution of thinking. It required a paradigm shift to change the human condition and overall quality and standard of living. One of the collateral consequences of this shift, Cauvin tells us, was the transmogrification of the loosely-knit belief systems into organized religion that revolved around conjured-up divine figures or figures described in human terms and language. In other words, it was a paradigm shift in the human imagination that culminated in the evolution of organized religion. And this "transformation of imagination" led humankind to think a touch grandiosely that it is they who occupy the "central place" in the universe. That's to say, humans began thinking of themselves as rulers of nature, implying that everything else in the universe was created for them and thus subservient to them. This sense of grandiosity, bordering on hallucination, marked a tremendous shift that helped transition from animism to institutionalized religion.

Having been born in Mesopotamia, institutionalized religion and agriculture were later exported to Egypt, Persia, and Indo-China. It was only a matter of time before an entire pantheon of personalized and humanized gods took shape, and over the next ten thousand years, to borrow from Reza Aslan, God became, literally, human.

Oil, Grease, and Lubricant

The road to civilization turned out bumpier than expected. From village to town to urban centers didn't come easily and automatically. It had to be earned. Village societies adapt seamlessly to the immediate natural environment. They quickly develop good chemistry and equilibrium with Nature. Civilization is a different matter. It doesn't come naturally; it has to be designed consciously. The urban centers are like machinery, and the denizens are moving parts of this machinery. For this machine to function smoothly, particularly in challenging circumstances, individual parts should function in collaboration with each other with minimum possible friction. To achieve a touch frictionless working state, periodic oiling, greasing, and lubrication of the machine is needed. Any potential clash has to be handled with caution.

Contrary to ordinary machines, oiling and greasing are done in a societal machine with new and robust ideas, stories, and narratives. However robust, the ideas based solely on logic, reason, and rationalism, can prove dangerously ineffective or even counter-productive. Care must be exercised while delivering new ideas.

Humans are prisoners of emotion. Emotionally appealing ideas, never mind substance-less and empty ones, always work better to rally even the most intelligent and wise skeptics. People believe in crap - fiction, nonsense mythology, and preposterousness - provided it is delivered in an emotionally touching gift-packing.

As the early Mesopotamian societies gave roots, the civilization simultaneously began shaping itself; trade and transaction gained momentum. Profit and loss became a topic for fireside gossip and dinner table talk. People became more concerned about material gains to advance and improve their living standards. Trade demanded inventing transaction methods, and as the barter picked up oral contracts, trusting each other's word and keeping promises became mandatory. New guidelines and conventions needed to be devised and popularized to smoothly handle trade and everyday give-and-take affairs in the bazaars and neighborhoods. People came to regard the so-called "values" like honesty, truthfulness, love, compassion, kindness, mercy, and so on in a new light. Suddenly, "values" - those abstract concepts or myths (virtual mental templates or ideation) - gained primary importance when trade, transaction, and exchange of goods picked up over time. Values became virtues, and virtues assumed shape and life of their own, metamorphosing into the fully-fledged and influential currency of morality. The religion quickly seized the opportunity to claim ownership of the "institution of morality and ethics" and accord it divine origin.

As civilization was being designed, religion, like everything else, created its space. Operating from that space, religion greatly influenced civilization's formation and maturation. Religion did it then, and it does it today. It never lost its sheen or its relevance. It occupied a central place in the civilizational journey partly because it possessed a pretty good corpus of oral mythology, legend, and stories and somewhat because another curious development took place along the way that worked in religion's favor. That new development pivoted on a new technology that changed the whole equation of interaction and transaction. Religion could now, like a mighty sword, slash the most formidable barriers of the hearts and minds of the people. It did so by harnessing the new technology: the written word.

Word or Sword

Whether agriculture necessitated the settled way of life or the settled lifestyle promoted agriculture is still moot; what is not moot, though, is that it was primarily the change in the lifestyle that initiated urbanization with all its complex network of nodes, connections, and interactions. As can be recalled from the previous discussion, gossip, and word of mouth alone handled much of human interaction until before urban civilization came up. With the advent of urbanization, as the amount of information exponentially increased, oral transmission alone couldn't efficiently handle the information load. In the oral Mesopotamian society, as in the rest of the ancient world, with increased trade and business transactions, "memory became a highly prized commodity." Any mechanism that would help improve the working memory of individuals would certainly be welcome simply because the possession of enhanced working memory would give a great deal of leverage to any society.

In his book *Babylon*, Paul Kriwaczek observes, "All that was needed to increase the capacity and efficiency of day-to-day working memory was a simple reminder, 'something as neutral as a sign of a left-pointing finger, which can be read as 'go left.'" Just a sign made all the difference. Pretty easy! It was a no-brainer to increase working memory, wasn't that? Then, why didn't anyone think about it before the Mesopotamians? No one thought because it simply never occurred to anyone before them. Unbelievable. Even more unbelievable is that a tremendous revolution could begin with a modest idea – an idea as modest as a sign 'go left.' It was not the first time history witnessed revolutions born from simple ideas. Rather, every great revolution has sparked off from a simple idea. Gossip, story, and religion were all simple ideas, yet they created a cumulative culture that underpinned the Neolithic revolution and civilizational progress. So did word – only, that this time the Southern Mesopotamians created the real recorded history by the reed – yes, a reed that turned out to be far mightier than the sword. The Mesopotamians invented the art of "Writing"!

In its primitive form, "writing" provided simple signs and symbols to record things. Then, these symbols became more valuable and recognizable to others when "lexical lists" were created. From this elementary and modest beginning, a never-ending journey started. Soon an extensive repertoire of symbols was created and organized in systematic order. Initially, only symbols and signs were recorded on clay tablets – baked and unbaked – but the Mesopotamians soon recognized the limited utility of symbolical recording for effective communication. Effective communication depends on thoughts being translated and transported to one another clearly and comprehensively. The symbolic representation couldn't do that as well as language.

The thoughts are innately multi-dimensional. Expressing thoughts through the written word necessitates rendering multi-dimensional abstractions into a two-dimensional reality; symbols and signs are simply insufficient to achieve that.

"For a long time, the idea of representing speech in a two-dimensional fashion in

the form of marks on clay tablets simply did not occur to anyone," writes Paul Kriwaczek. Again, the Southern Mesopotamians were the first to tinker with that idea, as they did with symbols, probably as a matter of fun or perhaps as an expression of their eagerness to record their existence in permanent form. Be that as it may, the undeniable fact is that ancient Mesopotamia changed the course of human history for all times to come. "The idea of writing was surely [the] greatest gift to the world" that came from Nineveh (present-day Mosul, Iraq) of Mesopotamia, says Kriwaczek.

Writing put history into its Third phase – the era of written history. Over time, an effective system of communication was developed through which the three-dimensional world of human thought could be translated in its entirety into a two-dimensional world of the written word. As Paul Kriwaczek aptly observes, "From now on, whatever happened in the world need never be forgotten!" There was no need now to depict sacred history as incomprehensible and indecipherable cave art. It could now be written as a live and rich body of literature laden with all hues of emotion.

"Writing" is undoubtedly humankind's one of the greatest inventions. It changed everything. As soon as the Sumerians invented the cuneiform script, other Mesopotamians eagerly adopted this technique. The Babylonians, for example, in the southern lands of Mesopotamia, created a treasure of literary works and inscriptions, and the Assyrians in the North used writing for political documentation. These ancient societies left behind a treasure of archives and records in cuneiform writing. Temple records provide details about various cults and religious sects and a massive wealth of myths, legends, and stories. This written "sacred history" allows access to the earliest and fully developed religious systems ever devised by humans. It provides us an opportunity to take a deep and focused look into the psyche of the ancients. Through this prism of ancient sacred history, many layers and colors of the human thought processes and religious perspective can be examined better than in prehistoric sacred art.

The Mesopotamians were not the first to create a sophisticated religious system, though, but they certainly were the first to write about religion. Their writing about it allowed religious ideas to spread faster and farther. It became far easier to "manufacture the consent" with the help of this new technology of writing. More importantly, writing allowed talking about gods or divinity in lofty terms and painting a vivid picture of their attributes and qualities that quickly fitted human imagination and emotion. A concrete shape was given to the mythical narrative, and gods and divine beings were portrayed as thinking and acting in human language and human terms.

How else could humans write about gods? After all, gods did not write about themselves in their god language. Perhaps it didn't occur to them to devise a script and language of their own; maybe, they trusted humans' linguistic capability more than their own; or perhaps they relied on humans' generosity – after all, humans have given them credit for everything good. Whatever the reason, they couldn't simply invent a God language themselves. And humans were free to project human personality, nature, attributes, and understanding onto the divine, for humans could only use the human imagination, not the gods'.

Humankind created beatific fiction, mythology, fantasy, stories, and narrative – the sacred history – and established an institution of religion. Further evolution of this institution resulted in an organized hierarchical system with the necessary infrastructure. History's sargons, kings, rulers, despots, bigots, zealots, and all others who grabbed and then terribly misused power mostly did so under cover of this institution. It happened then, and it happens today. Religion has historically been so formidable an institution that it can't be questioned or challenged, neither for committing wrongs nor rights. It drew and still draws most of its power from that unfounded fear of the future. It's precisely by instilling fear about God, gods, and retribution in the afterlife that religion could control the mightiest and the weakest alike.

In essence, religion is nothing but a political tool that has historically been used by the wise to control others.

Religion that meets the eye is subservient to unfounded fear. It works incessantly to reinforce that fear in the hearts and minds of people. The notion that religion is powerful is a misplaced one. It is the fear that is powerful. Religion simply rides on that power. Humankind tenaciously clings to religion as something sent from above. It will probably continue to do so for ages to come, even though it is precisely humankind themselves that shaped religion in the first place. Be that as it may, the fact is that religion is an invisible sword that slashes deep into the hearts and minds of the people, leaving a permanent mark in places hard to see with the naked unaided eye.

Chapter – 03

Mesopotamia - Salt, Marsh, Water, and God

The Land of Ziggurats

The Mesopotamians had a pantheon of thousands of gods. They had a god for everything that they found difficult to explain – wind, storm, rain, light, darkness, love, or hate – anything you could come up with. Then, there are god's attributes and attributes that are gods. Take, for example, wisdom. Wisdom was an attribute of some gods, that is, gods with wisdom, not necessarily wise gods. Then there was the wisdom god, for example, *Enki*, who could bestow wisdom. Likewise, you had a fire god, *Girra,* and others. Just as we have plant taxonomy, the Mesopotamians have god taxonomy. In one word, Pantheon. Why did Mesopotamians designate things as gods? It was useful.

In the Paleolithic era, people called on their deceased ancestors to intercede with nature. This was a brilliant idea but it was then. Paleolithic or Old Stone Age was simple. In the Neolithic era that followed the Paleolithic, human society was much more evolved. People looked at things of the old through a new prism. They wanted to understand the forces of nature, perhaps address nature without getting their deceased ancestors in between. That was quite an evolution in thinking but they lacked a crucial thing: knowledge, proper knowledge about nature. To avoid trouble they took the easiest approach: you don't know how rain falls? No problem. It is rain-god pissing. Did the rain god piss? Really? That wasn't important. What was important was to find a way to communicate with gods and call them by name and by implication tackle the forces of nature. This set the wheel of inquiry in motion.

Considering that ancestor worship was already firmly established in the Paleolithic, it came as no surprise that this custom (ancestor worship) morphed into god worship. At the fundamental level, the human mind was struggling to understand the forces of nature or nature as a whole. Personifying natural phenomena was the first step in that direction. That's how the Sun came to be the sun that shines in the sky and the sun-god, *Shamash*, simultaneously. *Shamash* could now be beseeched directly without ancestors' mediation. When urban centers came up the Mesopotamians connected gods to their cities. Each urban center was assigned a specific god or deity that looked after it. *Enlil* was the guardian god of Nippur; *Inanna* of Uruk and so on. In each city, a dwelling place – *Ziggurat* – was built for the respective guardian god. Unlike the temples of later days, the *ziggurats* were not meant for worship. They symbolized the city center where god lived.

The Neolithic revolution and urbanization marked a period of great shift of ideas, values, and behavior of the ancient societies. A fierce battle of ideas got underway. Urbanization was an attractive idea but it was also a disruptive one in the sense that it pushed people out of their comfort zone. The attraction however was the psychological lure that guardian gods take care of the cities and, by analogy, the city denizens. What better guarantee could have been thought of than a god or a deity himself establishing a particular urban settlement?

Take *Eridu*. He supposedly established the city of Eridu, previously a desolate place, where there was nothing other than sand and dust in a beastly hot climate. The legend went that *Eridu* sent water and churned out fertile land out of sand and dust and made his dwelling place here. Ever since he protected his city and people from enemies. The reality lay somewhere else but that didn't matter for Mesopotamians. Scholars speculate that this stretch of "salt and marshes" might have transmogrified as a result of some colossal event, most likely a meteorite strike millions of years ago. The groundwater released by the meteorite strike changed the quality of the salt and marshes and the heat of the burning sun boiled it into fertile mud. We can debate how that happened exactly. But for the inhabitants of Eridu and other Mesopotamians what mattered were *Eridu* and his *Ziggurat* and his watchful eye.

Here was a clear and unambiguous message for others: Look at our god and his dwelling place and see for yourself how we live under our god's merciful watch! The *Ziggurat* served as a model for other settlements and tribes to emulate. Over the years, other communities also built temples to their gods and the entire Mesopotamia became a dazzling land of

Ziggurats. People forgot that *Ziggurats* were built by their forefathers. They remembered them simply as "houses of their gods."

Enki, Inanna, and Cow

In cuneiform script city names were written in three parts – a sign for god, another for his name, and the third for the place. Gods could be represented by symbols. Their names could be written. And stories about them could be written. It was a paradigm shift. A new era had dawned. Sacred history was now recorded in the written word. New stories poured in and new gods sprang up from nowhere. All sorts of attributes became personified and transformed into independent gods or subalterns of other gods with colorful stories backing their biography, kind of. The written word gave impetus to poetic sensibility and out came poems, bard, and songs in praise of gods (and later goddesses also). In that literary gush, even the names of gods changed.

The god of Eridu came to be known as *Enki* – the god of civilization – who supposedly bestowed the Mesopotamians with intelligence, knowledge, and understanding. It was *Enki* who divided the tongues and made all the different languages spoken by different people. By the way, in the Biblical version of the story (Genesis. 11:1-9), the God of Abraham confused people and each began speaking a different language. By contrast, the Mesopotamians' version of the story is clear and precise. The Mesopotamians were very proud of *Enki's* role in founding their civilization and they recorded the story at length. When a later day Babylonian priest wrote the history of Mesopotamia, this is how he praised *Enki*: "He taught them to construct cities, to found temples, to compile laws and explained to them the principles of geometrical knowledge. He made them distinguish the seeds of the earth and showed them how to collect the fruits." The Biblical version seems a corruption of the Mesopotamian story of *Enki.*

Not far from Eridu, another settlement known as Unug, which later became Uruk, developed around a temple that was dedicated to the great goddess of love, *Inanna*. She symbolized womanhood and motherhood – she was "the beautiful cow to which the moon god in the form of a bull sent healing oils." She was represented by symbols like the "door of cowshed" and was supposed to be present in the holy "Cattle Pen." Cow and bull were central to the cult of *Inanna,* and as we shall see in chapter 4, ancient

Hindu scriptures describe cow in a metaphorical sense not unlike that in Mesopotamian myths. Possibly this Mesopotamian legacy of revering the cow was carried to India by the Aryans as agriculture spread to the East.

Inanna controlled the power to reproduce. If she absented herself from the world, the human race and the domesticated cattle would perish as depicted by the following hymn:

No bull mounted a cow,
No donkey impregnated a jenny,
No Youngman impregnated a girl in the street;
The young man slept in his private room;
The girl slept in the company of her friends,
That was a serious issue.
(*Myths of Mesopotamia*, translated by Stephanie Dalley)

The cattle and the beasts of burden formed the backbone of the agricultural economy. If the cattle were to stop reproducing the economy would come to a halt. That is to say, the Mesopotamians believed that anything that could annoy the goddess *Inanna* would have had huge repercussions for them. Understandably, they tried their best to stay away from any such risky endeavor. Here was a goddess who was impressive and powerful enough to control the fertility of the cattle - the farming community was not only hooked but even scared of her. They joined the crowd to worship her. There would be no cudgels with *Inanna.* She was paid respect and reverence. Awe-inspiring emotive stories and poetry were written and sung in her praise.

Inanna's sexual relationship with *Enki*, the god of Eridu was described at length by myth makers apparently to romanticize sex and love.

The Mesopotamians believed that *Enki* after creating civilization in Eridu had hidden the "principles" or "secrets of civilization" in *Aspsu,* the lake. *Inanna's* love affair with *Enki* ensured that she acquired the hidden secrets from *Aspsu.* That was what had made it possible for Uruk, the city of *Inanna,* to become the world's first urban center, they believed.

Toward the end of the 4th millennium, Uruk was a vibrant city abuzz with trade and business activity. Temples, buildings, shrines, and gathering places thrived around the *ziggurat* of goddess *Inanna.* The temple of the sky god *Anu,* it seems, had also come up in the vicinity of *Ziggurat*. In her influential book *Mesopotamia, the Invention of the City*, Gwendolyn Leick points out that these temples, although not yet places of worship were nevertheless open to the priests as well as the general public. As this city was coming to life around its temples and in their name, so was a totalitarian religious belief putting out deeper roots into the collective societal consciousness. That is to say, a theocracy controlled by the priesthood was taking a formal shape. The priestly class as is always the case, thoroughly used religion as an institution to systemically manipulate and exploit the "beast" — to borrow Alexander Hamilton's term for "people" — threatening them of retribution by the gods and goddesses if they disobeyed. That way, the priesthood maintained its grip over society and indirectly ensured the stability of the then-primitive state.

Religion was good at forging harmony and unity among unrelated tribes and communities within a particular settlement. That however didn't mean that minor differences in belief patterns and rituals would go unnoticed. These minor differences invariably mutated into contentious issues and different urban settlements rallying behind their respective gods adopted their particular belief patterns. Some even denigrated others' gods, which made clashes inevitable. Religion became synonymous with culture and culture defined the turf for wars. As the wars turned out profitable to victors in terms of booty, the war-mongers encouraged the people to fight. Wars for booty became a lucrative enterprise for this fragile agricultural economy. In the case wars would be threatened by peace, the clergy, and the power brokers would activate the whole religious propaganda machinery to "manufacture the enemy."

Old Order Erased

No sooner than Urukian civilization reached its peak, it suddenly tumbled down. What exactly happened is hard to establish. In around the 3rd millennium BCE, trade routes between different urban centers of Mesopotamia ceased to function, people emigrated out or got displaced, accounting and recording of business transactions were abandoned, the writing was forgotten, agriculture ignored and crops were left unattended and fields were not weeded. The economy collapsed bringing to an end the centuries-long cultural dominance of Uruk. Scholars blame floods and other natural calamities for the decline and fall of the Urukian civilization. That may be true. What is also true is that the destabilizing forces within the society itself might have led to anarchy and then collapse. Whatever it was, it was strange.

Primitive agrarian societies were fragile. The infrastructure was underdeveloped. Any sudden shift in the equilibrium would have been gravely inimical to the stability. Society would easily collapse. It has happened in many instances in the past and quite recently too, although, not to the extent of complete annihilation and extermination. The Urukian economy, for instance, not unlike yester years Communist Russia, was a tightly managed economy controlled by the clergy. Slavery, bonded labor, and peasant exploitation could well have resulted in rebellion. Otherwise, why would the temple lands, as scholars point out, be usurped by the farmers? That points to the breakdown of state machinery and some form of anarchy seizing control. In other words, people turned to loot, plunder, arson, and violence. Everything came to a standstill. For primitive agrarian societies, it simply meant irreparable losses, starvation, displacement, and death. People were forced to migrate to other places, leaving the town desolate.

In Uruk, as the data reveal, the drama probably played out thus: people first accepted and supported an ideology, say theocracy. As the ideology was put to practice it proved an inefficient and exploitative model of governance. As people became disillusioned and showed resentment and resistance, the alarm rang for the elite. Driven by fear of losing power, they responded aggressively unleashing indiscriminate force to curb the resistance. As is the case, the crack-down provides only temporary relief; the trouble usually simmers below the apparently calm surface. Unsurprisingly, the Urukians became increasingly estranged; the productivity suffered and the revenues of the temples fell. The state coffers too suffered and the power structure shook. The society was gripped by a civil war-like situation. People abandoned Uruk to save their lives. This all is supported by the evidence unearthed by a recent expedition of experts from the University of Chicago that comprehensively studied Uruk's archeology and history.

Societies are delicate machines. Ancient civilizations were even worse, extremely fragile, and founded on a rigid framework of religious ideology. Founding civilization on religious ideology is a recipe for failure. When people lose faith in a particular ideology or system, no amount of coercion or force can keep them leashed for long. The world of Urukians collapsed because they lost faith in their religion and temple-run government. Both *Inanna* and her religion were shelved in the archives of history. The official

Sumerian history of the day bluntly sums up the downfall of Uruk in one sentence: The older order was erased.

The First Book and the Market

With the Uruk's days over in the 3rd millennium BCE and the major population centers embroiled in strife and violence, much of the greater Mesopotamia was put to devastation and ruin resulting in wanton death and displacement of its people. In these gloomy days Nippur, the city of *Enlil*, became the center of gravity for hordes of displaced and homeless people. The ziggurat of *Enlil* witnessed frenzied activity. Here supplies, materials, and men and arms were collected and coalitions and confederations worked against each other's interests. Rivalry led to conflict and terror, infighting, and bloodshed – a kind of civil war. What is interesting is that in contrast to Uruk, here in Nippur during this warfare and turmoil, simultaneous construction of destruction also took place. Absent that war and wartime construction, we probably wouldn't be discussing Mesopotamia, for it was precisely because of the wartime competition that the Mesopotamians laid the foundations of what we call civilization.

The Mesopotamians were a passionate people. Their passion for inquiry, observation, and record-keeping was unmatched. They were ingenious enough to come up with the first of their kind books on clay tablets. A famous one, called *The Farmers Instructions* was a handbook designed to teach farmers how to get a better yield of crops. It asks them to perform certain religious rites to protect the crop from mice and pests. That looks absurd by today's standards, but other instructions like, say, how to better prepare land for crops – using hoe, demarcating the area, cutting weeds, leveling the field, etc. – are by all standards accurate and scientific. This is one of the many documentary shreds of evidence that life continued to happen despite all the turmoil, bloodshed, and war. Destruction, construction, war, and peace didn't hold back the Mesopotamians from founding civilization.

After the chaos settled a bit, Sumer rose to dominate the sociopolitical scene of Mesopotamia. Sumerians outrightly rejected the Urukian style "temple command economy." *Inanna's* religion also was forgotten however, *Inanna* didn't lose significance completely. As trade and barter began to flourish once again the concept of "market" was born for the first time and the first seeds of "market economy" were sown. The success of a market economy depends on the honesty and fairness shown by individuals in their dealings with one another. As formal transactional business picked up it was inevitable that stress began to be laid on values and virtues. The public display of honesty, integrity, and promise-keeping became an integral pillar of the now-evolving market economy. Religion again came in. Public display of religious observance gained prominence as never before. That is to say, religious observance in public became an index of righteousness and virtuousness of the people.

As markets flourished, wealth accumulated in fewer and fewer hands. A class of "haves" came into being. The parvenu "haves" slowly withdrew themselves from the traditional temple-centered communities and created a power structure to control the trade and economy. Backed by the clergy, this power structure led to the creation of the Institution of Kingship – one of the most important achievements of the Sumerians that laid the foundation of the institution that we call Politics.

Historically, the first kings came from a city called Kish. The situation was such that cities needed to be defended against the brigands of raiders, looters, and dacoits from neighboring townships. The different communities in a city would finance trained men and fighters to defend them against robbers – not a reliable method of defense against suddenly charging brigands. A sort of professional army was needed. But the army had to be fed and provided with remuneration, weapons, and lodging on a regular and systematic basis. Who would do that?

The nouveau riché had the resources and the wherewithal to finance a standing army. They were the "big men" or in Sumerian the "Lugalene" – the oligarchy that would eventually run the urban centers in the name of the top "Big man" or "the King" who was divinely ordained but recognized and anointed by the clergy.

As the oligarchy of Lugalene assumed control, they conscripted men to fight. In other words, they made an investment. To earn the profits on their investment, they had two options: either tax their populace (which could, well, prove precarious) or annex other territories to collect tribute (which meant fighting wars). That's to say, war was always a business. The world of business has always worked like that. Today we have big corporations, governments and churches, mosques and temples but the foundational principles of these big businesses remain the same as that of Mesopotamian Lugalene.

The army needed to fight wars but the business of war needed to be legitimized. Religion did precisely that. It called these wars the "business of gods in heaven" carried out by men on earth under the leadership of a King (a representative of gods). In other words, fighting wars became a holy business. As religion gave the green signal, the bloodshed didn't matter. This Mesopotamian legacy was faithfully observed by the later-day Abrahamic faiths as the holy war or Jihad. That's how the world of business works. Otherwise, why would one religious group fight another to grab war booty and make one or the other pay tribute? Holy wars were a lucrative business.

"Men fight and destroy the cities but the actual argument is between the gods," thus spoke the people of Lagash and Umma, who fought each other well over a century. The story goes: The King of Kish had been ordered by the god *Kadi* to mark the borders of the cities. The king of Umma, at the command of his god, usurped the land and entered Lagash. The king of Lagash, commanded by the god *Enlil,* went into battle with Umma. The battle was fought on *Ningirsu's* (another god) beloved field. Both sides fought hard. The battle ended but the war continued.

In his book *Babylon,* Paul Kriwaczek mentions that according to "Cambridge Ancient history, one temple alone in the city of Lagash furnished 500 to 600 men from its tenants for the military navy." It is estimated that as many as 10,000 warriors may have been involved in such wars, leading to unnecessary bloodshed and loss of lives.

Small or big, wars are wars. They incur costs. The Mesopotamians on both sides were hugely squeezed and badly affected by demands put by the war on social capital. Both sides had their respective gods at stake. Both sides had their respective "commandments of gods" to adhere to and defend. The result was a vicious cycle of protracted bloody conflicts and wars between different kingdoms where each aspired to win and dominate the other. Each aspired to build the civilization according to their version of religion.

Even though the differences in rituals and religion were quite minor, nevertheless, these differences created a bitter animosity among the different Mesopotamian communities, settlements, and cities. This is not quite unlike what we see today. Different sects of the same religion fight each other on matters relating to interpretation. One such example in the modern world is the "Shia and Sunni" conflict in the house of Islam. Despite minor differences in matters mainly relating to religious politics, Shias and

Sunnis have shed tonnes of human blood over more than a thousand or so years. The ancients were no different; in fact, we are no different from the ancients. After all, it is we who carry their genes. The Mesopotamians couldn't resolve whose god was better and they resorted to holy warfare. We can't resolve whose religion is correct. And we fight and kill each other. That's Life.

Divine Kingship and Hero Worship

Despite wars gods didn't change. Religion did as did business. As economic and socio-political order underwent a haul during Sumer's dominance, deep fault lines appeared in the religious perspective of Mesopotamia. Until then city gods, temples, and clergy carried undisputed importance in the socio-political life of Mesopotamians. Now, the new power structure had grown increasingly dissatisfied and disillusioned with the religious system revolving around city gods. The elite wanted a bigger share of the pie. Their support emboldened the kings to directly claim for themselves divine status. That raised the king's status from mere mortal to semi-divine monarch, which is to say, the "Divine right to Kingship" was formally sealed.

The Royal Graves excavated in Sumer indicate that some of the kings buried here had claimed to be gods. That is, a transition had happened from city god to king god. With that power center shifted from temple to palace, commencing the era of Royal patronage of religion. Sumer had become a real theocratic state. The King and the ruling family would now extend direct power and control over the temple property. That sounded alarm for the priestly class. Disgruntled dismayed and gripped by fear of losing relevance in a fast-changing scenario, they put up a united front against the royals. They called the action of kings blasphemous instigating the masses to mount rebellion against them. The clash between the priesthood and the rulers, each claiming the exclusive ownership of religion, brought Sumer to the brink of collapse.

During the reign of King Urukagina, the conflict further deepened pushing the society over the edge of the precipice. The records throw great light on this story. Both the palace and priesthood unscrupulously exploited the masses. The kings snatched temple property – lands, fields, and oxen – and used it as their royal holdings. Priests directed their wrath on farmers. A priest could enter a poor man's garden and with total impunity cut down his trees or take away his fruits and produce. Or when a commoner died, the priests would force the bereaved family to pay burial charges. Religion, instead of bringing solace, brought untold misery and exploitation to the poor. It proved powerful organized machinery in the hands of a few to extort wealth from people by creating fear about the unseen. Anybody daring to speak out against religious exploitation would simply be excommunicated. Period.

This politics around religion alienated the masses who ultimately ended up resisting the power structure. It didn't manifest as an all-out armed or violent rebellion, though. Instead, the masses put up a non-cooperative and stubborn attitude toward the state, imparting a signal that given the opportunity, they may even use the economic weapon. In ancient societies, the economy wholly depended on manpower, and people could use "labor" as a formidable weapon against the kings and their state except they seldom chose to do so. The reason: Ancient states were much more brutal than we can imagine, the peasantry was poor, ill-fed, ill-equipped, and at the mercy of feudal lords or Lugalene in Mesopotamia for a morsel of food. The enfeebled and emasculated workforce was seldom allowed to cooperate and scheme against the merchants of religion and the state machinery. But in rare situations, when the Lugalene would switch sides throttling the supply of food grains and commodities to the state, or when after crop failure due to drought or famine or after some disease epidemic when the labor force severely diminished, the state machinery would severely suffer and collapse. In Sumer, too, events unfolded so inimically that sooner or later it had to fall under its own weight. It did. Not abruptly, though.

Decades earlier *Lagash* had inflicted a humiliating defeat upon *Umma*. But then it was *Umma's* turn to revenge on *Lagash*. This event coincided with the dawn of a new era – the era of hero worship and empires. Sumer was caught amidst transformation which rose to a fever pitch. Religious politics assumed a new façade.

In 2230 BCE the first true empire emerged under the leadership of one known to history as *Sargon*. He ruled in the name of *Ishtar*, the all-powerful goddess of war, love, aggression, lust, and procreation. All the Southern Mesopotamian gods and goddesses like *Enki, Ea, Utu, Shamash,* and *Inanna* paled before *Ishtar*. Sensing opportunity Sargon made a bold somersault. Rather than founding a city in *Ishtar's* name he founded *Agade* in his own name. *Agade* was the Sumerian name for what is *Akkad* in Semitic languages.

For the next 1500 years, Sargon, the founder of the Akkadian Empire came to be regarded as a patron saint by all the subsequent Mesopotamian empires. With the emergence of empires and hero worship Mesopotamia's religious perspective and outlook noticeably changed.

Up until Sargon's era, the common belief was that gods created human society for their own (gods') benefit; cities were divine entities; a particular god resided there and life on earth was no more than a shadow of the *real life* that gods lived in some supernatural domain or the heavens. By the time Sargon's Empire was in place, the religious discourse had shifted from the *world of gods* to the *world of men*. Now "people" instead of gods became the protagonists of stories. People longed to take control of their everyday world in their own hands. It was a transformation in thinking. Religion followed suit in content and connotation. Men became "heroes" worthy of "worship" like gods, and interestingly enough women were coming forward to take an active interest in religious affairs.

Sargon's daughter became the Head Priestess of the temple of *Nanna*, the moon god. She formally introduced an element of hero worship into religious practice to quite successfully shift the emphasis from gods to humans. She became the first "in [recorded] history to express a personal relationship between herself and her god" and boldly and eloquently argued and demanded recognition of her status from the goddess *Inanna*.

The Akkadian empire, though powerful by the standards of the day, was nevertheless innately fragile. It couldn't develop adequate means and technology to handle the myriad pressures, forces, and vagaries of nature. There was practically no transportation system or road network. The expansionist policy pursued by the empire ultimately worked against it by stretching the boundaries beyond its capacity for consolidation. The annexed lands and settlements couldn't be held for long under the control of the central administration. Rebellions erupted and the empire was gripped by chaos.

Mesopotamia was an agrarian economy at its core. Any predominantly agrarian society was necessarily fragile owing to primitive technology and the inability to harness resources for growth. They had only two things to survive on: crops and religion. Any disturbance in these two could easily tip the balance toward economic disaster. In the case of the Akkadian empire, like others before it, the forces that led to the fall were primarily economic. The Mesopotamians, however, didn't buy the idea that purely economic reasons caused their decline. They sought to find the explanation in religion. They maintained that "this disaster" was due to "gods' anger" against arrogant emperors and their blasphemous practices. The Mesopotamians were clear in their understanding, "Nemesis had necessarily followed and the gods had punished arrogance by altering the course of nature and causing starvation." Interesting! Does it look different from how most people think today?

When Akkad was crushed by the Gutis, people quickly blamed their kings' and elite's blasphemous practices. Now that the Gutis imposed their over-lordship upon them, the Akkadians felt humiliated. It was a crisis time for Akkadian society. Cursing themselves, they sought refuge in gods and religion and beseeched for pardon before their gods. In desperate hope for a better future, they turned to all sorts of ideas and abstractions to help them patiently tolerate their enemy's over-lordship of them. The belief that "our gods will not betray us again" kept them going in the hope of a better tomorrow.

Scapegoats

Humans engage in conflicts, rebellions, battles, and wars yet religion and the gods provide a rallying ground and inspiration for that all tussle. When an atmosphere of war is threatened by peace or when relative peace is interrupted by war, religion suddenly becomes the most important entity. Ordinary rituals and routines take on ceremonial significance and the guardians of religion attach to them all kinds of spiritual meaning and metaphysical dimension. And surprisingly, people oblige. They set aside their differences on economic and political issues and come together on a common religious platform. They quickly identify with each other through shared stories, shared rituals, and shared nostalgia. Everybody longs to revert to the old and supposedly pure religious practices of their forefathers. Every time trouble befalls them they castigate their irreligiosity, never blaming gods for not hearing their supplications.

Out of fear and uncertainty about the future, historically people have been reluctant to embark on innovative religious paths. They prefer to be over-cautious in their actions and religious discourses lest the gods may punish them. And crisis times are tricky. They carry a risk of pushing a society toward religious fundamentalism. That is to say, any reform has the risk of being completely rejected and dubbed blasphemous. Innovative and critical voices get silenced. Such brittle periods in sacred history are usually molded, managed, and accentuated by the contagious character of the religious "crowd mentality." People either follow the leaders obsequiously or they get paralyzed by the chaos. They want answers but remain pathologically chained to the past. As a result, they fall into a perpetually vicious cycle. They fall back on the mistakes of the past. Frustration increases. As the ghosts of the past haunt the collective mind and memory; the society finds itself warped by the inertia of the past and fails to dissect its actions and critically examine its behavior. Blame gets laid on all kinds of scapegoats. It provides an exit route out of frustration.

Akkadians made Sargon their chief scapegoat. He was accused of chipping away at the ancestors' religious rites and attempting to erode ancient belief patterns; an ignoble deviation from ancestral religion, responsible for bringing disaster on people. His introduction of hero worship was an outright blasphemy, unforgivable by gods. As the priesthood had been particularly uncomfortable with Sargon's religious policy, they saw an opportune occasion to beat up the drum: abandon hero worship, this blasphemous innovation, immediately lest the anger of the gods and their punishment would be perpetual!

Sargon in his hubris and complacency had quite underestimated the priesthood's clout. These shrewd guardians of religion were patiently waiting for the fault lines to appear, and now, at the slightest hint of people's dissatisfaction, they threw the gauntlet. As the rhetoric turned vitriolic they took the bull by its horns. But Sargon was long gone then. It was the Gutis who faced the Akkadian wrath.

How Opium Worked

Utu-hegal spearheaded the revolt against the Guti occupation to restore the Akkadian empire to its former glory. The Akkadians considered Gutis barbarians and uncivilized because the latter turned down their gods and refused to acknowledge the religious practices of the former. This was a serious matter implying that the occupiers planned to impose their pagan religion, and by analogy pagan culture, on the Akkadians. They needed to resist. The rebellion built up as the religious sentiment was at its peak to bring back the glory of the Akkadian gods. "It was '*Enlil*' the king of gods, who had decided to kick the Guti out of Mesopotamia, and had chosen me for the task," announced Utu-hegal to his supporters. This was quite a move to garner support to overthrow the occupiers of the land. Utu-hegal was "inspired by god, himself". The aspirations ran high. "There was a sure-shot victory waiting for us [the Akkadians] as god himself had sanctioned it," Utu-hegal shrewdly assured the people. The religious proclamations and invocations naturally boosted the confidence of his supporters as they were to face an enemy stronger in military prowess than them. Only those blind in reason can risk their lives to go ahead in the battle against a powerful enemy and Utu-hegal was well aware of that. He carefully chose his words, adroitly and craftily intoxicating the Mesopotamians with the word-opium to fight until death.

Utu-hegal stopped at the temple of the goddess *Inanna*, allegedly to keep her informed. Then, he stopped at the temple of *Ishtar*, the god of storm, and addressed the citizens: "*Enlil* and *Inanna* had chosen me to lead the campaign against the occupiers of our land." Everybody zealously joined his ranks. The rest, as they say, is history. With the fall of the Gutis, the foundations of a remarkable social system were laid.

Around 2100 BCE, Sumer built a new city called Ur. According to Max Weber, Ur became a large imperial state that ruled over almost entire Mesopotamia. The social set up was strictly patrimonial. That is to say, the population arranged itself in a hierarchy led by a father figure – the king. Despite the king's occupying the top position the government was run by an oligarchy of nobles and wealthy. The carrot and stick approach was used to keep the masses in line. The Sumerian ruling elite understood well that to run the administration smoothly an aura of power and strength should be created around the king. Accordingly, they projected him as an all-knowing, all-powerful persona.

Shulgi, the greatest king of Ur, like Sargon before him took a calculated risk which turned out his masterstroke. He declared himself a god. As Ur and Mesopotamia in general were enjoying relative prosperity and peace after long periods of instability, people didn't question their king's blasphemous proclamation. Again, Hero worship became fashionable. Shulgi's reversion to an allegedly ignominious practice of the past was nothing but shrewd political posturing of his; it worked in his case as the economic situation in Ur was favorable in contrast to that in Akkad. Soon hero worship and personality cults were firmly reestablished in the empire. The king now instilled awe and fear into the hearts and minds of their subjects.

Glowing tributes were paid to King Shulgi in the temples. Chants and hymns were sung in his honor. Shulgi was no more a great ruler and warrior only but an embodiment of supernatural powers and attributes; an embodiment of the Sumerian (Mesopotamian) history and civilization; and, well, a personification of divine qualities and powers. He made Sumerian the official language of ancient Mesopotamia. And with that, the protocol for the future kings was officially laid down in writing.

History abhors stagnation. It has its unique way of happening. Its law of inertia is always at work, whether we perceive that or not. As a result, history repeats itself, or at least rhymes, to borrow from Mark Twain. Ur would have a much-cherished status quo, had it not for old age to whittle this city-state. Time weathered the Urukian Empire, breaking it down into warring territories ruled by individual chieftains. Ur, like its predecessor, Akkad, couldn't withstand the pressures and challenges of its own making. Ur had expanded beyond capacity. The rebelling territories under their respective chieftains wanted to go their way. The economy suffered severely. Again religion had come in the way of unity. The records show that one community worshipped a territorial or local god, *Amurru*, who hadn't been allowed a place in Ur's pantheon. They put the spark in a heap of straw. The fire of religious persecution was set ablaze which ultimately burnt the whole empire to ashes. As luck would have it, the infields, as the people of Ur called the worshippers of *Amurru*, finally won the day. History knows them as Amorites.

The Amorites rose from the ashes and rebuilt Mesopotamia into a dazzling civilization of the day. It was under Amorites that this civilization reached its new apogee. The new world order was in the offing. History had reached a point when the "sacred histories" of the world would intersect, and the place where they did so was none other than Babylon in Southern Mesopotamia. After two millennia of North's dominance the seat of power slipped over to the South. It was time for *Marduk* to be the all-powerful god – the god of Babylon.

A long walk to the *Hijab*

It was after a long walk on the bumpy path that sacred history finally laid to rest the age-old belief that city, land, people, crops, and livestock are the property of gods. A new socio-political system was birthed in Mesopotamia.

For the first time territorial units called the political states came into existence. Mesopotamia was divided into Northern and Southern units. The North went to Ashur and the South to Babylon. For a touch long Babylon was ruled by kings who didn't promote any particular god officially. That is to say, South Mesopotamia was enjoying a more or less secular government. That trend was broken by one Hammurabi, supposedly the greatest king of Babylon, who officially invoked the god *Shamash* as guardian and protector of his empire. It was *Shamash* who, according to Hammurabi, revealed to him his new laws, famously known as Hammurabi's code.

By the time Hammurabi ascended the throne, the class division (like the Caste system) had created deep fault lines in the society. The *Awailum, Mushkenum,* and *Wardum* were the three dominant classes. The *Wardum* were the slaves, the *Awailum* were the ruling elite and the *Mushkenum* were the commoners. Hammurabi might have been hard-pressed to handle the class conflict; the reason that he came up with the "revelation thing" from *Shamash.* He was the first king in recorded history who took a somewhat softer view on slavery and slaves: Debt slavery was strictly limited to three years in Hammurabi's code! This is in sharp contrast to later religious scriptures like the Torah, the Bible, or the Quran which are the "word of God" for their respective followers. All of them are silent on the question of the abolition of slavery.

In Babylon, vibrant sociopolitical machinery was consolidating itself, and the old Sumerian cultural dominance was fast becoming a thing of the past. The populace was supposed to be "loyal to the king" and respect the ancient myths, legends, and sacred history. *Marduk* replaced other gods as the chief deity of Babylon but the foundational religious beliefs and rituals didn't change much. There were no sacred texts and no written theological doctrines to set the rules and regulations of worship.

A significant change slowly took place in Babylonian society like never before education was becoming a systematic and structured discipline. What we today call "Science" was shaping its beginnings here in Babylon. Some keener minds were getting drawn to the study of life forms (Biology). The earliest records of observation and classification of the living world belong here. For the first time, education, learning, and intellectualism were valued.

A conspicuous shift in the thinking led to a shift in the religious outlook of the Babylonians. Their relationship with gods transmogrified and they began to question some of the old religious dogmas. As they pondered the order and the logic behind the workings of the world, they turned to the study of medicine, astrology, geometry, and mathematics exploring new ideas and new horizons of inquiry.

As the Babylonian state reached its zenith it began to show its brittleness. Like other agrarian economies before, it reached a tipping point when its decline became inevitable, as it suffered from the same limitations as the empires before it. With no road and transport network in place and no effective means of delivering administration to annexed territories, the revenue base got steadily chipped away. With the decline in the economy, the traders, the priests, and the workers started migrating away from the capital. The urban population declined and fewer people were left to defend the city-state. Chaos, uncertainty, and despair gripped Babylon. Sensing opportunity, the neighboring tribes and states attacked the city from all sides.

Long story short: In the tussle a people, from Upper Mesopotamia known to history as Assyrians, emerged winners. Babylon was sacked and Hammurabi's dynasty was put to an end. The political chaos, however, refused to settle immediately.

The conflict over suzerainty between Assyria and the enfeebled Babylon continued for centuries. Finally, in 1120 BCE, the Assyrian Empire (also known as the *Assur* Empire after the god *Ashur*) was formally established by King Tiglath-Pileser I. However, after his death, the empire quickly disintegrated. Interestingly, the political instability and uncertainty brought about a robust transformation in the overall attitude of society. People turned to novel ideas. The religion was more or less identical to that of the old Babylonians. The Assyrian god *Ashur* replaced the Babylonian god *Marduk* as the official god. However, other gods like the moon god, the sun god, and the goddess *Ishtar* of Nineveh with *Venus* were also worshipped freely.

The religious discourse and narrative too changed profoundly, permanently impacting the shaping of the future sacred history. The Mesopotamians carved out new theological principles that would go on to become the foundational traditions for the later Abrahamic religions. Many Mesopotamian cultural and philosophical traditions were inconspicuously carried within the densely worded scriptures of the world's major religions.

Some of history's harsh and cruel laws came into being here in the Assyrian Mesopotamia. Women especially were severely punished for acts like abortion. Abortion was considered a particularly abominable crime inviting harsh punishments on women. Convicted women were impaled in stakes and their burial was prohibited. Adultery was punished by death or disfigurement. A woman would be punished for her husband's crime but the husband bore no responsibility for his wife's behavior. Men enjoyed far more liberty than women under the new laws. They could divorce their wives or throw them out of their houses with impunity.

The implementation of harsh laws against women was a U-turn from the old traditions of Mesopotamia when women played a far greater and constructive role in society. Female goddesses were prevalent, popular, and powerful then; women actively participated in religious matters; and some notable women were appointed as high priestesses in important temples. The recent change in the perceived status of women, in the Assyrian society, was undoubtedly the result of a great, though, negative, shift in the overall religious outlook of the society.

Women were now bound by law to follow the prescribed dress code – the *Hijab*. As Paul Kriwaczek notes, "the earliest known requirement for women to wear what is now called the *hijab* is found here [in Mesopotamia]," except that the slave girls had no right to veil themselves; if found veiled, their ears had to be cut off. The harlots were dealt with in the same manner. *The hijab* was simply not meant for slaves and harlots. Anybody, even a member of the upper class, who had seen a slave girl or a harlot in *hijab* and had let her go, would be punished with fifty lashes without any regard to his status or nobility. *The hijab* became a status symbol and cultural heritage. Later scriptures (e.g. the Quran) maintain that observing *hijab* or *Parda* was a divine injunction sent upon the Muslims.

Ancient Assyria established a "model for female seclusion" for the future. "Indeed there is a direct continuity from the harem of the old palace in Ashur, right through the Babylonian, Persian, and Hellenistic eras, to the Byzantine royal court, from which imperial Islam, in turn, inherited so much of its preference for women's public invisibility," notes Paul Kriwaczek in *Babylon*. That is that.

The Omnipotent God

During the Assyrian dominance, religion evolved and transformed to absorb different cultural influences. Much of the religion of the forefathers was abandoned, except that the foundational traditions persisted as vestigial rituals. As can be recalled from the discussion a couple of pages earlier, ancient Mesopotamians held the belief that gods were the owners of everything connected to humans and the earthly kingdoms were simply a replica of the heavenly kingdom of gods and thus the old Mesopotamians personified and deified nature and the forces of nature. Their pantheon of gods was quite elaborate and exhaustive. Come Assyrians, and all that slowly changed.

There was nothing strange or preposterous about the older Mesopotamian religious tradition. It fits the socio-political frame of the day. As the sociopolitical and economic systems evolved, religion evolved side by side. Or maybe religion evolved first and the socio-political evolution followed. From a utilitarian standpoint, it didn't matter which came first. What mattered though was how power could concentrate in the hands of the few who in turn would keep their firm grip on the masses. What better could man think of than harping on the perpetual fear of retribution in the afterlife to establish the house of power? It was far easier to instill the fear of the future in the hearts and minds of people than engage in fine talk with them to get them to follow the smooth-talking leaders. The concept of "invisible power behind everything" was an abstract idea born out of the fertile human mind. But abstractions are abstract. They are not things.

Humans are comfortable with things. To make abstractions look like things, the ancients personified ideas, concepts, and abstractions as things (deities) and things (water, fire, earth, sky, sun, storm, rain, hail, flood, etc.) as ideas and attributes. Thus water was the rain-god's attribute, fire of fire-god's, and so on. That way abstract could be touched, felt, assimilated imagined, and communicated with. That is to say, the deification established a connection between everyday mundane affairs and some imagined higher-order entity (a particular deity, sub-deity, or a group of closely related deities). Now different attributes could be projected onto different deities and they in turn could then be beseeched and supplicated for things, non-things, wishes, desires, and on and on, the list can be infinite.

In ancient Mesopotamia, politics was not as complicated as it is today. Religion was a powerful tool for handling political affairs, partly because of a lack of a better idea and partly because religion was probably the only option. Religion was politics and politics was religion.

Different people gave different names to the same things and the same gods meant different practices, rites, and rituals, and thus different religions to the same people. The religious practices and customs as an integral component of the society's cultural milieu were completely synonymous with cultural identity. Cooperation between different communities, settlements, or societal units became increasingly difficult and even dangerous to contemplate. Over-enthusiasm of one group to cooperate could be viewed by the other as an unwanted attempt by the former to interfere in the latter's matters and tip the balance. Clashes would happen at a moment's notice. Sectarian clashes could at times become ugly. In urban centers, such clashes could temporarily be handled but the potential pressure points and the fault lines persisted leading to chronic bouts of violence and damage to state property. As a result, the city empires' economy suffered, supplies fell, expenses to maintain peace skyrocketed and the coffers depleted, all contributing to the eventual collapse of state machinery under the weight of sectarian religious-tribal conflicts. It was by far a common phenomenon in the Mesopotamian civilization. The truth is that no empire could survive past its old age not because religious strife brought it down but because all ancient empires were economically fragile. Religious conflict simply brought the economic fragility of the empires to the tipping point.

Centuries of living settled life transformed the human perspective. A curious shift took place. As mentioned earlier, gods that hitherto represented natural forces now became entities beyond and above nature and natural forces. In other words, faith in the "transcendence of gods" replaced the old religion of "gods dwelling in ziggurats." Now the gods were contemplated as "entities dwelling in some unknown realms of distant heaven," that could only be reached indirectly through some form of contemplation or inspiration. These gods communicated with kings and big men through a "messenger." The messenger supposedly handed over to "big men" some sort of a "writing tablet" with the message engraved by a "stylus" implying it was the god who had written some order on the tablet. Be that as it may, the transcendence of the gods permanently redefined humankind's relationship with nature.

The Mesopotamians came to believe that humans were created in the likeness of gods and by corollary humans are above nature (or the natural world). This theology imparted the Mesopotamians a sense that humans overall by nature were superior creatures and everything else was subservient to them. That's to say humans rightfully could claim their dominion over the seas, rivers, land, cattle, and everything living. The sense of superiority, imparted by religious discourse created a whole lot of complex issues in the Mesopotamian (Assyrian) civilization – Men gained dominance over women who in turn were debarred from participation in public religious liturgy and worship, particularly during menstruation and immediately after childbirth. The royal edicts, as reported by Paul Kriwaczek in *Babylon,* were unambiguous, "No menstruating woman was allowed into the presence of the Assyrian king. Priests had to be careful to avoid sexual contact with their wives during menstrual days and had to carry out elaborate rituals to purify themselves after sharing the bed with their wives. The women were regarded as a danger to men's half-divine nature."

Another curious transformation that quietly happened in Assyrian Mesopotamia was this: gods, now independently transcendent entities separate from nature and their dwelling places, could be worshipped anywhere. That is to say, it was no longer necessary to worship god near *Ziggurats* or temples or in his particular city for worship to be effective. This in the Assyrian case meant that their god Ashur could be worshipped anywhere, and there was no need to build Ashur's temple in every conquered city. A 'Central temple' in the main city was enough for organizing the systemic religious activity.

The worshippers could occasionally visit the "Central temple," which practice metamorphosed into the ritual of pilgrimage. Soon some major pilgrimage sites emerged (usually around ziggurats). All kinds of stories and myths circulated to attract people to these "places of pilgrimage." The city centers and ziggurats became hubs of religious and economic activity. This Mesopotamian legacy of pilgrimage then continued into the Abrahamic and non-Abrahamic religious traditions following the fall of Mesopotamian civilization.

Toward the end of the second millennium BC, religion in Mesopotamia (now Assyria) had in a sense molted as it had grown. It had cast off much of its baggage as it metamorphosed into its almost entirely new form. With *Ashur* being detached from its strings transforming *him* into an

Omnipresent from a strictly Assyrian god, the path was cleared for *him* to evolve into an "omnipresent, omniscient, and omnipotent" Single God. Soon the whole Mesopotamian Pantheon got assimilated under the all-encompassing, blessed, and merciful persona of this single god – *Ashur*. That was a remarkable evolution of religion. By a sleight of the invisible hand of theology, solid foundations of monotheism were laid here, in Assyria.

The Judeo-Christian-Islamic tradition wasn't anything new but a continuation of a religious-cultural milieu that had taken firm roots by the late Bronze and early Iron Age in northern Mesopotamia. The Assyrian kingdom expanded over the years and spread its agriculture, influence, and above all foundational principles of faith and religion to distant regions, touching the heart as well as the body of Asia. God became God and the story of faith evolved uninterrupted. All along, scared history refined itself by smoothing out rough edges here and there. It was then only a matter of a few centuries of focused discourse that monotheism would be formalized, not in Mesopotamia proper, though, but in its unassuming neighborhood, Judea.

PART 2

India
Violence, Sacrifice, and Throes of Ahimsa

Chapter – 04

From Cattle Rustling Aryans to Cow Revering Community

The Transformation

"We are meaning-seeking creatures and, unlike other animals, fall very easily with despair if we cannot find significance and value in our lives," writes Karen Armstrong. Traditionally, humankind has looked to religion for answers and explanations to some basic existential questions. Yet, many a great mind were baffled by the apparent mysteries of the world. Absent a systematic form of inquiry and investigation (that we now call Science), it fell on religion to answer questions like who are we, where did we come from, and where are we going, etc. In that struggle to answer such questions, religion inevitably stumbled onto what we call spirituality – a connection (or, more accurately, a sense of reference) to something bigger than us, such as God or spirit. Ironically, this "search for meaning" was accompanied by violence between different sects professing different methods of search. Peaceful spirituality and peaceful spiritual quest have largely been ineffective in preventing this violence (religious violence). However, spirituality brought about a paradigm shift in the religious evolutionary process. Yet the vast majority of the people of faith refuse to acknowledge the slow and steady maturation of religion and faith. To many, the shift seems to have happened abruptly at some point in human history by the invisible hand of the divine; to others, there was no shift the divine agency perfected religion at the outset, but humans distorted it. In reality, the paradigm shift resulted from the long drawn-out cascade of spiritual and cultural processes whose fingerprints can be seen everywhere from Mesopotamia to India to Europe and the Arabian deserts. It is a different matter, though, that this shift didn't translate into complete dis-association from violence in the name of religion. That would be much to ask of it. Absent violence, you would probably not be reading this book. At least.

In the late Bronze Age (3300 BCE – 1200 BCE) and throughout the Iron Age (1200 BCE – 600 BCE), religion was in the midst of a serious evolution. A new thought had begun to stir human consciousness at a much deeper level culminating, over time, in a significant shift in the religious outlook. Before the Bronze Age, rituals, particularly animal sacrifice, mattered. By the time the Iron Age was at its peak, the emphasis had shifted from ritual to human behavior. The roots of Ethics and religious morality were firmly laid. In the words of Karen Armstrong, "What mattered now was not whether you believed in city gods or not, but how you behaved." That is to say, as religion expanded its scope and sphere of influence to include morality and ethics, it claimed complete guardianship of all the matters of everyday life. The direction of the debate and discourse shifted accordingly, and religion took more responsibility for itself. Responsibility meant a tremendous opportunity to profoundly change humankind from within, i.e., behavior and outlook. That was a monumental task. Religion underestimated the magnitude of this task. In the struggle to transform the human being, religion itself evolved. Religious thought matured over the centuries, adjusting to the needs and challenges of developing societies. Scholars say the collateral manifestations of this continuous thought transformation and evolution of religion were seen millennia later in the form of the Renaissance and Industrial Revolutions. That conclusion may seem farfetched; however, it is hard to deny. Tim Lewens aptly argues in his book *The Meaning of Science* that "all of today's scientific disciplines started life as speculative branches of philosophy itself." Philosophy, in turn, started life as a discourse mostly around religion and religious matters.

Contrary to the commonly held belief that religion is immutable, it turns out it is as malleable and evolution-prone as anything else – a fact darn unsettling for the believers in the divine origin of religion. As religion descended from God, they believe, there could be no evolution or modification in what came from above. The people, however, transgressed divine law and corrupted the original pristine religion, they maintain. Yet, the study of history tells a different story. German philosopher Karl Jasper identifies a specific historical period when everything human, religion included, underwent the most extraordinary transformation and evolution. He calls that period the "Axial Age." The Axial Age roughly corresponds to the late Bronze Age (1500 BCE- 1200 BCE) and the Early Iron Age (1200 BCE - 700 BCE). Contrary to the commonly held belief, the transcendence of gods, monotheism, and spirituality took root for the first time during human history's Axial Age. The sacred history of the day duly reflects this change in the religious landscape.

The Idea of Sacrifice

Around 4500 BCE, pastoralist people lived in a loose network of tribes on the Caucasian steppes of today's Southern Russia. We call them the Aryans. They were hardy and tough-skinned people. They had to be. The perpetual peregrinations put extraordinary demands on them. The resources were meager, and making out a day's meal was quite a deal. Yet, when they finally settled in the plains of North India, they became the first people whose records that have come down to us reveal that they practiced the spirituality of the Jasperian "Axial Age." Long before they migrated to India, the individual Aryan tribes increasingly started drifting apart, organizing themselves into nomadic communities. Finally, two tribal groups dominated the steppes – the Avestan and the Sanskrit speaking (Avestan and Sanskrit are two dialects of the same language). Over time, these two tribes also drifted apart, although they didn't immediately cut off their ties with each other. Both persisted with the foundational principles of their shared cultural and religious traditions for a long time.

One foundational principle of their religious tradition was that an "invisible force" exists in the "nature" surrounding them. Everything manifested from this invisible force. They called it *mainyu* in Avestan and *manya* in Sanskrit. Everything, then, was a manifestation of *mainyu/manya*. In a sense, it was an Aryan way of saying what we now call monism. But the concept of *manya* didn't prevent them from creating, like the Mesopotamians before them, a pantheon of hundreds, or perhaps millions, of gods. Any phenomenon or event that defied explanation within their limited arsenal of knowledge and everyday language was venerated as a god. The good thing about that wanton awe of things, real and imaginary, was that it helped them understand and bond with each other better. As can be recalled from Chapter 1, a common religious vocabulary is of tremendous help in building rapport, creating communal groups, and establishing "cumulative culture." Never mind, much of religious vocabulary was a product of childish ignorance. Yet ignorance has served humanity to accomplish incredible feats. For instance, it helped achieve huge cooperative endeavors like building nations. To borrow from Ernst Renan, nations are built by getting history wrong. That is one of the ways by which ignorance is rewarded.

Fire, storm, thunder, sun, moon, stars, etc., defied explanation. They still do, to some extent. The Aryans, like other ancients, took the easy route. They made them gods. The god is inexplicable and incomprehensible; god is a name given to a bunch of abstractions. Scholars cheerfully, if a touch disingenuously, argue that god became god because *he* could not be explained logically or physically. The concept of god saved people from a lot of drudgeries. Seeing god everywhere and in everything was a more accessible and palatable way for the ancients to handle natural phenomena, adjust daily life accordingly, and streamline individual and collective behavior. It helped evolve a set of rules, traditions, and belief systems and establish a peculiar cultural milieu within the existing "cumulative culture." Over time these traditions and beliefs became dogmas, and various dogmas became so ingrained in the individual and collective mind that questioning them, even in good faith, meant inviting unnecessary and disproportionate trouble.

Belief in gods became an article of faith. Tribes began to identify themselves with particular gods. Each tribe had its preferred deity out of a pantheon of gods. That meant one specific god had to be respected and revered by everyone who wanted to identify with a particular tribe or community. Switching from one deity to another tribal deity by a member or a group of members amounted to a rebellion against the parent tribe. Understandably, switching sides was an exception rather than a rule. However, in contrast to later religious traditions, the ancient Aryan religion (before and immediately after migration to India) was not well-organized. It didn't strictly forbid the intermingling of belief. It didn't impose a strict moral code on the faithful. Later religious traditions, as we will see in forthcoming chapters, are known for adopting a relatively extreme position in matters of faith. Take Christianity. According to it, God puts a "seal of faith" on the heart of a fetus even before it is fully developed in the mother's womb. In other words, as per Christianity, religious morality is etched on the "heart of man" by God himself. Nothing of the kind was seen in the Aryan religion.

The Aryans called their gods "*daevas*" or "*devas*." No *Deva* could qualify as an omnipotent god by himself. Each *deva* was supposed to submit to "*Rita*" – an all-powerful, higher sacred order "which held the human society and the universe together as one whole system." In other words, the individual gods were, in essence, the workhorses of *Rita* incessantly laboring to maintain the order of the world. The so-to-say-incessant labor exhausted *devas*, draining their energy. From time to time, they required energy replenishment; otherwise, the exhausted *devas* could let the world slip into disorder and chaos – so went the story. The surest way to meet the energy demands of *Devas* was Sacrifice – the ritualistic sacrifice. In a sense, the Aryans were no ordinary players. Like other ancients, they could concoct and conjure up anything from nothing! They found a brilliant solution in "Sacrifice." It was, the Aryans concluded, an appealing and efficient method for transferring nourishment to gods.

The sacrifice ritual had another practical benefit: it helped the Aryans overcome the taboo of fear of killing a living creature. Killing cattle and beasts of burden was a particularly fearful and loathsome act. But, by the fourth millennium BCE, the priorities had changed. New challenges had arisen. Food requirements had increased due to the increased population. To meet the demands of food for a growing population, it became necessary to slaughter the cattle, but the fear of killing was proving a stumbling block for this enterprise. The fear had to be done away with, and the best way to achieve that was by making sacrifice a religious ritual. It was a brilliant idea. Immediately sacrifice became a sacred duty. That eased the fear and encouraged the people to adjust to killing cattle for meat procurement. Ritualistic sacrifice removed the burden of guilt that would otherwise fuel the reluctance of people to kill the animals. People almost broke free. It was only a matter of time then that the Aryans mustered the courage to engage in raiding, rustling, and looting to pick the cattle for holding grand sacrificial ceremonies and communal feasts.

Initially, the sole incentive for engaging in cattle rustling activities was the Collective Sacrifice. Over time this raiding and rustling became a profitable enough enterprise to attract more people's participation. The Aryans beautifully rationalized their rustling business. No Aristotle of the time could have conjectured a better syllogism. Deducing syllogistically, the Aryan chieftains and priestly class argued that the universe couldn't have originated except through a "sacrificial offering" – a pure conjecture that the Aryans accepted as a matter of fact and truth. They weren't alone in this business of conjecturing fantasy. Humans have engaged in such things since the dawn of civilization: when the need arises to justify actions, humans have all the imagination to do that. They can rationalize, explain, and justify anything.

Humans possess this marvelous brain and mind. The mind creates reality out of non-reality, constructs out of concepts, and meaning out of meaninglessness. Nothing surpasses the human mind when it comes to imagining. That the Aryans and other ancients didn't have the science and technology we possess today didn't matter much, their mental faculties were no less fertile than ours. Their immediate need was food procurement. Cattle slaughter could easily cover their requirements for meat. Yet slaughtering cattle was a taboo. To overcome this taboo, the Aryans ingeniously invoked a *deva* or god, an alibi not quite so different, in principle, from the later Abrahamic faiths. By resorting to such theological maneuvering, the Aryans lavishly ate meat, drank *soma*, sang, danced, and enjoyed. And gods were free to receive whatever nourishment they wanted. Only humans are capable of using a sophisticated sleight of ideas.

The Sacrifice, *Sati*, and the Power of Money

Ideas matter. But only when they are propagated. Propagating an idea requires a strategy. A good strategy is the use of a story. Storytelling runs deep in our DNA. We cherish stories—more so preposterous ones. We thrive on the edge of preposterousness: the more incredible a story, the more appealing it is to our imaginative mind! When stories get interwoven into a tapestry of narration, our rational mind easily glosses over the element of fiction in it. Since w live under the influence of a complex frame of our acquired belief patterns, we tend to pay little attention to the fictional aspect of stories. Naturally, then, fact and fiction meld into each other like the warp and weft of a fabric. They become one inseparable whole. And that is what makes a story a powerful tool of communication.

The Aryans had perfected the art of storytelling. They were master storytellers. They conjured up so ingenious a creation story that its influence continued to trickle down from generation to generation until today. The story, as recounted by Karen Armstrong, goes like this: Gods created the "sky" out of a hard shell, and then they created the "earth" which rested like a "dice on water;" in the center of the earth, gods placed a unique Trinity – bull, plant, and man – and the "Fire;" but everything was lifeless. To endow the world with life, gods "sacrificed" the Trinity – bull, plant, and man – and the Sun started moving; clouds began forming; rains came, and crops began growing. Animals shot out of "bull," and the human race emerged from "Man."

In this beautifully woven story, it is hard to miss that *Sacrifice* is the central theme. It is no longer a simple act of killing an animal, instead exemplifying a "creative" process behind all "life" – a thoroughly legitimated process. In other words, human life depended on the death of other creatures, which in turn lived on others, and so on, obviously and indefinitely, the cycle continued. Doesn't this remind us of what is known as the "Food Chain" in biology speak? It does. The Food Chain is an irrefutable fact of practical life. We know that. The Aryans knew that, too, but in the 25th century BCE, they couldn't be expected to see the science of biology behind the "food chain." Instead, they saw gods. They put the Food Chain in perspective through a paranormal story. Each age has its peculiarities and idiosyncrasies. We are good at doing science; the ancients were good at doing stories. They told stories that resonated well with the masses then, and do so even today.

Gods were inserted into the drama to make the food chain story credible. As mentioned a page or two earlier, the invocation of the gods made a huge difference. In the name of gods, anything went. Stories looked good and credible enough to thoroughly legitimize slaughtering the cattle. Could they have done otherwise? Probably not. With a touch of ingenuity, they attributed the storyline to *avatars* and *rishis*, who allegedly received the inspiration of sacrifice from the "sky god." The Mesopotamians had done that before; later, the Greeks and others did the same. They all invoked their respective gods. The Aryans were no different. Stories were indispensable to them to get the gullible masses hooked. Stories helped establish sacrifice on a firm footing, making it an institutionalized undertaking or perhaps an institution in itself. Over time, unfortunately, the sacrifice ritual didn't remain limited to slaughtering cattle and animals. Like in ancient Mesopotamia or the late Paleolithic age, humans were sacrificed at the altar of some gods, such as *Kali*, in India. In its vestigial form, the ignominious ritual of human sacrifice shamefully persisted as the infamous custom of "*Sati*" – requiring a widow to voluntarily (allegedly) plunge into the funeral pyre and burn herself to ashes. *Sati* was practiced in India until the late nineteenth and early twentieth century.

The Aryan sacrificial ritual was considered a lofty spiritual practice; nonetheless, the elite could hardly ignore its material implications. On the one hand, it was alleged that the *devas* personally attended the Sacrifice ceremony to replenish their energy. On the other hand, the *devas* were expected to reciprocate. That is to say; it was no free lunch for them. They were supposed to ensure the prosperity, health, and overall well-being of the community or family that offered the sacrifice. Sacrifice was a finance-driven undertaking. It was an investment in gods. The bigger the sacrifice, the more favors from gods were expected. Not everybody could afford a big sacrifice. To perform a grand sacrifice, one had to be prosperous enough to undertake expenses, and whosoever could afford that luxury would be raised in status and influence in the society. The sacrifice ritual became a means to show off wealth and material power. Whether or not the gods would bestow the favors on them, the society, all the same, acknowledged the sacrificers as the favored lot of the gods, which fact, enhanced their material power more, and even legitimated their exploitation of the weak and poor. The rich were the lucky ones. The gods gave them wealth, and stealing them was a sin. The poor were poor because they couldn't make the gods happy. They ought not to harbor evil designs and ill will against the rich. The rich received more since they spent in the way of gods. They practiced religion and ritual in the best possible manner.

Unquestionably the material benefits of religion were of primary concern. The spiritual benefits were secondary. Take, for instance, the afterlife. In the beginning, the Aryans did not entertain the existence of the after-life; however, as that perspective changed over the centuries, they considered the after-life an extension of worldly economic prosperity. If you were an Aryan and would like to go to heaven after you died to stay there in the company of gods, you ought to be wealthy enough to perform sacrifices. Sacrifice guaranteed a visa to heaven. The more sacrifices one had in the account, the easier it was to obtain the visa. In short, money talks.

Taming Horses and the Violence

The Aryans lived relatively peacefully in the Caucasian steppes. With the advent of the Bronze Age, much of that changed. Globally a few comparatively advanced civilizations, like Mesopotamia, Egypt, Armenia, etc., emerged in the ancient world. The legend goes that in 2107 BCE, the Armenian hero, Hayk, defeated Belus, the Babylonian God of war (Armenian folk tales miss many details, but with dates, they are punctilious, which makes them great stories.) In the highlands surrounding the mountains of Ararat, Armenia flourished around 4000 BCE.

When the Aryans came in contact with these more advanced civilizations of Mesopotamia and Armenia, the inevitable cultural osmosis transformed the Aryans' socio-cultural outlook. Taking a cue from the Armenians and the Mesopotamians, they took to taming wild horses, an attractive enterprise that conspicuously transformed the Aryan agrarian society. The use of the horse, like the airplane in the 20th century, dramatically cut distances saving time, energy, and human resources. It freed time otherwise spent lugging sac-fulls of loads and burdens. Within no time, a revolution that did to the ancient societies what airplanes did to the modern world was underway in the Aryan society. Total transformation. Like the Mesopotamians, the Aryans quickly learned horse riding and demonstrated excellent skills turning it into an enterprise. On horsebacks, they now swiftly and ruthlessly, not unlike warriors, carried out rustling and raiding activity. Like lightning in a fell swoop, the Aryan hordes now stole the cattle and crops of the neighboring settlements. Raiding and looting became more of an adventure bringing in better dividends. Over time as competition ensued, the rustler tribes turned against each other. The resulting feuds culminated in acts of arson, terror, and killing each other. Where earlier, there was a sedentary and relatively peaceful society, violence became a new norm.

How could a relatively, so to say, non-violent society reconcile with this brutal change of behavior? To find the answer, we need to look at religion.

As we know, religion has proved quite a tool in the hands of the powerful to manipulate the masses. Civilizations were made in the name of religion and also upended by religious fervor. Religion is an idea wrapped in the cloth of a story. Ideas are contagious. When hedged with a powerful storyline, they spread like an epidemic. A good storyline loaded with idiomatic nuances hypnotizes the masses to lose sight of the thin line that demarcates fact and fiction. A preposterous storyline with a touch of mystery, delivered with subtle punches, works remarkably well. The Aryans didn't find it hard to weave good stories. They possessed a foundational story and created a perfect role model - *Indra*, the chariot-riding Lord of Vigor, the Warrior

God – a god known to incite and excite conflict. People had a strong faith in *Indra*. What they needed now, as they say in psychology-speak, was a sense of cognitive closure to get rid of the inhibition, if any, toward violence. It turned out that was no big deal. The Aryans took an idea and created an unrealistic belief in that idea. It worked.

It doesn't matter whether you believe in fact or fiction, in the seen or unseen, in the rational or irrational, or in right or wrong; what matters is how strongly you believe in what you believe in. The Aryan rustlers invoked *Indra* to rationalize and justify cattle rustling as the Aryan populace had an unwavering faith and belief in their omnipotent god, *Indra. He* was the role model, and *he* called them to action; in *his* name, anything could go. *Indra* communicated his thoughts to the *Rishis* and the *Avatars*, who lost no time in announcing them to the masses. The rishis convinced the masses that they had dreams, inspirations, and, as the later religious traditions put it, revelations through which *Indra* communicated with them. That was hard to refuse. Herd mentality is a tough nut to crack. It sets the ball rolling. A belief system emerged, and story upon story was added. That's to say, the Aryans took to living in *Indra's* name. Their stated purpose became earning a livelihood in *his* name, never mind the brutal violence done to fellow creatures. Violence became an accepted fact. A new norm. All kinds of paranormal stories – stories that gave meaning to violence – shot up. As is, perhaps always, the case stories made life a struggle worth carrying out.

Indra, the god, imported

Cattle rustling and other associated violent activities were not a cakewalk that anybody could engage in. Understandably, not all the Sanskrit-speaking Aryans could muster the courage and strength to participate in such an endeavor. The non-participants were left behind. The left-behinds suffered economically as well as socially. They steadily got marginalized, suffered disadvantages, and ultimately were compelled to migrate out of the steppes. Descending southward, they reached the northern plains of India and settled on the banks of the river they called *Sindhu*. The word Sindhu means river in Sanskrit. In his book *India A History,* John Keay tells us how Sindhu became Indus. "In the ancient Persian or Avestan dialect (a sister language of Sanskrit), the "S" is rendered as an aspirate. *Sindhu* is thus *Hind[h] u* in ancient Persian. When the Greeks came across the word *Hind[h] u* they dropped "h," and it became Indus." Long before the Aryans, a great civilization called the Harappa flourished on the fertile plains fed by this river. By 2600 to 2300 BCE, some major cities like Mohenjo-Daro (now in Pakistan), Harappa, Lothal, and others made this a civilization bigger and grander than that of Mesopotamia. However, by the time the Aryans finally reached here, Harappa had already fallen from its zenith.

Ironically, the immigrant Aryan tribes who fled from steppes to escape violence inflicted on them by their more aggressive compatriots resorted to all kinds of violence in the foreign land, the Indus valley. Adept in horse riding, the Aryans certainly had an advantage over the indigenous Harappans, who were unfamiliar with horse and horse-driven transportation. As they moved swiftly, inflicting damage on the natives, horse-riding Aryan invaders quickly got the upper hand in the new land. The Harappans, already enfeebled physically and economically by the floods, disease, and devastation, proved no match to the Aryans, who quickly subdued and displaced them. Nothing could stop the Aryans from imposing their writ and religion in the foreign land. Rustling the cattle and raiding the indigenous settlements became a profitable religious activity. They imported *Indra* to the Indus valley, and by the time they fully settled in *Sapta-Sindhu* (land of seven rivers, now called Punjab), *Indra* had risen to the status of Supreme God for them. In his name, anything would go – violence, rustlings, loot, sacrifice, feasts, you name what. In their eagerness to control the fertile lands, they would be presented with plenty of opportunities to resort to violence in *Indra's* name and prove their god's superiority. Violence in *Indra's* name became a ritual.

Soon *rishis* and *avatars* sprang up from everywhere. They propagated the stories of their inspiration from on high. Many complex and multilayered myths were conjured up by them around the cult of *Indra*. Ind*ra*, a god of vigor, became the creator god of the universe. The "how and what" of the universe was now in the hands of *Indra*. The stories and myths had divine sanction, so they were the ultimate truths. Not to be challenged. They stood firm on the legitimate ground, and their impact on society's collective psyche was humongous. Nothing could stop these stories from becoming inalienable bedrock for the edifice we call the Aryan culture. The later Hindu civilization would nostalgically trace its roots to this very culture claiming it to be India's indigenous religious-cultural achievement.

The stories with alleged divine signatures are perfect for indoctrinating the masses to accept preposterous myths without questioning their authenticity. Once indoctrinated, the crowds follow herd behavior, refusing to see what they see. Herd behavior defies logic. Since the dawn of time, the power brokers have shrewdly taken advantage of the herd behavior of the people. It's no surprise that the Aryans, like all of us, accepted, believed, and faithfully followed what the *rishis*, priests, and theologians proclaimed from time to time. Karen Armstrong tells us this about the Aryan belief system: "*Indra* killed the three-headed dragon, *Vritra*, and made the earth habitable; *Indra* fought terrible wars to attain the goal of making the world habitable; *devas* were engaged in protracted wars in the heaven to establish the dominance of one god over others, not unlike the later Greek gods; the wars and battles were to be fought on earth to replicate the heavenly wars." The Aryans, like multitudes among us, never questioned such a religious premise. Stories, howsoever embedded within one another, are, after all, stories. However, the Aryans were not the only people who were reluctant to question such stories. The entire Axial age and before was an Age of stories. Questioning the stories was simply not safe. Stories were the fabric of wisdom. It was dangerous to be unwise. Even today, it is dangerous to be too foolish to question religious stories.

The Holy Death

The Aryans, no doubt, faced economic problems after settling in the foreign land. Willingly or unwillingly, they had to engage in conflicts with indigenous people. They required resources to feed their families and their immigrating compatriots that were pouring in from the steppes in wave upon wave. Naturally, then, what they needed was to control and own big swathes of cultivable land and livestock. One way of doing that was to usurp the lands of the natives and displace them, and another way, a harder one, was to clear forest tracks or grab fallow lands. No easy undertakings. Both required might and muscle power. Both required establishing their supremacy over the indigenous population. And both required getting involved in fighting and violent conflicts, though forest clearing would entail conflicts on a lesser scale.

The immigrating Aryans, having experienced tough skirmishes in the steppes, were conscious that battles were not easy to fight; neither was it easy to sustain the courage and the will of the people to fight for long should the battles unintentionally stretch over prolonged periods. Motivating and holding people united through the difficult times of war can be challenging. It mandates running robust propaganda aimed at rallying the people after a cause. Propaganda is one of the most, if not the singular, vital component of war machinery. In fierce competition, there is no better technique to rally the people than using religion when survival is at stake. Religion legitimizes warfare as holy, thereby completely concealing the real purpose of war. Under religious indoctrination, people refuse to know that wars tend to be fought for economic gains.

To survive in a foreign land, the Aryans needed to cooperate closely with one another. Kinship and tribal affiliation alone wouldn't be sufficient to achieve coordinated cooperation. Religion would. Religion binds and bonds. It draws together even different tribes and communities as if through a common language. Willingly or unwillingly, they had to come under one roof provided by religion.

The religion of *Indra* helped create cohesiveness in the Aryan tribes. Additionally, it helped them become fearless fighters sending shudders through the spines of indigenous communities. The Aryan invaders fought ruthlessly, sincerely believing they were performing a holy duty in *Indra's name.* They were fighting holy wars.

Which brings us back to the human mind. As recalled from the first couple of chapters, the human mind is unique. So unique that it defies explanation. Its remarkable capacity for abstract thinking allows us to play and replay a physical drama in the world of our thoughts with the minutest detail and precision. The mind can create tremendously colorful virtual, mythical, or fictional templates that are hard for the brain to differentiate from reality. Our perception influences our thinking so strongly that the boundary between the real and the imagined gets blurred. The tricks of imagination get transmogrified into infallible truths. The Aryans were no exception. Like others before and after them, they conjured up a religion best suited to their needs. And it worked for them. With a bit of modification here and there, all peoples and tribes have conceived their respective religions, best suited to their needs and day. Religion's role in the Aryans' and other peoples' civilizational success can easily be de-emphasized. What, however, can't easily be wished away is the stoking of fundamentalism by religious zeal. Religious fundamentalism has cost History heavily in terms of life and limb.

In India, too, the affluent and the elite would use their power against a fellow tribe or community for petty reasons. Mutual resentment and anger of tribes resulted in terrible, violent campaigns against each other. The reasons for rivalry could be as trifling as one can imagine. For instance, when a tribal head or a well-to-do person was not invited to a ritual sacrificial ceremony, it was considered an affront to the whole tribe. As believers and worshippers of *Indra*, the aggrieved tribe felt duty-bound to attack (in this case, the patron of the sacrifice), kill the people, and carry off the booty. Not doing so would amount to disrespecting *Indra* on the part of the affronted tribe - a severe violation of the custom and convention.

Another dangerous consequence of this belief system was the consecration of the death of raiders as martyrdom if it happened during the rustling and lifting of cows and cattle. The cattle rustlers and raiders were regarded as warriors. Rustling and raiding was a dangerous and deadly game of contest to earn a livelihood. Though there was nothing spiritual in it, rustling was regarded as a holy affair. In this game, the warrior, no matter how strong and swift, was at a real risk of getting killed, nay martyred, at the hands of the enemy. These martyrs were believed to join the world of gods immediately after their martyrdom – an honor that was previously reserved only for the wealthy (by dint of making many sacrifices). Such and other kinds of religious sacralization of death, whether in the name of god or for political or economic gains under the shadow of religion, reached us as an inspirational legacy. No wonder we witness the glamorizing of death by suicide bombings, holy wars, and political and economic wars between nations. The concept of "holy death" or martyrdom wasn't unique to the Aryans; neither did the Aryans invent this concept in the first place. The idea might have already existed in other civilizations and disseminated far and wide in the ancient world through trade, migrations, and demographic displacements. Or maybe it originated here in the Indus Valley and spread to other parts of the world. No one knows for sure. To borrow from Voltaire, it remains up to history to prove that anything can be proven by history.

The Axe of Varna's Might

The economy is notorious for leaping and limping. It abhors stagnation, yet it is pretty unpredictable in its behavior. People need help to understand economics fully. The economy behaves capriciously, presumably under the influence of what Adam Smith called the "invisible hand." The market and economy remain great enigmas, partly because many read too much or too little into markets. Great economists confess that the economy has a hard-to-comprehend abstractness attached to it. And, now and then, it does smile like a god on a chosen few. The Aryans happened to be in the good books of this god, i.e., economy, at least for some time. Things improved, especially for those who were more aggressive in rustlings and raids, as they claimed a bigger and better share of the booty. Slowly, as wealth became concentrated in fewer and fewer hands, leaders or tribal heads (big men) came to control the decision-making apparatus. Religion suited them well. They displayed power and influence by performing enormous sacrifices more often. In the Aryan speak, they pleased the gods better to secure for themselves a place in the afterlife. They were regarded by everyday folks as the specials or nobles, calling them *Kshatriyas*. Later, the rustler warriors, commanders, and fighters also claimed the title of *Kshatriya* and the "big men." Thus an elite or aristocratic class got shaped. The elite then identified people who could be grouped under other class lines or *the Varna* system, by which they could maintain a primitive form of record not unlike the census.

Varna system started life as a divinely sanctioned class system which later transmogrified into the notorious Caste system. Three more classes, *Brahmins*, *Vaishyas*, and *Shudras*, sprang up in addition to *Kshatriyas*. In his commentary on the Bhagavad Gita, Dr. Radhakrishnan defends the Caste system as more effective and less drastic than the system of Slavery and colonialism by the West. However, the fact remains that *Varna* created inevitable fault lines in society, leading to complex conflicts and formidable challenges. The inter-caste conflict cost Indo-Aryan civilization dearly in terms of unity and political power. The class conflict created messy tensions, sucking more and more people into chaos with each passing day and leaving no time for economically productive enterprises. The conflict-ridden early Aryan society groped with a sense of cynic pessimism as testified by *Rig Veda*, the earliest known Indian scriptural text, which, it is believed, correctly reflects the overall mood of the Aryan society. The hymns of Rig Veda tell us that *Rishis* – the learned and the supposedly enlightened folks – were wantonly complaining and lamenting the distress and the despair caused to society by class conflict. Remember, these *rishis* claimed to be the messengers of Rig Vedic gods. As such, they allegedly conveyed to the masses that the gods were unhappy with human affairs - quite an ingenious damage-control exercise by the *rishis* aimed at handling the class conflict that threatened the stability of the tribal and economic structures of the Aryan society.

The Kshatriya class's power, wealth, and domineering influence created an eerie restlessness in other sections of the society, who viewed this tilt of power with a degree of envy and antagonism. However, mere opposition by others couldn't undermine the *Kshatriya* nobles' hold on the power structure. On the contrary, the axe fell on those who voiced antagonism. *Vaishyas*, or clansmen (people of less noble class), found themselves silenced and marginalized. Since they were less enthusiastic about violent rustling, raiding, and fighting, they eventually alienated themselves from these raiding hordes. As a result, the Vaishyas were to stay put toiling on lands and rear livestock. They got down to a more settled and docile way of life. They took to farming as their full-time vocation.

Another class, the *Shudras*, comprising predominantly non-Aryan indigenous natives, found themselves entirely at the receiving end. They became a soft target. They could be plundered, enslaved, and subjected to forced labor – with total impunity. They were left to struggle with the sweat of their brow, not claiming any right over their labor. They subsisted on others' throw-aways. They had no rights, no property, nothing. What we call human rights didn't exist for *Shudras*. Not unlike stray dogs, they were supposed to live on the morsels thrown to them. The Aryan scriptures and gods proclaimed them untouchables. They were the filth, created by God out of dirt, and thus were supposed to live with the crud. They had no right over life, no right over decent livelihood. For them, life was harsh and society merciless. These, so to say, unfortunate creatures were human in appearance but worse in status than the most despised creatures. They were made to live such a wretched life that a morsel of half-rotten food was a luxury, not every *Shudra* could afford. For them, it was forbidden to cross the path of an upper caste person, intentionally or otherwise.

For Shudra, it was a horrible crime to look eye to eye with a Brahmin or Kshatriya; for him, it was a sin to even think of religion or heaven, let alone talk about heaven in the marketplace. Society strictly monitored Shudra's thoughts, feelings, and emotions. He was the denizen of hell, both here and in the after-world. That was a foregone conclusion. No Shudra could even come near a sacrificial altar, let alone take part in or perform a sacrifice. Their job was to clean the shit, collect the garbage, and eat from the leftovers. In short, they were human scavengers. The *avatars* and the *rishis* had condemned the *Shudras* to suffer; the gods' revelation had ordained them as nothing more than the lowliest animals. Yes. Nothing could save them. They were born to grow up as the most despised creatures.

Why were *Shudras* predestined to suffer humiliation and torture? Was it that "the sky god" and the other gods of the Aryans were biased and judgmental towards the *Shudras*? Or was religion simply an instrument in the hands of the power to manipulate and exploit the weaker sections? Or was it that the Aryans, like others before them, conceived God from a human perspective and attributed human psychological undercurrents to this imagined figure, God, to legitimize the cruel human game of life? These are uncomfortable questions. Asking such questions means inviting trouble. Most people prefer to remain silent and obsequious and deliberately feign ignorance. Some modern scholars, though, seem inclined to question these age-old truisms.

The Economy, the Kings, and the Gods

Having dominated the fertile basin of Indus, the Aryans, by the 10th century BCE, had grown in people. To handle the increasing demand of foodgrains, they embarked on territorial expansion to control eastern India, later popularly known as *Arya-Varta* (land of the Aryans) – a stretch of land bordered by two important rivers of North India, Ganga, and Yamuna. During their advance, they burnt down dense forests, clearing long tracks of land. The use of fire was a significant technological advancement of the ancients, undoubtedly mesmerizing and enigmatic to them. The fire was no less than god. Indeed for the Aryans, it qualified as a god. It was called god *Agni* having descended on earth from the heavens. The fire god, *Agni*, occupied a prominent position, almost replacing the earlier god, *Indra,* during the eastward expansion phase, which brought inevitable conflicts with the indigenous population. Aggression and violence (duly sanctified by religion) ensued during the usurpation of new lands. The indigenous people were effectively subdued and displaced. It turned out that religion, especially the Aryan one, was a brilliant weapon that could cut through the hardest of the stuff.

The Aryan religion, in contrast to later monotheistic tradition, was never a monolithic one. It yielded to the societal demands undergoing maturation, transformation, and evolution as society progressed. In the Indo-Aryan socio-cultural milieu from which it arose, it smoothly transmogrified into an unimaginably malleable and maneuverable institution assimilating into its fold all kinds of gods, devas, avatars, customs, and legacies.

The Aryans, keen to find a religious connection in everything, devised new rituals to sanctify their expansion policy, never mind the violence, strife, and misery that expansion brought. In line with this policy, ceremonial proceedings with all the necessary rituals would be organized to re-enact the storyline of *Agni's* victorious progress into new territory. *Agni* invoked reverence because of its ubiquitousness in the universe — in the sun, thunder and lightning, household hearths, communal sacrifices, and so on. *Agni* became the patron god, and fire became sacred. A burning hearth was now always ritually carried by the frontline Aryan warriors clearing forests, tracks, and fallow lands. Fire came to symbolize power and, of course, the Aryans' ability to control and manipulate the environment and the enemy. The new settlements would be inaugurated with fire. Only after the victorious warriors built an altar to light a fire would the newly occupied territory become legitimate. If the residents resisted, they would be killed in the name of *Agni.*

After the Aryans expanded and settled in new territories economy improved. The relative improvement in lifestyle and quality provided ample time to *Kshatriyas* and *Brahmins* for politics, debate, and discussion. When stomachs are full, the socio-political upheavals and the evolution of religious thought quickly happen. The Aryan elite embarked on philosophizing and rhetoric. All kinds of discourses ensued: Who are humans? Who are gods? Whence they come from? What is reality? Who is supreme? Philosophizing abstract stuff inevitably ignited people's interest in debate, discussion, and storytelling. As a result, society's outlook changed, and religion also evolved. One of the significant themes that shaped religious evolution was the discourse ignited by the concept of supreme reality and its transcendental character. In Vedic *rishi* speak, the supreme reality was called *Brahman. Brahman* was no simple god or *deva;* it was an inexplicable, indefinable higher reality having no 3-dimensional representation. It was a multi-dimensional construct of some unfathomable something.

The concept of *Brahman* may seem un-provoking and dull to many, but on digging a little deeper, one encounters many commonalities between *Brahman* and Abrahamic god. That, however, is not the point here.

Interestingly, Brahmanic discourse set off a wave of transformation of the overall Aryan religious thought process. It marked no less than a cognitive quantum leap that catapulted the Aryan or Vedic religion into new levels of complexity. However, this was no abrupt change; neither did the cognitive quantum leap happen in India alone. It was a global phenomenon during the Axial Age experienced far and wide by almost all cultures, religions, and civilizations. Humans compelled religion and god/gods to adapt to abstractions, conceptions, and imaginations of the human mind. One of the drivers of the engine of religious evolution was the economy. Toward the end of the Iron Age, priorities had changed, means of transportation had improved, and agricultural enterprise had become relatively mechanized; plow, spade, shovel, and sickle were widely used. Cattle were used for plow driving, leading to increased productivity. But the human population had also proportionately grown due to a better food supply and improved economy. Demographic spurt meant that the challenges faced by human civilization became more complex, demanding new approaches, new insights, and of course, new thinking.

Back to *Brahman*. In the Arya speak, it represented a principle rather than a simple divine being. In practice, it signified "one invisible divine" matrix that, as Karen Armstrong points out, supposedly held within it the collective "essence of all the gods." *Brahman* came to imply the omnipresent, omnipotent, omniscient, and all-encompassing principle that held the universes together – physical on the earth and the invisible, call it metaphysical or spiritual, in the heavens. No one could see *Brahman; however*, anyone could experience *Him*, according to the priests and *rishis*, by carrying out certain rituals; hence the rituals were necessary. As the economy, primarily temple-controlled, stabilized, *Indra* was no longer a useful god. Since necessity is the mother of invention, *Brahman almost completely replaced Indra*. Henceforth, when the warriors or the raiders returned with plunder and booty, their victory was attributed to *Brahman*. The leader or commander (or later, the king) came to be regarded as the viceroy of *Brahman* on earth. The leader, it was argued, happens to be in a "state of oneness with *Brahman*" because of supernatural powers conferred on him by *Brahman*. When kingship was established later, the kings were supposed to be divinely chosen – not unlike in ancient Mesopotamia. The invisible, inconceivable, enigmatic *Brahman* showered *His* favors on the king, thereby ensuring the economic prosperity and success of the kingdom – so went the story. The institution of kingship, duly backed by religion, thus enjoyed an unchallenged legitimacy.

Despite the lofty philosophy surrounding the Brahmanic religion, it left many *rishi* (teachers, guru, or mystic) scratching their heads for answers to many questions. Many became deeply uncomfortable with some of the existing religious dogmas and constructs. Some influential *rishis* resorted to fine-tuning the grotesque antinomies with which the creation myths and the concept of heavens and gods were loaded. Others couldn't get their head around the story of *Brahman*. In frustration, they turned to alternative narratives. Some subjected themselves to penitence, voluntary starvation, and self-punishment. A kind of turbulence called spiritual restlessness, for the lack of a better word, gripped the religious elite and paved the way for the appearance of some radically divergent religious thought processes.

Purusha, Prajapatti, and Peasants

Rituals, sacrifices, and other established religious practices benefitted only a select class of people, i.e., Brahmins; the rest shouldered the burden of keeping the gods happy. The Temple economy controlled by the Brahmins and Kshatriyas put the Vaishyas under the yoke of tax and levy, overstretching them in terms of labor to sustain their fragile agricultural enterprise. They had to pay a massive share of their produce to the temple and kings, leaving their underfed families starving. What they needed was blessings and help from gods or *devas*. Nothing was forthcoming. To complicate their woes, *Brahman* was an unfathomable deity that could not smoothly fit into ordinary folks' mental frame. The age-old indoctrination had made people more comfortable relating to gods as physical beings represented efficiently through idols, icons, figurines, etc. The idols and frescos satisfied people's urge and desire to touch, smell, and feel their gods directly and see them dwelling amongst themselves in temples or chosen garrets of their houses. They would worship them straight.

Some adjustments and fine-tuning were needed to reconcile the long-held paradigms and the abstract *Brahmanic* principle. It was not easy, though. Wisdom instructed that any radical departure from the accepted paradigms, however necessary, could have dangerous consequences for the *rishis* and the elite. So every step had to be craftily and carefully planned even though the tipping spiritual restlessness demanded an immediate paradigm shift. Some *rishis* did, however, show courage and eagerness to throw caution to the winds. Yet they were careful not to reject the religion of rituals altogether. They smartly customized the message to convince the target audiences.

Take, for instance, the following. A Rig Vedic *rishi* had a vision that he called "a revelation" from *Brahman*. He claimed that the universe had existed in the form of primal chaos. *Brahman* vigorously stirred it, and out came *Prajapatti* (the Creator god), a physical (perhaps idolized) representation of formless, invisible, and unfathomable *Brahman*. The personification of *Brahman* through *Prajapatti* helped address the enigma of the abstractness of *Brahman*. Embodiment, as *Prajapatti*, transformed *Brahman* into both "immanent" and "transcendent" – both within and without or inside and outside the universe. *Prajapatti*, by default, became the universe, the god, the "God of gods," and above all, an impersonation of *Brahman*, meaning, in other words, that one could worship *Brahman* like any temporal god. The invention of *Prajapatti* thus made *Brahman* conceptually accessible to worshippers. Now that *Prajapatti* was the vicar of *Brahman*, it made sense to offer sacrifices directly to him.

Notably, the Rig Vedic *rishi* also reframed the story of the *Triple Sacrifice* discussed a couple of pages earlier in this chapter. According to the new version, the first man, or *Purusha*, was not killed by the gods, but (*Purusha*) voluntarily offered his sacrifice, thus surrendering to the gods at his will. The new story surmised that *Purusha's* surrender – call it self-sacrifice – set the cosmic engine into motion. *Purusha* thus came to represent the prototype for the universe. Everything, literally and figuratively, sprang forth from his body. In a society where a sense of weariness due to violent rustling and raiding had set in, *Indra* was no more relevant, and *Agni* became a lesser *deva; the* new creation story set into motion a philosophical debate and discourse among the elite. Many of the hitherto established rituals and religious practices were questioned by them.

By then (10th century BCE), India was already caught in the throes of the "Axial Age" transformation. People, especially the elite and Brahmanical class who enjoyed the luxury of wealth and spare time, had begun to seriously question the wisdom behind raiding, rustling, plundering, and all the necessary collateral warfare for securing booty. The curious thing about this rustling enterprise was that the hard-earned loot would be consumed in elaborate sacrifice and communal feasts. It was okay when the Aryans were a fledgling community of immigrants, but more than 500 years down the line (i.e., by the 10th century BCE), it was no more relevant, surmised the rishis and the elite. It was a waste of resources. The circumstances had changed, and a fair majority of the Aryans had transitioned into a settled way of life courtesy of the agricultural activity and temple form of economy.

Furthermore, the hugely labor-intensive farming enterprise brought along its unique set of problems. The produce was meager, the know-how to introduce quality seeds and fertilizers to improve the yield was lacking, and crops were at the mercy of winds, rain, storms, and other vagaries of nature. The overall scenario was grim with agriculture, which put a heavy burden on the family units of the farming community. The revenues of the temples and palaces also suffered. Then was this rustling thing. The rustlers and raiders suddenly stormed in and out, practically snatching away all the possessions of communities in a matter of hours. Free loot and rustlings by a few adventurous hordes created insecurity, fear, and restlessness in the society endangering the politico-economic stability. These adventurers needed to be reined in.

Practically, farming has always been a terrible gamble. Add to it a culture of violence, raids, and counter-raids, and the Aryan farmers had plenty of things to worry about. The sacrificial rituals were no less quarrelsome and aggressive affairs. For trifles and petty matters, the ceremony would often degenerate into brawls and fights between the participating families and tribes, resulting in family feuds that would last for years. There would be acts of revenge and avenge against each other. Honor killings became a new norm.

In this chaos, it was the peasantry who would be severely affected. It shouldered the heavy burden of providing livestock and food grains for these elaborate and violent sacrificial rites. They weren't supposed to take sides with one or another rustler party. Should they side with one, another party would take it as an affront and plunder the settlement. The friendly party sometimes fought the looters to defend the farmers' fields. One of the rustler parties would win the skirmish. Whosoever would emerge as victors would take away the farmers' harvest and the livestock, leaving them utterly destroyed. In this sense, it was too dangerous to befriend the rustlers. That could cost the farmers dearly. As they say, grass would be crushed and trampled upon in the fight of elephants; farmers would get destroyed when two rustler parties competed. This all was becoming disgusting and unbearable with each passing day. Something needed to be done to assuage the peasants' misery to keep the temples and treasuries well supplied with donations and tax on their produce for the elite to feed on.

Slaughterless Sacrifice

When a particular religion or religious practice becomes unproductive and burdensome, sooner or later, a sense of dissatisfaction creeps into society. In the extreme case, the dissatisfaction may trigger a reaction whereby even the dedicated followers may abandon the said practices or even turn their backs on a respective religion when given an opportunity. In practice, though, an abrupt abandonment by the masses of one faith and conversion to a new religion is rare. More often, social transformation happens over prolonged periods. Usually, subtle perceptual and behavioral changes precede shift. A particular religious practice may get partially over-shadowed, superseded, or even replaced by some other ritual practice - usually, but not always, by a polished version. New rituals lead to new customs and dogmas, and the cycle continues. Over time a seemingly entirely new religion may replace the older religion. In reality, however, every new faith is rooted in the same old cultural milieu. Religion, after all, is a product of cumulative culture. With the evolution of thought, the rough edges of older versions of religion are smoothened here and there to customize it to a new socio-political outlook. That's how the socio-religious transformations look from the outside—a smooth and benign process. In reality, the new religious movements and revolutions don't always behave benignly. History shows that whenever a religious movement attained power and clout of numbers new religion was forcibly thrust on people. Everything from religious radicalism, fundamentalism, and persecution to forced conversions has been witnessed. No successful religion can claim that it wasn't involved in the heinous oppressions, persecutions, and slaughterous rampage in its name. Yes, there are differences in the scale and degree of force; some religions were brutal in applying force, and some were a little accommodative. But every religion's history is laced with the blood of innocents.

Civilizations didn't transform overnight. They went through a painfully slow process. Progress comes at a price. We are still nowhere close to becoming civilized enough to respect, accept, or even tolerate differing view points, religious or otherwise. Yet, slowly and steadily, the older established religious habits and customs get chipped away, a bit at a time, and replaced by new customs, new traditions, and new behaviors. Historically the economic benefits took precedence over other considerations like excommunication, social boycott, or resentment by others when it came to converting to a new religion. Yet there have also been people for whom spiritual matters far outweighed all other aspects. And these so-called seekers of spirituality have, for the most part, been responsible for religious movements, transformations, and revolutions.

As the 10th century BC approached its closing years, the whole Arya-Varta was in economic distress. People suffered from poverty, disease, and strife. It was a time of crisis, both spiritual and physical, for the Aryan society. Crises sometimes bring the best out of the human species through art, expression, and innovation. For the Aryans, the closing decades of the 10th century BCE were a watershed phase of sacred history. Religious reform was long overdue. The time had come for serious inquiry and search for new ideas, methods, and practices to redefine their relationship with the universe and other creations. The time had reached for the Aryan elite to embark on religious experimentation in search of spiritual meaning. An era took a life that brought out religious reforms to such an extent that not only did the socio-political and economic scenario change, but an unprecedented spiritual awakening sprang up in the Aryan society.

Which brings us back, meanderingly, to the ritual of sacrifice. Up until the 10th century BCE, the sacrificial animals were violently decapitated in the name of the god *Indra*. As mentioned in previous pages, towards the end of the 10th century BC, *Indra*-worship was on the decline. Hence there was plenty of scope for reconsidering the rationale behind *Indra*-sacrifice. However, no drastic retreat or abandoning the sacrificial ritual was on the cards. Instead, a seemingly minor modification in the method of slaughter was introduced. And surprisingly enough, that made all the difference. The critics of sacrifice had long argued that the violent killing of sacrificial animals had a revulsive effect on people's minds. They weren't paid heed to for a long time. But now their argument was winning. Many joined their chorus, and the intensity of the debate around decapitation became vigorous enough to call into question the rationale behind the sacrifice ritual. Before things could go out of control, the priestly class flung into action and got people's heads around the problem. Sacrifice wasn't abolished. The ritual was modified. The priestly class managed to safeguard its economic interests.

Instead of being slaughtered, the sacrificial animal could now be let loose. Anyone could pick it up, or the sacrificer could give it as a gift to the officiating priest. The slaughter of the animal was no longer deemed mandatory for the ritual. The implications of sacrifice without slaughter were impressive. It turned out to be a hugely important and crucially transformative event that sowed the contextual seed for the emergence of the concept of *Ahinsa* or *Ahimsa* (nonviolence). The violence and aggression committed towards fellow humans and other creatures were now openly criticized, condemned, and ultimately pronounced as a sinful activity, courtesy of debate on sacrifice. That was a unique and remarkable achievement of ancient Indian society. The world had seen nothing of the kind.

The festival-like crowded celebration witnessed during the sacrificial ceremony was abandoned. Only the sacrificer and his family were now supposed to be present at the sacrifice, and they could choose to either sacrifice the animal, set it free, or offer it as a gift. Symbolism replaced all the drama, fanfare, and violence of the older days' sacrificial events. The officiating priest would now make only some anodyne chants or subtle gestures. Some plants and herbs were pressed to extract the juice or *Soma,* which now symbolized the reenacting of *Indra's* slaughter of the demon of drought (*Vritra).* A total transformation was underway.

The Cow

The committing of violence and warfare, the burning down of the dense forests and the enemy property by the Aryans during their march into *Arya-Varta*, was initially sanctified as a religious duty called *Agnicayana*. By the 10th century BCE, the Aryans legitimately claimed ownership of the whole land – *Arya-Varta*. There was hardly a pressing need to continue with the *Agnicayana*. The time had now come to render it symbolical. It was, no doubt, difficult for the warrior Aryans (mainly *Kshatriyas*) to modify their behavior; however, they fell in line because the *rishis* claimed to receive revelations from *Prajapatti*, the creator god, lending a solid religious backing and authenticity to their message. In a superstitious society like India, it was hard not to listen to the *rishis*. Even the most obstinate warriors and strong men couldn't muster the courage to disobey the *rishis*. It was no surprise that people silently accepted the symbolic version of *Agnicayana*, reducing it to a simple ritual: pick up the firepot, stand face to East, take three steps, and then set the firepot down. That was that. *Agnicayana.*

According to the story mentioned in *Brahmanas* (technical ritual texts compiled during the 9th century BCE), the Rig Veda records that *Prajapatti* revealed to a *rishi* this message: "*Prajapatti* and *Death* performed a sacrifice together, competing in the usual chariot races, dice games, and musical compilations. But *Death* was soundly beaten by *Prajapatti*, who refused to fight with traditional 'weapons.' Instead, *He* used new ritual techniques and defeated Death and swallowed him up. *Death* had been eliminated from the sacrificial arena," and like the patron in the reformed rites, "*Prajapatti* found himself alone." This story recast *Prajapatti* as an archetypal sacrificer. It implied that any sacrificer while performing the ritual of sacrifice need only imagine as vividly as possible a mental scene of "conquering death by the sacrifice." That is to say, the sacrificer had only mentally to re-enact *Prajapatti's* victory over death. It followed that the sacrificial ritual would now be re-conceptualized as a simple three-step mental algorithm: first, picture in mind *Prajapatti's* sacrifice; second, focus on this mental picture to, kind of, assimilate the whole event; third, proclaim "*Death* has become *atman* ("self" with small "s"). Sacrifice was effectively reduced to mental gymnastics. It was a turning point in the sacred history of India.

Which leads us to the climax of Aryan ingenuity. The *rishis* were sages. The gullible and superstitious masses believed they spoke the word of gods. As *rishis* proclaimed, humans don't need to make a physical sacrifice because *Prajapatti* had already sacrificed for them. The elite and the commoners obsequiously followed suit. It seems that this Rig Vedic theology of *Prajapatti's* sacrifice was in no way unique to Aryan theology. It was a cross-cultural religious paradigm. Centuries later, the paradigm "Prajapatti had already made a sacrifice for the humans" repeated itself in the context of the theology of Jesus' crucifixion. By replacing *Prajapatti* with Jesus Christ, quite ingenuously, Christianity claimed its proprietorship of an ancient mental sleight. It built a remarkably resilient castle of sacrificial theology around the crucifixion story of Jesus. To borrow a phrase ascribed to Mark Twain, History may not always repeat itself, but it often rhymes. All human reason and rationality of succeeding two thousand years have failed to produce a dent in that castle of Christianity.

Whether right or wrong, ideas refuse to die when backed by faith. The Aryans shrewdly stretched ideas. They floated the idea that symbolic ritual was as good as the age-old physical sacrificial ritual in that they both exalt the sacrificer to become "one with *Prajapatti.*" However, the flip side of the symbolic ceremony was that fights, raids, and rustlings weren't essential to reenact what the gods had been doing in the heavens. Especially when the Cow itself had become a symbol of wealth, prosperity, and sacredness, it was harrowing to rustle and lift the cows. By now the "Cow" was a sacred animal. As we are told, for instance, by A H Vidyarthi, in his book "*Mohammad in Hindu Scriptures*," the later hymns of Rig Veda testify wealth was counted in terms of a cow; the more cows a family possessed, the more affluent it was. The cow was a unit of barter. Currency. Or *Lakshmi,* in Hindu religious parlance. Wealth exchange happened through cows: you give me a cow, and I provide you with grain. The cow was the backbone of the agricultural economy. No cow, no heifers, no calves, no bulls, no milk, no curd, and no grains. The economy and society's well-being pivoted on Cow. It came to be revered as a mother. Cow rustling was no longer allowable.

As the economy became firmly rooted in agriculture, fine-tuning the creation story and popularizing ritual symbolism became necessary. Economic stability provided more free time for inquiry, contemplation, and idea creation, heralding an era of experimental spiritualism in India. Millennia later, the Indian-origin spiritualism and religious philosophy would disseminate far and wide, impacting the religious outlook of whole nations worldwide, as we shall see later. For the moment, hang on with *Prajapatti.*

As *Prajapatti* emerged as the model god of the Aryans, the religious discourse, too, saw a radical shift. It became more intellectual, linguistically elitist, and strewn with idiomatic complexities, as exemplified by the commentaries of the four Vedas and the *Upanishads* (the religious texts that followed the Veda). According to the Upanishadic thought, the sacrificer becomes a victim himself. To enter the so-called realm of gods (heaven), he must imagine dying a "ritualized death." And to achieve immortality, becoming a 'killer like *Indra*' was no longer necessary. Afterlife, too, began to be viewed differently. In Rig Vedic time, it simply meant entering into the realm of gods. *Upanishads* explained it as a "state of being" attained by entering a "state of a release" called *Moksha* or *Nirvana* in later Buddhist theology. The concept of *Moksha/ Nirvana* marked the beginning of another paradigm shift in religious discourse in ancient India.

Until then, the Aryan religion, like the ancient Mesopotamian one, stressed that the physical world is merely a temporal replica of the unseen world of gods. Now, the goalposts changed. The thrust shifted from physical to mental, from material to spiritual, and from the real to the imagined aspects of religious practices. Seeking "meaning" in life and the world became a well-meaning preoccupation of people from almost all walks of life (except Shudras and peasant Vaishyas). People would crave what they called spiritual experience - certain fleeting states of "rapture" or intense religious experience brought about by mindfulness practices.

The symbolic rituals demanded specific mental effort and observation of procedural protocols on the performer's part under the supervision of experts or priests. This fact created a robust opportunity and avenue for the priestly class, who was always well versed with the procedural ritual technicalities as part of their job. They were all along involved in officiating at all kinds of sacrifices and ceremonies. As a part of their job, they were responsible for helping people get "mentally" engaged in the ritualistic process. In return, the priests would get gifts in kind or coins. That is to say, it was a priest-client relationship. Whenever a client wanted to do a ceremony, the priest would chant specific mantras, and the client would perform certain rituals according to a set discipline. The priest would guide the client to imagine every hymn, action, and minute sub-ritual. While chanting mantras, the specific intonation and monotonicity of the priest's voice would put the client into a trance-like state, construed as heightened awareness and self-consciousness by the latter. Through this guided mantra-chanting, the officiating priest would suggest to the client-ritualist "meaning" to every action or mantra and even connect things to the cosmic reality.

Over time, the ritual practices evolved into guided meditations and other mindfulness techniques. Slowly the foundations were laid for a discipline that later became known as *Yoga* - originally meaning, as Karen Armstrong writes, "yoking" or involving oneself in connecting and "yoking together of different levels of reality."

Atman or the Self

By the 9th century BCE, *Prajapatti* was exalted as the originator and the source of all reality, physical and cosmic - *Purusha, Devas, Asuras,*

Vedas, etc. He became an all-encompassing entity. As recorded by Karen Armstrong in her book *The Great Transformation*, the story goes: "All these entities [physical and cosmic] were part of *Him [Prajapatti]*, but when *He* was exhausted and fell asleep, the 'reality' dropped away from *Him*. Upon awakening from slumber, *Prajapatti* had to put them together. Again, *He* accomplished this feat for *Himself*." Such myths gave credence to the "meaning-seeking" narratives attached to symbolic sacrifice or sacrificial fire (*Agnicanaya*). Building a new fire by a sacrificer symbolized reconstructing and reenacting the creation story of *Prajapatti* and, by corollary, participating in sacred creation through the power of *Agni*. Imagining became a dominant component of the religious liturgy. It demanded a focused mental effort on the part of a believer – a thing unheard of in the earlier version of the Aryan religion.

As new versions of the old stories appeared, they were relatively polished. Some creation myths were framed *de novo* to close the existing loopholes in the older versions. The divine origin of the myths was specifically stressed – a well-known trick employed by religious elites all over history – to silence the skeptics. *Prajapatti* now revealed "new insights" directly to the prominent sages and *rishis*. Period.

The impact of the reformed ritual and liturgy on the overall religious outlook in ancient India was profound. The concept of revelation played a significant role, drawing its legitimacy from the authority of the respected rishis. The "revelation" from on high was frequently invoked, though it wasn't always called revelation. "Enlightenment" was a preferred usage. All the same, the Aryan theology (now referred to as Vedic religion) was caught in a vortex of conceptual revolution, paving the way for the emergence of an entirely novel religious thought process. The beauty and strength of this new religious thought lay in its relative simplicity, both in description and practice. Soon it almost entirely eclipsed the old religious outlook. The ease with which it could be grasped by even the uninitiated translated into an emotional appeal. People became more receptive to change, readier to transform their behavior, and shunned the hitherto sacralized war games and rituals of the older religious tradition. The metamorphosis of the rituals into contemplative exercises and meditation paved the way for this transformation, which can be viewed as the outstanding achievement of the Axial Age in India.

The priests and sages actively debated and deliberated on subjects like *self* or *atman* (the spirit or soul). This debate fashioned the discourses recorded in the *Upanishads* (scriptures that came after the *Vedas*). As the debate continued and the discourse evolved, the sacred history widened in scope like literature did in the later days of civilization. Yet, despite the clergy's and sages' deftness at handling tricky questions, a bunch of complicated and controversial issues assumed prickly dimensions. For instance, if a person had become an expert in ritual, understood the meaning of rituals, and was proficient in contemplation, implying that he became one with *Atman* (Self with capital "S") and *Prajapatti*, did he still need to perform liturgy publicly? Could he contemplate the whole liturgy and ritual in silence and still become "one with the 'Higher Self' or *Atman*"? Such and other issues created a theological conundrum. Its outright resolution favoring writing off public liturgy would theoretically render the priestly class jobless. No rituals, no income for priests.

The priestly class resisted the reformers' attempts to strip religion of liturgy. To avoid confrontation with the clergy, the sages gave in. And they adroitly turned to philosophy to pacify the clergy. Given the clergy's clout in society, it was essential to bring them on board. A bit of philosophy can sometimes work wonders. Slowly the reformer sages got the clergy's head around the argument that any form of ritual, whether public or private, that leads to experiencing the "state of one-ness" with the whole universe and its creator was a legitimate form of worship. Thus, personal contemplation by an individual – a form of mindfulness practice called meditation – was recognized as equivalent to ritual worship. As time passed, meditation became quite popular – a form of prayer in its own right. Appropriately executed meditation could raise the meditator to a level at par with gods – so went the argument. That is to say, a master meditator could qualify to become *Atmayajnin* – a self-sacrificer, meaning *Prajapatti* incarnate. Thus like gods, a master was exempt from worshipping anything. So went the philosophy.

The recognition of private worship (meditation) was no more than an intellectual defeat for the clergy. For the vast majority of people, meditation was cumbersome. They still preferred rituals. The reason was that there was no set protocol for meditation. There was no universal and uniform method. That is to say, there never was one correct way of meditating. Each master floated their own complicated and cumbersome form of mediation.

The result – a simple and elegant concept became exquisitely complex and controversial to be translated into practice. It was next to impossible for everyday folks to aspire to become *Atmayajnin*. The clergy had all the reasons to celebrate. Their customer base remained intact.

"An *Atmayajnin* was supposed to follow a rigorous discipline and speak the truth at all times," stressed the sages. "By acting in accordance with the truth and reality," they emphasized, "he would attain the power and energy of *Brahman*." It was a new direction in religious thought – an adventure to explore the inner "self," or what we call the mind in today's scientific parlance. The Aryans had formally embarked on the path of spiritual quest. The discourse shifted from gods to metaphysical abstractions, fuelling polemics, rhetoric, and philosophical inquiry. Soon the Indian religious perspective would be revolutionized so much that quite an intellectual rebellion against gods was in the making. Barely three centuries from the 10th century BCE would the Indus valley and the Arya-Varta civilizations make fertile ground for new religions and new theological movements to germinate and blossom.

Individual householders were at liberty to establish an altar for the "sacred fire" in their homes. The public liturgy was no longer a prerequisite for meditating on "self," and the entry into "the world of gods" after death was no longer directly proportional only to wealth. Yet stripping religion of its liturgy left behind a bland theology that hardly charmed people. Most people still preferred public liturgy over meditative contemplation. But in the minds of some prominent thinkers, doubt was sown about the classical religion and its effectiveness. Yet the apparent simplification of rituals led to that weird inner sense of incompleteness and tugging curiosity that compelled these men to resort to extreme measures to address their discomfort. Perhaps. They adopted rigorous physical and mental practices that involved inflicting torment and torture on their bodies in the solitude and silence of the dark corners of jungles and caves. Unsatisfied still, some renounced their families, totally abandoning the luxury of the settled life of the villages and communities. These renouncers became known as *Sanyansins*. The *sannyasins* became instrumental in shaping another religious evolution and reformation in India.

Trance or the Religious Experience

The *Brahmins* (one of the four *Varnas* mentioned earlier) had become full-time priests. All that was needed to ride on the backs of the gullible people were a few enigmatic mantras here, and a few unintelligible chants there was. The Brahmins wantonly exploited the unsuspecting people. Soon a powerful and prestigious Brahmanical priestly class was established that would least hesitate to ruthlessly impose sanctions and codes on the society. The Brahmins held the keys to power through their monopoly over the oral scriptural texts they took care to pass on to their generations as a closely guarded secret so that knowledge wouldn't disseminate to non-Brahmins. The *Brahmins* painstakingly memorized the hymns or the mantras of the Rig Veda. They masterfully performed the religious rituals in a stepwise manner following an established chronological order, all along taking care to impart training only to their sons and male relatives. As guardians of the scriptures, they ultimately set their hold, influence, and power over the entire socio-political machinery. Through their artful manipulation of the institution of religion, they also tightened their grip over the Temple-and-Palace-run economic system of ancient India.

By the 8th century BCE, the *Brahmins* had jumped to the topmost echelon in the power hierarchy. To use the modern lexicon, they were "religious technocrats" who would oversee and perform the religious rituals and rites with remarkable precision and focus, whether in ordinary households, in the warlords' houses, or kings' palaces. In return, they received generous remuneration. As their status in society rose, they came to be respected and honored as a "visible deity" or *Prajapatti* incarnate. The knowledge of scripture made them "one with the being of *Brahman*" in the eyes of the people. *Brahmin* was no mere mortal. As an "embodiment of holy life." he was expected to reveal his supernatural power during the rituals as and when he wished. Under the spell of a *Brahmin's* alleged magical power, the client or ritual performer could make a momentary "mystical ascent to gods or heaven," experiencing a state akin to "rapture." So went the logic.

In modern psychological parlance, "rapture" exemplifies a state of heightened awareness that monotonous hypnogogic mantras, chants, and voice intonations can induce. That's to say, the rapture is a hypnotic trance state. A trance state tremendously increases the suggestibility of a person. In meditative trance states, the subject can be led to fantasize and reconstruct images and scenes, for instance, of gods, heaven, ghosts, and all other kinds of stuff. People can be guided to imagine tunnels, fire, hell, paradise, etc., which they interpret as visiting a previous life. People who called themselves mystics and sages misconstrued induced trance state as a "religious experience." These so-called "religious experiences" provided them, they believed, a window of opportunity to dive deeper into the realm of the unknown and thus connect with the A*tman* or "Self." For an unsuspecting initiate, it was a curious experience. Just like people get addicted to euphoric states after consuming psychedelics, some meditators long for hypnotic trance states. They enjoy daydreaming under the spell of meditative hypnosis. Some erroneously call such imaginative contemplations a deep sense of selflessness, nothingness, mystical rapture, etc., you name it. In essence, all mediation is self-hypnosis.

Meditation is time-consuming and not always easy, however blissful it might seem to some. For the ordinary working class of the Aryan society, the daily chores of life would prove an impediment to engaging in these so-called "religious experiences." It was a hard choice for them–you go after "religious experience," or you toil to earn bread.

Some indeed were so tempted by this "religious experience" that they left everything behind - fields, cattle, family, and all - seeking extended periods of such experience. Some even wanted to stay in "rapture" almost all the time. Such crazies renounced families and worldly life to relieve themselves entirely from the responsibility of earning bread. They turned to jungles and forests. The solitude of raw nature, they believed, provided them with a perfect environment to explore the enigmatic spiritual life, abandon public liturgy, and turn to inner experiences. It was these renouncers who, in Karen Armstrong's view, pioneered the art of "*internalization of religion*" - one of the hallmarks of the Axial Age of India.

Some renouncers (*Sanyansins)* became hermits. In contrast to renouncers, the hermits established mini-societies in the forests with their wives, children, and family around a "sacred fire." Both renouncers and hermits practiced strict forms of asceticism and *tapas* (meditative worship). Fasting, *tapas,* and celibacy were the prerequisites for attaining spiritual growth. An esoteric interpretation got attached to fasting and *tapas.* They were viewed as a sacrifice offered by the silent sage to the internal and external *devas. Sanyasins* held the view that devas lived within the "self" (internal devas) and outside the "self" (external devas), both being controlled by *Brahman* and *Prajapatti.* The *Sanyasins* who adopted celibacy as a matter of principle were known as *Brahmacharyas.*

Teacher and Disciple

Humans seek meaning. This meaning-seeking tendency has driven the evolution of religious thought along varied paths. One of the collateral effects of this evolution was that religion became institutionalized and religious education attained great importance amongst the elite. The necessity of learning the art of meditation, contemplation, and *tapas* popularized the institution of *Guru* and *Shishya* (teacher and disciple), providing an opportunity to learn to non-elites. The sages and *rishis* of the later Vedic period – The *Upanishadic* period – devoted much of their time and energy to esoteric meditation and *tapas* in an attempt, they believed, to touch, feel, and sense the so-called "essence" of life. They strived to fathom the ultimate meaning of human existence. In doing so, they would experience "self-hypnotic trance states" induced through monotonous meditative chants, postures, and breathing exercises. These hypnotic trance states, perceived by them as "deeply serene feelings" of "ecstasy and peacefulness," were erroneously labeled by them as "authentic religious experiences." Right or wrong, trance states changed the sages' understanding of religious phenomena. That was crucial.

In a society where the popular Vedic religious belief that a "religious experience" could only be achieved by performing a particular sacrifice or ritual was deeply etched on the collective consciousness, even a minor paradigm shift was a massive achievement in the direction of religious reformation. As the material condition of the ancient society improved, public opinion also changed, as it always does. The *Upanishadic* sages were quick to use the opportunity to introduce new paradigms, creation myths, and philosophy. Some openly challenged the older Vedic religious dogmas insisting that a state of peace, serenity, and union with gods, particularly *Prajapatti,* could only be achieved by living "differently" and not by performing rituals alone. By "living differently," they meant practicing contemplation and accepting "truth" as one of the foundational "values" underlying moral principles. They emphasized that "bliss and serenity" was an attainable goal – perfectly achievable by following a proper incrementally progressing religious discipline. No ritual, no sacrifice, no worship, and no liturgy, they said, could replace disciplined living. Although studying sacred texts was necessary, they argued that textual learning alone was insufficient to live blissfully.

The scriptural teachings, the sages stressed, were meant to be contemplated upon, experienced, practiced, and lived. And that was where an apprenticeship with a guru could help. Only a guru could lead the pupil, stepwise, through that long and challenging process – "introspection into 'self.'" *The Upanishadic* student was to live a humble life and obey his guru completely. That was okay for many. For the warrior Aryan class, a dash of "obedience and obsequiousness" was as strange and foreign as it was absurd. It hurt their self-esteem and challenged their sense of hubris. How could a people with a high sense of self-esteem bordering on hubris reconcile with such an absurd discipline? The answer? A story.

Stories backed up with appropriate religious metaphors are powerful. They persuade. In one sentence, the gist of the story, which put to rest all skeptics, went like this: "*Indra*, who was a war god, also had to gather wood for his teacher, look after his fire, clean *Prajapatti*'s house, and be chaste, give up warfare and practice *ahimsa*." The *Indra-Prajapatti* story was explicit: "If *Indra* would denounce violence and obey his teacher, *Prajapatti*, so were the warrior Aryans duty-bound to learn from *Indra*. That was to say, shun violence, adopt and practice a life of obedience and ahimsa, and pay respect to the sages and gurus." Who could defy *Indra* and *Prajapatti?* Even the most obstinate *Kshatriya* warriors gave in. And gradually, Indian theology began to touch new horizons of possibility. Religious inquiry and debate had already sparked a revolution of thought. Now was the time for it to unfold.

Kapila and *Samkhya* thought

Upanishadic religion – call it spiritual philosophy - couldn't satisfy the inquisitive curiosity of some sharp-witted people, its apparent philosophic brilliance notwithstanding. To ordinary folks, it hadn't much to offer. It didn't promise solutions for their immediate economic problems. No theology does, despite the claims by the faithful to the contrary. No theology is a perfect code or solution for life's problems. Perfection in itself is detrimental to theology. It builds monotony; monotony breeds rigidity, and rigidity kills theological evolution. *Upanishadic* theology survived and evolved because it unwittingly left gaps to be filled by later theologies and philosophies.

Because of its noticeable gaps, the renouncers and sages grew uncomfortable with the Upanishadic theological framework. They raised questions about the rationality of its precepts. Some influential thinkers rejected *Brahman, Atman, Purusha,* etc., as mere impersonal constructs and concepts defying dimensionality. "How could the identity of a being merge into an abstract construct?" asked one. And "How could I merge with *Brahman* without losing my identity?" questioned another, and on and on. These people, looking at the world unceasingly working, wondered: "nature" seemed to be at play in every sphere of human life. How could nature, *Brahman,* and man be reconciled into "one" whole and then construed as subservient to *Prajapatti*? Questions like these created a thorny philosophical tangle. Others sensed that contradicting this line of religious belief was pretty dangerous. They preferred the status quo approach fearing excommunication from the community. However, some sages ultimately did muster enough courage to embark on a revolutionary, though not a totally radical, path.

One of the most courageous sages of the day was Kapila – a 6th century BCE sage who introduced a revolutionary concept famously called *Samkhya.* The *Samkhya* philosophy took a different perspective vis-à-vis *Purusha*: As per it, p*urusha* (with a small "p") represented merely an aspect of the *Purusha* (with a capital P). That was another way of saying the "human" and "being" of "human beings" are principally different, but together, they become one whole. The *purusha* in *Samkhya* merely denoted the essence of the human being and not of the universe, unlike the Vedic *Purusha*; *purusha* (with small p) interfused with the '*Prakriti*' – the nature of the human species as a whole. *Prakriti,* according to *Samkhya,* was another name for impulses like emotions, feelings, desires, wants, and so on that keep humans attached to the external world. These impulses, the *Samkhyans* maintained, hinder human conflation with that of its *purusha*, thus obstructing human "knowing" of the eternal dimension of the *Purusha.* How could humans understand and know this essence – the *purusha*? Through meditation. Through meditation alone, Kapila answered, one could understand the entanglement of *Prakriti* and *purusha* (nature with spirit). That understanding, he argued, would open up before a S*amkhya* practitioner the precise path to the "true self."

This familiar-looking yet innovative, in its own right, philosophical perspective – *Samkhya* – marked the beginning of a revolution that would reach a fever pitch in the succeeding centuries. Remarkably enough, *Samkhya* shifted attention away from *Brahman* and *Prajapatti* – the divine – to the humans and their psychological moorings. *Samkhya* gained acceptance partly because it was theologically simpler though not necessarily quite straightforward and partly because it provided a feasible alternative to the doctrine of *dukkha* – a pessimistic legacy from ages that life was a real suffering (*dukkha*). The contemplation of this perpetual *dukkha* was quite unnerving to sages, rishis, and commoners.

"Is there a way out of this *dukkha*?" was a question that loomed large in everyone's mind. People felt helpless. There was no hope of a *dukkha-less* future. *Samkhya* offered some hope, a glimpse of light at the far end of the dark tunnel. This proverbial light attracted people to *Samkhyan* thought. *Samkhyans* called it the "bliss" – that same bliss that would finally release humans from their eternal bondage of suffering.

The word about Kapila spread. He became a star, a saint. His was an uncanny method for achieving the enigmatic "release": "Meditate upon 'release' itself to acquaint *self* with complexities of human predicament; by acquainting with *self*, one can hope to transcend *self*." That was a milder way of saying, "don't worship or meditate on *devas*, gods, or *Brahman* but on the human 'nature' or '*purusha/Prakriti* interaction. Only then can you transcend *dukkha* and become eternally liberated." Undoubtedly, it was the first-of-its-kind unequivocal recognition of innate human power to control and modify the destiny of humanity.

Samkhya philosophy deserves credit for accomplishing a landmark feat. For the first time in the Sacred History of the world, a philosophy uncannily succeeded in excluding the role of divine beings and gods in human affairs and still managed to survive as a theology at its core. Remarkably enough, *Samkhya* stubbornly refused to rely on the shenanigans of revelation and inspiration, arguing instead from the standpoint of logic and rationale. Quite surprisingly, in the dangerously tricky religious atmosphere of the day, the *Samkhya* thought managed to carve its place as a distinct religious movement. *Samkhyans'* strategy was cold-blooded and calculated. Their arguments were veiled, wrapped within the thick garment of incomprehensible and unintelligible abstract conceptualizations. They sparingly and calculatedly used idiomatic abstractions. However, they quite often used a far sharper sword – syllogism – to slash at the heart of the arguments with such cunning precision that even the Aristotle of the day would be left jaw-dropping.

Take *prakrati* (nature). *Samkhya* would go like this, there are three *Gunas* (the original traits) – *Satta, Rajas,* and *Tamas* meaning intelligence, energy, and inertia, respectively. The three *Gunas* (original traits) are in equilibrium, but the *purusha* create chaos. New realities like *buddhi* (intellect), *ahamkara* (ego), etc., emerged because of *purusha*'s ignorance and obstinacy. Thus *purusha* gets trapped in a false "self" dictated by *ahamkara* (ego), which is the root cause of *dukkha* (suffering). The *ahamkara* (ego) creates the confabulating "illusion," putting the human being into a state of "ignorance." Ignorance confuses the *purusha* (human being), and he becomes subservient to desires, whims, and longings. Humankind pays attention to these ego trappings and mistakes them for the authentic "*self.*" Henceforth come all the woes and sufferings.... Brilliant. No Socrates, Hegel, or Bakunin could match this sophistry of *Samkhyan* rhetoric. No wonder the poor sages and *rishis* of the day couldn't counter Kapila when he pointed out their mistakes and insisted on meditating upon *buddhi,* which according to him, reflected the *purusha* in the human intellect. Mediation on *buddhi,* Kapila said, was the only path to ultimate liberation or *moksha.*

Rebellion against gods

The *Samkhya* theology's cautious portrayal of gods as helpless creatures, perpetually struggling against their natural weaknesses and not powerful enough to change the humans' condition, was a real turning point of the Axial Age religious discourse in India. Its claim that the gods did not exist in some external supernatural realm but within *purusha* seemed thoroughly outlandish – rebellion against the gods. Yet it went unnoticed. The *Samkhyans* inferred that they could boldly teach that there was no need to beseech the gods for help, and there was no need to reenact the model of heaven and gods. They began to argue what was needed, instead, was the "awareness about self," which could be cultivated through a contemplative practice so that the "self" hidden within the garment of ignorance could be "released." The *Samkhyan* sages encouraged followers to cultivate a greater self-awareness to find liberation from miseries and the *dukkha.* "Such a state of awareness," they boldly pronounced, "had nothing to do with the divine or the supernatural – it was simply a goal to be attained, for the 'fulfillment of human nature," and "achieving this state is within everybody's reach." Strive and attain. The monopoly of gods is over.

Truly, the *Samkhyans* were the first religious secularists of ancient India. The Buddhist and later Zen practices, or even psychoanalysis, hypnosis, and self-hypnosis, can be traced to these revolutionary insights of the *Samkhyan* sages. The emergence of *Yoga* as an independent discipline was, to an extent, one of the immediate results of this revolutionary thought process. Patanjali may have taken the credit for systematizing *yoga* as a discipline; nonetheless, the fact remains that by the 6th century BCE – more than six hundred years before Patanjali – *yoga* had already become a widespread religious practice, courtesy of *Samkhya.*

Like other religions that came and went, *Samkhya* theology, too, couldn't retain its original form for long. It melted away to diffuse into the inter-atomic spaces of other theological elements. Historically, various theologies melted and mixed in the Indian religious-cultural crucible, lending and borrowing each other's ideas, concepts, and constructs that led to a cultural mosaic. *Samkhya,* in its time, tried its best to do away with the tedious, cumbersome, and economically burdensome Vedic and *Upanishadic* religions. But.

Established religions tend to be pretty resistant to weathering effects of time. The Vedic religion withstood *Samkhya's* assault despite the latter's audacious attempts. In doing so, ironically, *Samkhya* theology itself became a casualty in the winds of change. It would have been wiped off from the memory of history had its rebirth in the form of Jainism, Buddhism, and other religious-philosophical movements not saved its vestiges. It is also true that in the ensuing competition and struggle, the Vedic and *Upanishadic* religions also couldn't escape unscathed. They, too, had to adjust to the changing circumstances. But they proved more resilient.

What prevented the beautifully simple, brilliantly philosophical, and economically un-burdensome *Samkhya* religion from becoming popular? The answer lay in a problem overlooked by Kapila and other *Samkhyan* sages: as a religion, *Samkhya* was difficult to practice despite its apparent simplicity; it didn't promise immediate rewards as expected of a new religion. People are impatient by nature. They want quick-fix remedies for their existing problems. Historically, religions that benefitted people economically and politically, particularly the aristocracy and the elite, quickly and reliably won the day. The *Samkhya* religion did not put the Aryan society at much disadvantage, but it did not help it handle the economic challenges either. It prescribed no communal feasts, grain collections at the temples, or charity institutions. Neither could it muster the support of political and religious aristocracy. Instead, it demanded a life of solitude and renunciation from its followers. That was impractical for the peasantry and the nobility of the day. Later, through *Yoga*, though, *Samkhya* did manage to touch people's lives on a much larger scale; however, by then, the scenario had changed, and enthusiasm about this religion had already waned.

Despite its failure as a religion, the *Samkhya's* contribution to the religious discourse was tremendous. It sparked a robust and well-constructed dialogue and argument, which compelled the thinkers and the seers to engage in the fine talk – instrumental in bringing about a paradigm shift that cleared the decks for great religions like Jainism and Buddhism. These two great religious philosophies catapulted the *Samkhya* doctrines to fame. Down the line, all this transformation had a long-lasting and tremendous effect on the collective consciousness of human civilization worldwide. The global reverberation of these religious movements is felt in the modern world as strongly as it would have been two and a half millennia ago. It doesn't matter whether anybody remembers Samkhya or not. What matters is that Kapila managed to carve out a place in history that nobody could occupy. Humankind owes him a lot.

Chapter – 05

Buddha or Bhagavad Gita

Karma

Religion couldn't afford to restrict itself solely to matters of the spiritual realm, partly because the boundary between the spiritual and the temporal was historically indistinct and partly because religion feared the loss of its institutional role. Religion could never alienate itself from economics and politics despite the claims of a fair majority of believers to the contrary. The matters in India were no different. Political economy per se necessitated religion's birth and organization in the first place. However, religion consistently failed to provide a comprehensive, complete, inclusive roadmap for societies and city-states. That's not to say that it didn't remain deeply entrenched within the fabric of human culture. Not the least. For good or bad, religion has always been instrumental in shaping the ethos and cultural milieu of our civilizational history. Ever since the appearance of humans on this planet, religion has taken center stage in politics, economics, and sociology. The reason is that humans have always sought answers to deeply mystifying, mind-boggling questions about creation and existence. No religion so far has given a complete set of answers, solutions, or guiding principles to be universally adapted to address the aspirations of all the diverse groups, cultures, and racial subsets comprising the vast human society. There is no one-religion-fit-all option. That is too much to ask of religion.

Humans are dichotomous. Their world and their experiences are dichotomous. Like every other living creature, humans experience the physical world around them through the five senses but what makes humans human is that they are capable of imagining and possess foresight; the real and the imagined interact and overlap in mind, putting humans on the knife's edge. The human mind that defies space-time and can cross the horizon of the remotest and unfathomable universe makes it hard for us to be satisfied with one way of doing things. Times change, our priorities and challenges change, our world changes, and so does our imagination. What is relevant today may not be such a decade or century hence. What was relevant to the ancients isn't relevant today. With changing circumstances, religion feels the heat.

Religion is unlike Science. Science grows by changing and adapting with time, discarding what doesn't work. Not religion. Religion builds on certain foundational dogmas which are hard to abandon. What it does at the most is evolve and restructure itself, albeit at a slower and relatively imperceptible pace. It would be a mistake to ascribe the emergence of modified versions of the older thought to the invisible hand of the divine. Religion has always yielded to the pressures of politics and economics. India's sacred history demonstrates the point remarkably well that time after time, prominent and influential religious saints introduced revolutionary ideas, even ideas bordering on atheism.

Take Yajnavalkya. He was a prominent *Upanishadic rishi* who compiled *Brhadaranyaka Upanishad.* He enjoyed the patronage of the King Janaka of *Videha.* Yajnavalkya was among the first to put forward the revolutionary idea, in the late 8th century BCE, that the "ultimate reality can be discovered within the depths of self or *atman.*" Over time, the doctrine of *Atman* became the central theme around which all the subsequent religious thought lines in India would revolve. Yajnavalkya became controversial when he brought up his other doctrine, the doctrine of *Karma.* Yet within three centuries after his death, *Karma* became a defining principle of individual and collective behavior in Indian society.

Karma became the recurrent theme for subsequent religious reformation. What is Karma? It is the sum of a person's actions in this and previous life, which decides the fate of future existences. Yajnavalkya's *Doctrine of Karma* was a particularly controversial theology because it prefigured a weird yet abstract idea of an unending cycle of death and rebirth. Evil *Karma,* arising out of the natural desires of a human being, could lead to rebirth as animals, plants, insects, worms, and *Shudras* (untouchables, lower caste) or enslaved people. The afterlife, a gloomy affair, became more despairing by adding Karma to the equation. What made things worse was the idea that all the old Vedic rituals were useless for extricating a person from bad *Karma.* The only piece of good news was that *Yoga* could be helpful. The caveat, however, was that *Yoga*, especially in the 8th century BCE, was no simple thing. It was still raw and un-systematized. It demanded an amount of effort incompatible with regular life. A *Yogi* had to completely divorce himself from everyday activities to avoid falling into the trap of *Samsara* or a life of desires.

Market, Dukkha, and Self-deception

With the emergence of the Kingdoms of Magadha and Kosala, urbanization picked pace by the sixth century BCE. The changing political atmosphere reinforced the power struggle among the *Varnas* (class or caste). During the first few centuries of the Iron Age, Kshatriyas' power had dipped slightly in favor of *Brahmins*. Now they again usurped the prominent position of controlling power. With the barter system giving way to a 'coin-based' (Monetary) economy, markets expanded, and trade flourished. It also opened up new opportunities attracting Vaishyas to switch from farming to business. Before long, a new merchant class emerged. Simultaneously new towns like Varanasi, Kapilvastu, and Kaushambi sprang up. All in all, a primitive type of capitalist economy was underway. *Brahmins* found themselves pitted against the predominantly *Kshatriya* power structure.

As trade and agriculture brought along more wealth and comfort, people began to realize the futility of performing the *Vedic* and *Upanishadic* religious rites. Seeing how the *Brahmins* (priestly class) exploited them in the name of religion, they began to question sacred economics. However, it was too early for ordinary folks, not yet organized enough, to revolt openly against *Brahmanical* exploitation. There was no rebellion, but sure enough, the new economic awakening had ignited a smoldering fire that could burst into flames anytime to engulf the prevailing old religious thought.

Urbanization pushed class divisions further and deeper, the inter-class tussle taking an ugly shape creating deep fault lines in society. The Brahmins and Kshatriyas found a common foe in Vaishya's parvenu-rich urban class. They shelved their differences and united against the parvenu rich trying to establish themselves in the higher echelon of urban society. In the coming centuries, this class war would go on to define the socio-cultural milieu of the Indian civilization permanently.

The many upsides of urbanization and economic boom are usually accompanied by equally intense unseen-in-the-villages problems, such as the surge in infections and diseases. The urban ghettos and crowded places spark epidemics of infectious diseases, gambling, drinking, prostitution, crime, etc. Tavern life, crime, and disorder go hand in hand. People can turn merciless in money matters. In ancient India, too, trade and urbanization created wealth, but they also created insurmountable challenges. For everyday folks, life came to represent nothing but total *dukkha*. Strife, infightings, and aggression were the norm. Economic prosperity didn't translate into peace. The kings coerced the subjects into paying heavy taxes, greedy merchants turned competitive, and money lenders were ruthless. The powerful lived a luxurious life, and the poor went under. The Vedic religion refused to come to the rescue of the oppressed.

People wanted respite. Religion gave them none. *Karma* was intimidating, and religion did not bother, demanding extensive rituals and burning fires. The perpetual death and rebirth cycle was frightening to contemplate, but the priestly class, the guardian of religion, ran after power and wealth. People immediately needed something to handle the problem. Something new. Something solution-oriented.

Dukkha ran as the common thread through the theological discourses of 5th century BC India. Inevitably and understandably, everything accentuated *dukkha*. Life was *dukkha*. Karma was *dukkha*, and desire was *dukkha*. The sages preached handling "desire" with *Yoga*, meditation, and certain forms of asceticism. Not everybody could afford that luxury. The few who did (renouncers) were hailed as courageous and extraordinarily gifted. They were held in high esteem, believed to symbolize the embodiment of divine power, and would be called the "enlightened ones."

People always want a shortcut to a better life and success, free of cost and labor—a gift from the gods. The ancients believed that pleasing the gods and gaining their favor would bring them good fortune. But pleasing gods was easier said than done. In earlier days, people performed sacrifices. Now those days were gone. Nothing short of strict individual discipline and renunciation of worldly life was required of the aspirants who wanted a favor from the gods—bad news.

No worry. People can always wriggle out of any conundrum through self-deception backing the latter with the sleight of rationalization and logic. The ultimate genius of the human mind lies in creating something out of nothing. Only humans make nothing look like everything. Like everywhere in India, the witty conjured a fantastic solution to their dilemma. It was simple. Go to the *sanyasin* (ascetics and hermits), tell them about your woes, please them with alms and gifts, and the *sanyasin* will mediate for you with the gods. You would enjoy worldly success and a place in heaven after death for a small fee.

The sages and hermits enjoyed high status and prestige. People believed in them and graciously attended their discourse to learn about religion. Some sages taught revolutionary ideas, which the disciples disseminated far and wide, attracting a big following. The common folks genuinely revered these sages and their teaching for centuries after their death testifying to the influence they wielded on the collective consciousness of society.

Mahavira

Vardhamana Jnanitrputra, the *Mahavira*, was a renouncer, an influential teacher, and a founder of a great reformist theological movement. Mahavira practiced strict asceticism and penitence. He subjected himself to extreme repentance, fasting in the torrid heat of the Sun, and refused even to wear clothes. The purpose behind penitence was to release his true "self," which he did. At least, he claimed so. He became convinced that *Ahimsa* (strict nonviolence) leads to liberation and, thus, *Moksha* (release or rapture). He believed he had become an "enlightened" one, and the people agreed. In truth, under intense and prolonged fasting, he might have momentarily slipped in and out of a state of an altered consciousness, which he construed as a religious experience. There is nothing esoteric or supernatural in such incidents. People have experienced horrid images and scenes after trauma which some describe as "near-death experiences." In the so-called "near-death experience," people claim to have a brush with past and future life; some even put out preposterous claims of visiting heaven and hell. In Mahavira's case, prolonged fasting and starvation might well have induced a brain state that he called rapture (Moksha).

Mahavira was reluctant to give a detailed description of his religious experience, or he genuinely couldn't explain the phenomenon in words, calling it "nothing but at the same time something." He argued that anybody who followed in his footsteps would automatically attain *Moksha* and become *Jina* (or Jain). Mahavira claimed, as Jain seers would later believe, that he was the last in the long line of *Jinas* who had conquered *dukkha* and become liberated. No Jina would come after him, but anybody could become a Jina in his name, vicariously. That sounds Christian.

Since Mahavira was the top *Jina* and didn't spell out what Moksha was, every other aspiring *Jina* had to follow a specific discipline and hope "something" would happen to him. That was to say that every Jina could interpret "something" as some spiritual experience, which, after all, was a good thing for the followers of Mahavira. It opened the door for debate and discussion among them, and they erected a whole body of elaborate metaphysics and philosophical discourse after Mahavira's death. For Jains, *Karma* was no longer an infallible destiny but simply an impurity that touches the clean slate of the 'soul' as a consequence of undisciplined behavior. Change your behavior, change your *Karma,* the message went. That was to say that the man had complete control over his *Karma.* A huge relief, after all.

A Jain was required to take five vows of abstinence: Abstinence from violence, lying, sex, stealing, and owning property. He had to see everyday life's activity through the prism of these five vows. *Ahimsa,* too, was reframed with a touch of metaphysics, making it the central dogma of Jainism. Mere abstinence from killing would not suffice; instead, a positive benevolence toward all living creatures was what Ahimsa got to envisage. Interestingly, in Mahavira's formula of things, gods weren't mentioned at all. And, still, Jainism made its mark on the sacred history of India as an organized religion.

The gods had no place in Mahavira's religion. *Mahavira* was the first in the history of humankind to categorically refuse to acknowledge the role of a god or gods in human affairs, a remarkably bold thing to do in ancient society. In Mahavira's words, gods had no business bestowing *Moksha* (liberation/ enlightenment) on human beings. Attaining *Moksha* was a human enterprise, an enterprise that entailed discipline, mindfulness, and change of behavior, totally within the power of each one of us. That was a pretty rebellious announcement. Earlier *Samkhya* tradition, as recalled from chapter 4, had also hinted, but indirectly, at such a possibility. Mahavira was unambiguous and unequivocal: everything is within the power of humans. Period. With one stroke, he shifted the direction of theological discourse from "divine" to "human." That was a significant and profoundly revolutionary shift in fifth-century BCE India.

Atheism as religion is quite an oxymoron in our modern day. Modern atheists shy away from declaring atheism as their religion or faith, seeking to hide under the cover of rhetoric and scientific evidence. In proclaiming a revolutionary – no, dangerous – philosophy, Mahavira displayed humungous courage and became a famous saint, the only saint in history who openly declared atheism as his religion. It seems absurd to run a considerable risk, but Mahavira could afford it because India at that time was caught in the throes of the Axial Age transformation. Furthermore, ancient India was a melting pot of ideas, philosophies, and religions; anything went in that environment. Hardly any ancient civilization has demonstrated as secular an outlook as that of old India.

Mahavira and his followers quickly attracted royal patronage – quite an achievement – which, for obvious reasons, gave this movement a tremendous boost. As long as the royal patronage continued, a good chunk of tradespeople and the merchant class persevered with *Mahavira*'s creed (popularly called Jainism). Over time as the Jains continued to insist on the strict observance of the five vows, especially of *Ahimsa* and the refusal of property ownership, Jainism faced problems. The five vows became a stumbling block for Jainism as a religion. The masses, especially the merchant class, began showing a cold shoulder to this religion which, like socialism of the 20th century, forbade them from owning private property and, by corollary, wealth.

History shows royal patronage or political power has been the most significant, nay the rate-limiting, factor for the survival and spread of any religion. Jainism couldn't hold on to royal patronage for long. The consequence – Jainism's support base shrank. Without acceptance in the power corridors and among the elite, no religion has ever succeeded in making a reasonably significant number of converts. Jainism missed the ball, unwisely, ignoring the premise that people judge a religion not by its spiritual standards alone but by its economic friendliness.

Jainism unwittingly set itself against odds with its bad economic policy. People seek a means to an end; they look to the gods for prosperity; they pray to avoid losses, calamities, and trouble. Spiritual Enlightenment, no doubt, is welcome as long as it positively impacts the material well-being of the people, but Enlightenment alone, without tangible material success, doesn't have many takers. Most people look to religion to achieve a better life. They turn to religion to handle the problems they can't handle alone.

When a religion, rather than making life easier, puts more demands on the individual and their family, sooner or later, they will turn away from such a religion, however brilliant and beautiful its theology and metaphysics might be. Most people are less concerned with their faith's philosophical beauty; they want their faith and religion to satisfy their immediate needs. That's why temples, churches, mosques, religious places, and pilgrimage sites are bustling with people 24×7.

Jainism couldn't build a large support base, no doubt, but it did succeed in sparking a revolution casting doubt on the power and prerogative of gods of the Vedic Pantheon. Asa result, the theological discourse of the day diversified. The older traditions didn't die out. They accomplished a comeback, the resurgence, and revival leading to an atmosphere no less different from today's religious fundamentalism, especially towards the end of the Axial Age. We shall revisit this later. Here, we will peek into another development that took place toward the end of the 5th century BCE.

Yoga of Compassion

A prince named Siddhartha from the Sakka kingdom snuck out of his bedroom one fateful night and left for the jungles. Despite the elegant lifestyle he enjoyed in the palace of his king-father, with all the servants and lavish wealth, something deeply disturbed this young prince's mind. It was neither material lack nor abundance that gave him sleepless nights. He worried about some philosophical mysteries, of which there were plenty. *Karma,* death, rebirth, gods, heaven, hell, suffering, disease, etc., you name them. Plenty of things to worry about. If *Karma* and rebirth defined life, there was nothing to be cheerful about. Life a purposeless wandering first in the world, then in the heavens, and then again in the world in the form of a dog, beast, worm, or an untouchable Shudra, and so on, infinitely, was no fun, rather depressing, and despairing to contemplate. The ultimate future was pain and suffering. Many fine people struggled to untangle the knot of *Karma* and rebirth. Mahavira's solution didn't bode well with all.

The young Siddhartha possessed a fine mind. He genuinely worried about the randomness that underlies the events of the world. Witnessing the suffering, pain, and injustice troubled him deeply. He struggled with his "dark night" of the soul. We are told he had all the wealth, all the luxuries, and everything at his doorstep; he was the king in the waiting. All that material abundance failed to fill the void in his soul. He sought fulfillment, liberation, and release – his definition of the ultimate truth and meaning – not to be found in the wealth and luxury of the palace life. Where could he find it? Not in his father's palace, at least. He had made up his mind to say goodbye to his princely life. In the middle of the night, when his wife and kid were asleep, he quietly sneaked out of the palace.

He became a disciple of Uddakala, a great teacher and practitioner of *Yoga*. Soon he found that Uddakala couldn't impress him with his trance states and his disciples' metaphysical interpretations of these trances, as *Nibbana* or *Nirvana*. Siddhartha possessed a curious mind. It wasn't easy to impress him. Uddakala's *Yoga* was good for achieving a momentary and fleeting experience of stillness of mind; Siddhartha sought a total and permanent release (liberation, rapture) from the *dukkha* of life. That wasn't possible with *Yoga*. Siddhartha rebelled. He insisted on putting everything to the test and rejected the doctrines and dogmas taught by the sages if they failed the test. That created friction, and finally, he parted ways with his teacher and fellow monks and took to silent meditations on his own.

All alone now, he devotedly engaged in fasting and practiced mindfulness. Not long after, he had his eureka moment when he put his finger on the crux of the problem. He announced calmly, perfectly sagely, that he had received spontaneous insight, a significant breakthrough for him. In stark contrast to Mahavira, he forbade physical penitence, insisting instead on cultivating "innate tendencies" that would lead a person to the release state or *Nibbana*. Interestingly, he described *Nibbana* as a "state of mind" and abandoned his so-called "fight against body," cultivating an attitude of "mindfulness" or "awareness" of thoughts instead. He called for accepting "change" as the fundamental prerequisite that keeps life and the world going. If humans resist change, he warned, they are bound to be caught up in a perpetual, never-ending *dukkha*. The only path, he insisted, leading to happiness and bliss was to accept change and be a part of the change. This attitude frees the heart and mind from the fear of uncertainty and judgment by others. "Enlightenment," he explained, meant " freedom from anxiety and fear, compassion for all and hatred for none, a state of total lucidity and calmness."

Siddhartha was the first prominent sage in India who unambiguously denounced the popular punitive ascetic practices as futile. Cultivating systematic self-discipline and compassion through "mindfulness" was what he considered the chosen method of meditation – *Yoga* of Compassion – a healthy substitute to all rituals. In principle, "*Yoga* of Compassion" is self-hypnosis. Twenty-three centuries ago, Siddhartha was unwittingly laying down the foundation of "mind science." He was the first philosopher-saint to talk about "ego" and "egotism" in his characteristically brilliant way. He didn't use the word ego, though. Semantics alone doesn't matter. Principles do. He realized that craving, hatred, and ignorance keep humans emotionally fixated on suffering. To deal with these three vices, he devised the famous action plan – "Asht Marg," or the Noble Eightfold Path.

Siddhartha famously called Nirvana "nothing and everything at the same time." His "Yoga of compassion," he insisted, guides a practitioner to the *Nibbana* or *Nirvana.* Like Mahavira, he too confessed that his vocabulary failed him to define *Nirvana* in linguistic terms, yet, as he clarified later, he found nothing supernatural about this state of liberation or *Nirvana. Nirvana,* to him, was a purely transcendental state that led to inner awakening. It could be experienced by following the prescribed discipline of "Yoga of compassion."

Gautama Buddha

As Siddhartha had attained *Nibbana/Nirvana,* he was an enlightened (spiritually awakened) man, now called *Gautama Buddha.* In simple translation, he had transcended into a permanent state of release where greed, hatred, and delusion were extinct. He had attained, in his words, "the supreme goal, a certain serenity, and self-refuge." It meant a lot to him, and he was keen to share his success story with fellow humans. Passionately, he called people's attention to the inner processes of "self" and innate human nature. His supremely revolutionary idea, based on logic and not backed by a powerful story, was hardly reassuring for the elite.

The disciples struggled with the problem that *Buddha* had consistently refused to acknowledge the hand of gods in *Nirvana.* Sure, he had even doubted the existence of gods in the first place. To him, it made no difference whether gods created the universe or universe created gods. In his case, a divine revelation or inspiration story to back *Nibbana* philosophy, historically the easiest and most effective way to convince the people about new religious ideas, was ruled out. In revelation stories, gods revealed insights to *rishis* and sages, who then delivered the messages to people. In *Buddha's* case, that won't go.

To circumvent the god question, the Pali Buddhist texts resorted to an ingenious trick: The gods, they say, came and knelt before the *Buddha* and prayed to him "to please teach this 'dharma' to humans." The Pali texts reversed the pattern – gods beseeched *Buddha* to take pity on the human race and save humanity, and Buddha agreed to teach his dharma out of compassion for fellow humans. That is that. *Buddha* became a teacher, seer, enlightened, and Lord, a Lord with a difference: with his power, he "submitted the gods to his will."

The above story may seem incredible and preposterous, but it worked. After all, how did all religions establish themselves? Of course, through stories. Outlandish stories fascinate us. They build our belief in the unbelievable. What else does religion need? The Pali Buddha story captured the imagination of the gullible masses. Soon Buddhism drew large crowds and big groups of *Kshatriyas* and *Brahmins* into his following; before long, *Buddha's* order became a sizeable *Sangha* (organization). Early Buddhism was a relatively successful movement, attracting common masses into its fold in fair numbers. Yet, for more than 200 hundred years following the death of *Buddha*, it never grew into a mainstream religion, existing, instead, as nothing more than a fringe religion, with some scattered pockets of support in Magadha in what is now South Bihar. During these formative years, it failed to penetrate the power corridors of the Magadhan Palace, without which it was impossible for Buddhism, like any religion, to make that significant leap from a fringe religion into a mainstream one. During those two hundred-odd years of struggle following *Buddha's* death, the leaders of the *Sangha* worked incessantly, refining Buddhism's postulates, smoothing its rough edges, and presenting it as an attractive religious philosophy. To their dismay, the royalty seemed to have no appetite for this new creed.

The day's political elite was not keen on the doctrine of *Ahimsa* (nonviolence) taught by Buddhism. Politics hinged on violence and warfare; the more the king fought wars, the more his perceived power. In such circumstances, religions like Buddhism or Jainism that stressed nonviolence could potentially undermine the palace's power. Furthermore, Buddhism was still struggling with its foundational principles, the *Asht Marg*, whose varied interpretations cropping up soon after the death of the *Buddha*, had left the concept of *Nibbana* or *Nirvana* as fluid and un-outlined as one could imagine. The different interpretations dragged the creed of Buddhism into the throes of instability.

Another paradox that cost Buddhism strategically a lot was that of the hierarchy. Buddha's place on the ladder was unsettled. Was he a god, avatar, or mere mortal "enlightened through discipline and practice of mindfulness?" *Buddha* himself had never claimed to be divine or to have divine revelations. He loathed, we are told, to even talk about the gods and creation story. A century or so after his death, nothing of that seemed to matter; most of his followers looked to him as a god. A minority disagreed. The internal friction pushed this struggling creed to the receiving end. It desperately needed a savior lest it died out.

Ashoka the Great

After two hundred years of struggle, the tide turned in Buddhism's favor. Ashoka the Great, the grandson of Chandragupta Maurya, embraced Buddhism. He converted to Buddhism after the famous battle of Kalinga, which left thousands of people dead, families devastated, streets stinking of corpses, fields soaked in blood, and infections raging like epidemics. Ashoka was deeply traumatized by the horrors of this war. A dragging sense of remorse and guilt left him in depression. Overwhelmed by that so-called "dark night" of the soul, he turned to Buddhism for solace, becoming a Buddhist by conviction – a humble monk-king and a missionary of Lord Buddha's *Dharma.* With this, Buddhism, at last, jubilantly entered the power corridors. Within a decade, it saw its metamorphosis from a fringe religion into a global one. A glorious chapter of the sacred history of India was about to be written.

We usually consider Buddhism a philosophy. Not so. In Ashoka's time, it became a state religion that set the trend of proselytization for all faiths to follow. The state assigned the Monks the task of creating missionary institutions to supervise financing, patronizing, and establishing *Gurukuls* (religious schools), orphanages, and *Viharas* (Buddhist temples). The empire spent lavishly on ecclesiastical propaganda machinery.

Ashoka's religious zeal and obsession with missionary activity led the empire to cut defense expenditures and divert funds to religious work, which left the army complaining. The capital-intensive investment for missionary and proselytizing enterprise, which brought no material return to the empire, was proving a massive drain on the empire's coffers. With the army out of work and no further plans of territorial expansion to bolster the empire's revenues, the coffers suffered severely. The officers were demoted, the soldiers laid off, and the regular army was finally disbanded. The emperor was blinded by faith. Why fight when *Nibbana* and *Moksha* are just at arm's length?

Religion and spirituality were hotly sought after by the decision-making elite. The debate and discourse focused on spirituality, i.e., endless and empty talk. Under emperor Ashoka, Buddhism flourished throughout India, spread from Kandahar to Kanyakumari, and was carried by missionaries to Sri Lanka and other Asian countries. The quick spread of Buddhism didn't translate into economic prosperity. The hollow spirituality emptied the empire's coffers. Over time, religion and spirituality proved disastrous to the state and state policy. The theocratic mindset brought down this strong empire that had just begun to make its mark on the world scene, from the pinnacle of glory to utter despair, poverty, starvation, and death. With Ashoka's death, the empire crumbled like a pack of cards.

During Ashoka's life, an eerie calm prevailed in the empire. The empire diverted resources to pursue the afterlife, leaving this life at the mercy of the winds. The state's only top priority was converting people to Buddhism. In religious fervor, the state ignored infrastructure building – a fatal mistake, as the time would prove. There descended no mass *Moksha* but mass restlessness. The irrigation projects suffered, dilapidated water reservoirs were not repaired, and roads and bridges weren't upgraded. As the crops suffered and trade and business declined, the economy went into recession.

Nature doesn't give a damn about the whims and fantasies of humans. It does what it always does – follow a pattern and law. In other words, nature does physics, chemistry, biology, etc., without bothering about kings, religions, philosophies, or spirituality. No Ashoka or Buddhism could change nature's laws. As it does, nature brought in famines, droughts, and disease, destroying crops and livestock and leaving the people starving. The state only watched. Powerlessly. All it could do was try digging the wells when the fire rages. It was too late. The welfare work and infrastructure should have been put in place long back. Then, it wasn't done, and now it can't be done. The great Ashoka managed to keep the pieces together, courtesy of his charisma. After his death, things quickly scrambled, and in a matter of decades, the great Mauryan Empire met the same fate as the empires before them, getting buried under the rubble of history. Only Buddhism survived the mayhem.

Idol, Art, and God

With the collapse of the Mauryan empire, India entered a challenging phase of history. Chaos replaced socio-political stability. Buddhism, though still popular, was losing its luster. Now that it had assimilated metaphysics and supernaturalism into its theology, it ceased, for all practical purposes, to be the old Buddhism. The factionalism had intensified within its ranks. By the time the 3rd Buddhist conference was held under the patronage of Ashoka, doctrinal differences had already become a matter of concern for Buddhism. In the new competitive religious atmosphere where the Vedic religion was all set out for a serious comeback, Buddhism desperately needed continued royal patronage. The sigh of relief came in the early 1st century CE when the Kushan king Kanishka established sway over an area stretching from today's Afghanistan to Kashmir. But, when it came time for the 4th Buddhist council to be held in North Kashmir under the patronage of Kanishka, splitting Buddhism into *Mahayana* and *Hinayana* sects was a foregone conclusion. This split was the beginning of the end of Buddhism. At least in India.

The sectarian conflict and split were partly a reaction to the pressure created within Buddhism by the resurgence of the Vedic religion (now referred to as Hinduism) toward the closing centuries of the 1st millennium BCE. It was the time when India as a whole was reeling under political and economic instability. There was no empire in place, and there was no hope that a viable empire could emerge soon. All politics hinges on hope. No hope, no political stability. Anarchy, chaos, and insecurity were what India was going through. The subcontinent was divided into small kingdoms, satrapies, and feudal strongholds—all warring with each other. The political elite busied themselves more with dispute resolution than attending to state and state-building affairs. The aggressive religion-centric debates and discourse made inter-religious conflicts a new norm, leaving them with no time for empire-building. India desperately needed a *Chanakya* to mentor another Chandragupta and teach his *Arthashastra,* a treatise on political economy, to the political elite. That had to wait some six hundred years. Finally, in the 4th century CE, Chandragupta Maurya's namesake Chandragupta Vikramaditya came along and established the Gupta Empire that, after centuries of uncertainty, brought some political stability to northern and central India for a couple of centuries.

While, on the one hand, during the tumultuous pre-Gupta period, religious disputes and conflicts left India fractured and fragile, yet, on the other hand, the reviving Vedic religion (still an oral tradition), took on an evidently "visual" character. Religious art and representation underwent significant mutation during the pre-Gupta period. The artful depiction of gods became a prominent feature of this period's sacred history. Iconography suddenly imparted added meaning and vigor to the hitherto abstract mental rituals and worship. Idol worship opened the portal for direct contact with the gods. The worshipper felt more confident when he held a picture of his God before him.

As the new trend of temple art picked pace, the culture of devotion to images and idols of different gods spread quickly. Accordingly, Buddhism was tugged to follow the trend and adapt its theology. *Buddha* became an avatar, and then God. His images and idols appeared everywhere to compete with Hindu gods. The followers worshipped him inside and outside of Viharas. If *Buddha* were resurrected, he would be surprised to see himself elevated to the pedestal of a god.

But then, times had changed. The new millennium was different. *Buddha* would be hard-pressed to consider that his creed (and Jainism) was left with no option but to adapt to the change or perish in an environment of intense theological competition and changing discourse. Since he had taught that change is the law of nature, Buddhist theology tried to adapt quickly to the changing scenario. Would the resurrected Buddha approve of it? Nobody knows. What we know, however, is that comprise with the foundational principles in the name of adapting to change did, undoubtedly, not augur well for Buddhism. It eroded its identity as a "religion with a difference," an identity it had guarded over the centuries.

Mass support alone isn't enough for a religion or philosophy. Without overt or covert patronage by the power structure, no religion, idea, or philosophy has ever been effective in having a significant civilizational impact. Buddhism had the good luck of getting two full terms as a state religion. By the time Kanishka, Buddhism's second bulwark, died, Hindu revivalism had attained celerity and sharpened its onslaught on Buddhism. Jainism by then had already retracted. The Vedic tradition fast reclaimed its proprietorship of *Ahimsa,* sensing rightly the opportunity to create new theological constructs in the fluid religious landscape.

The Avatar

Samkhya yoga, the revolutionary movement of the late 8th century BCE, was a pivotal, transformative trigger that helped define religious discourse for centuries to come. During the closing three centuries of the 1st millennium BCE, even the reviving Hinduism revisited these old *Samkhyan* constructs and ideas, cleverly repackaging them to dilute Buddhism's influence effectively. Furthermore, during this period, Hinduism incorporated the concept of a "personalized god," an extremely significant idea that completely reshaped India's religious landscape in the following centuries. In that tide, *Vishnu* overshadowed *Prajapatti* and became the personified *Brahman,* the unfathomable and incomprehensible reality. Without *Vishnu's* blessings and grace, no *Moksha* or *Nirvana* was possible. The Yogins (renouncers) said that only *Vishnu* (God) had the power to liberate the renouncers and the meditators from the painful cycle of *Samsara* and *Karmic* burden. Hinduism returned emphasis on gods, accusing Buddhism of spreading heresy. It wasn't lost on people's memory that Samkhya, Jain, and Buddhist philosophies pushed the gods to the periphery during their heyday. They put human capacity and human power above that of the gods—an outright blasphemy.

Hinduism's nostalgia for its Vedic past gave vent in a sophisticated narrative. Obscure gods sprang to prominence. For example, *Rudra* had never been a prominent deity in Vedic religion, but now he has become the "lord of the universe" and merged with *Shiva. Vishnu* rose to become the omnipotent "creator and destroyer" – an all-powerful god, only slightly lesser in scope and status than *Brahman.* If Brahman was the human body (*Purusha* reality), *Vishnu* was no more than the thumb of the hand. Accordingly, in depictions, *Vishnu* was portrayed as a thumb-size.

By the 1st century CE, had evolved a coherent-looking theology amalgamating *Brahman* and *Atman*, *Karma* and *Nirvana*, with *Samkhya yoga.* In the absence of science, these concepts, born out of the necessity worked well to tackle the unfathomable-to-ancients mysteries of the universe, life, and gods. Naturally, they served as scaffolding for religious discourse. For instance, the renouncers and *Yogin* stressed love – love for self and others. The *Yogin* (pleural for *yogi*), the *Samkhyan,* and the Buddhists interpreted love, a touch vaguely, as a form of *Ahimsa.* On the contrary, Hinduism, using iconography, simplified things. To ordinary folks, an idol perfectly represented the idea of a Vedic God. The physical depiction of gods, avatars, saints, and rishis effectively shifted the paradigm. The idols made the gods accessible to humans, and idol worship helped turn the clock back – worship became synonymous with love for the deity. And, in one fell swoop, old forgotten deities sprang back to life.

"Love of a deity" became an independent discipline called *Bhakti* (devotion). Bhakti underscored that the deity loved and cared for his worshippers who surrendered before him. Over time, "surrender before a deity" transmuted itself into the theme of "Self-surrender" – the motto for the *Bhakts* (devotees). The devotee was required to acknowledge his helplessness before the deity and selflessly "love the lord." In return, the "lord would help and take care of him." The acknowledgment of "human helplessness" before God became an accepted theological contract. Gone were the days of *Buddha's* version of human self-sufficiency and the powerlessness of gods. The time had come for God to enter people's homes and for an exciting scripture, *Srimad Bhagavad Gita*, to become a household name.

The *Bhagavad Gita* became an important scripture by the 3rd century BCE. The reason the Gita attained importance had, among other things, much to do with the Hindu revivalist movement. To effectively counter Buddhism's complex yet seductive metaphysics, the holy Gita was the perfect stuff – a plain and comprehensible sacred word told in the form of a story that stuck. No dense metaphors to leave the brains scratching for meaning, Gita's similes worked wonders with the masses. Armed with the scripture, the Brahmins got the ball rolling to lead the theological battle against Buddhism. They had long been watching their losing grip over the power corridors while the Buddhist priestly class took over. The *Kshatriyas,* too, felt uncomfortable with the complacency of the traditional Hindu elite. The overall subconscious urge of the elite was to forcefully counter the Buddhist theological onslaught. Only a nudge was required to get them going. The holy Gita helped spark the nudge.

The *Bhagavad Gita's* storyline suitably sketched the syncretic philosophy in metaphoric language. The Gita handled the thorny issues and concepts of the day artfully through characteristically flowery prose using similes, mythology, and supernatural imagery. Quite a feat of wordsmithery! The Gita is traced to a famous epic drama called the *Mahabharata,* written by one Vyasa *rishi,* supposedly under divine guidance. In Gita's narrative, God takes a human form called an *avatar.* The Hindu avatar, like the Christian "son of god," engages in everyday human life's ordinary affairs and conflicts. The concept of an avatar didn't exist in the old Vedic religion. It appeared on the scene of the Indian drama of sacred history late in the Axial Age.

The Wake-up Time

After Alexander reached India, defeated king Porus, and installed his governor to rule India, the entire Gangetic plains came under the eye of foreigners. Had Alexander not died prematurely, India's history would have been different. There would be no Chandragupta and no Mauryan Empire. Perhaps. As Alexander left, the Scythians and Persians moved into the fertile Gangetic plains wave upon wave. The Indians (by now, the Aryans had become Indianized and the Indians Aryanized), self-domesticated through centuries, disliked these outsiders, despising their habits, customs, and cultural practices. Fearing foreign dominance and subsequent dilution and even assimilation of the Vedic culture by the foreign one, the Indians zealously renewed their struggle to revive the Vedic religion aggressively. Cultural osmosis, however, couldn't be prevented despite putting barriers. In particular, Greek visual art was impossible to resist. India had just turned to visual religious art to reshape their sacred history. The Greeks were already proficient in this enterprise. There was much to learn from them and much to lose from protectionism. Reluctantly, Hinduism chose to learn.

The Greek invasion coincided with a period of history when various indigenous religious and metaphysical movements had created an environment of dissonance in Indian society. Sectarian harmony was becoming fragile by the day. With Chandragupta's toppling of the Greeks, Hinduism became optimistic about seizing the opportunity to revive itself. But with Ashoka's conversion to Buddhism, Hinduism's hopes were dashed. It found itself at the receiving end for the next three hundred years, molding and adapting to new currents of thought.

The Hindu priestly class and the *Kshatriya* elite had good reasons to be worried. Jainism, never a threat as significant as Buddhism to Brahmanical power, had already been effectively reduced to the status of a fringe religion.

Buddhism, on the contrary, was on the surge. Being a state religion, it pushed its influence to the north from Kashmir to Kandahar. The tide turned only after the death of Kanishka. As the Hindu kings ascended the throne, Buddhism was systematically wiped out from northern India. The Buddhist Viharas, art, and iconography were destroyed, and the Hindu zealots used all force to suppress Buddhism.

The economic distress and political instability allowed the Hindu priestly class and elite to foment almost an open religious conflict. The masses were galvanized into action by the slogan "reclaim the glory of the Vedic religion." Buddhism found itself in a tight spot. This heretical religion was squarely blamed for all the economic woes: it had led people astray, abandoning their age-old religious customs and gods; the gods, in turn, also abandoned the people, and the droughts, famines, and floods ravaged the lands; and disease, hunger, and poverty left people crippled; the hopelessly depressing state of affairs could worsen if the people don't return to the old and original Vedic religion, the theologians frightened the gullible masses to submit to gods and Hinduism.

Karma and *Ahimsa,* by now, were well-established and influential doctrines, each in its own right. At their core, though, lay contradiction. Reconciling the two doctrines, the opposing ends of the spectrum, entailed significant theological fine-tuning. For instance, to get rid of the bad *Karma*, you needed to follow a strict religious discipline and perform certain rites and rituals (including sacrifice). *Ahimsa* called for total abstinence from all types of violence and aggression, minor and major. Buddhists, arguing from logic, encouraged adopting *Ahimsa* to handle the dilemma of "rebirth and karma" – quite a rugged solution for soft problems. According to Buddhism, *Ahimsa* wasn't something passive. Instead, it was an "active principle" to be practiced in everyday life by the commoners and the political elite. The difficulty lay in applying the Buddhist version of *Ahimsa* to the affairs of the state and kingdom. It was squarely in contradiction with Chanakya's *Arthashastra,* which by the 1st century had reclaimed a fair audience among the political elite.

The emperor couldn't be expected to shun violence. Everybody couldn't be Ashoka. He had inherited a vast empire, and despite his administrative qualities and skills, he consciously chose to devote his life to religion and missionary activity, delegating the empire's affairs to others. He could do that. His literal interpretation of Buddhism and religious zeal tumbled his great empire. No violence was synonymous with bad politics. Bad politics is far deadlier than bad *Karma* for the state. Buddhism had nothing to offer to politics except *Ahimsa* and *Asht-Marg*. That left much to be desired. Asoka didn't care. And Kanishka, too, to a lesser extent, though. After a long slumber, the Vedic religion had woken up to respond with new vigor. The Bhagavad Gita emerged precisely at this crucial juncture. Its polemic successfully countered the Buddhist narrative and won the day.

Sacred Violence

Life on Earth has thrived on violence. Much of natural selection and evolution of life forms have come about courtesy of violence. No violence, no natural selection, and thus no complexity, and the beauty of life on the Earth. The capacity to commit (or withstand) violence has ensured the survival of the fit species. Only the fit and resilient species could tackle the pressures the food chain imposed on life. Take animals. A pride of lions will survive if they devour the pretty but unarmed (and weaker) gazelle. The gazelle can outlive the onslaught if it has learned to run fast. A minor slip and the game is over. It is killed. Mercilessly. No ethics here. When a hungry lion goes out for lunch, only the might pays him. Humans are no different. They kill and devour weaker animals and plants in countless numbers. They compete and kill each other to secure control over the food chain. In the struggle for survival, there are no friends or foes, only the self-interest of the individual, group, tribe, community, state, or country. The winners rule the roost.

Violence underpins the whole game of survival. "Survival" may mean a better life for some, peace at borders for others, power, influence, and status for some, and economic supremacy for others, regardless it entails struggle. Often bloody. Civilizations can't be built peacefully. Building civilization entails humungous amounts of violence.

While interpreting *Ahimsa* as the total exclusion of violence from everyday life, Jainism and Buddhism were unwittingly going against the flow. By the 1st century CE, this version of *Ahimsa* was becoming increasingly defunct. The doctrine needed to be refined and redefined. Buddhism resisted. It struggled to stay within its prison of the past, missing the writing on the wall. The tipping point had come, the times had changed, and paradigms were shifting. Not Buddhism. It stuck to its version of *Ahimsa*.

Violence can't be eliminated from the drama of life entirely. In the animal kingdom, we see a lot of violence, ethics don't matter, mercy is unknown, and weakness is an invitation to death. Things are a little different for humans, though the underlying laws of life are the same. We are rational animals. We suffer when we carry a psychological burden of guilt, resentment, depression, etc. To avoid the psychological burden, we invented ethics, morality, and religion to help us justify and rationalize our actions, including violent behavior. Take Aryans. They justified violence by taking refuge in the god *Indra* and legitimated cattle rustlings and raids as a religious duty. Other civilizations before and after them did the same, on a different, maybe, scale. Against this backdrop, Hindu revivalists consciously struggled to reconcile *Karma* and *Ahimsa* somehow.

Which brings us back to the closing centuries of the first millennium BCE. *Vishnu* and *Shiva* were popular gods. *Vishnu* was the four-armed savior of mankind, and *Shiva* was the three-eyed god of both destruction and benefaction. It would seem childish to invoke *Vishnu,* like *Indra* in the Vedic Aryan days, to justify violence. Now that the sages and *rishis* were claiming to receive direct revelations from God in contrast to Vedic Aryans, the stories, too, had to fine-tune themselves accordingly. For Vyasa *rishi*, the author of *Mahabharata*, it would have been a daunting task to develop a spicy and palatable storyline. Vyasa's God, like the Abrahamic one, omnipotent and omniscient, could have revealed that it's okay to commit violence when circumstances demand it. That would have ended the debate on *Ahimsa*. But no. Vyasa's God intended to create a climax.

The story that Vyasa's God revealed (i.e., *Bhagavad Gita*) is a story of a war between evil and good forces. There were many stories about wars circulating at the time, but what made the Bhagavad Gita stand out was its narrative that evoked a feeling, a mental picture, and a vivid visualization of the battlefield scenes, warring soldiers, conversation of avatars, etc. All that made a folksy story extraordinarily compelling, absorbing, and unforgettable. It shifted the balance in favor of Hinduism. Buddhism's dry discourse paled before the Gita. Despite its lofty discourse, Buddhism utterly lacked the story component in its brilliantly revolutionary religious philosophy except for what the Pali texts put out. The *Bhagavad Gita* (or the Gita in short) brilliantly trumped the Buddhist reading of *Ahimsa*. With a brilliant stroke of genius, it beautifully contextualized violence. Depending on the situation, violence could be either a horrendous sin or a sacred necessity for the survival of a society, taught the Gita. It removed all fog. The people were free to interpret the story any which way. Particularly the Chanakyans of the day felt hugely relieved by the sacralization of violence.

By the way, the sacralization of violence is not specific only to the *Gita*. All religious stories follow a more or less identical line of thought. Only the plots differ.

We, humans, by nature, are complex creatures. We thrive on stories. Culture, civilization, and history are, in essence, a story, a human story. Religion is no different.

Karma Yoga

Story helps. It changes our mental frame. We, then, view the events through a different prism. That makes all the difference. The paradigm shifts. The perspective changes. A nasty act takes on the meaning of a righteous deed. Take killing. When you kill a person, it is murder. When you kill in the name of religion, that is? You are right. Sacred. In scripture speak, it is *karma yoga* – a form of worship without meditation. The human mind is extraordinarily remarkable when it comes to hallucinations.

In the *Bhagavad Gita,* the climax comes when *Arjuna* (protagonist) gets embroiled in a war with his cousins – the *Kauravas*. Pious at heart, Arjuna loathed having to fight and kill his kin to gain the worldly kingdom. *Krishna* (the God disguised as a man) counsels him to consider that "even a warrior who is fighting a deadly battle can achieve *moksha*." In other words, what Krishna wanted him to keep in mind while fighting was *Karma yoga*. Krishna explains, "The warrior must fight in the path of truth without being concerned about the results," arguing that the deeds on their own don't matter, but the "attachment to the fruits of the deeds" causes humans to suffer in an endless cycle of death and rebirth. That is to say, "detachment" is the crucial component of Krishna's word; when you detach from the result, your deeds become sacrosanct. Hence, cultivating a sense of detachment can justify any action, whether war, violence or even *Ahimsa*.

In stark contrast to Buddhism's insistence on the power of logic in religious and spiritual matters, the Gita makes a point through Krishna-Arjuna dialogue that rationality and logic don't always work with humans. Krishna's reasoning did not convince Arjuna, as reported in the Gita. Krishna hadn't revealed his identity to Arjuna as yet. When he did, for a minute, Arjuna couldn't believe what he had heard. Krishna, the God-incarnate! Really! It left Arjuna spellbound. In awe, he immediately bowed before Krishna, the son of Lord God *Vishnu,* and submitted to him. When Krishna announced, "Whatever God said was truth and nothing but the truth; there is always a purpose behind God's decision, which may not always be evident to mortals," Arjuna didn't argue.

God had decided that Arjuna's kin were to be defeated and killed, and even if Arjuna, Lord Krishna revealed, didn't want to go ahead, that would not change the fate of the Kauravas. Their fate was sealed. With a pen stroke, Gita's author sacralized killing (even of the kin) in the name of God and religion – a massive relief for warriors and kings to use religion to resort to violence to meet political and economic expediency.

The *Bhagavad Gita* left some gray areas for theologians' debate, for instance, when should violence qualify as holy, when should holy war be waged, or who will decide that particular war was a sacred religious war? Left to their own, the political demagogues could instigate wanton persecution and suppression of other sects for political reasons, potentially transmogrifying a political feud into a religious war against other denominations. And it happened. Buddhism found itself at the receiving end of history. Buddhist temples were razed down, and the great art was left to die. Buddhists were reduced to a minority.

The *Bhagavad Gita* vividly depicts the drama of war between the *Pandavas* and *Kauravas* (between good and evil). Yet, there is no unambiguous historical proof or circumstantial evidence to support that this war took place. Neither did the *Bhagavad Gita* even try to make a historical point. Sacred history, as always, hardly ever bothers about the historicity and chronology of the record. Much of what we know about many religious wars and battles comes from secular sources. For instance, in medieval times, kings would employ regular historians to document expeditions and wars. In ancient times with no paper, history writing was not an established enterprise except in the form of edicts, stupas, and stone carvings. Whatever records are available, never mind meager, it is hard to miss that the base storyline has hardly ever changed throughout human history: economics has necessitated the invention of religion. Power equals ethics. Arjuna, for instance, fought and killed his kin at the insistence of God; others fought in the name of tribe, community, or religion; the succession wars of medieval kings were given a religious undertone, not unlike Arjuna's battle. Aurangzeb, for example, mercilessly killed his three brothers to ascend the throne, justifying the heinous violence in the name of religion and the sultanate. Power is a magnet. As iron filings change their behavior when they come in contact with a magnet, so do humans when they taste power.

A literal reading of the Gita conveys that Krishna's sayings were meant to legitimize violence against perceived evil. The scholars disagree with such a literal reading of the *Gita,* arguing the story was told to reinterpret *Ahimsa* and to expose and dismantle Buddhist fallacy. The *Gita* reinvented *Ahimsa* as a doctrine, not as a troublesome and obstructionist one, hindering politics, but facilitating the attainment of political ends and encouraging, not obfuscating, expansionist policy. For resurgence and self-determination, there was a pressing need to accept violence conceptually and stop hiding behind the shadow of *Ahimsa.* For that, the *Bhagavad Gita* supplied the requisite narrative.

As the battle of ideas intensified, persecution of Buddhism became inevitable. Violence, bloodshed, and damage to religious property became unstoppable, the *Viharas* (Buddhist temples) were destroyed, and those that remained intact lay abandoned. Buddhism's architectural glory in central and northern India was extinguished. Hinduism reclaimed its place, and Buddhism was pushed to the fringe. What remained of Buddhism was memory engraved on dilapidated stupas and recorded in manuscripts in *Gunpas* (Viharas or temples). Now it was Hinduism's turn to control sacred and genuine histories.

With the breaking down of Buddhism, Hinduism became an undisputed candidate religion to claim royal patronage. Royal patronage was essential because there still was no shortage of enemies. There was no dearth of hardcore "others" to be suppressed, banished, or killed unless they relented and accepted the way of life of those who now called themselves the proud followers of the *Bhagavad Gita.* The first millennium became the undisputed millennium of Hinduism in India.

The scientific Religion

The followers of the *Bhagavad Gita,* now formally known as *Hindus,* find tremendous comfort in this great book. For instance, Dr. S. Radhakrishnan, the second President of Independent India, tells us how convincingly comfortable he is with Gita. In his Commentary on Gita, he writes, " [It] sets forth in precise and penetrating words the essential principles of a spiritual religion which are not contingent on ill-founded facts, unscientific dogmas or arbitrary fancies." Dr. Radhakrishnan talks from faith. He is convinced, like those religious scholars and theologians who see nothing but Science in their respective sacred texts, about the scientific integrity of the Gita. For a non-Hindu, it isn't easy to see the Gita in the same light as Dr. S. Radhakrishnan did. They miss the divine light that a Hindu sees in the Gita. They don't see what their minds don't look for. Absent objective verification of the stated scriptural truths, experiential knowledge, and subjective evidence on which all sacred history is built allows only the faithful to see the highest degree of perfection in their respective scriptural texts.

A little later in the same essay, Dr. Radhakrishnan goes on, "The teaching of *Gita* is not presented as a metaphysical system thought out by an individual thinker or school of thinkers. It is set forth as a tradition that has emerged from the religious life of mankind. It [Gita] represents not any sect of Hinduism, but Hinduism as a whole, not merely Hinduism but religion as such in its universality, without limit of time or space." In other words, he affirms that the *Bhagavad Gita* holds a universal message that can fulfill humanity's needs for all times to come. Not surprising. Believers of all faiths regard their respective religions and scriptures as universal, unique, and all-encompassing.

One may disagree with Dr. Radhakrishnan, but that is not the point. The fact remains that *Gita's* compact text and flowery narrative ensured its central place in the religious ethos of the Hindus at the cost of its receptivity outside India, contrary to the Buddhist texts. The reason that the Gita failed to impress the outside world has partly to do with the fact that after Ashoka the Great, India could never emerge as a robust imperial power. Absent military might, India, a composite of disintegrated polities, lived on the wrong side of history, attracting predators. All eyes were set on India. As a result, it never attained the economic and imperial might to influence global and regional geopolitics meaningfully. Barring Ashoka the Great, no ancient and antique Indian emperor was confident enough to even peek into the outside world. *Bhagavad Gita* remained, and remains, merely a collection of allegedly lofty ideas wrapped in metaphorical stories relevant to the Indian context. They could never impress the outside world.

Until recently, until the industrial revolution came around, religion was the only robust employment-generating enterprise available. The economy, politics, social welfare, etc., depended solely on religion. Wars, battles, territorial expansions with contingent booties, enslaved people, and tributes from the vanquished were all driven in the name of religion. Politics was religion, and religion was politics. When empires emerged, they obliged religion, keen to acknowledge political success as a blessing from their gods and religion. The vanquished would equally quickly recognize the prowess of victors' religions and gods. The result was that victor's religion promptly attracted followers. Add to that missionary zeal, and the victor religions rapidly spread far and wide.

Hinduism and the *Bhagavad Gita* sorely lacked the luxury of great imperial power. The Gita is a beautiful scripture, no doubt; however, this theology was targeted to a specific audience familiar with the typical centuries-old cultural paradigm we can call Hinduism. In that context, the Gita only connected the dots in the philosophy and spiritual discourse. Surprisingly before the 1st century CE, Indian society didn't show much appetite for violent reformation or revolutions. Ancient India was an open and mellow society. Religious debate and reformation entailed not much violence. The seers could fearlessly talk of atheism. Take Mahavira. He openly denied the existence of God, and guess what? He comfortably drew a considerable following. Buddha also did not acknowledge God or a creator, yet, he was a saint, an avatar, and a god and openly and freely taught his views. Before them, Kapila and other *Samkhyans* also propagated their atheistic views with impunity. On the contrary, in the 21st century, it is dangerous to talk about atheism in as democratic and modern a country as the United States.

The Tolerance

Despite its weaknesses and shortcomings, ancient Indian society was reasonably tolerant of other religions. In that ruthless world of the old, it was a miracle that religious harmony prevailed. One reason for this miracle could be the institutionalization of *Varuna* and Caste, as Dr. Radhakrishnan has observed. A fairly vast majority of the population consisted practically of the slave-like untouchables (*Harijans* and other low castes), and these people were not even allowed to come near a priest or temple, let alone question others' faith. The game of religion was the domain of the upper caste people. They wielded power. They had the privilege. They engaged in debate, discourse, and difference of opinion about liturgy, worship, and rituals. The silent majority (lower caste people) earning a morsel of food with the sweat of the brow would be left with no spare time to create trouble unless goaded by the privileged and powerful merchants of religion.

When Buddhism permeated the power corridors, as discussed a couple of pages ago, the *Brahmins* (Hindu priestly class) were naturally left out. They felt weakened and threatened before the new priestly class, making them quickly irrelevant in matters of state. As the people toed the line of the new priestly class and its propaganda, the Brahmins could see their support base shrinking among the elite. A dangerous development in the long run if allowed to persist. Suddenly, they had this reawakening that Hinduism was in danger. The only way to save Hinduism, they contemplated, was to convince the elite to revert to the old religion. A thorough, new narrative was the need of the hour. In such circumstances, the *Bhagavad Gita,* a product of the contemplation of people like Vyasa, came in handy. It became the "foundational text" of Hinduism. For the next 2000 years after the death of Ashoka the Great, the Hindu religious discourse revolved around this text.

The *Bhagavad Gita* emphasizes the personal God, *Ishvara*, who created the world in his nature, in his image, and is responsible for the destruction of the universe. This scripture beautifully laid the framework of a syncretic diversity typified by its concept of the Trinity long before Christianity stumbled on its Trinitarian theology centering on Jesus. The *Gita* put forth the Trinity through subtle theological sleight, without much pomp, evoking almost no reaction from the masses or even the elite. The Trinity traversed the path of sacred history somewhat unnoticed; the people quietly and almost unanimously accepted the concept with no overt or covert signs of resistance.

On the contrary, it took centuries of protracted persecution and coercion in the Christian world to establish the Trinitarian doctrine. In India, there was no need, in principle at least, for applying force as the collective societal psyche was ripe to receive new conceptual innovations. That, however, doesn't mean that there were no sectarian conflicts in India after the decline of Buddhism. No. It was simply more uncomplicated and relatively straightforward for a Hindu, Buddhist, or even a Jain to some extent to accept that wisdom, love, and perfection God's three attributes, despite being separate and independent, are nonetheless unified and interdependent. God is all these things, and all these things are God. The attributes are personified in the Hindu mind as *Brahma*, *Vishnu*, and *Shiva*, depending on how you classify them. In plain talk, the Trinity of *Brahma*, *Vishnu*, and *Shiva* is fundamentally one reality, godhead, if you will, conceived three-fold. In *Gita*, for instance, the aspect of *Vishnu* overrides the other two. *Krishna* (God) becomes an aspect of *Vishnu*.

The Trinitarian concept never creates a subconscious conflict in the Hindu mind. By the time the Hindu trinity evolved, Indian sacred history had already witnessed over 800 odd years of a philosophical discourse ranging from gods, atheism, and spirituality to an omnipotent God. Even though the atheism of Jainism, Buddhism, or even *Samkhya* was abhorrent to the mind of a Hindu, it hardly precluded the growth of these religions for quite an era. But, when it came time for the reassertion of the old Vedic religious legacy, people equally quickly responded positively to Brahmanical propaganda to somersault. After a long gap, a religion seriously and unambiguously Hindu sprung up from the ashes. People owned the storyline enthusiastically, catapulting the *Gita* to prominence. Through the *Gita*, people now revisited the past to reinvent the glorious ethos of the Indus valley and Aryan civilization.

The Aryan religious-cultural legacy became authentic again, and it wasn't long before loyalty to this cultural legacy was perceived as a religious duty of the society. All this took time. It was no quantum leap. The process began as India entered the "dark period of history" after the collapse of the Mauriyan Empire. By the time India reached the so-called "Golden Age" under the Gupta dynasty, the religion of the Bhagavad Gita was fully established. Buddhism and Jainism were pushed entirely to the fringe.

Chandragupta, the founder of the Gupta dynasty rose to power by riding the wave of social and religious change. India had become unstable and new migrations of Sacas and Kushan tribes descended from the north and new kingdoms were appearing in the south. Like a modern demagogue, Chandragupta used the opportunity to engage with religion for the promotion and expansion of his kingdom. Two things came in handy to him. One, the religious discourse and awareness had penetrated the masses (previously Brahmins were the sole guardians of religious talk) and second, the multitude of deities had more or less distilled into two chief gods, Vishnu and Shiva – a focus point for the still-diverse community. Chandragupta made good use of both strands of change.

After the death of Chandragupta, Samudragupta won the war of succession and proclaimed himself the king. Under his rule, the Gupta Empire expanded briskly across northern India but not into the western and southern portions of India. Like, Ashoka, he was filled with religious zeal, an ardent supporter of religious activity, and desperate to portray himself as a guardian over the empire's spiritual well-being. To that end, he reinstated a religious practice – the *Ashwamedha*, or horse- sacrifice – discontinued and abandoned by the illustrious Mauriyan emperor, Ashoka.

The *Ashwamedha* was a costly affair requiring elaborate preparations. For a year the chosen horse was allowed to roam freely across the land. Wherever the horse went the land was demarcated and claimed by the king personally. After one year of roaming, as the horse returned, a huge gathering of Gupta society would prepare the ground for the sacrificial ceremony that would last three days and nights. A fire was kept burning with the fat and blood of continued animal sacrifices. On the second day, the chosen horse pulled the chariot, in which stood the king and the chief Brahmin. All of the king's wives assembled and the Queen decorated the horse, after which it was smothered to death. The queen lay down by the side of the dead horse feigning copulation which symbolized the "union between the ruling couple and the gods." The dead horse then was dismembered with a golden knife and its blood offered to the sacrificial fire.

On the third and the last day of the ritual, twenty-one cows were sacrificed and the king gave gracious and plentiful gifts to the priests and wives. The ceremony's focus on the king and queen carried the crucial message that they were the guarantors and guardians of the "peace, stability, and divine goodwill" of the society. Through the *Ashwamedha*, Samudragupta asserted his quasi-divine status. The Brahmins were still an important force within the society and couldn't be ignored. They received royal gifts in the form of land. During the Gupta regime there was a vast increase in land grants and the Brahmins ultimately became influential land-mangers employing rural inhabitants for cultivating huge stretches of land. These feudal lords would control the economy of India. An internal tussle was set off.

In the coming centuries, India's outlook changed in many ways. It metamorphosed from a tolerant society to one deeply mired in religious conflict, hatred, chaos, and the worst form of discrimination, whose echo reverberated long and whose ghosts still haunt India's collective consciousness.

PART 3

Greek Hegemony and the Birth Pangs of Israel

Chapter – 06

The Mediterranean

The Alphabet in the Dark

When I was in the ninth grade, our Geography teacher puzzled our class with a question – Give the characteristics of the Mediterranean region. I didn't know the answer then, and I am not sure I know it now. However, I know that since then, the word Mediterranean has stuck with me. It always created a strange feeling inside me for reasons unknown to me. After decades as I returned to this subject and to kind of offload me, I named this chapter "The Mediterranean."

Topographically the Mediterranean region is peculiar. By definition, it is the region of lands around the Mediterranean Sea, from Macaronesia in the West, including the peninsula of Anatolia minus central Turkey, to the Levant in the East, bounded by Syrian and Negev deserts. Geographically it is thus a meeting point of three continents: Europe, Asia, and Africa.

Europe lies to the north of the Mediterranean, but much of Southern Europe falls in the Mediterranean zone. The Iberian, Italian, and Balkan peninsulas directly extend into this zone. The mountain ranges like the Pyrenees, the Alps, and the Balkan separate this zone from the temperate zone of Europe. The cultural history of the Mediterranean region is vital for understanding the Greek, Phoenician, Hebrew, Persian, Roman, Christian, Islamic, and other cultures. For ages, the Mediterranean Sea was, and still is, the superhighway of transport, trade, and cultural exchange across three continents.

As recalled from the previous chapters, the proto-urban civilization of the 8th millennium BCE, an extension of the Neolithic revolution, evolved into the urban culture proper in the 5th millennium BCE in Mesopotamia (and to some extent in Egypt). During the Bronze Age (4th to 2nd millennium BCE), when the Mesopotamian urban civilization was maturing, it developed writing systems, bureaucracy, and empires. As the Bronze Age approached its closing years and Mesopotamia tumbled, the Hittite, Mycenaean, and Egyptian empires dominated the Mediterranean region. When the Bronze Age collapsed and the Iron Age set in, the urban centers with their palace economies vanished, replaced by disparate villages of the so-called Dark Ages period. As the iron-working technology that originated in Romania in the 13th century BCE began spreading, the Mycenaeans and the Hittites were already collapsing. There was a sudden cessation of trade for half a century (1206-1150 BCE), and almost every city from Troy to Gaza was engulfed by violence and destroyed. In that din and chaos, no one was in a position to claim suzerainty over the other until the Dark Ages period gradually ended by the mid-10th century BCE with the rise of Neo-Hittite Aramaean and Neo-Assyrian kingdoms.

The Bronze-Age technological advances had not touched the western zone of the Mediterranean; however, the Iron Age culture spread to the entire coastal region courtesy of the Phoenicians. They had become the masters of the sea (1200 BCE-800 BCE) and transported cargoes from the East to Iron Age Greece, Italy, Iberia, and other regions. It was they who, during their trading activity, carried alphabetic writing to other areas, which became the hallmark of Iron Age Mediterranean civilizations, almost eclipsing the cuneiform system of Mesopotamia and the logographic and abugida systems of the Far East and India.

Culture of violence

As mentioned earlier, by the 12th century BCE, the Mediterranean sociopolitical structure was in shambles, urban centers were violently destroyed, and the village economy replaced the once-vibrant Palace economy. The underlying reasons for such a terrible crisis could have been purely environmental, probably droughts and famines, rather than entirely political. The shortage of food grains might have triggered a cascade of violence, arson, looting, and wanton killings. As the civil unrest engulfed the whole of the Mediterranean zone and its domino effect spread to other parts, Egypt began disintegrating, and the Mycenaean empire almost died a silent death in Greece.

This dark period of the Axial Age cost many proto-empires and urban centers their life. It only ended after the emergence of an entirely new social system of the Iron Age. All great historical transitions are preceded by chaos, usually violent. When under pressure, history reshapes itself. It never stops happening. History, like mathematics, follows the universal "Scaling Laws" to fill the void created by the unexpected chaos with new civilizational order on the remains of the older onc. The civilization of Greece took birth on the remains of the Minoan and Mycenaean civilizations, while on the other shore of the Mediterranean, Israel shaped herself into existence.

The Minoan civilization flourished during the early Bronze Age from 2700 BCE to 1500 BCE and ended long before the Iron Age set in. We don't know much about this civilization, but scholars believe it was replaced by the Mycenaean civilization, which survived for the next 400-500 years. The records suggest that Minoans were a highly evolved mercantile society whose religious practices revolved around a pantheon of female goddesses.

The Mycenaeans were warriors who developed efficient public and military administration compared to the Minoans. Yet, they could not hold on for long. It couldn't have for simple reasons that, like any primitive agrarian society, it could not control an extensive territory and establish robust and resilient administrative and communication networks to guarantee a reliable flow of wealth into the state's coffers. There were no efficient roads or means of transport to control extensive territory, so expansionism created instability in the long run rather than being a boon. Expansionism meant making more enemies who could sometimes prove dangerous, given an opportunity. The Hittites, for example, had established their dominance in the adjoining Anatolia (modern Turkey) in 1600 BCE. When they turned their attention to the Mycenaeans, the latter completely collapsed, never rising again from the fall. The fall of the Mycenae set off the domino effect that brought the whole geographic region to the brink of devastation. The raging flames of instability and chaos didn't even spare the Hittites themselves. They also got engulfed in flames and burnt down to ashes. In the din, the Greeks appeared out of nowhere.

The Greeks traced their roots to the steppes – remember the Indo-Aryans? – and spoke one of the Indo-European dialects, and practiced religion not fundamentally different from the Rig-Vedic religious traditions of the Indo-Aryans yet so dramatically metamorphosed that it no longer seemed to retain any commonality with the foundational principles of the Aryan tradition. Except maybe the Fire, which continued to remain central to Greek religious tradition. The Aryan blood in their veins, however, endowed the Greeks with a warrior instinct that helped them withstand the Dark Age's pressures and, later, establish their sway over the fallen Minoan and the Mycenaean kingdoms.

As the Dark Age period receded, the future seemed rosy, except that it wasn't. The storms don't always come with a warning. The real trouble began with the collapse of the Mycenaean civilization. The Greeks had stood their ground and expected the clock of history to stand still. They basked in their past glories, throwing caution to the winds. Cherishing the memories of the past victory, they quite quixotically refused to acknowledge the dangers of changing political scenarios. The Trojan War had become established not merely as a legend but as sophisticated mythology. The martyrdom of Achilles in the Trojan War had assumed a rich, meaning-laden connotation superseding its mythological connection, and Oedipus of Thebes, for example, had become an alive and organically rich character in the collective consciousness of the masses.

As the crisis deepened and seemingly never-ending chaos engulfed the whole region, Greece too was about to be swallowed up by history had Athens not survived a touch miraculously. With no serious contender left to counter it, Athens somewhat unrestrainedly established its socio-politico-economic structure to dominate the later history. The spectacular feat of Athens left a deep imprint on the collective Greek consciousness. Athens' victory was so improbable that the Greeks thought it could not have happened without *Theseus's* invisible hand driving the course of events.

Theseus was a mythical king whose day was celebrated with all religious fervor. It was Homer who immortalized him through his drama. The Homerian epics depict Theseus like *Indra* of the Aryans. Like *Indra* was a god of war, *Theseus* symbolized strength, power, and a warrior mentality. Like the Aryans, the Greeks conveyed through the persona of *Theseus* the message that violence was necessary to survive.

The Greeks purposefully depicted scenes of violence through stories, dramas, and epics. Given violence was unavoidable, they had to either shy away from violence and find themselves on the wrong side of history like others or better accept and adapt to violence as a way of life. The propagandistic depictive art helped them choose the latter. However, that didn't mean right-minded Greeks never abhorred violence. No. But the world order was such that without resorting to violence, survival could be threatened. Given the prevailing circumstances, there was little room for compassion, love, and peace. Greece found itself in a typical "do or die" situation; ethics and morality had no place, and the answer to violence was violence. The Greeks normalized a "culture of violence," not bothering much about ethical niceties. They had to. They simply couldn't afford any setback.

The "culture of violence" didn't come easily to Greeks. They had to create it dedicatedly. A complex tapestry of mythology that they constructed helped them with that endeavor. The mythology assumed a religious character and helped mold the collective social psyche accordingly. Violence became a virtue. Thus began the Greek story. The Greeks' violent behavior would send shivers through the enemy's spine.

The culture of violence paid dividends. In no time, the Greeks came to dominate the Mediterranean region and a significant chunk of the world. Greece became a superpower. The natural after-effect was that Greek thought and philosophy would dominate the thinking of the whole world for no less than 2,000 years into the future. Greek philosophy (science was synonymous with philosophy) touched almost all civilizations' sociopolitical and cultural life. It was accepted as gospel truth by all the cultures of ancient and antiquity. No civilization, culture, or society had the courage and the audacity to challenge Greek science until the renaissance brought it under serious scrutiny for the first time. By then, however, Greek thought had become a widespread folk knowledge, finding its space in the religious traditions, especially of Judeo-Christian-Islamic faiths. The truisms had become scriptural truths, hard to challenge. Challenging them implied challenging the authority of revealed religions bearing in mind all the consequences. Be that as it may, the truth is that by any metric, the magnitude of the soft power the Greeks managed to wield over human civilization was enormous and remains unmatched even today. But, this all didn't come naturally to the Greeks. The Greek society had to struggle long and hard against the odds to attain soft power.

War of Gods

The much-celebrated Trojan War might have been a turning point in Greek history, but it was a comparatively later phenomenon. A couple of centuries before the Trojan War, the Greek world was collapsing during the crisis of 1200 BCE. It was a national tragedy. The nightmare of impending annihilation shook the Greeks. They had to resurrect themselves, so to say, from the ashes during the intense struggle ahead. Usually, people turn to religion during tough times, but for Greeks, the old faith and the old religion were not of much help in assuaging fear and uncertainty of the future. They urgently needed a new religion, theme, and narrative to reassemble and re-organize around, never mind the theological foundations of the new narrative. A new narrative that provided a powerful theme, a causus belli, to rally the people effectively.

The tragic past left a lasting impression on the collective psyche of generations of Greeks. Standing on the memory, they would use visual art, creativity, and storytelling effectively to replay and reframe the past so that it would not only register in the minds but also help galvanize the new generations to take up arms against any hostile tribe or enemy. After all, stories work wonders.

The Greek stories depicted gods and the supernatural, a touch like their predecessors in the steppes. The physical world was a shadow affair of the supernatural. But the artful stories extended a purpose to the shadowy affair, compelling the Greeks to look back into their past with a new perspective and zeal, arousing in them the yearning to reawaken their dormant power to resurrect and reassert their existence and identity amidst utter chaos. The survival instinct ignited patriotism in them that strengthened religious nationalism. Religious revivalism and nationalism were the natural consequence when the going got tough. Religion motivates, moves, and rallies the people behind a cause. That is, it identifies the purpose of the meaning-seeking creatures humans are. We fight the enemy in the name of religion, but behind the curtains, we are driven by our survival and status instinct.

Religious sanction makes anything legitimate and worthy - even something that doesn't make logical sense. We, humans, are exceedingly brilliant at making sense of the nonsense. From a neuroscientific point of view, we live in a state of perpetual self-deception. Our brain conjures up a mental world with all its colors, characters, dimensions, and relations for us to live inside it. We think we observe reality through our eyes. That is not the case. What we see and experience as reality "out there" is a reconstruction built *inside* our brains. In other words, what we see is the brain's "model" of the world - a hallucination, if you may—a deception. Of course, in self-deception, we still need to be accurate; otherwise, we may ram ourselves into walls. For accuracy, we have five senses. But they deliver only partial information to our brains. Rest the brain conjures up. Will Storr recapitulates quite brilliantly the present neuroscientific perspective on "reality" (in his book *The Science of Storytelling*) in this paragraph " the job of all the senses is to pick up clues from the outside world in various forms: light waves, changes in air pressure, chemical signals. That information is translated into millions of tiny electric pulses. Your brain reads these electrical pulses, in effect, like a computer code. It uses that code to actively construct your reality, fooling you into believing this controlled hallucination is real. It then uses its senses as fact-checkers, rapidly tweaking what it's showing you whenever it detects something unexpected."

"It's," he continues, "because of this process that [sic] we sometimes 'see' things that aren't actually there. Say, it's dusk, and you think you've seen a strange, stooping man with a top hat and a cane loitering by a gate, but you soon realize it's just a tree stump and a bramble." What happened was that you saw what your brain conjured up out of the input it received in the twilight. As you drew near, "and new, more accurate, information was detected, it rapidly redrew the scene, and your hallucination was updated," the stooping man vanished.

We see things that *aren't* there; similarly, we *don't* see things that *are* really there. Our tendency to make sense of things goads us to accept the unknown as known and the un-seen as seen. Our power of imagination is strikingly unlimited, un-confinable within space and time. Fiction and fantasy come in easy and handy to us. Our minds can deftly ride on the waves of heightened imagination to conjure up deja vu scenarios when confronted with the unknown and inexplicable. We invoke the "unseen" gods, divines, or supernatural forces just to assuage our sense of uncertainty. Otherwise, who doesn't consciously understand that the supernatural is nothing but a figment of human imagination?

The Greeks were tremendously well-versed in the art of storytelling. They went to great lengths to capture the unimaginable, the unfathomable, and the unseen in their myths, stories, and fiction. But there was a catch. Why should benevolent gods create a world full of violence, mercilessness, and disregard for the weak? Why a dog-eat-dog world? This question tickled the minds of the people all along. It was hard to reconcile with this aberration, yet they were clear in their minds that success and survival required mercilessness, ruthlessness, stone-heartedness, and brutality to kill, subjugate, and humiliate the enemies. What was woefully infuriating to some, not all, of the Greeks was that the gods seemed to be totally indifferent to the mayhem occurring day in and day out in the world.

On the one hand, the gods were benevolent; on the other, they were indifferent. This created a dilemma, mustn't it? The Greeks, like other civilizations, needed to do something to handle this dilemma.

Like Mesopotamians and Indo-Aryans, the Greeks imagined the world as a shadow (of the world of gods), but unlike them, the Greeks saw violence as an operative principle in the birth and death of gods. For the Greeks, their gods birthed and died just like humans did. When the gods fought each other, humans were automatically driven to violence by an invisible hand. What gods did in the skies, the humans automatically re-enacted it in this physical world. That is to say, the heavenly world served as the template for the physical world.

The Greeks' concept of the universe rejected the idea of peace and order. For them, the divine realm sustained only hatred and conflict. Only *Chaos* and *Gaia* could be the ultimate defining forces of the existing universe. These two forces existed in perpetual hostility toward each other, *Gaia* the creator and *Chaos* the destroyer. *Gaia* gave birth to *Uranus*, the Sky God. *Uranus*, the oldest, slept with his mother, *Gaia*, and his six sons and six daughters – *Titans*, the so-called first generation of gods – were born. *Uranus* disliked these children of his. So he tucked these Titans back inside the womb of *Gaia*. But when *Uranus* tried to have intercourse with *Gaia*, one of the Titans, *Cronus* bit off his genitals and threw them away. *Cronus* then wiggled out of the womb, proclaimed himself the chief God, and released all his brothers and sisters from the womb prison.

Suppose you have read this far into the book. In that case, you will probably find it hard to miss that the *Gaia* story is the Greek version of the *Prajapatti* story of the Indo-Aryans, except that Prajapatti, unlike Cronus, isn't born out of sexual intercourse. In Greek myths, the gods do sex, love, and family feuds just like humans do. *Cronus*, now Chief God, turned out no different than his father, *Uranus*. He married his sister, *Rhea*, and sired five sons, who became second-generation gods. Surprisingly, in the ancient Indian epic *Mahabharata*, there were also five *Pandavas* (Avatars). It is hard to miss that the principle theme is identical in the Greek and Indian versions of the story. The plots, however, were customized to the respective audiences. In the Greek version, for instance, when *Cronus* learns that one of his sons will overthrow him, he devours each of his five sons immediately after birth. When *Rhea* was pregnant with the sixth baby, she reported to *Gaia*, who agreed to protect her newborn from *Cronus*. As the infant was born, *Gaia* took him away and hid him on the island of Crete. This infant was named *Zeus*. He grew up on the island, and when he returned, he fought his father *Cronus,* defeated him, and forced him to vomit out his stomach five brothers of his that he had devoured. The five brothers took up residence on Mount Olympus.

The family war of gods wasn't over with the fall of *Cronus*. There was yet more to come. The Titans united against *Zeus* and his brothers, and the war between them continued for ten years. The Greeks called it the "Olympian War," which only ended with Zeus's victory. He buried his father and his confederates deep into the depths of the earth. The Olympian War story is not any different from its Indian counterpart (*Mahabharata*), as told in the Hindu scripture, the Bhagavad Gita. Except for the protagonists (five Pandava brothers), they don't bury their kin after killing them. The resemblance of these religious stories can't be a coincidence, given that a common thread runs through almost all the major religious stories. Somewhere in the timeline, the different sacred histories intersect; the exact point of their intersection and collision in the time-space, though, is hard to pinpoint with the present tools and technology. In the future, scientific advances may be better positioned to dig deeper into the "deep" history and hopefully uncover many, if not all, secrets and mysteries ascribed to religion and faith. Hopefully.

At the moment, turn to the Jewish foundational story. We are told Moses was born when Pharaoh Ramses II passed on the orders that all male newborns should be killed immediately after birth. Like *Cronus,* the Pharaoh had learned (allegedly from soothsayers) that a male infant born in that particular year would overthrow him later on. He ordered all male infants born in that specific year to be killed. The infant Moses survived because his mother, following some preplanned arrangement, hid him in a chest and threw it into the river. The chest floated along seamlessly till Pharaoh's daughter noticed it and picked it up from the water. Upon opening the chest, she was overtaken with empathy and joy when she saw the infant, Moses. She picked the infant and took him into the palace. There, Moses grew up under the doting care of Pharaoh's household. The grown-up Moses ultimately fought his adopted father, Ramses II, until the latter drowned in the parted waters of the sea while chasing Moses and his followers.

Compare Moses's story to that of Zeus. Both escape death serendipitously. And both become important and influential figures in their own way. Depending on the story's plot, one becomes a prophet, and the other is a god. The plots differ, no doubt, but what about the foundational thread of these stories? In principle, it is identical. Its fictional character stares in the face. But the sacred history hardly bothers. It maintains a thin line between fiction and reality.

Sin, Punishment, and Fear of Death

Which leads us to another chapter of the god story: The *Primal Chaos.* It seems the Primal Chaos became distraught with the Titans' behavior. To handle the Titans, it gave birth to a frightening and revengeful generation of gods called *Erinyes,* whose task was to punish others for their crimes. The Olympian gods like *Zeus, Cronus,* and others were indicted before *Primal Chaos* for severe crimes and deserved a horrible death. The *Erinyes* were assigned to inflict punishment on them for their sins. And on the story goes. The idea behind these stories was to fit the rationale of punishment with sin because in Greek religion, the concept of "sin and punishment" comprised one of the foundational principles.

The modern Greeks may find it surprising or even amusing that "sin and punishment" were pivotal in ancient Greece's religious discourse. Yet the fact stares in the face that Christianity's concept of "original sin" is a thematic continuation of the old Greek theology. Nothing surprising in that. Greek philosophy and thought ruled the rest of the world relentlessly for the next two thousand or so years. Greece had originated through a woefully horrendous struggle against insurmountable odds, and no wonder that violence occupied a deep and meaningful place in their life. Violence was like a *miasma,* contagious. Violence begot more violence, pushing Greek society deeper and deeper into a mire from which the exit seemed impossible. Despite violence becoming a new normal, violent behavior wasn't entirely bereft of a sense of guilt, though apparently, the Geek society appeared to have no scruples in resorting to wanton violence. Humans, by nature, are thinking creatures and a feeling of guilt is a normal reaction and needs to be assuaged. Humans need what we call "cognitive closure," lest guilt becomes burdensome.

Guilt implied that violence necessitated atonement. Without atonement, the Greeks feared plagues, catastrophes, and misery would haunt their world. They were not to be blamed for such a mindset – their forefathers had seen the devastation and terrible suffering during the Dark Age period and never wanted to slip back into the mess, for they hadn't, still, fully recuperated from the past wounds. Despite their valor, they also suffered from inherent psychological weakness like others.

During the years of struggle to regain their pre-Dark Age glory, they naturally turned towards religion. Religion, a glue, kept them together and gave them meaning resilience, and emotional strength to cooperate in founding a robust polity. Within a couple of centuries, the Greeks again became prosperous and powerful, establishing an empire that reached its zenith by the 5th century BCE. All along, they remained faithful to their ideology of fatalism, firmly believing in the power of the Olympian gods to hold them together. The Greek destiny was in the gods' hands.

The Olympian gods were impulsive and whimsical, and they could do whatever they liked, even destroy and create human life at will – the Greeks had no doubts about that. Yet they supposed that *Erinyes,* though ruthless and pitiless in pursuing the punishment of wrongdoers, had some sense of objectivity. This strange religious perspective underpinned by a firm belief in fatalism and the confusing unpredictability of gods was utterly frustrating. The Greeks were at a complete loss to predict the gods' temper, intention, or reaction. They had to put up with that uncertainty.

But that was a story, a story devised to reflect a reality: that the Greeks had seen adversity, turbulence, uncertainty, and violence very closely. They had learned a harsh lesson. Survival comes at a cost. It entails violence. Uncertainty is a natural component of life; they would not risk slipping into complacency for a moment. Accordingly, they shrewdly customized their gods' behavior to serve them as a constant reminder of the uncertainty of life and the capriciousness of the winds of fortune. If gods and the supernatural are unpredictable, so would the physical world. Such religious understanding kept them going.

Uncertainty translates into struggle, fights, and wars over resources. Wars are hard to fight, especially protracted ones. Not all societies readily engage in them. They must be lured into battles. The booty and spoils of war are good baits to convince some, not all, to risk their lives in the violence of wars and conflicts unless some abstract purpose, like religious duty, nationalism, or racial superiority, supports the bait. Shrewd use of religion always simplifies the task for men at the top. Faith makes woeful violence and bloodshed holy. But religion needs a compelling narrative and propaganda to deliver the uncanny punch. In the case of the Greeks, religion's task was simplified by the popular belief that the gods do commit ruthless violence against their closest kin. Then a question could be asked as to why humans should loathe violence when the gods have no scruples and when gods' kinship and families didn't matter, why should our kinship and family bonds matter? That was an exceedingly brilliant theological argument. But it still was only one side of the coin.

On the face of it, the Greek religion seemed to do its bit to legitimize and, in a way, even sanctify violence, as Greece's survival and hegemony in the ancient world order depended on it. However, there also was a subtle nudge, call it, subliminal messaging, attached to the Greek religious narrative and philosophy. As mentioned a couple of pages ago, the Greeks held a fatalistic view of life. So their theology, in a way, didn't attach much importance to worshipping and supplicating the gods for favors – a rather subtle way of underlining that the gods didn't even have their own house in order, so how could they bring order to the human world? Yet it emphasized that the gods did whatever they liked, irrespective of what the humans asked. They were gods! They punished whom they wanted and blessed whom they wished.

In a way, such theology prepared the people for the worst by presenting both sides of the story and urging them to face reality as it was. The Greeks possibly wondered, "in that case, why should the people be overburdened with the guilt of sin, murder, and violence? Why not throw morality and ethics away to the winds and do what the gods do with impunity? Violence." And they did. They went on with their violent lifestyle, bothered less and less about the wrath of gods, and succeeded in establishing a civilization and philosophy that went on to have a lasting and transmogrifying impact on the collective consciousness of the world of the Greeks and beyond.

The Greek religious liturgy and traditions were rooted in fear and sorrow, like many other contemporary religious traditions of the time. With the help of these traditions, stories, and rituals, they looked the fear in the eye: experienced it, understood it, and then faced it. All religions revolve around fear – fear of the unknown – but not all help their followers live it through. The Greek religion clearly stood out by showing the Greeks to do precisely that. Take, for example, the festivals of *Hera*, *Demeter*, *Thesmophoria*, or *Dionysus*. All these festivals, in a way, enacted and played out the theme of circumventing the fear of the future. They concluded with certain purification rites, symbolizing that the gods were appeased and new life and hope were on the horizon. Through these rituals, the Greeks would experience the fear of death, sorrow, mercilessness, uncertainty, and chaos in preparation for tomorrow's renewed life. Their physical death, the rituals signified, was simply a transition to another state. Why fear state transition? All the same, the Greeks were careful to accept that life can bring tragedy that will always stay as a companion to life, to be accepted and reconciled with.

Olympia, Nudity, and Hallucination

The arduous and turbulent years up until the 8th century BCE were, in the true sense, formative years of Greek thought and perspective that only refined later in the succeeding centuries. One of the gifted intellectuals who recast the events of the 8th and the preceding centuries in a more or less historical perspective, most significantly influencing the Greek religious-cultural landscape, was the Great Homer. He fixed the famous epics, the Odyssey and the Iliad, in permanent memory through the written word. These Homerian epics, like *Ramayana* and *Mahabharata* in India, came to occupy a central place in the Greek ethos, culture, and sacred history. The Odyssey and the Iliad were instrumental in erecting the much-needed legacy of older traditions and the Pantheon of gods, particularly during the Greek civilizational history's transition phase.

While the Greeks were courageously stepping into a new phase of their history that would usher in prosperity and power, they desperately needed a new religious platform to kind of amalgamate different sets of beliefs and perspectives into a more or less unified religious-philosophical paradigm to glue together diverse communities. While they did not deviate radically from their past polytheistic tradition, they introduced new drama and effects into liturgy and theology, managing (quite successfully) to establish a new religious ethos on the foundational principles of their age-old tradition.

Simultaneously, the Greeks were making their presence known on the world political scene of the day. They were courageously embarking on experimentation with new ideas, calculatedly using religion to legitimate their political ambitions with the home audience. It didn't bother them much that their religious ethos and politics were poles apart. As it came to making bold decisions, they would seldom dither. They were the first to experiment with self-governance, essentially a crude and primitive form of a union of federal states. Under this scheme, the urban centers or city-states (*poleis*) enjoyed a fair measure of independence from the central federal government. Each city-state was fenced and had its temple, assembly of elders, and harbor. The marketplaces usually ran on the vast open spaces within the city-states.

The right to citizenship was open for all except enslaved people and women. Public speaking became important as everybody was supposed to develop debating skills because pressing matters were discussed and debated in assemblies. People enjoyed participating in these debates and discussions. The farmers also would join in the debates to argue their case. The argument, after all, was no less than a contest, and whoever could argue their case impressively would be the victor. Eloquence mattered. Debate and discourse became instrumental in transforming the behavior of the citizenry.

The innate competitiveness of the Greeks was pretty evident even in their debating. Combativeness was alive in them. The transition to smooth argumentative talk didn't extinguish in them the warrior instinct they had inherited from the steppes. In contrast, the Aryan Indians retracted into a withdrawal mode during and after the Dark Ages. The fertile lands of India lured them into cultivating and livestock-rearing activities and trade, eventually abandoning the warrior behavior critical for establishing supremacy on the world political scene. Quite plausibly, this Indians' kind of cocking a snook at the stark realities of the existing world order ultimately paved the way for foreign militaristic tribes to subdue India on many occasions. Some plundered and left, and many, including the British, French, and Portuguese, ruled it with an iron fist. Regrettably, there was nothing that predominantly agrarian India, politically and geographically fractured as it was into countless independent serfdoms and tribal kingdoms, could do but carry a deep grudge against these victors.

Contrary to the Indians, the Greeks willingly put up with the violence, embraced it, and restructured their religion to accommodate violence, war, bloodshed, and ruthless competition. They had to. They had inherited a geography that was not as conducive to agriculture as that of Aryan

Indians. They were more practical – and a touch insouciant–than what their mythology suggests. Even the later Greek thought led one to believe that these people were more preoccupied with philosophical sophistry and abstractionism than military endeavors. That wasn't the case. The 8th century BCE attitude – goal-oriented, practical, brute, and even vicious in political matters – lingered on with the Greeks.

Harshness, brutality, and calculated barbaric aggressiveness paid their dividends. Greece became an affluent society. Material affluence pushed for the exploration of new vistas of opportunity and progress. The Greek elite enthusiastically voted for the creation of the *poleis* (city-states) and advocated using force to compel villages and communities to join the *poleis.* The violent re-settlement drive created communal conflicts within the city-states. Add to it that each new polis faced fierce competition from its neighboring polis, making the already complicated situation fragile enough to lead to a prolonged state of mini-war among individual city-states. Throughout those turbulent times, it was Pan-Hellenism that bonded them, as religious nationalism does, through the regular festivities and religious-cultural events sponsored by the state. Had it not been for this sense of Pan-Hellenism, the Greek civilization would have been torn apart long before it could sprout.

The athletic competition at Olympia was one such important festival that started in 776 BCE with the predominant, if not the only, aim of reinforcing cultural unity. Initially, it was a part of the big religious festival held in honor of Zeus. In 776 BCE, the athletes – all male citizens of the *poleis* – from every corner of Greece participated, and one Koroibos, a cook by profession, was declared the winner of the stadion race. For the next 12 centuries, the festival was held every four years. It was pretty typical for the contestants to run naked. Nudity in the Olympian festival owed its origin to a Spartan tradition that began in the 8th century BCE. The Olympian Games continued till 393 CE in Greece and then were stopped, as the Greeks had lost their power and influence by then. In 1896, after a gap of 1503 years, the modern Olympics were held in Athens after years of hectic canvassing by a French aristocrat, Pierre de Coubertin.

The ancient athletic competitions at Olympia involved a brutal display of deadly warrior skills to enact a symbolic victory over death. The champions would die in the contest, a noble death – a necessary component of the whole drama. These horrific contests were designed with the purpose to kind of motivating the masses to overcome the fear of death. The champions were hailed and emulated, even worshipped, as heroes. Hero worship being an important feature of the Greek religious ethos, all the dying champions were profusely honored like Supermen, and the graves, particularly of the victorious warrior-champions, were elevated to the status of places of worship like any other temples in the poleis. Worshippers visited these tombs and performed religious rites as they did in temples. Over time this custom of visiting tombs and grave worship was assimilated by other cultures and continued to be practiced by adherents of all three Abrahamic religions. It survives into the present day, and despite claims to the contrary, all religions accommodate hero worship and tomb worship. Such ingrained practices of ours, quite clearly, bear testimony to the extent of influence the ancient Greek thought continues to have over our collective mind, however vehemently we may deny it.

Apart from the temples, shrines, and tombs in a *polis*, another unique cult thrived in association with *Delphi*. In a mysterious temple of *Delphi*, the prophetess or advisor to the *Apollo* god, *Pythia*, was supposed to dwell. Here in the premises of this temple, a kind of mystical religious cult thrived, and people frequently assembled to allegedly consult with that all-pervasive *Pythia*. Here, they discussed ideas and charted out the strategies as a part of a ritual, not a serious brainstorming exercise, on matters as diverse subjects as sowing seeds, everyday life's transactions, politics, war, expeditions, etc. In *Delphi*, under the supposed aegis of *Pythia*, performing rituals lent the people a sense of certainty and confidence about victory in battles and wars. Faith matters!

Before launching the offensive against their enemies, especially, the Greeks engaged in esoteric, mystical, or religious rituals, as is still universally seen in cultures irrespective of the professed religious beliefs. In medieval times, for instance, Christian priests carried the Holy Cross to invoke the blessings of Jesus as the crusader armies marched against Muslims. These psychological tricks were devised to motivate people to overcome their fear of death and willingly risk their lives despite knowing the death trap lay ahead. How else could humans face terrible wars and challenges with their survival at stake if they weren't made to hallucinate things like a noble cause, the holy war, crusade, Sacrifice in the name of God and religion, etc.?

The Iliad and The Odyssey

Long before philosophers stumbled on dictum – "you are what you think about" – the Greeks practiced it through their belief in Pythia. Thc hallucination about Pythia's infallibility gave the Greeks confidence for victory in the political fights, battles, and wars. They succeeded overwhelmingly in expanding their sway into far-off regions of the Mediterranean. Their ferocious expansionism, blessed and sanctioned by no less a god than Pythia, set a massive wave of colonization into motion. As a result, by the 7th century BCE, the whole Mediterranean region had practically become a Greek colony.

Colonial imperialism brought the Greeks in contact with eastern traditions and religious ideas, setting off cultural osmosis that left the religious-cultural thought on both sides deeply influenced by each other. Many eastern traditions got seamlessly assimilated into the Greek religion and theosophy. Some scholars argue that the influence of eastern religious traditions was so profound on the Greeks that they modified their Pantheon to emulate the Eastern line of thought. They point out that gods like *Apollo*, *Ishtar*, or *Aphrodite* and *Adonis* weren't Greek in origin, but were imported from the East, accorded an honorable place in the Greek religious liturgy, and subsequently raised to the pedestal of influential gods in the Greek Pantheon. Whether the Greeks imported the gods or not didn't matter to them more than their dramatized depiction and celebration through the Great Epics of the time, these epics profoundly impacted Greece's overall socio-political and religious-cultural consciousness.

The popular epics gave meaning to violence, murder, and barbarianism. In the ruthless world order of the day, the Greeks had, broadly speaking, only two options: either kill or get killed. Therefore, before blaming the Greeks for committing wanton violence, it is worth considering that they were quite disquieted by violence rather than totally indifferent to violence. Guilt pangs hurt their souls. Yet, even if they did not want to commit violence, the circumstances were such that, willingly or not, they would be dragged into it. To kind of offload the burden of guilt, they intelligently projected violence over to the gods. Homerian epics like the Iliad and the Odyssey served as influential pieces of propaganda that celebrated this project.

For us, the epics of Homer are nothing but fiction, mythology, and drama told in difficult-to-understand and flowery language. Not to the Greeks of the 8th century BCE. For them, it was plain and simple God's word. Had that not been so, Homer's work probably wouldn't have survived until our day. When print and electronic media didn't exist, these epics were hugely popular and remarkably influential in reframing the Greeks' perspective on religion and worldly life. For us, the ancient Greek metaphorical language poses a difficulty, but for the ancient Greeks, it was simply Greek. The message to the ancient Greeks was clear: there is nothing of what we call "order." The universe is underpinned by chaos and conflict; precisely, harmony had to be sought out of this chaos and conflict. More importantly, harmony was unlikely to be achieved through loving deeds and compassion alone; aggression was as much needed as nonaggression. Compassion, kindness, love, and forgiveness were no substitutes for aggression when it came to survival and hegemony. That was to say, violence and peace, as two opposing components of life, are necessary to achieve balance. Yin-Yang interaction if you like.

The epic drama left the audience emotionally charged, agitating their conscious and subliminal faculties of inquiry by unequivocally stressing that the gods are violent. As the human world is a shadow of the gods' world, there was no wrong for humans to engage in violence amongst themselves. Thus, a religious garb was wrapped around violence to obscure its stigma, which facilitated the political machinery to put its hand on a woefully sinister propaganda tool.

The propaganda fanned out a subliminal suggestion that men were remembered only by their glorious deeds, and the glorious deeds were possible only by overcoming the fear of death. When an ordinary man died, he "simply" went - out of sight and, after some time, out of mind. What keeps men alive in people's minds is heroism, success, and glorious deeds. The religious philosophy and propaganda promoted heroism. It suggested that being egotistic or obsessed with achieving honor, status, and prestige, even if that meant unscrupulous indulgence in violence, war, killing, and exploitation of the weak, was perfectly acceptable.

The Iliad and the Odyssey glorified violence and warfare through intelligent artistic and metaphoric language. Their message was clear and cut to the point: mortals were okay to engage in violence and warfare when the gods in the heavens were busy in perpetual wars. Like a modern self-help or motivational story, the epics ignited the people's religious-nationalistic fervor, stimulating them to fight brutally and ferociously to establish Greek supremacy over the rest of the then-known world. That would give them control over global commerce, trade, and business to ensure their empire's monopoly over the revenue supplies.

Ethics, Empire, and Religion

Ethics and morality have always been tickling issues for humans, especially when they adopted a settled way of life some 12000 years ago. Whether or not we humans are meaning-seeking creatures, which Karen Armstrong insists we are, all the same, we are mystified by Life, creation, God, survival, and the like. All along, we have been subliminally cognizant of our need for cooperation for survival, which has, historically, pushed us to devise and explore different strategies to fulfill that need. And we are the only species that has successfully developed, implemented, and then carried forward to our subsequent generations methods and strategies to help achieve and sustain targeted cooperation of the crowds to attain goals. But the path to materialize meaningful collaboration has been quite bumpy and bloody. Entire civilizations were imperiled and even destroyed at times when things went awry. After blood baths and wanton destruction, whenever humans introspected, the need to draw a set of paradigms and frameworks that would address the moral and ethical basis of our actions and reactions topped the agenda. And religion led from the front seat to implement moral and ethical standards.

The two fundamental questions have perplexed the human species from the beginning of its existence. They are: Why do we die after all the hard work, struggle, and investment in living? And what happens after death? These fundamental questions have defied all logic. There is no convincingly satisfactory answer to them. Had there been one, religion perhaps wouldn't have been invented. Religion was churned out of socio-cultural ethos to answer these puzzling issues, which it couldn't. It simply ended up with clever circumlocutions. Never answering the two prickly questions definitively, it characteristically maneuvered them to bully the people with the fear of death and after-death, which served the political and economic ends of the societies.

For instance, in the case of the Greeks, the urgent problem was political and, to some extent, economic, which made war and expansionism a necessity rather than a choice. Quite understandably, it brought economic benefits to the palace and the elite in terms of booty, tribute, and taxes, but it caused distress for the general population. In the long run, it was too dangerous a policy for the empires to pursue. Irrespective of its lures, it brought about the decline of the kingdoms and empires. Yet the short-term benefits and the need to safeguard their status made the political elite desperate to drum up the narrative to exalt the beauty and holiness of warfare. Absent religion that was easier said than done.

The idea of nationalism was too abstract to strike a chord with the Greek populace. To circumvent the problem of abstractionism, a loose tapestry of narratives, borrowed from an "imagined" past, was finetuned and splendidly fabricated into an organized story – religion. It looked entirely new and refined to an outsider.

Ideas, things, and even paradoxes of everyday life, such as happiness, worry, wealth, etc., were personified as the gods. Thus, we had the God of wealth, family discord, happiness, and the like. The individual gods were profoundly antagonistic to one another, but together, they exemplified "unity in diversity," sort of. To the Greek mind, diversity portrayed the complexity of life with all its paradoxes or conflicts. They hardly bothered about gods being wholly good. They were Okay with the premise that every God had a dark side. They seemed not to be particularly worried by their gods' nonchalance toward morality and ethics. The collective Greek mind was programmed, at least during the formative years, to accept that conflict and chaos in the heavens were, in fact, a template for earthly strife and chaos.

The Stupid Prophet

Things don't remain static for long. Time flows. History happens, and Sacred history, too, adapts to the circumstances. Even though the Greeks had become thoroughly programmed religiously, it didn't take them much still to revolt against that unfounded dogmatism. One spark ignited a colossal fire as their society reached a tipping point.

The economy had seemingly stabilized, and it seemed the people would enjoy prosperity. Yet that turned out to be a mirage. Before long, the people would pick the fruit of a robust economy, and the relentless crisis began engulfing the Greek world. By the middle of the 7th century BCE, a dangerous split was emerging in society. The farmers were becoming increasingly restless and disillusioned by the burdensome political system. The unrest turned into an ugly peasant rebellion. The working class joined the farmers in their accusations of the Homerian gods' indifference to their sufferings. That brought religion into question, jeopardizing the trust in gods. As the institution of religion came under attack, the merchants of religion were at a loss to fix the damage. Luckily a prophet appeared on the scene. His timing was opportune as he claimed to receive revelations from *Zeus*. This prophet was Hesiod.

Hesiod, it seems, built his story on the old Indo-European "Four Ages" mythology, which he might have been fully acquainted with. The myth goes like this: In the Golden Age (cognate with *Satyug* in Indian mythology), humans lived happily like gods, without labor enjoying abundance. Then came the Silver Age (*Tretayug* in Indian mythology), and humans became reckless, exploitative, violent, and disobedient to Olympian gods. *Zeus,* in a fit of anger, replaced them with a new race of humans. This event coincided with the beginning of the Bronze Age (*Dwaparyug* in Indian mythology). But it turned out that the new human race was no less aggressive than their predecessors, terrible, warrior type, and violent, destroying one another. *Zeus* was compelled to replace them with Heroes – reformed and justice-loving men. However, the Heroes fought the Trojan War and were annihilated. The end of the Age of Heroes coincided with the Iron Age (*Kalyuga* in the Indian version). In this Age, men then engaged in wanton violence and destruction on the Earth.

Now, what Hesiod claimed was that Zeus, in a show of generosity, decided to condone their crime and shower his blessings upon men. That gave him a perfect alibi to preach, "life is suffering, but the men do have a choice," they must either submit to the goddess of Justice called *Dike* or "abandon themselves to the sin of hubris." Hesiod's smooth talk essentially focused on resurrecting the honor and respect of the gods of the Greek religion. He argued that the concept of Primal Chaos arrogated "clarity, order, and definition" to the universe, and it was this *Theogony* of Hesiod that paved the way for inquiry about the origin of the universe, cosmos, and even Primal Chaos itself by the later philosophers. Another undeniably outstanding contribution of Hesiod to Greek religious thought was his emphasis on the human element in the so-called mysterious "order underlying the universe." Hesiod refrained from contradicting the notion that humans – in the beginning – lived alongside gods in heaven. By the way, this man-living-in-the-heaven thing was faithfully carried into all three Abrahamic faiths, as the Adam-Eve story.

Hesiod, however, in his characteristically unique style, reframed the creation story introducing the character of *Prometheus* in his recast of the original story. We are told, he wrote: After the gods left the humans alone to their fate, they had only one way of connecting with the former – by Sacrifice. But *Prometheus* thought that this was unfair to humans. So he tried to trick *Zeus* into "accepting bones of the victim (offered in sacrifice) so that men could devour the flesh." But *Zeus* cleverly declined *Prometheus's* offer, immediately proclaiming that gods didn't need any portion of the meat or bones of the sacrificed animal; they were superior creatures, and as such, the energy of smoke from the sacrificial fire was enough for them. This, according to *Prometheus*, was a ploy devised by Zeus to frustrate humans by stopping the fire from burning. So *Prometheus*, to help humans, now tried to steal the fire from *Zeus*. But he was caught, and Zeus punished him for cheating him. In a fit of rage, he also decided to punish humankind. He sent *Pandora* – a beautiful woman carrying "suffering and misery" in a box. As she opened it, "suffering and misery" escaped and took hold of humankind.

That was Hesiod, reasoning about Sacrifice and human suffering. His rationale behind Sacrifice pivoted on the premise that even if gods don't eat flesh and bones, smoke and smell reach them. Quite ingenious and, at the same time, stupid. Yet, most importantly, in that superstitious Age, he attempted to get humans, perhaps at least the Greeks as he was more interested in them, into the creation equation; otherwise, there was no dearth of god stories and Primal Chaos in the existing folklore. Unfortunately, the fatalist in him prevented him from elaborating further on the characteristically chimerical idea of human participation in the god story. He failed to articulate the premise that humans were self-sufficient and didn't need gods' blessings to tackle their miseries and suffering, as Kapila, Mahavira, or Buddha in India did. As the coming centuries demonstrated, his failure to shun fatalism was utterly stupid of this great prophet and wise man.

The Seed of Democracy

Not all believed Hesiod received revelations. His attempt at religious reformation provoked resistance during his lifetime, but that didn't prevent the subsequent evolution of Greek philosophy and religious discourse. Unbeknownst to him, he had cast the die. Yet, in reality, he was far from being practical. He couldn't see the trouble brewing as the economy was failing, the peasantry was up in arms, and the political elite reacted disproportionately. Take what he advocated in his pamphlet *Works and Days* at this crucial juncture. Without putting his finger on the pulse of the people, he proposed "Passive Compromise," allegedly revealed to him by Zeus. His contemporaries immediately rejected that. It was not a viable formula to solve the immediate political and economic crisis the Greeks faced. Greece's problem was rooted in the inefficient management of economics, and here Hesiod is directed by *Zeus* to teach compromise. It proved to his critics that he was not in tune with the mood of the masses.

The first rebellion had begun in Corinth in 655 BCE. The leader of this rebellion was famously called the "Tyrant." Although he was overthrown in a subsequent mass uprising, his rebellion awakened the hitherto oppressed masses to the possibility of effectively countering the ruling elite. Through cooperative uprisings, they could now effectively influence the political decisions of the city-states.

War, and not philosophy and religion, made such mass uprisings possible. The weapons were relatively freely available during wartime. Anybody could get enlisted as a soldier, even the peasants, provided they could afford the *Hopla* (spear). Hoplite fighting was carried out in formations, or units called the phalanx (a row of soldiers packed shoulder to shoulder.) Hoplite fighting permanently transformed the technique and the character of warfare. For the first time in history, war became a cooperative enterprise. The individual members of the hoplite phalanx were required to cooperate for the success of the whole phalanx. Over time the individual hoplites would understand each other better, become friends, and develop a sense of camaraderie in the units. The natural consequence of rapport, mutual trust, and reliance was that entire units would get mobilized in the blink of an eye should the need arise.

Hoplite warfare mandated more human resources than the conventional one practiced before and created a pressing need to recruit more commoners into soldiery. As more commoners flocked into the rank and file of the army, society's then-existing old and rigid class hierarchy was diluted to the extent that even the peasants now came to rub shoulders with the erstwhile military class and elite. The farmers and laborers quickly began to copy and adapt the aristocratic outlook. In a matter of years, the poleis were inhabited by more or less one class of "warriors." This shift helped deepen the sense of belonging and patriotism in the masses, and Greek society was nudged to proceed toward democracy.

Sparta became the torch bearer of the hoplite culture. Young aspirants were trained for warfare not in mock drills, as had previously been the case, but in real battles organized in Sparta. Blood would flow from the left, right, and center. Only those who emerged victorious in these local battles would then make it to soldier ranks to fight in wars against other cities and kingdoms. Sparta also became a prototype for warrior *poleis* where the power of the people or *demos* came to reside in the assembly constituted of warriors. The seed of democracy was sown, albeit not in fertile soil.

In 510 BCE, Sparta invaded Athens (a neighboring polis) to install a Spartan governor to administer there. The Athenians put up strong resistance and succeeded in repelling the invading Spartans. After the war, Athenian magistrate Cleisthenes took over as chief administrator of the polis. He introduced some sweeping political reforms. Though an oligarchy of nobles could still rule the city, they were now subject to checks and balances through an assembly of people. This precarious yet bold political experiment became popular in no time, with other poleis following suit. The people could now freely participate in the debates of the assembly, provided they followed specific rules of the debate and behaved intelligently. This system was designed to impart a hands-on political education to the masses. Over time it made resorting to brute force to run the government almost redundant.

Spirit of Intellectualism

Although Athens never ceased to be a deeply religious city, the new political system helped spark a robust philosophical discourse and debate bordering on secularism. For instance, Heraclitus (540-480 BC) boldly put forward his views about the cosmos and life, stressing that every human should engage in introspection. Coincidently, it was at the same time that Heraclitus's contemporary from India, Buddha, encouraged his followers to resort to contemplation. Did the two visionaries exchange some correspondence? There is no evidence of that. Yet it seems plausible that the ideas traveled through trade routes far and wide, influencing people far removed geographically from each other. According to Heraclitus, Cosmos is in a state of perpetual flux underneath its apparent stability. He regarded *flux* as the immutable law of nature, yet flux and stability, he stressed, were not antagonistic to each other instead, they were complementary. It was the interaction of these two states that kept the cosmos in a state of equilibrium with the universe, he passionately argued. Soon other philosophers joined the discourse. The proverbial cacophony of discourse was leading the Greek elite to an unthinkable, by the standards of the day, conclusion: it was possible to amend the tribal political system without the permission of gods. That was a characteristically chimerical direction of thought, a spirit of intellectualism resting on outright blasphemy.

Xenophanes (560-480 BCE), another contemporary of Buddha, was emboldened to even reject the Olympian gods altogether. He argued that these gods were nothing but the imagination of the mind. He is among the first who pointed out the anthropomorphic character of gods. Being cognizant of the fact that he was treading a dangerous path, he cleverly shifted the heat away from him by clarifying his stand on the Olympian gods. He explained there were not multiple gods but only one, "*Nous*" (mind/god), who governed everything from the human world to the world of gods. Furthermore, like Hesiod before him, Xenophanes claimed to receive divine revelation apparently from *Nous*. Perhaps he was deeply influenced by the eastern religious tradition, which is quite possible, since, by the 6th century BCE, eastern and western regions of the Mediterranean zone had come much closer through trade, business, and war to undergo cultural osmosis.

Parmenides, another philosopher, propounded the "static universe" theory – that same theory that caused trouble to twentieth-century genius Einstein in his day while formulating his famous theory. Such was the extent and depth of influence that Greek science wielded on the subsequent world order from mundane to extraordinary matters. Parmenides claimed that the universe was fixed (so did Einstein and classical physics believe), and no change was possible because "reality" was essentially existent only in the body of one complete and eternal "Being," and the rest is the shadow of that "Being." Any perceived change in the universe and its working, thus, was essentially an illusion. The likes of Aeschylus, Sophocles, Euripides, and other less prominent playwrights subsequently joined the chorus questioning everything from the nature of gods and the stated values of the Greek civilization to the meaning of life. Mohi-ud-din Ibn al Arabi, a 12th-century mystic, clearly influenced by this ancient Greek philosopher, vigorously defended the philosophy that the physical world is merely an illusion, substituting Parmenidean "Being" with God, the absolute "reality."

At the face of it, Athens was a terrific society, and the city-state was becoming prosperous. Quite naturally, Athens attracted attention from all. Suspicions grew about Athenian politics. Sparta perceived Athens as a potential empire readying imperial grunts to establish hegemony over the Mediterranean zone. As the suspicions grew, the tension escalated, bringing these two neighbors face to face. A long and costly war ensued, breaking the back of both warring states. Finally, in 466 BCE, a truce was negotiated, and the Greek world was divided among two empires. However, that didn't end the trouble for the Greeks. The real danger was closing in on them. A giant lurking around the corner was watching them closely and waiting for the opportunity to gobble them both up.

The mighty Persia posed a real threat to Greece, sending shivers through its spine. The semblance of political stability post-truce furnished no guarantee of survival in the face of a Persian onslaught. The news of the Persian cavalry and navy's preparations for invasion sent the Greeks berserk. Their fate was hanging by a thread. Frantically, they set on preparing for defense. Normally, in a dire situation like this, they should be devoting all their energies to preparing for the war and letting go of philosophical hair-splitting. But no. The Persian threat couldn't dampen the spirit of intellectualism; instead, the disruption intensified intellectual innovation and progress. Prominent figures like Zeno, a student of Parmenides, a member of his Eleatic school of thought, and in his thirties by 466 BCE, were hell-bent on expanding the sphere of influence of their teacher's philosophical thought. Parmenides believed the universe was changeless and immobile – static with the earth as its center. Zeno defended this view by arguing that motion was impossible. He launched his argument with his famous puzzle, "The Achilles," grounded in cold logic. Zeno's thesis continued to fascinate philosophers for centuries after his death. As Charles Seife points out, everybody knew Zeno's statement was false, but nobody could find a flaw in Zeno's argument.

What was Zeno's argument? In one sentence: the motion was a succession of measurable "immobilities." Starkly weird but a logical puzzle that put the Greek philosophers in a dock for centuries. The silly statement that nothing in the universe could move – of course, that is not the case – gave restless nights to mathematicians for two thousand years. What irrefutable logic did Zeno provide as proof of his riddle? He demonstrated it by example: Achilles can never catch up with a tortoise in a race. Of course, that is not true in the real world, but Zeno proved it was true – logically. Zeno did something like this: Imagine Achilles runs at one foot per second speed and the tortoise at half that speed. As the tortoise slugs a foot, Achilles covers that distance in half a second. By then, the tortoise moves another quarter of a foot. Achilles covers that distance in a quarter of a second, but as he reaches the point where the tortoise is, the tortoise has moved by eight of a foot. It happens each time. Achilles never catches up with the tortoise. The philosophers knew Zeno was wrong, but there was no way to refute his logic – his deduction was correct. What did the philosophers not understand? Infinity. Yes, infinity. And void, too. They had no mathematics to deal with the infinite. Their mathematics was essentially geometry, not number-based. As Zeno divided motion into tiny and tiny steps, the Greeks assumed it to go forever. There was no zero where the positive would end, and the negative would start (+1, 0, -1). Zeno, too, didn't possess a solution to his paradox, but that didn't bother him as long as it served his philosophy and his master's teachings.

Another philosopher, Anaxagoras (508-428 BCE), refined Xenophanes's philosophy. He paralleled *Nous* to cosmic intelligence that gave rise to everything. He argued cosmic intelligence was real, not supernatural; a form of matter, not spirit; it was in perpetual motion and not static. Everything else that moves, including the Sun, the Moon, and the stars, is driven by this cosmic intelligence. Later, Aristotle generously drew on Anaxagoras's thought when he introduced his concept of "prime mover." At some point, Anaxagoras changed his mind. He began inching toward materialism but stopped short of taking a conspicuous leap. That was left to Democritus (466-370 BCE), who, taking a quantum leap of thought, proposed that things were formed from small particles (later called the "atoms"), which continuously collide with each other. His startling conclusion that the collisions of atoms lead to the formation of objects around us upset the philosophers of his time. It was courageous – and reckless on the part of Democritus – that he sought materialistic thought to explain the everyday phenomena in a world dominated by superstition, black magic, and other infantile belief systems. He was playing with fire that could consume him anytime. It was blasphemous to introduce the "atom" as a physical entity, and he deserves credit for laying the first seeds of Particle Physics at the wrong time, though, in the wrong kind of soil of the Greek mind.

The Protagorean Materialism and Socrates

Another class of intellectuals called the Sophists or the wise men, known for their contribution to bringing philosophy into the everyday life of the Greeks, wielded tremendous influence on Athenian thinkers. Later philosophers, though, criticized sophists woefully, perhaps unwarrantedly severely. Like Buddha and his followers, the sophists stressed self-sufficiency; they taught their students how to understand the workings of the mind. They claimed – and quite correctly – that once a man learns and understands that "all thought is subjective," he can be better placed to handle delusions like superiority, self-righteousness, grandiosity, egotism, etc. According to the sophists, the students and disciples must develop the "habit of questioning" everything from mundane to extraordinary to the supernatural. To sophists' minds, every phenomenon witnessed in the world was "relative" – one person's perception may not match that of another's, and that is normal rather than aberrant – this all was not so different from what Buddha allegedly taught, remember!

One of the influential sophists, Protagoras, taught that the Truth or the "Reality" or the "Absolute" wasn't something situated in remote, inaccessible heavens but something entirely within reach of every human being. Here, Protagorus and Buddha seem to be on the same page, independent of each other. Both believed that to experience "Reality," what was needed was to direct attention inward, and everything depended on the humans themselves; there was no transcendent authority or supreme God. Buddha's audience was okay with this line of thought, but Protagoras was doing a dangerous experiment; he was crossing the line. In his boldly written treatise on gods, he emphatically stated there was no way to ascertain whether gods exist, and since their existence can't be proved by logic, they (the gods) should not be a subject of study or *logos*. Protagoras had forgotten that he lived in ancient Athens and not in India, where anything could go. For instance, Mahavira and Buddha drew followers despite openly denying God's existence and were respected and honored as saints. That was in ancient India. The Greek world was different. There was uproar.

Protagoras could've been outrightly killed, but the authorities decided to expel him, instead, along with his philosopher friend Anaxagoras – perhaps in an attempt to contain the volatile situation. They, too, had some followers, and capital punishment of them might have caused violent clashes. Despite being removed from the scene physically, they never left the people's minds, sparking a fire in the intellectual landscape of the day. Difficult questions were now being constantly raised about gods by many influential thinkers – of note being the famous playwright Euripides. He, for instance, couldn't hold back his skepticism about the Greek religion. He lashed out at Greek religion in famous plays like *The Trojan Women* and *Medea.*

Protagorus was reportedly held in high esteem by the likes of Socrates, an ardent critic of sophists. He pointedly targeted the sophists for focusing solely on cosmology and the supernatural and ignoring the practical problems of life. Socrates conceived what is known as *dialectic* – a dialogue technique – for exposing false beliefs and eliciting the truth. Where Protagoras had restricted himself to mindfulness alone, Socrates went ahead with its practical demonstration through his dialectic. He stressed that true knowledge was attained only by introspecting and examining own thoughts. The knowledge acquired thus paves the way for deconstructing erroneous beliefs, ideas, or dogmatic truths. He forcibly argued that the truth or knowledge about the future would always remain uncertain unless the past and the present were examined.

Socrates saw no idea or dogmatic truth as perfectly flawless. He dissected every proposition with his dialectic to reveal its inconsistencies. Dialectics had opened the doors of knowledge to him, and he passionately appealed to his students to use dialectic – his technique of cross-examination. He reckoned knowledge as the fundamental virtue and was never ashamed of acknowledging his ignorance about certain matters of importance to philosophy. Rather, he took pride in his ignorance, emphasizing that ignorance opened up the opportunity for him to learn from others. To him, "knowledge was morality," and a virtue attained only by interrogating other fundamental assumptions a human being or society held. Socrates despised confining the meaning of courage to "bravery on the battlefield" alone. For him, real courage meant practicing Justice, temperance, wisdom, and goodness.

Another significant contribution of Socrates to philosophy was his invention of the concept of the "soul." He was among the first to regard the soul as a separate entity, which, according to him, already existed before an individual's birth, accompanied the being through their worldly life, and was not destroyed by death. To Socrates, the ultimate indicator of an individual's success was the "cultivation of the soul." According to him, action taken after careful consideration of whether it helps in the cultivation of the soul or not, wrong is not always retaliated with wrong, and displaying loving behavior to both friend and foe, demands courage. The action that benefits the soul consists of right and just deeds and living a disciplined life based on knowledge of the truth. The ultimate road to happiness lay in following a virtuous path, and self-introspection was crucial for cultivating the soul (psyche).

Socrates' philosophy represented a marked departure from the Greek conventional religious wisdom allegedly sanctioned by the Olympian gods that vengeance and revenge were the sacred and legitimate course of action in dealing with opponents. Such departure, especially when Athens was going through a crisis at war fronts, was inopportune and inimical to the national interest – or so the Greek political elite thought. Eventually, when Athens was defeated in the war, the politicians squarely blamed philosophers, particularly Socrates, for preaching blasphemy, thereby infuriating the gods who forsook Athens at a crucial moment bringing disgrace and defeat upon it. Socrates landed in trouble. He was indicted for denying the gods and corrupting the youth. The jury brought him before the trial, where he failed to convince them of his innocence. He refused to go to exile at his ripe old age of seventy and chose to drink hemlock and die smilingly.

Earlier, Protagoras was similarly brought before trial, but he chose to accept exile. Socrates refused to go into exile because, having lived into old age teaching courage, he now wanted to create history by demonstrating ultimate courage – by "looking death calmly in the eye." And he did. He washed his body, took the glass containing hemlock in his hand, looked at it, smiled, and drank it. Then, he patiently waited till the poison killed his body. All along, he remained serene and calm. His followers, friends, and disciples watched the nightmare, unable to intervene with the master. With his death, Socrates proved to them what he preached all through his life – humans can enjoy serenity amidst pain, fear, and suffering, but that depends on how the mind perceives and accepts the events.

Plato and the Cosmic Religion

Socrates never wrote a word during his lifetime. It was his pupil, Plato, who immortalized Socrates through his writings. Plato was highly distressed by his master's death at the hands of Athenian democracy in 399 BCE. Having been deeply influenced by Socrates and his philosophy, he held him in high esteem. It was now depressingly hard for Plato to live in the conflict-ridden city-state of Athens, where the unhappy and disillusioned "demos" took to violence on trifles. A depressed and disturbed Plato turned to the Pythagorean School, looking for solace. The Pythagorean School attracted primarily students and intellectuals interested in mathematics rather than philosophy. For Plato, it turned out to be a wrong choice, driven by compulsion rather than passion. Temperamentally, Plato was not cut out for mathematics; he felt choked by the Pythagorean system. Deeply contemplative and philosophical as Plato was, he found the school's environment unsuitable for venting out his thought burden. Soon he left and went his way.

Plato established his school called the Academy, where he conducted teaching according to the Socratic "dialectic" and "logos" for some time. Then he slowly drifted away from Socratic principles as he became convinced that excavating the truth is an arduous task requiring rigorous training and dedication on the part of the practitioner. Furthermore, he learned that detaching oneself from intuition and imagination, as taught by Socrates, was impossible. Then there was this democracy he initially supported but now came to despise. Plato began to view democracy as unfit to handle the existing political morass. Democracy, he argued, was incapable of providing the "good government" that Athens desperately needed. The solution he had in mind – which he was reluctant to put out in black and white – was outlandish, given the fragile Athenian socio-political atmosphere. Plato played safe and shrewd and refrained from derogating ancient philosophical and religious concepts and dogmas. He intentionally clothed his ideas in a dense language of metaphors and double entendres, focusing only on his targeted audience, who knew where the master was coming from.

Plato was careful not to divorce himself from the ancient Greco-Mesopotamian convention that the earthly world has its template in the heavens. He only intelligently paraphrased the popular concept. Calling the "Reality" the "Essence," he said although the "Essence" manifests in time and space, it is superior to manifested worldly objects. He went on to argue that violence (also included in the "Essence") existed in objective reality on a higher plane than the worldly one, i.e., on the plane of the soul - cleverly invoking Socrates for support. And also, to avoid contradicting Pythagoras, Plato acknowledged that the cosmos worked on a fundamental mathematics of ratio and geometry, but, he added, the underlying mathematical principles of cosmology weren't within reach of the ordinary intellect. By doing so, he kept both the Socratians and the Pythagoreans happy. Perhaps.

In private, Plato believed these mathematical principles should be explored and understood further as it was well within the capacity of human beings to do the mathematics of the cosmos intelligently. But for that, as he put it, one needs to awaken the "Essence" that lies buried deep - and forgotten - within the layers of consciousness. Like Socrates, he believed in the existence of the soul, but unlike the former, he also thought the soul was born many times and had all the previous experience within it. Where Socrates had claimed that the soul is outside - somewhere out there, not within the body, Plato subscribed to the concept of immortality and transmigration of the soul. Plato seemed to win the argument. Incidentally, it was during the same time that the Bhagavad *Gita* was gaining popularity in the Indian subcontinent as a divinely inspired religious book. It would be only a matter of time before the Greeks would move toward India, invade it, and establish a never-ending cross-cultural exchange of ideas with the Far East.

While elaborating on the Essence, Plato spoke metaphorically of beauty as akin to God because, to him, the essence of beauty was "Absolute *God-ness*." A firm understanding of "Absolute God-ness" would prevent a person from living an immoral or unethical life. It transforms a man into an immortal, like God, because, argued Plato, in "god, all things become one." According to him, just as God was indescribable, so were beauty, goodness, and *god-ness* in ordinary language bereft of metaphors and parables. In his later works, *The Republic* and *The Laws*, Plato is a different man - authoritarian and even intolerant - quite unexpected for a philosopher of his caliber and fame. He ceases to be the Plato that Socrates perhaps would approve of. Where Socrates desisted from imposing his ideas and perspective on others and cautioned others against doing so, Plato did the reverse. Maybe he understood better than Socrates that convincing the power corridors with dialectic alone was hard. That is, at the most, a guess. Accordingly, he took a hard-line approach in *The Republic* and *The Laws*, which, in any case, didn't work any better for him. It nearly cost him his life. He narrowly escaped execution but failed to escape the impact this incident left on his thinking.

Plato's philosophy of the Essence sold exceedingly well to the Greek religious opinion makers. Soon a trend picked, and these people began to discuss religion, the cosmos, and mathematics with a certain Platonic flair. Sensing the mood of the elite, Plato finetuned his ideas. He started to speak eloquently about creation story and metaphysics (though he didn't coin the term *metaphysics*). "Absolute perfection," Plato emphasized, was well within reach of humans, and they didn't need gods to ascend into the divine realm – which they couldn't anyway; everybody knew that. Again, cautiously holding on to Socrates, he advocated a disciplined way of life to attain knowledge. Knowledge sets humans free.

Plato unambiguously acknowledged a Creator – not an omnipotent, though, who is involved in the everyday world, whether as a doer, seer, or supervisor – but his further involvement had no relevance because the created universe maintained a set pattern. That underlying pattern, he asserted, could easily be observed, investigated, and understood empirically. That is to say, the universe, according to Plato, works according to a plan already laid out for men to try to understand through the cultivation of an intelligent mind – or maybe a mathematical reason. He cited the example of the regular motion of the Sun, moon, and stars as typifying a mathematical truth. That way, Plato tied philosophy proper, religion, and science of the day into one bundle, paving the way, centuries later, for the reconciliation of Christianity with Greek philosophy.

It was Plato's philosophy that roused later generations to take an active interest in the mysteries of the cosmos. To him, the mysteries of nature were the mysteries of the Divine, and whosoever investigated the Earth and the stars were, in actuality, delving into the mysteries of the Sacred. This Platonic cosmic connection ultimately led to the demotion of the Olympian gods to "nature spirits" or angel-like entities – a status of middlemen between God and humans. Plato did not categorically reject the old Greek religion but regarded it inferior to cosmic religion. Sensing the impressive receptivity of the masses for the cosmic religion, he turned to brazen religious fundamentalism in his approach toward socio-political issues.

In *The Law,* Plato completely shunned the principles he had previously stood for. The religious belief, as held by the ancestors of the Greeks, which he despised – though not publicly – was now essentially fundamental to him for morality. Without faith, there can't be any ethical behavior, emphatically proclaimed the master. Gone was Plato, who once mourned the execution of Socrates. The new Plato was so disenchanted with his teacher's philosophy that he advocated severe punishment for the people who expressed "doubt about the existence of the Olympian gods" or asked "searching questions about them." Hadn't Socrates encouraged Plato to look at everything with a measure of "skepticism" and "doubt" and investigate the "essence of the universe" rationally? Yes, but.... Perhaps old age was taking its toll on him. He had grown narrow-minded, irritable, and probably insecure. In a fit of anger or maybe depression, Plato upended the whole edifice of Socrates' dialectic. In the words of Karen Armstrong, "he [Plato] became coercive, intolerant and punitive," and "he sought to impose virtue from without, distrusted the compassionate impulse and made his philosophical religion wholly intellectual." Sad.

Aristotle and the Prime Mover

Plato died in 347 BCE. In his last years before death, he became an angry old man, anguished by his apparent failure to influence the masses hugely. But he left a brilliant legacy in the person of his pupil, Aristotle. Aristotle studied under Plato's tutelage for 20 years and left Athens for Macedonia only after Plato's death. In Macedonia, he received employment with King Philip as a personal tutor of the latter's son Alexander. Like Plato, Aristotle, too, in his later years, chose to divorce himself from his master's line of thought – not entirely, but to some extent – turning to a diligent study of the physical world. In a sense, he became the first Greek philosopher who insisted on observation of the living and nonliving world to do philosophy.

Aristotle conceived "change" as inherent and natural to the world. Rather than resisting "change," it was more meaningful to accept and celebrate it, he insisted. Though Aristotle saw the universe as static and perfect, he didn't exclude change as one of the ingredients of wholeness. Without change, there would be no point for the universe to exist at all, he surmised. It was the transformation that lies at the core of the universe's existence, and only transformation brings diversity, and diversity imparts meaning to existence – so thought Aristotle.

Aristotle regarded the mind (*Nous*) as divine, and it was *Nous* that built the bridge and connection between man and gods. According to him, the *Nous,* through rational thinking and logical reasoning, can activate in man the divine principle and bring him the experience of the ultimate bliss. Reason and logic lead to clear thinking, and only through clear thinking can man rise to a level high enough to explore the secret life of God. Aristotle not only accepted religion, but he also finetuned the concept of the "First Cause." According to him, as the universe was eternal and functioned on its own, the First Cause played the role of an "Unmoved Mover." He reasoned that the "cause and effect" argument inevitably leads to a starting point purely based on logic, and the Unmoved Mover – call it God – was needed to close the gap in the "cause and effect" argument. No metaphysical or mystical understanding was required here. It was a matter of logic and reason. Aristotle had a point – a point so strong that it hasn't lost favor with philosophers and religionists even today to defend the "God hypothesis" – that God's eternal and supremely divine existence can be deduced from logic. By the same logic, though, Aristotle questioned the existence and role of the Olympian gods but did not pitch for abolishing the cult of the Olympian gods. He understood that people had a yearning for gods and that respecting their way of worship did him and his philosophy no harm.

Aristotle was less interested in founding a new religion than understanding the mental phenomena underlying "religious experiences" that people perceived as a "heightened state" or "rapture." Like a modern psychologist, he doubted the existence of rapture or mystical experiences as independent phenomena except that they were names given to certain emotions and feelings. But he skillfully avoided targeting religion in his critique, feigning no interest in the affairs of religion and gods. Likewise, other philosophers of the 3rd century BCE like Zeno, Epicurus, Pyrrho, and others who made a tangible impact on the intellectual discourse of their day, avoided getting involved in the religious controversy.

Aristotle upheld, as mentioned in chapter 1, the views of Thales, Parmenides, Zeno, Anaximander, and others, making them the standard Creation Myth. Over time, this Greek myth became the mainstream narrative for more than two thousand years, finding its way into influential religious scriptures like the Bible and the Quran. Aristotle formalized his model of the Universe based on Anaximander's views, believing Earth was the center of the Universe, totally unmoving - the view also in line with Parmenides, another Greek philosopher who postulated the "static universe" theory that even Einstein feared to transgress. According to Aristotle, the Sun, Moon, and stars nested within invisible crystal spheres and moved around Earth; the Sun was the source of light, and the Moon, and the stars, were lit by reflected light. Aristotle viewed gravity as an attracting force that pulled everything to Earth and levity as a counter force that pulled things away. His premise that heavy objects would fly off into space if Earth were not the center of the Universe, forced him to conclude that to keep everything in place - that is, spheres within spheres - a greater than levity and gravity power held the whole Universe in place. He called this force the prime mover, the First Cause as mentioned a page earlier. It was this prime mover who gave life to everything there was. In the mind of a religious person, that prime mover is God.

Aristotle's most significant contribution – if it may called contribution, disservice maybe a better word to use – to the Greek civilization and the world lay in putting down a body of philosophical truisms - erroneously called principles - that remained unchallenged for more than 1,500 years. His thought, mostly conjecture, ruled the minds of philosophers, thinkers, and ordinary masses from the East to the West. Paradoxically, Aristotle's thought didn't influence significantly the immediate religious discourse of Ancient Greece, but the same can't be said of the sacred histories of later religions, especially the Abrahamic ones. His many unscientific truisms were carried in the scriptures of the Abrahamic faiths as gospel truths, hard to be challenged.

For the ancient Greeks, Aristotle's philosophy didn't matter much. They continued with the age-old religious rites, rituals, and festivals. Aristotelian thought really mattered when it came time for the Greek civilization's soft power. Aristotle's pseudoscientific nonsense quickly became common sense wisdom for the Middle Eastern and other cultures. The Greeks genuinely longed to control and contribute to world history through might and muscle in a meaningful way, but they collapsed and were lost to the winds of change. If anything Greek was to endure the weathering of time, it was that thought – Greek science – call it philosophy. It did some good to humanity, but it mostly stalled hard science's progress for nearly two thousand years. The ancient Greeks might have never contemplated anything like that happening.

Nevertheless, if the Greeks are remembered, it is because of the voices that spoke, albeit subtly, against the unfounded and erroneous religious beliefs of the Greeks. The world knows about Greek civilization because of the Sacrifice of men like Socrates, who sowed a seed of doubt in the people's minds about the infallibility of religion and religious taboos and dogmas underpinning the brutal religious politics. The politics of religion drenched poleis in human blood and threw the Greeks from one abyss to another. Violence is violence, and no amount of religious legitimacy and sanction can transform violence into virtue. Violence can never lead to peace, and any religion that, historically, embraced violence as its ideology – or part of ideology – to bring about peace and order in the society, was apt to fail. The Greek religion is a stark example.

Chapter – 07

Moses to Midrash

Kosher and the Kashruth

The Sumerian civilization that flourished on the ruins of Mesopotamia came to an end by the 3rd millennium BCE, jolted finally out of history by the Amorites. The Biblical books Numbers 13:9 and Joshua 5.1 tell us that Palestine was already inhabited by the Amorites and the Canaanites when the Israelis entered the scene. Scholars date this event to the 21st century BCE based on the evidence provided by the Egyptian Execration Texts. Archeological evidence suggests that the Canaanites occupied the fertile agricultural lands of Palestine and thus had every reason to flourish economically, culturally, and politically. Despite the intervening civilizational shocks, the cultural continuity seems to have remained unbroken up until 1200 BCE. In all probability, it was during this time that the distinctive cultural landscape of Palestine might have taken firm roots. The Old Testament speaks in no uncertain terms of this cultural Palestine of which the Patriarchs (Abraham and his progeny) were a part. Abraham is supposed to have lived somewhere around the 18th or 17th century BC. However, to ascertain the veracity of this claim, there is no record or evidence except what the Biblical sources offer.

Abraham supposedly left his town Haran at 75 years of age. Twenty-five years later, a son was born to him. He was named Isaac. Jacob was born to him when Isaac was sixty years old and later migrated to Egypt at 130. Scholars question this biblical story for its lack of corroboration with what the excavations at Jericho have revealed. Skeletons found at Jericho tombs demonstrated that the average life expectancy of the people when the Patriarchs supposedly lived was thirty-five years. The Patriarchs' exceptionally long ages can't simply be explained except as a story to suit a particular audience.

The biblical books (Genesis, Exodus, Leviticus, Numbers, and Deuteronomy) were written more than a thousand years after the Patriarchs (precisely toward the middle of the first millennium BCE). The story goes that Abraham left his birthplace in Mesopotamia, Ur, temporarily resided at Haran, and then migrated to settle in Canaan permanently. Abraham's grandson, Jacob, also known as Israel, migrated to Sheohem, present-day West Bank of Palestine. Jacob was luckier than his forefathers, who had one or two sons each. Jacob had twelve. The progeny of the twelve sons of Jacob came to be known in the Jewish traditions as the twelve tribes of Israel. They were compelled to migrate to Egypt when Canaan and its adjoining neighborhoods were reeling under hunger, impoverishment, disease, and death during a severe famine. By the time the descendants of the twelve sons of Jacob had multiplied, becoming twelve tribes, they had been enslaved by the Egyptians. Centuries later, in around 1300 BCE, Moses led these slave tribes out of Egypt to freedom. They now returned to Canaan only to vociferously claim their right as Abraham's only and actual descendants.

Going by their historical narrative, the truth was that Israelites had long ago ceased to be a homogenous people. They comprised nothing more than a loose confederation of various ethnic groups. Over the generations, the bonds of kinship had diluted, and the tribal affiliation was held intact only through shared customs, habits, culture, stories, and myths. Their religion was in many ways different from what Moses supposedly preached. Despite all the troubles Moses allegedly bore for them, he hardly found a sympathetic audience in them. They persisted with their reluctance to comply with what he taught and professed. The monotheism that Moses preached was, it seemed, foreign to them.

This brings us back to the biblical story detailed in the Book of Genesis (12:4). Abraham and his descendants lived in Haran, albeit temporarily. It is assumed that Haran is the biblical name of a Mesopotamian town now in Turkey called Harran or Eski-Charran. Interestingly, there is also a small town called Haran, far away from Turkey, in the summer capital of Indian Kashmir, Srinagar. According to scholars like Fida Husnain, Holger Kersten, and others, historical data and archeological excavations have provided some clues "that in around 1730 BCE" the wandering Hebrew or Jewish tribes "began to make their way towards Egypt under the leadership of Jacob" from Kashmir. Kashmir is a province of the northern Indian State of Jammu and Kashmir. The archeological evidence dates the Burzahom civilization of Kashmir to 3000 BCE, a touch older than the Harappan civilization. There are more profound than what meets the eye cultural similarities between the Kashmirians and the Israelites. The Jews are known for observing *Kosher* or *Koshur* dietary habits – a cultural legacy they call *Kashruth*. What is not so widely appreciated is that the Kashmirians are also very possessive about *Kashruth*. Like the Jews, it connotes a distinct cultural legacy, including dietary habits. Etymologically, the word "*Kashir*" or Kasher (Kashmir) is derived from *Kosher* or *Koshur*, and the Kashmirians are called *Koshur* (singular).

Holger Kersten writes, "The inhabitants of Kashmir [Kasher] are different from other peoples of India in every respect. Their way of life, morals, character, clothing, language, customs, and habits are all of a type that might be described as typically Israeli. Like present-day Israelis, the Kashmiris [*Kashurs*] do not use fat for frying and baking: they use only oil. Most Kashmiris like fish called *fari*, [eaten by Israelis] in remembrance of the time before their Exodus from Egypt." Furthermore, many Biblical names, especially towns and places, are still in vogue in the Kashmiri vernacular. These names have changed little. The towns like Agur (Agurn in Kashmiri), Ajah (Ajas in Kashmiri), Amariah (Amariah in Kashmiri), Amon (Amonu in Kashmiri), Aroer (Aror in Kashmiri), Baal-poer (Balpoor in Kashmiri), Beth-peor (Beth poor in Kashmiri), Haran (Haran in Kashmiri), etc. mentioned in the Bible haven't changed their names up until today. Similarly, the Biblical names of tribes, clans, villages, and geographical regions have persisted in the Kashmiri vernacular. On the contrary, there is hardly any biblical town or geographical area identified in present-day Mesopotamia (Iraq and Turkey) or the entire Middle East.

The Promised Land

Some scholars believe that Abraham might well have migrated from Haran of Kashmir to Canaan rather than from Harran (or Eski-Charran in modern Turkey). That, they say, is partly borne out by the existence of deep cultural links between Kashmir and Israel. For instance, the traditional dress code of the Kashmirians is similar to that of the Jews; and the age-old dancing traditions of Kashmirian women, the *roff*, can safely be called Jewish. During *roff*, the girls sing and dance in two columns facing each other, linking their arms, and moving forward and backward in rhythmic steps. Furthermore, after childbirth, a woman in Kashmir remains in seclusion for forty days for purification – again, a Jewish custom. At the end of the forty days, the woman takes a bath and becomes clean.

Take burial practice. The Islamic graves are peculiar because a side chamber is dug out in one of its walls where the dead body is laid in a North-South orientation. However, in Kashmir, there is also an age-old tradition of burying the dead in the so-called "Mosae Qabar" or Mosaic Graves that lack a side chamber. The present-day Mosaic graves no doubt face in a North-South direction, but many of the older graves unearthed in Haran and Awantipora and other towns of South Kashmir are oriented in an East-West direction. In one of the oldest cemeteries in Bijbehara in South Kashmir, a stone and a bath called Moses bath have been unearthed. Interestingly, here a Hebrew inscription was found in one of the graves.

Back to the Bible. After crossing the Sea of Reeds, Moses could well have led the Israelites to their destination via the northern route or Beersheba. Instead, he went South and ended up in the wilderness for 40 years (figuratively, 40 years may mean 40 ages!). The book of Deuteronomy (34:1-6) also tells us in great detail that Moses gave his last Sermon on the Mount of Nebo and looked over the Land of milk and honey one last time before he died, but the same chapter (34:1-6) adds, "... but no man knoweth his [Moses's] sepulcher unto this day."

It is a pity that Moses's grave hasn't been located either in Israel or elsewhere in the Middle East. If Moses were a historical person, surely he would have been buried with great pomp and show, and many would have attended his burial. The book of Deuteronomy, in a sense, hints precisely at that. It gives a detailed description of the place where Moses died. It mentions the names of places like Mount Nebo, the plains of Moab, Beth-peor, etc., where Moses visited. In the backdrop of a reasonably detailed discussion of Moses's death and his having looked over "the Promised land" from the mountain top of Nebo, why is it that his grave remains unidentified so far in the Middle East? Is it possible we are looking for his tomb in the wrong place? Or is it that the Promised Land doesn't belong where it is believed to be situated? That is to say, is the Promised Land, not the real one because the geographical landmarks of the Promised Land provided in the Bible have been ignored? Perhaps.

Mount Nebo and Beth-peor are two important landmarks mentioned in the biblical text. Holger Kersten writes that Beth-poer literally means "a place that opens up" – in other words, a valley. Behat-por or Beth-poor (homonym of Beth-peor) is the name, since ages, of a small yet broad valley at the termination of the river Jhelum (*Veth*) in Kashmir. The river Jhelum runs from the South to the North across the valley of Kashmir to fall into the famous *Wular* lake. The valley Beth-poor is formed by Jhelum just before it enters the *Wular*, 70 km north of the capital (Srinagar) of Kashmir. Presently there stands a modern town called Bandipur. To the North-East of Beth-poor and Bandipur, there is another small village called Hasbal (the biblical Heshbon) near "the slopes of biblical Pisgah (now also called Pishnag in local dialect)." Pisgah also forms a valley called the "Plains of Mowu" (it corresponds to the plains of Moab as mentioned in the Bible). On the North-West of the Plains of Mowu (Moab) is the Nebo Baal (Nebo mount), also called Niltop in the local dialect. It offers a view of the entire landscape.

The Book of Deuteronomy (34:6) says, "And buried him [Moses] in a valley in the land of Moab, over against Beth-Peor…." At the foot of Nebo mount, there is a village called Buth (Beth), barely 12 km from present-day Bandipur. In this village, on the foothills of Nebo, there is a stone column – the tombstone allegedly marking the grave of Moses. It is here, according to the local folklore, that Moses was buried. The descendants of one *rishi* family have been tending this grave for more than 2700 years. Geographically this location conforms to the biblical landmarks. In addition, other places bearing a connection with Moses are Muqami-e-Musa (Moses's Place), near Heshbon (Hasbal in local dialect); Sang-e-Musa (Stone of Moses), also known to the local inhabitants as the Bath-place of Moses near Ka-Ka Bal in south Kashmir; Kohnai-e-Mosa (Corner-stone of Moses) near Shadipor in north Kashmir.

Interestingly Kashmir is also known as Bagh-e-Suleiman (Garden of Solomon). In the summer capital of Jammu and Kashmir, Srinagar, the remains of a structure – called the Takht-e-Suleiman or the throne of Solomon – still stand for visitors to see. King Solomon is supposed to have stayed in Kashmir and built a channel through which water flows into one of the famous lakes of Kashmir, the *Dal*. It is interesting and curious that the tomb of Moses, Beth-poer, and Mount of Nebo, the Bath of Moses, Sang-e-Musa (the stone on which Moses allegedly sat), and the throne of Solomon happen to be in Kashmir. They speak of the deep cultural relationship that the Israelites have with the land of their ancestors, Kashmir. The accumulated dust of ages has obliterated history and turned brothers into strangers.

Which brings us, meanderingly, to the Promised Land. Historically, Mesopotamia has been considered the Garden of Paradise or Eden. The Book of Genesis (2:10-14) says that the Promised Land lay in a Paradise in the East where four rivers flow. However, there are only two rivers in Mesopotamia (modern Iraq) – the Tigris and the Euphrates – instead of the four mentioned in the Bible. In that four-river equation, Kashmir fits better. Apart from being historically famous as a land of milk, honey, and grapes, it boasts four rivers – Jhelum, Indus, Sendh, and Lidder. Kashmir is also – a perfect description of the biblical Promised Land.

Furthermore, in the fortieth chapter, the Book of Ezekiel says that the prophet Ezekiel had a vision or revelation from God in Babylon. He saw a particular temple in the Promised Land that he identified as the landmark for the final destination for the people of Israel. The temple he saw stood on a high mountain overlooking a magnificent river. Interestingly, in South Kashmir, a famous temple called the Martand Temple stands on a high mountain peak overlooking a spring and the majestic river, Jhelum. Researchers have unearthed ruins of older walls underneath this temple that predate the Christian era. Did Ezekiel mean the now-buried temple on which the present Martand temple stands? Perhaps. And this all squares well with the biblical geography of the Promised Land.

Am Yahweh

The Bible is a fantastic book. In reality, it sketches a story of an entirely new chapter in Middle Eastern religious thought evolution. God promised to give Abraham and his offspring mastery over the entire land of Canaan (Palestine). However, centuries later, the famine compelled these Abrahamic descendants to migrate to Egypt. They initially prospered there but eventually were enslaved by the Egyptians and forced to live miserable lives. Finally, in 1200 BCE, their god, known as *Yahweh* in the Bible, took pity on them and helped them achieve liberation from the cruel Egyptian subjugation. Moses – also from their tribe but miraculously saved by *Yahweh* from being murdered at the time of birth, as can be recalled from the previous chapter – was chosen by *Yahweh* to lead them out of Egypt and back to Canaan on the other side of the un-navigable Sea of Reeds. The

Yahweh did a miracle: He parted the Sea's waters for this flock of enslaved people to cross to the other side dry-shod. As the Egyptian army chased them, the parted waters rejoined and drowned them all with their King, the Pharaoh. *Yahweh* then made a covenant with these formerly enslaved people – now, people of Israel – on Mount Sinai, giving them "the Law." They were now the holy or "the chosen people," supposed to enter the "Promised Land." Here the story could end, except that it didn't. Like in any drama, the twist followed. Rather than being grateful to God, the Israelites allegedly transgressed. *Yahweh* punished them for their transgression, leaving them to wander for forty years in the wilderness searching for the Promised Land. Moses became severely distraught that his labor bore no fruit. Already an older man at the time of the Great Escape (Exodus), he died before fulfilling his dream of entering the Promised Land. So goes the story in a nutshell.

The Israelite folklore about Moses and his Exodus was carried down as the foundational scriptural truth in the Torah and retold in the subsequent Middle Eastern scriptures like the Testament and the Quran. The Bible's authors were less concerned about the narrative's historicity. For them, the epics and national sagas per se were more critical to establishing the Israelites' identity. Scholars doubt that the Exodus happened in the first place; they even dismiss the notion that Moses existed outside of the story simply because, as they argue, there is no direct or indirect evidence for his being a historical figure. Furthermore, there is no parallel historical evidence of Abraham, Isaac, or Jacob existing except for what the scriptures narrate. It is strange, many argue, that an event as grand as Exodus and the drowning of Pharaoh and his army in the Sea of Reeds doesn't find a place in the Egyptian records. Yet there is indirect but faint archeological evidence that a chunk of people who ultimately became the people of Israel may perhaps have come from Egypt and settled in Canaan. Indeed, some major demographic shifts due probably to mass migrations did happen during a period of crisis (13th through 10th century BCE) in the Mediterranean region.

Around that time (13th through 10th century BCE), the whole of the Mediterranean region was reeling under tremendous hardships created by hunger, famines, disease, and violence. The epidemics of the plague did take a heavy toll on human life. The primarily agricultural and pastoral economy was as inefficient as insufficient to sustain the demand for food and grains. Different tribes, clans, and communities fiercely competed over meager, even by the standard of those days, resources. The invaders, raiders, and looters lifted crops and livestock wherever possible. As crops and harvest were to be guarded against lifters, the people felt the need to build confederations between different tribes and villages. Cooperation against a common enemy among tribes who typically competed over ownership of lands for agriculture and grazing pastures was challenging. To survive in that harsh environment, the handful of Israelites desperately needed a new way of looking at the past, present, and future. They required the most cooperative effort to handle the challenge to survive. Creating a sense of identity was crucial to that effect, which compelled them to visit the past and, to borrow the phrase from Earnst Renan, get history deliberately wrong. Here the Israelites were quite successful. They created a religious-nationalist bond that helped different tribes to converge as a unit.

Over time the theological discourse evolved, allowing the Israelite religious elite to shape and structure the narrative robustly. By the time the Torah was written (a few centuries later), they vociferously proclaimed and insisted on their unique historical legacy and special relationship with their god. They became the first-ever people to experiment with monotheism successfully in a structured and systematic manner. The Israelites proved that monotheism was a viable option. That, however, doesn't mean that they were the originators of monotheism. No. According to the Middle Eastern religious narrative, there has been only one authentic religion of humankind since the beginning of the material world: monotheism. From this religious point of view, God himself had taught monotheism to Adam, the first man.

Yet, in recorded history, monotheism was first practiced by *Akhenaten*, the pharaoh from the eighteenth dynasty of Ancient Egypt. Traditionally, the Egyptians worshipped *Shu* or the Sun god. *Akhenaten* did not show much devotion to *Shu*. Somehow, it did not satisfy his curiosity or perhaps did not help him deal with the many challenges he faced as the ruler of an empire. Or, possibly, his rational personal inquiry into the creation mystery might have led him to contemplate seriously revolutionary ideas by the standards of his day. In his day, Thebes was the traditional capital city of ancient Egypt, and *Amun* was the city god. In honor of *Aten*, Akhenaten shifted the capital to another place he named Aket-Aten, the "One God." He claimed to have found the real God in his quest and wanted his people to believe he was in intimate touch with Him. He asserted that the idea of a change of capital was revealed to him by God. Initially, his new monotheistic religion was tolerant of other gods and temples, but things changed as they always do, later. *Akhenaten* turned his attention to rival religions: he prohibited the worship of other gods, got the idols of gods smashed and the names of gods erased from monuments – by definition, it was a form of religious fundamentalism.

He then resorted to violence to altogether suppress the traditional Egyptian religion. To some extent, *Akhenaten* could force the people into submission, but his persecution policy turned into an unwise and deleterious strategy in the long run for his newfound religion of monotheism. After his death, it too was buried in the grave of history. It remained buried under the sands of the hot and arid Egyptian deserts for the next thousand years. Ultimately, though, the Egyptians turned to monotheism again, but it was not the same monotheism that had originated on their soil.

Contrary to the Egyptians, the Israelites transitioned to monotheism slowly but steadily. They diligently worked on the ordinary folks through dialogue and discourse, only sparingly using coercion and force. They wisely factored in their disadvantageous position numerically, politically, and economically. So, religion was a priority for them but not the only one. They understood – and for good – that they needed religion, but they didn't need to live for religion. For Israel, the priority was to survive the onslaught of raiders, invaders, and marauders. To that end, they were hardpressed to strengthen their tribal ethos to glue together the miserably incoherent lot they were. Historically, social relationships and tribal bonding were mainly determined by kinship, especially in hunter-gatherer communities. That is not surprising, considering the small size of these communities, with their circle of interaction mostly limited to their immediate groups. With the settled lifestyle, group size increased, and the circle of interaction also widened slightly, though not hugely, because of the absence of efficient transport technology. Hunter-gatherers, for instance, traveled on foot, limiting their territory of influence to hardly ten miles in diameter. With the domestication of cattle some 10 thousand years ago and the utilization of beasts of burden for transportation of goods and crops, the sphere of human interaction increased. Taming horses further revolutionized transportation, drastically cutting the distance and bringing in many other improvisations. However, it was nothing close to the modern world's technology. Even in medieval days, when the means of transportation were far better than in ancient, man could travel no more than 1600 miles a year on average (1200 miles on foot and the rest by carriages). Compare that with the post-industrial world of today. It is unbelievable. In today's world, a human being traverses a cumulative distance of more than 60,000 miles a year on average (40,000 miles by automobile and the rest by train and airplane). It should not be hard to see that filial relationships alone can't sustain the complex interaction network in a modern society like ours.

In the barter economy of the ancient, tribal unity thrived on kinship. However as the size of the settlements grew, inter-tribal cooperation gained significance. Kinship alone couldn't maintain inter-tribal peace and harmony. Kinship needed to be augmented artificially to make it a more effective mechanism for inter-group unity. To that end, shared stories, beliefs, and religious affiliations became crucial to establishing artificial kinship to rally people for a common cause. For example, the Covenant of *Yahweh* helped extend a sacred kinship bond to all the twelve tribes of Israel. *Yahweh* became the undisputed high god of the Israelite community – in other words, a national God – giving the early Israelite settlers a feeling of belonging toward one another irrespective of blood relation. They now came to be "*Am Yahweh*," a community of followers of *Yahweh*, thus transmogrifying from a collection of a disparate and disunited conglomerate of competing tribes into a well-knit religious nationality.

Crossing the River Jordan

Ancient tribal societies lived in perpetual warfare and violence, making tribal confederation building a necessity rather than a luxury. If any tribes were attacked by an out-group, it was construed as an attack on the whole confederation, thus calling for collective action against the attacker. Such and other cooperative efforts helped strengthen the tribal bonds. No doubt, the economic gains lay at the heart of the confederations, but the matter didn't always end there. Brute economic gains alone, bereft of psychological underpinnings, couldn't always serve as a strong justification for violence for the simple reason that humans are susceptible to the moral aspects of their actions. Violence ultimately weighs down on our consciousness, and we invariably seek some moral justification for our actions. Here religion comes in handy. Like others before and after, the Israelites sought refuge in the religion of Yahweh. Now that they called themselves *Am Yahweh*, invoking god and customizing religion to their economic needs was far more straightforward. There was no need to pinpoint economic aspects when the "holy war" could serve as an excellent surrogate for rallying the masses to meet violence with violence. The "institution of the holy war" or *Harem* played a significant role in charting the course of Sacred histories of the Middle East as elsewhere.

Religion is a powerful motivating force to drive a sense of collectivism in societies. One of the reasons for the failure of purely economic considerations to rouse a streamlined collective response of the masses against others is the inequality in the distribution of wealth. In the older days, like the present, people who managed to grab significant shares of the profit invariably caused soreness in the eyes of the rest. The profit and loss tussle could quickly bring down the confederations. With religion, things are different. Here things allegedly done in the name of Yahweh, for instance, provide exceedingly better scope for creating a Temple economy to handle financial discrepancy within or between the tribal units or groups. By putting more stress on religion and Temple, economics took care of itself. The Israelites were correct in assessing the challenges they faced. Religion helped them kill two birds with one stone—nothing extraordinary, though. However, the Israelites' genius lay in inventing a robust form of religion structured around a uniquely imagined sacred esoteric cult. Their version of religion served them well in the harsh and challenging circumstances the Israelites found themselves in, providing them with a purpose to strive for and a rallying ground to cooperate against a common enemy.

The Israelites invented no ordinary religion. It didn't come to them spontaneously, as is erroneously thought by many. Rather their religion was a result of centuries of concerted experimentation. Scholars maintain that the Israelites turned to monotheism only after the 6th century BCE. Up until then, their religion and rituals were no different from those of the other communities or tribes living in and around Canaan. By the 6th century BCE, the transition to monotheism happened smoothly, as the changing socio-political and geo-political scenario in the 6th century BCE had created new pressures and frustrating challenges for Israel.

Contrary to the Biblical narrative, the historical evidence shows that the sacred history and the religious myths of Mesopotamia and Babylon did influence the Canaanite civilization and its spiritual evolution, and, as a result, the Canaanites developed a complex body of stories similar to the creation story of Babylon's *Marduk* and *Tiamat*. The Israelite folklore has it the best: Abraham and his descendants worshipped *El*, the high God of Canaan, who had two sons, *Baal* and *Yam*. *Baal*, the god of the storm (a warrior god), battled with *Yam* (the god of sea and rivers), defeating him in a decisive battle, but *El's* wife intervened and forced *Baal* to spare *Yam*, thus making it possible for *Yam* to threaten the Earth with floods and rains forever. The perpetual struggle between *Baal*, who made the Earth fertile, and *Yam*, who inundated the Earth with floods, became a recurrent theme in Canaanite mythology.

One day *Baal* dies and is taken up by *Mot*, the god of death and despair. When *El* learns about *Baal's* death, he comes down from his throne to save him (his son) but cannot. Then, *Baal's* sister and wife, *Anat*, seizes *Mot* and cleaves him with a sword snatching *Baal* away. Where *El*, the high god failed, *Anat* succeeded in reuniting with her beloved husband and brother, *Baal*. This reunion of Baal and Anat featured as one among the many religious themes of that day, ritualized by the Canaanites as the death of god, the quest of the goddess, and the return to the divine realm. Commemoration of the alleged "reunion theme" reminded the Israelite men and women to cooperate and share a struggle for the continuation of their race to spread on the Earth.

Scholars maintain that some earlier verses of the Bible, written somewhere around the 10th through 9th century, do, in fact, point to the possibility that Abraham also practiced the older religion rather than monotheism as claimed by the later writings of the Bible, especially those that were put down toward the end of the 6thcentury BCE. Later, as the cult of El merged with that of Yahweh, the former lost much of its significance; over time, it was totally overshadowed by the latter. *Yahweh* was initially depicted as a warrior god like *Baal*, or more like the Aryan cult of *Agni* and *Prajapatti*.

The Canaanites underwent a difficult transition between the 5th and 4th centuries BCE. Life was so violent that surviving was no less than a miracle. During these fragile times, the people desperately yearned for an invisible hand of support from on high to respond to violence with violence. Festivals and ritual processions came to be organized to hammer down religious messages into the hearts and minds of the people. It was then that *Harem* – fighting in the name of Yahweh – was made a sacred duty, the holy war or Jihad. Yahweh became the source of motivation and hope that kept the Israelites' fighting spirit alive.

It would be misplaced to view the Festival of Gilgal, commemorating the victory of Joshua, one of the four founding fathers of the Israelite nation (the other three being Abraham, Moses, and David), purely as a festival of sacrifice or prayer for economic prosperity. It was a ritual that, kind of, sanctified military campaigns. The recruits for war went through a purification ritual, underscoring fighting against the enemy as a religious duty, the holy war. These rituals contrasted the Hindu, Mesopotamian, and Greek traditions that primarily highlighted mythical sacred wars fought by gods. The Israelites showed no interest in celebrating mythic holy wars. The festival of Gilgal, for instance, commemorated the memory of a victory achieved by a historical figure, Joshua, in human time and space on this Earth. Even the songs and poems – like the Song of the Sea – chanted during the Gilgal festival dealt with the subject matter of human courage and victory. The "Song of the Sea" was later incorporated into the Biblical Exodus story.

The Song of the Sea described the miracle when *Yahweh* allegedly led the "chosen people" to the "Promised Land." They had been living in the wilderness for forty-odd years and had suffered immensely before they finally crossed over to Palestine under the leadership of Joshua. Originally the song depicted the story of Joshua's crossing the river Jordan to reach the Promised Land and his massacring of the local populace to settle the Israelites. It celebrated the so-called first victory of "Israel" when the odds were hugely against them.

The El

For long, the Israelites continued to acknowledge other gods alongside the supreme God, *Yahweh*. It was much later that they turned away from the cult of *Baal*, becoming strict monotheists only by the late 6th century BCE after *Yahweh* was officially canonized as the one, single God. However, it was hard to erase El from the scene quickly. His memory persisted, despite *Yahweh*'s rise to the status of the single omnipotent God. Yet the shift had become more explicit than in the 9th and 8th centuries BCE when the Israelites were generally reluctant to contemplate the idea of one god. By the 5th century, the religious discourse had almost morphed to speak about

God in anthropomorphic terms, as generally depicted in the Bible. By contrast, the 8th century BCE Bible was clearly hesitant to talk of God in anthropomorphic language. It didn't commit to themes like "God speaking to Abraham" or "God telling Jacob," etc. Attributing human qualities like speaking, hearing, or listening to God amounted to blasphemy. Until then, God was regarded only as an "essence" and thus lacked physical dimensions. The biblical authors circumvented this dilemma by introducing the concept of an intermediary – the angel – between God and Abraham. For instance, God talked to an angel, Gabriel, who then conveyed God's message to Abraham.

The prevalent Pagan religions of the day were still territorial in their character, i.e., a god's jurisdiction was limited to a particular temple of a village, town, or city, like in the Greek world and ancient Mesopotamia. In contrast, the Israelites were all set to make their god an omnipresent "universal deity" regardless of whether his Temple stood at a place or not. This significant paradigm shift paved the way for a much more profound transformation and evolution of the collective Israelite mind.

The Bible now boldly spoke of Jacob receiving revelations and experiencing spiritual epiphanies. It is replete with passages like: "when Jacob left Canaan, God promised him that He will protect him 'wherever he went;' when Jacob woke up from sleep at one place, so much overtaken by his dream, he identified that particular spot as "Bethlehem" or the house of God." The stone that he had used as a pillow was sanctified as a "marker stone" for Jacob's spiritual ascent. Jacob then made his god, *Yahweh*, his *Elohim* – meaning *Yahweh* would protect him and give him prosperity and everything he desired in the world and hereafter. *Elohim* is generally translated as "everything that God can mean to the human being." This trend-setting paradigm shift set the wheel of the future monotheist religious perspective and thought process into definitive motion.

The Torah says the Patriarchs had complete faith in *El* (God), not because they saw him face to face or could prove his existence but because faith in ***El*** worked for them as *He* took care of them – indeed, a pragmatic kind of religious thinking almost unknown in the global religious perspective and discourse up until that time. The Israelites substituted the new view for the ancient world view that "gods live in a metaphysical realm and the human beings only reenact the drama of the heavenly world." Furthermore, the Torah rejected the popular ancient theological view that gods were totally indifferent to what humans faced on Earth, for instance, death, deprivation, disease, hunger, violence, etc. Instead, it steadfastly shaped the concept of "faith," depicting Abraham as a prototype for "faithful." Abraham put unflinching trust in *El* (and then *Yahweh* of the later version of the Bible.) The Bible phantasmagorically demonstrated that the faith in El worked for Abraham and Jacob and all others who followed them.

When the Old Testament authors recounted the Patriarchs' story and their epiphanies and conversations with God, they didn't care about exact historical chronology; instead, they were driven more by storytelling to make their point about *El's* power and oneness. The events were recorded retrospectively, into far removed past of at least a thousand years prior. In the absence of written history, the scribes drew heavily on legends and folklore, conforming to the familiar religious discourse and thought process of the 8th and 7th century BCE Israel and caring less about the narrative's historicity. As a result, we have a scripture that is more a throwback of the 8th century BCE perspective into the thousands of years of the past than anything remotely akin to genuine history. We call it the Old Testament.

Take Exodus. It is the foundational story of the nation of Israel and Judaism. However, many serious modern scholars believe that the Exodus is a myth. Exodus didn't happen at all. But that is a different matter. The Israelites were not interested in what and when of the Exodus. They were interested in the story. The story of the Exodus and its aftermath may seem to modern scholars a saga of a discriminatory, jealous, or brutal God and his chosen people, but that is immaterial when faith comes in.

This story depicts *Yahweh* as passionately partisan, a behavior characteristically expected of a tribal god. The scholars maintain that initially, *Yahweh* was no more than a tribal deity, like the city god of Mesopotamia or Zeus of the Greek pantheon, who parted the waters of the Sea of Reeds to make way for his people to escape from Pharaoh. As they crossed over dry shod to the other shore, *Yahweh* drowned and killed the chasing Pharaoh and his army. *Yahweh* couldn't have acted otherwise. In a world of "your god, our god," it was too early to expect the ancient Israelites to contemplate the idea of a "universal god." For them, the choice of words was more important than the theological nitty-gritty. That *Yahweh* saved them and killed the powerful and the mighty carried more meaning than *Yahweh* being the God of the whole world. Despite what can be said for and against the Exodus story, it was a brilliant theme to ignite faith in *Yahweh*

– faith that made a deep and lasting impression on the people's mindset, especially the 6th century BCE Canaanites (Israelites). This story helped the later rabbis permanently implant the seed of monotheism in the fertile minds of the Israelite generations to follow.

The Israelites clearly and obstinately began to imagine that *Yahweh* was on the side of the impotent, the weak, and the oppressed. This theme and its later elaborate interpretation and representation inspired and impassioned the Israelites to establish a society where social justice based on faith in one God would comprise one of the essential governing principles. Toward the closing years of the 6th century BCE, monotheism was an official and authentic creed of the Israelites. For the first time in recorded history, the experiment of monotheism succeeded. There would be no looking back. Monotheism would now become the fulcrum of the sacred histories to follow. The credit goes to the Israelites (later Jews).

God and the Market

The Israelites, as mentioned earlier, were not the originators of monotheism. Before the Israelites, Akhenaten had advocated monotheism as such, but this Egyptian Pharaoh of the 12th dynasty fell in disfavor because of the force of the stick he used to make his subjects accept his idea of "one God." People resisted *Akhenaten*'s forced imposition of religion and persecution of other faiths. Approximately two hundred years after *Akhenaten*, an ancient Persian prophet, *Zarathustra* or Zoroaster, also protested against the prevalent Persian polytheism of his day. Like Akhenaten before him, Zoroaster proclaimed that there was "only one God, *Ahura Mazda*, and no other gods." However, *Ahura Mazda* initially didn't mean god. It simply meant "that who has no name, but embodies wisdom, truth, love, immortality, and all other attributes." That was something strange for the people in 11th century BCE Persia. It didn't register in their mind. Consequently, during the first ten years of preaching, Zoroaster managed to convert only one person to his creed. With Zoroaster's death, his version of monotheism was buried in the furrows of history.

The Israelites took a different but systematic approach to the "one God" idea. While *Akhenaten* and Zoroaster claimed their respective individual authorships over the concept of "one god," the Israelite thinkers and scribes considered monotheism a shared cultural legacy and doctrine. Accordingly, they brilliantly manufactured their scared history to serve that end. They fell back on the past to retrofit the events and conjure up a national history first, and only then, the national identity. Furthermore, they so meticulously constructed the sacred history that fact and fiction merged seamlessly into each other, becoming one story. Over time, the story was cast in stone, leaving no scope for aspersion. However, it didn't happen overnight. Undoubtedly, theology and doctrine evolved over a reasonably long-stretched period.

The steadfastness with which the Israelites worked on the project of national importance paid them dividends. It ensured their survival as a distinct religio-ethnic entity though at a humungous yet avoidable cost in terms of life and blood. History put them through insurmountable hardships and challenges on many occasions, but they did not lose their heart. In hard times, rather than retreating, they focused more intensely on their goal, working out their way pragmatically and relentlessly to take their experiment with monotheism to its logical conclusions. They laid the foundations of a pragmatic faith, theology, and concept of God that profoundly affected the future religious discourse and evolution of theism, at least in the Middle East. They successfully reframed the discourse about gods, angels, and high God. God became God, who looked at the Earth, helped the humans, showed concern, worked for them, and occasionally punished them for transgressions. The Israelites shrewdly avoided falling into the trap of metaphysics. Instead, they focussed on fine-tuning their idea of "one God" to fit with everyday life. So long as a particular theological idea worked for them, they stuck to it, yet they never hesitated to reframe even the foundational dogmas. The merger of *El* with *Yahweh* is one of the many examples of fine-tuning that ultimately resulted in the birth of the theology of an omnipresent, omnipotent, and omniscient or "universal God."

The Bible is a masterpiece of literature. It captures the ups and downs of this ongoing religious movement in such a masterly fashion that one can't help getting transported into the past. The events, as it were, seem to happen just before the eyes. *Akhenaten* and *Zarathustra* were born in the wrong places at the wrong time. Their revolutionary idea failed to capture peoples' imaginations. The Israelites' movement succeeded precisely because their leaders put all their imaginative might to work. They had to. Their license to survive in a world order governed by "all or none" and "an eye for an eye and a tooth for a tooth" principles was religion. Awareness of their weaknesses and fragilities sensitized them to seriously worry about their tribal cohesion and integrity. They succeeded in creating a robust mechanism of "thought control" through a sacred history built out of fiction. After all, it doesn't really matter whether the fact is born out of fiction or vice versa. What matters is what works better – fact or fiction? In the case of Israel, fiction worked pretty well. Yet they often missed out on the principle that "might is right" under the blinding influence of religion and repeatedly paid heavy prices. They should have known better.

In the Exodus story, the Old Testament subtly clarifies that the Israelites did not believe that Yahweh was the only God during Moses's day. Indeed worshipping one God was something that didn't come naturally to the Israelites. As described in the Book of Exodus, approximately one year after the Exodus, when the Israelites were encamped at the foot of Mount Sinai, God instructed Moses to build an Ark to commemorate the Covenant they worship only *Yahweh*. Many successive prophets, too, urged the Israelites to remain faithful to the "covenant" that Moses made with *Yahweh*.

By the 6th century BCE, the religious thought and discourse had matured enough for the Israelite tribes to have united under a single god. More than 600 years after the Exodus had allegedly occurred, almost all the tribes now subscribed to one God, *Yahweh,* their "Elohim." They were now the "Chosen People" of *Yahweh,* supposed to enjoy his "unique favors and blessings." But if they transgressed, they would suffer or even get destroyed. That was what the Covenant was supposed to emphasize. The successive Israelite prophets reinforced that message from time to time because, as was the case, people turned to *Yahweh* in times of distress and war; yet they quickly reverted to the age-old practices of worshipping *Baal*, *Anat*, *Asherah,* and other gods. Which fact mandated that the prophets and rabbis (Jewish priests) be on high alert, all along, to counter other cults through *Yahweh*-centered religious movement!

When Solomon wanted to build a sanctuary in honor of *Yahweh* in Jerusalem, a city captured from the Jebusites by his father David, he ensured that the new building resembled other temples of the Canaanite gods. This "Temple of *Yahweh,*" as it was called, housed in addition to the Ark of Covenant, an altar and a representation of *Yam* (primordial sea and god of destruction), and other Canaanite mythological gods, like *Asherah*. It took another four hundred years before the Pagan religion was wholly overshadowed by "monotheism" or the Yahweh cult. That the pagan cults were still prevalent despite the repeated warnings of prophets like Joshua, David, Solomon, Elijah, and others, was testified by the presence of relics and iconography of pagan gods in the temple of Yahweh – a temple that symbolized Yahweh's heavenly court on Earth.

A transformation occurred during those four hundred years from the 6th through 2nd century BCE. New ideologies came up. The religious discourse and theological debate subsequently took concrete shape, moving exceedingly closer to strict monotheism. Scholars claim that the relatively quick transition to monotheism during the second half of the first millennium BCE in ancient Palestine happened because, as Karen Armstrong puts it, "the new religious systems reflected the changed economic and social conditions." The kings and the chieftains still controlled economic machinery, but the balance of power was somehow beginning to shift due to improved trade with far-off regions. Due to its peculiar geography, the Middle East was always an important meeting point for trade routes crossing the globe from East to West and North to South. The improved trade changed the dynamics of the power structure here with a slow and steady emergence of a powerful merchant class. The wealth and power slowly shifted from the political establishment to the market, resulting in wealth getting distributed among more hands. The new wealth sparked new intellectual and cultural awareness resulting in ideas emerging and spreading through trade routes far quicker than in the remote past. Religious movements spread their influence faster and farther, and new religious perspectives overtook the older ones with comparative ease in the Middle East's emerging and rapidly developing markets. In the words of Karen Armstrong, "the idea of God" in the Middle East "like other great religious insights of the period, developed in a market economy in a spirit of aggressive capitalism."

Elohim, the King of the kings

By the 8th century BCE, two kingdoms established themselves in the strip of land southeast of the Mediterranean Sea. The Greeks called it Palaestinea (present Palestine and Israel). The Jews, Christians, and Muslims call it the Holy Land. It is synonymous with biblical Israel and includes parts of modern Jordan, Lebanon, and Syria. The northern part of the Holy Land was called the Kingdom of Israel, and the southern part was the Kingdom of

Judah. Powerful empires of the day surrounded these two pieces of land, and an atmosphere of violence and war prevailed in the region. The Kingdom of Israel became a vassal state of mighty Assyria, aggressively pursuing expansionist policy to subdue the neighboring kingdoms in anywhich way. Israel was forced to compromise. The Palace enjoyed prosperity, but the masses suffered. The Palace economy ensured wealth accumulated in the hands of an oligarchy of nobles and influential priests. That created strain and tension within the society as the peasants and workers, who fed the power structure, continued reeling under a tremendous tax burden.

King Jeroboam of Israel, a vassal of Assyria, was heedless. He levied exuberant taxes on the populace to pay tribute to the suzerain and maintain a standing army and bureaucratic machinery. As a result, the public felt increasingly alienated in that atmosphere of injustice prevailing in the northern Kingdom of Israel. They held Jeroboam responsible for all the mess. Economic exploitation suffered by the masses compelled them to latch on to religious pretexts. The prophets challenged the king in the name of *Yahweh*. Backed by the strong religious sentiment, they decried injustice as a blatant violation of the divine decrees. Soon the whole society was galvanized into action, mounting pressure on the Palace. The prophets, who claimed to receive revelations and orders from the divine, put out the word that God urged them to raise their voice against the so-called transgression by the king and the powerful elite.

The Israelites were already distraught over their vassal status, and their anguish against the foreign over-lordship and the political incompetence of Jeroboam had stupendously deepened. The economic exploitation of the masses hit the last nail in the coffin. Jeroboam's buckling before the Assyrian king and accepting the status of a vassal king was seen by them as a blatant negation of the unique position of the Israelites and the omnipotence of the Israelite god. It was an affront to their self-esteem. "Had *Yahweh* forsaken them, or was it that their misbehavior coupled with the transgression of their king had put the nation of Israel in a perilous socio-political situation?" they wondered. The prophets added salt to the injury by warning them of the perils of their chosen path in contradiction to God's commands. They prophesied failure and disaster. The wrath of *Yahweh* was to descend upon them. This time *Yahweh* would not be on the Chosen People's side as he had been at the time of the Exodus should they persist with transgression, they sternly warned. That was an ominous prophecy.

It was clear from the prophets' warnings that *Yahweh* demanded the Israelites mend their behavior rather than perform rituals. Otherwise, *he* was to wipe them off the face of the Earth soon. The prophets instilled fear in the hearts and minds of the people by spreading the narrative of "punishment by *Yahweh*.". They deliberately chose the new fear-based narrative to compel their audiences to do some introspection and seriously cultivate sympathy, justice, and feeling for others. "The change was needed," the successive prophets complained, "because the people did not understand [the essence of] the religion of *Yahweh*." Almost every prophet regretfully observed that there was nothing left of the religious ethos except the elaborate rituals. "Nothing was left of the religion" became a recurring theme, a leitmotif, for the rabbis and the holy men. This theme hasn't lost popularity with believers of all three Abrahamic faiths.

The prophets emphasized what the Israelites needed to do to save themselves was to "know the *Yahweh*" – although they never spelled out unambiguously what they meant by "knowing *Yahweh*." They sternly prohibited the Israelites from Pagan worship practices, clarifying that the sacrifices and festivals were not enough to save them and the Holy Land from impending doom. Only their steadfast loyalty to *Yahweh* could save them. Such and other rhetorics helped successfully introduce the fear-based "ethical dimension" in the Israelite religion. Along these lines, the overall religious thought of the Middle East continued to develop unabatedly from the 8th century BCE onward. These evolving trends of the sacred narrative are detailed in the Biblical texts of those years.

In the earlier texts, the Bible described *Yahweh* in anthropomorphic terms [a projection of human imagination], but in the later texts of the Bible, *Yahweh* became transcendent. While, earlier, God talked to the Patriarchs directly, later on, God was described as a mere "presence" and communicated with the same Patriarchs, prophets, and humans through the agency of an angel. The anthropomorphic characterization of *Yahweh* amounted to an abomination. God was wrapped in a shroud of mystery, creating an intellectual and logical gap between humans and heaven. God could not be seen or experienced directly by ordinary people; only the prophets could communicate with *Yahweh*, that too, through the agency of angels. Although sporadically, stories of some southern Israelite prophets also circulated that they allegedly saw *Yahweh* in their visions occasionally. But only a few such accounts were taken seriously by the majority.

Take, for instance, Isaiah. He was a Judean (southern Israeli) prophet. He claimed he had a vision wherein he saw *Yahweh* in a temple. He then interpreted his vision as a sign confirming that *Yahweh* was now not only the *Elohim* of Israel but the *Elohim* of the whole world. That was unheard of in northern Israel. Based on a dream, this 7th-century BCE prophet from the South made an extraordinary claim. He had a reason for that. Isaiah lived around 740 BCE when the politico-economic crisis in the "Promised land" was at its worst. Neighboring Assyria was a rising power; in 745 BCE, a new king ascended the throne in Assyria. He turned out to be a shrewd statesman who lost no time consolidating his power. At the slightest evidence of a revolt in the Holy Land, he replaced its vassal king with an Assyrian governor who almost devastated the whole countryside of the Holy Land.

The Assyrians' iron hand policy in dealing with the adjoining kingdoms of the Holy Land created havoc and terror. The populaces and the rulers of these lands were terrified and paralyzed with fear. In that world of harsh competition for food, tribute, and territory – a dog-eat-dog scenario at its worst – the Assyrians meted them out terrible violence and inhuman treatment to beat them into submission. They submitted.

After subjugating the northern kingdom of the Holy Land, the Assyrian king put his grander plans into action. He imposed a sort of "uniform civil code" to create what could be called a prototype of federal polity – that was to say, one empire, one economic structure, and perhaps one culture. However, the problem was that each society or urban center had its god; some worshipped a national God, *Yahweh,* for instance, of Israel; *Ashur* of the Assyrians themselves, and so on. The Chosen People viewed the subjugation of Israel and Judah as a severe blow to their self-esteem and an insult to their all-powerful god *Yahweh.* They believed no earthly power could conquer them while they enjoyed protection under Yahweh's blessed wing. But that was not to be. To their utter astonishment and profound disappointment, *Ashur* turned out more potent than *Yahweh.* The Chosen People were overcome by grief, disappointment, depression, and doubt. These were times of extreme worry and uncertainty for them. Their society slipped into despair.

It was then, around this time of national grief, that Isaiah announced that *Yahweh* sent him to rescue his "chosen people." He set out to revive their religion and cultural ethos. To set the record straight, He claimed

Yahweh himself had revealed to him that '*He*' is not only the God of Israel but indeed the "King of the kings" and the "God of the world." Since *Yahweh* was the "God of the world," implying, according to Isaiah, that *Ashur* was also subservient to the God of Israel, and thus by analogy, Jerusalem was safe. "The people of Israel and Judah need not worry," he assured them, as "the fall of the northern kingdom of Israel happened because *Yahweh* has sanctioned it to teach a lesson to the Chosen people." Isaiah insisted that the Israelites should not engage in politics; instead, they should have faith in *Yahweh* alone and surrender their ego to Him in humble acceptance of His lordship over them all.

Isaiah preached a form of patriotism that, on the face of it, looked like a form of surrender but was, in reality, deeply rooted in defiance and subtle arrogance. It was also an opportunistic religious compromise. The Chosen people clearly had a disadvantage in a political situation where the Assyrians were the victors. There was no point in projecting *Yahweh* as a superior god from a position of weakness. In such a case, Isaiah's vision and prophecies served as a terrific alibi for escaping from the truth. Rather than debate which god was more potent, it suited the bruised psyche of the Chosen people to accept the premise that *Yahweh* was the ultimate God of gods and it was his choice to put his people to a trial. That way, they admitted defeat without needing to acknowledge their god's failure.

To carry on with life and struggle against enemies, the Israelites had to change their perspective, or their religion had to change for them. Isaiah wanted them to change their attitude. And they obeyed. This specific vision of Isaiah, namely "Yahweh is the God of all gods and the world," would come in handy for the people of Israel to withstand the future turbulences that history had in store for them. It helped them to tide over the crisis at an individual and collective level.

Furthermore, Isaiah didn't have to wait long for his prophecy to be fulfilled. The events, as it were, vindicated his alleged revelations. He became a hero when the glory of *Yahweh* was celebrated in 701 BCE after the Assyrian army under the command of Sennacherib invaded Judah, the southern foothold of the Chosen people. There it was. At the last moment of the battle, the hidden hand of *Yahweh* played havoc with the rank and file of the Assyrian army. They were struck with a plague and annihilated. Isaiah's vision came true. Now it was difficult not to listen to Isaiah. He boldly announced that Yahweh ensured the invincibility of Jerusalem – His

Jerusalem despite all the odds. This remarkable turn of events would go on for a long to justify the defiance and chauvinistic attitude of the Chosen people, albeit to their disadvantage. In the times ahead, history would become more turbulent and bloodier. There would be plenty of misery, destruction, and desolation for the so-called Chosen people of God.

Exportable Religion

Toward the middle of the 7th century, the Assyrians were declining, and Egypt again began consolidating its position. In 656 BCE, the Egyptian Pharaoh Psammetichus, after decisively defeating the Assyrians, brought the kingdom of Judah under his control. Josiah became Egypt's vassal king of Judah. He proved a good administrator, and Judah enjoyed relative peace and prosperity under his rule. During his reign, a significant reformation of the Israelite religion happened. It was during this period that Judaism, the faith as we know it today, not only took its final shape and formally became a "religion of the Book," but the scriptural theology became established as an essential feature of the Middle Eastern religious movement.

Josiah turned out to be smart and shrewd. His well-laid-out strategy, it is believed, effectuated the ultimate metamorphosis of the Israelite religion into the "religion of the Book." That all started with his order to resume the repairing work of the Temple of Solomon. As the repairing work was on, the workmen stumbled on an old scroll. After examining the find, Josiah and the priests concluded that the scroll was the lost *Sefer Torah* (the original Law of Moses) given to Moses by *Yahweh*. Since this *Sefer Torah* had been missing for ages, the actual teachings written therein, they forcefully and convincingly argued, were never implemented in letter and spirit. So, Josiah, the vassal king of Judah, put in place a program for reimplementing the Torah under his watchful eye. Under this program, all the ancient cultic traditions of *Baal* and other Canaanite gods were strictly banned. *Yahweh* was officially decreed as the sole God to be worshipped by all the inhabitants of the Holy Land. In support of this decree, Josiah referred to *Sefer Torah,* wherein Moses allegedly had insisted that the people of Israel would show no mercy and pity for the indigenous population of the Promised Land and that their religion should be wiped out. This outrightly brazen religious fundamentalism and chauvinism didn't worry Josiah much. Nor did the fact that Moses claimed to have received the Law on stone tablets bother him. He pushed through his agenda.

Josiah then relaxed the rules of sacrifice and slaughter of animals. He allowed the slaughter of animals for the people living far away from Judah at their respective places of residence. Until then, the animals were slaughtered at the central temple of Jerusalem only, and people from far-off places would come and collect meat from the temple. Sacrifices could also now be performed at altars far removed from the central temple. The priests were assigned to spread the message and officiate at the sacrificial rituals in their respective neighborhoods.

Judges were formally appointed to arbitrate the disputes. The tribal leaders, priests, and kings were made answerable to the law. The king ceased to carry the epithet "son of God" with his name. The scribes and the learned scholars were assigned the job of rewriting Israel's history and amending the Bible's text to customize it to the 7th century BCE socio-political and cultural milieu. The Exodus story was retold in a new context. That is to say, the story of Joshua's triumphant crossing of the river Jordan was also incorporated into the Exodus story. The new version of the Bible (Torah) reflected more the socio-political expediencies of the 7th century BCE Judah than the foundational leitmotifs of ancient Judaism. The political expediencies also guided the rethinking of Israel's relation to *Yahweh*. The myth that *Yahweh* dwelled on Mount Zion was also challenged and reframed.

The scripture now made it mandatory to give charity to orphans, widows, and poverty-stricken. For the first time in history, enslaved people were given the right to attain freedom. The socio-political and religious reforms were aggressively pursued by the rabbis, scholars, and theologians under Joshua's tutelage. Judaism became the first religion to formally adopt a written scripture presumed to be the "word of God." Now there was no scope for addition or subtraction of the text. The world's first "religion of the book" became strict and inflexible; the "word of god" became infallible; even minor deviations from the book would be blasphemous. The Israelites now did not doubt the purity and veracity of their religion. The *Torah* became a reference book for all matters. Be that routine and mundane issues of their daily life religious and philosophical issues, or political matters of national importance, the *Torah* had the answers for all.

History is strange. It is like the ocean, apparently calm at the surface but turbulent deep down with its mindboggling theater of life and death playing out at full speed. As history was playing out, Judah looked calm, apparently, but storms were brewing in the vicinity. A new socio-political and religious era was about to usher in. after the Assyrians' downfall, it was now Egypt's turn to go under and Babylon's to reassert itself after a long slumber. Israel would get trampled over like grass and bushes in the fight between these two elephants. However, they were better prepared mentally for the events and consequences this time. They had already undergone a subtle yet empowering collective transformation – a transformation from the fatalist "Chosen People" into self-introspecting Jews. They now put more thrust on preserving and defending their religious identity rather than capriciously continuing in their delusion of being the unassailable chosen people of *Yahweh*.

The Jews had now developed a robust form of conservative-progressive patriotism. Their religious discourse had shifted from the Temple of Zion to the *Torah* following the revolution set into motion by Josiah and relentlessly carried forward by the prophets. The Jewish prophets were no ordinary seers or enlightened individuals but men allegedly selected by *Yahweh* to convey *His* messages and prophecies to the Jews. "*Yahweh* chose whom *He* wanted to make a prophet to guide and lead the people on the path to righteousness" was the standard narrative the Jews believed in quite sincerely. The revolution in religious thought transformed Judaism as much as the Jewish concept of God. Hitherto the Israelites' ancestors had faithfully believed that *Yahweh* dwelled in the Temple of Zion in Jerusalem and thus protected them from all enemies; as long as *Yahweh* stood there in the temple, they believed, they were unconquerable. No enemy could be so powerful as to overthrow and overpower the Chosen People of *Yahweh*. They firmly believed that *Yahweh* promised the Patriarchs that a whole nation would prosper from their descendants. *He* was their protector, God, thus ensuring their safety, survival, and prosperity. But that was not to be. History happened otherwise. The Jews had begun to reconcile with reality and acknowledge their delusions and started to respect others' delusions. But they hadn't yet completely weaned themselves off their religious fantasies fully.

History has no friends or foes. It is merciless in its indifference toward the events. It doesn't regard one sacred history as superior to the other. The Jews got it late. History works through might and mind. Only those tribes, peoples, and nations get it to the top that learn to introspect, look for gaps, and try to fill them wisely. When history provided the Israelites with an opportunity, they fled out of Egypt to freedom. But they afterward allegedly blundered and landed in the wilderness for forty years till Joshua led them across the river Jordan into the Promised land, Canaan. In a fit of aggression and envy, they indiscriminately put to the sword the inhabitants of Canaan (older Israel) and its adjoining lands, massacring and driving them away. They usurped their lands and settled there. Yet they could not enjoy a peaceful life in their Promised Land. They endured severe hardships, misery, and misfortune, holding on literally by the skin of their teeth till the 7th century BCE.

As per the Israelites' belief, *Yahweh* lived amongst them in the Temple of Zion. Their religion revolved around the temple cult of *Yahweh.* They believed and accepted that Israel was conceivably invincible since their God was their most reliable protector against all invading enemies. To their dismay, things happened contrary to their beliefs and expectations. Their faith turned out to be nothing more than a delusion. History took a merciless turn. The kingdom of North Israel, as can be recalled, was razed to dust. The Israelites were deported, exiled, and also put to the sword. *Yahweh* and the Temple could not save them. They were thrown out to scatter on the globe. The only thing they could do now was to nostalgically look back to the kingdom of Israel and the temple of *Yahweh* and yearn to return once again to the promised land of their ancestors. Unfortunately, their yearning remained only yearning. Time played its age-old trick, and they assimilated into foreign peoples and cultures, and with that, the first batch of exiles disappeared in the fog of history.

The southerners (Judeans) learned a lesson from the tragic story of their northern brothers. They won't take things lightly. Yet, despite perceiving, and rightly so, the need for a robust edifice of religion and philosophy to save their ethnocultural identity, they failed to acknowledge *Yahweh's* powerlessness in protecting them from catastrophe. Their hubristic self-aggrandizement blinded them. Nonetheless, their hubris was not entirely unfounded. They faced tough questions: Was the "cult of *Yahweh*" a myth? Was their entire "sacred" history and religion a myth? Was their monotheism a simple fraud? – These and other questions undoubtedly stirred, shook, and jolted them. However, after the fall of the northern kingdom (or Israel proper), the situation became tense, depressing, and grim. Pressures mounted tremendously. A bit of introspection was, all the same, not out of place.

As can be recalled from a couple of pages earlier, the unearthing of the *Sefer Torah* during the repair work of the Temple of Solomon marked a turning point. Some believed it to be a trick played by Josiah, the king of Judah, but all the same, a fantastic one that helped solve much of the Judean Israelites' dilemma. It is alleged that he had deliberately planted these scrolls in the temple basement so that the repairers would inadvertently stumble on them. His plan worked. When the workmen noticed the scrolls lying there, they reported to Josiah. He quickly summoned his commissioned priests and rabbis to announce that the workmen had dug out the *Sefer Torah* (the original book of Moses.) This fateful event laid the foundation for a decisive transformation to establish a systematized and formal religion known as Judaism. With that, the people of Judah became the Jews.

Judaism was born only in Judah. Its further evolution happened in Babylon and elsewhere, where the Jews lived in captivity and exile. When Judah was invaded by the Babylonians and the Jews were thrown out, they were compelled to reframe their faith and customize it to changing circumstances. It was still fresh in their memory how their northern brethren had got lost and assimilated in the foreign lands. They didn't want to meet the same fate and decided to resist their assimilation into pagan ethnicities. However, that was easier said than done. Yet, under the visionary leadership of Josiah, the Judean Israelites had undergone a paradigm shift, and Judaism had already become a reasonably accommodative religion in its character, outlook, and philosophy. Judaism's well-thought-out and pragmatic reformation ultimately proved pivotal to the survival of the Jewish diaspora. This religion no longer remained chained to the Jerusalem Sanctuary and the Yahweh cult. It could now be carried through books, moral code, and the self-discipline of the Jews to places as far away from Jerusalem as today's Afghanistan. Judaism had metamorphosed into an exportable religion.

Exile, Synagogue, and Prayer

In 612 BCE, Assyria received from Babylon a fatal blow from which it never recovered. Judah automatically fell into the hands of the Babylonians. The Judeans, as usual, resisted the Babylonian over-lordship and mounted a rebellion – a foolish thing to do for a weak people. Emotionally traumatized, they forgot how big a price their northern brothers had paid for their foolishness decades back. The Northerners were battered, crushed, and finally eliminated. Now it was the turn of Judah to face humiliation, captivity, and deportation due to their idiotic stubbornness to fight a futile war against the mighty Babylonians. They sacrificed their lives and blood to earn nothing but exile and enslavement. In hindsight, it seems the Judeans could have acted a bit more patiently had they willed to be logical. They could buy time. They chose not to. They put all their eggs in one basket - the basket of religion that, to them, was infallible. Their leaders foolishly rallied the populace against the enemy in the name of religion - which had become an institution in itself - evoking a sense of nationality in Jews. They slipped into a fatal error that could perhaps have been avoided. Like their forefathers, they overestimated the power of their religion vis-a-vis their political enemy. Religion could, of course, help them rally behind a cause but that alone was no license to win a war. Winning required improved technology, fighting might, and adequate resources. *Yahweh* had provided them with none of them. Even in numbers, they fell behind. Yet, blinded by their religious zeal, they fatally underestimated the battle-hardened Babylonians' power, might, and ferocity. But then, when religious zeal fires up emotions, rational thinking gets clouded.

In 597 BCE, after three years of attritional fighting, Judah fell. Nebuchadnezzar evicted thousands of ring leaders and rabbis of Judah and sent them packing to Babylon as slaves. By the standards of the ancient world, Nebuchadnezzar was still a merciful way of dealing with the vanquished peoples. He could have completely annihilated them. He didn't. The Jews reckoned Nebuchadnezzar's forbearance as a mark of his weakness. They rebelled again within less than a decade, this time in league with the Egyptians. In 586 BCE, now Nebuchadnezzar laid a siege that lasted six months. This time Jews won't be spared. The puppet king and his sons were arrested. While he stood chained, his sons were put to the sword in front of him. His eyes were then gouged out before he was left to die - horrible, by any standards, a punishment. The Jews were deported to Babylon en masse. Only the poor and the sick were left behind to die of disease and hunger. The Jews, thus, destroyed themselves, their land, and their property. In their stupid arrogance, they refused to acknowledge that Judah was a small stretch of territory compared to the Babylonian Empire. In no time, the bustling Jerusalem was razed to rubble.

The adamant Jews ceaselessly harped on the same old trite conjecture that *Yahweh*, the all-powerful, universal God, intended to teach them a harsh lesson. Rather than acknowledging their foolish attitude, they construed the two recent defeats at the hands of the Babylonians as nothing but *Yahweh's* good intention to cleanse their sins. Nothing could shake their belief that Jerusalem was invincible as long as *Yahweh* dwelled on the Mount of Zion. So the remaining Jews rebelled the third time. This time, the Babylonians won't listen. They would finish Judah once and for all. The temple of Jerusalem was razed down. With that, Judah came to an end. Literally.

For 136 years after the fall of the northern kingdom, Judah strived to hold on but failed to withstand the assault of history. In that one and a half-century, Judah doggedly pursued single pronged agenda: to build organized religion and theocratic polity, irrespective of the geopolitical realities of the day. It found itself on the wrong side of history as the Egyptian empire fell. Babylon accomplished a significant military feat after 13 years of the campaign, finally crushing and breaking Judah into bits and pieces to bite the dust. Judah was put to the torch. The temple was destroyed. Everything that stood was razed to the ground. Smoke, dust, and debris, we are told, were seen by the mile. Judah was left desolate, numb, and lifeless. The Jews were evicted and forced to leave everything behind to consume in the raging fires. The Babylonians did all they could – break, vandalize, and burn everything that came their way, leaving almost nothing erect. They quite literally destroyed everything the Jews possessed, everything except one—the commitment of the Jews to their religion.

While in exile, the Jews engaged in profound contemplation. They channeled their nostalgia for Jerusalem and the Temple into a determination to set to work on the new chapter of their genuine and sacred histories in the land of exile, right under the nose of the mighty Babylonian Empire. The Babylonians turned out magnanimous. They treated them well; at least they didn't subject them to slavery. The Jews were allowed to establish their ghettos. Living in ghettos, however, was no guarantee against assimilating into other ethnic groups. What they needed most was a robust sense of brotherhood built on shared stories and shared religious-cultural ethos. Luckily, by now a comparatively polished and theologically robust religion, Judaism undoubtedly provided the much-needed glue to hold the Jewish diaspora connected at a deeper level. In contrast to the older version of

Judaism – which was bound and tied in space and time to the temple of Zion in Jerusalem – the new version had evolved a more accommodative doctrine. And more evolution was to come.

As can be recalled, the old Israelite religion was more a cult of *Yahweh* than a religion in the strict sense. One of the central themes of that cult was the ritual of sacrifice. Sacrifice could be performed only in the Temple in Jerusalem. The old religion had no scope outside the kingdom of Judah. It was strictly restricted to the territory of the Holy Land by dint of the Central Temple of *Yahweh* in Jerusalem (the Mount of Zion). In a broader sense, the Yahweh cult resembled ancient Mesopotamian and Greek religions of "city gods" more than Babylonian Judaism.

By the 6th century BCE, the geopolitical situation in the then-Middle East had become dangerously uncertain and volatile. After the annihilation of northern Israel, the people of Judah (now called the Jews) came under tremendous pressure to redefine their cultural and socio-political ethos. To catch up with changing scenarios, they quickly latched on to religion. In that process, they ended up redefining, rethinking, and revolutionizing their sacred history. The political agenda pushed through by Josiah, for instance, culminated in a well-organized religious reformation movement which in the next 136 years resulted in the creation of an exceedingly evolved organized religion – Judaism. In the formation of Judaism, the Jewish prophets (originally meaning wise men) played a pivotal role.

It wasn't easy for the Jewish prophets to talk the people into changing their beliefs and behavior. In the 6th century BCE Judah, preaching against a well-established and powerful cult meant treading a woefully dangerous path given the emotionally charged, deeply conservative society that Judah was. It would be pretty frightening for the folks even to contemplate abandoning what they believed in for generations. Given the Jews' mindset, would they be receptive to lofty ideas and novel concepts when they were essentially programmed through the ages to follow certain fixed principles? That was a tricky question for the reformers to handle. They knew that frenzied mobs killed some prophets for challenging the dogmas. Understandably, the prophets were careful to pronounce any ideas as their own lest they could be lynched. Yet, in that superstitious society, the ticket to safety was to communicate in metaphors, similes, and double entendres; invoke miracles, and make preposterous claims like receiving revelations from God. Such proclamations by the seers and prophets quickly struck a chord with the credulous minds. They gave in. And listened to the prophets, even enjoyed their talk. Perhaps.

In essence, the prophets urged the people to abandon the "Yahweh cult" that revolved around Sacrifice and the Temple of Jerusalem. It was too much to ask of people, especially the priestly class. It could easily have led to sectorial violence and bloodshed in Judah, given that there was no dearth of deeply committed and hardcore adherents of the "*Yahweh* cult." Yet the Jews, overall, adapted and reconciled to the novel concepts and percepts. When Judah fell to the Babylonians, the Jews were already fully prepared to regard Judaism not as a religion bound in time and space but as a universal faith that no longer needed a sanctuary or a temple for *Yahweh* to reside in. They were also prepared to accept that God did not require sacrifices; hence, it was no sin to abandon the Sacrifice ritual. The actual sin, though, as the prophets told them, was corruption, injustice, immorality, and disregard for humanity. The prophetic messages also transformed the role of priests. They now became "rabbis" or teachers of religion. Soon a considerable body of literature followed that permanently transmogrified Judaism into an institution in its own right.

The evolution of Jewish religious thought and discourse touched its zenith in Babylon. The Jews adopted new ideas, and the "cult of the Temple" and the "cult of *Yahweh*" were done away with, though not altogether. It was there in Babylon that the two most important tenets – Synagogue and Prayer – of Judaism originated. This Jewish invention, Synagogue, and Prayer – the landmark ideas of Babylonian Judaism – was destined to shape the religious outlook of the Middle East and the world at large in the following centuries. After their return to Judah during Cyrus the Great's reign over Babylon, the synagogue (the prototype for the Christian and Muslim places of worship and prayer) became a place for a religious assembly where the rabbis freely interacted with the people and taught them *Torah*, prayer, religion as well as politics. "Every morning," we are told in *Jerusalem-The Biography* by Simon Montefiore, "the trumpets announced the first prayer, like the muezzin of Islam. Four times a day, the blaring of the seven trumpets called the worshippers to prostrate themselves in the Temple." Later the Jews, wherever they lived, would pray only three times instead of five times a day. The synagogue and prayer gave Jews a sense and feeling of freedom from the rigid shackles of the cult of *Yahweh*. Now a Jew was symbolically free to communicate with *Yahweh* anywhere and everywhere. That created in them a sense of belonging in a distinct racial, ethnic, and religious-cultural group.

Furthermore, it assured their unity through a deep sense of religious nationalism. They began to consider themselves a distinct civilization possessing a resilient, accommodative, and exportable religion yet lacking overt iconography—a totally invisible faith. And, above all, Judaism could now be proselytized.

Yet, they never faltered in their belief that *Shekinah* - the Holy Spirit - resided in the ruined Temple on the Mount of Olives. Their longing for Jerusalem never diminished. Wherever they lived, they prayed three times a day, "May it be your will that the temple be built soon in our days." In *Mishnah*, we are told, they compiled every detail of the Temple ritual, ready for restoration. Each Passover Seder dinner (an annual feast and ceremony of retelling the story of the liberation of Israelites from slavery in Egypt, the Exodus story) ended with the words: "Next Year in Jerusalem." Jerusalem ceased to be a mere terrestrial town. It became a spiritual city. The Jews who lived far away wanted to be buried close to Jerusalem so that they would be the first to rise again on Judgment Day.

Word of God and *Midrash*

During the fifty years of exile in Babylon, the Jews underwent a physical and spiritual metamorphosis. They engaged in trade and flourished in it. In the libraries of Babylon, they dove into literature and internalized a wealth of knowledge. Their perspective changed. Their relationship with the Temple of Zion and Jerusalem was recast contextually, as mentioned earlier. Amidst all this positive change, as it were, history took yet another unexpected turn. In 560 BCE, the great Babylon - where Judaism attained its maturity - crumbled before the Persians. Its fall was steep and quick, as was its rise five decades earlier. This time it fell conclusively, never to rise again. Nothing survived of the great empire of Babylon except, paradoxically, Judaism. All the rest evaporated and vanished, leaving almost no trace of its existence. The death of the grand kingdom of Babylon marked the beginning of a new chapter in Jewish history. Unexpected to them, Cyrus permitted the Jews to return to Judah.

No sooner than many of the deportees had settled into the public life and trade, there was this call for a return journey to Judah. The newfound freedom jolted the Jews into a frenzy. For a fair chunk of the prosperous Jews, it was hard to leave behind their possessions and embark on a return journey. For them, freedom meant punishment.

Subsequently, not all returned to Jerusalem. Most of the Jews stayed, and many came to occupy high posts under the Persian Empire. Some joined the army and fought alongside the Persian rank and file; others joined the civil administration and proved very efficient; the rest continued in trade and business. Only a minority comprising mostly overzealous and religious conservatives returned to Jerusalem. As Cyrus the Great had rightly predicted, the Jews reconstructed and resettled the town and Temple of Jerusalem again. But the matter didn't end there. The more significant challenge was to follow: how to protect the Jewish race, identity, and civilization from assimilation and annihilation. It was an enormous task to accomplish. It was this enormity of the task they faced that inadvertently compelled the Jewish leaders to plant the seed for the later day Zionism in the collective Jewish mind.

The Jews established the office of the High Priest and obtained permission from the Persians to run this religious institution and follow a model akin to "Self-Government in Exile." The establishment of the office of the High Priest and self-government were just two of the significant historic achievements of the Jewish diaspora. Incidentally, two and a half thousand years later, the Tibetans adopted the Jewish model of Self-Government in exile. The return of Jews from Babylon to Jerusalem, popularly known as the Second Exodus, happened in two phases. One Ezra organized the second phase of the departure of the Jews to their homeland in 458 BCE. Ezra successfully cooperated with Nehemiah, who had handled this exodus's first phase and settled in Judah. It was during and after the Second Exodus that some of the most significant events of the Jewish socio-political and religious history took place. For instance, during the first phase of the second exodus, the Jewish leaders demarcated the geographical and political boundaries for their future homeland. When the second phase of the exodus was completed, the spiritual framework of the City of Heaven (Jerusalem) was laid down.

The rabbis now promulgated an ordinance banning intermarriage between Jews and non-Jews. (Interestingly, the Tibetan government in exile also forbade intermarriage of Tibetan refugees with other ethnicities). The ban on intermarriage, the first of its kind in history, was formally sanctified and established as one of the essential tenets of Judaism. It was a well-thought-out defense mechanism against any future religious-cultural dilution and assimilation. For the Jews, it was a landmark religious legislation that ensured their identity as a distinct ethnic and religious group. Later, Islam would adopt this law, albeit with a modification, to safeguard the newly established community of Muslims against possible demographic and religious-cultural dilution.

Ezra and Nehemiah made quite a duo in Jerusalem and brought many sweeping reforms to Judaism. One of the first things they ensured was the formal canonization of the scripture. The Book of Deuteronomy compiled in Josiah's time was revised and updated. Four more books were added to this compilation. The collection of these five books – Genesis, Exodus, Leviticus, Numbers, and Deuteronomy – is known as the *Pentateuch.* This collection of books came to be formally acknowledged as the "word of God" – the *Torah* –ascribed to Moses. Thenceforth no alterations were allowed to be made in the *Torah.* The canonized scripture was only amenable to interpretation or Exegesis. The concept of Exegesis didn't remain limited to translation and interpretation of the *Torah;* rather, it evolved into a well-organized *Midrash* (School) movement. That is to say, schools shot up everywhere where *Torah* was taught, and the students were trained in the principles of Exegesis. These schools produced formally trained interpreters or "exegetes" who came to command respect and regard in the Jewish communities. The concept of Midrash later metamorphosed into the *Madrassa* tradition in Islam.

It turned out that the Jews carried from Babylon to Jerusalem not only a refined version of Judaism but also the love for books they had cultivated in the Babylonian libraries. This love for books brought to the fore the stimulative intellectual life in Jerusalem. Synagogues were built in Jerusalem, where there were none. Soon they thrived there side by side with the Central Temple, practically transforming Jerusalem into a city of synagogues. Such a transformation was unimaginable before the exile of the Jews. It was preposterous to think of something like a synagogue alongside the Temple of Jerusalem. But that was then. Now the Jews had changed, the Yehwah cult had become Judaism, and Jerusalem followed suit. The synagogues wielded a manifestly colossal influence over the Jewish communities. They became places of learning, assembly, discussion, and debate; brainstorming sessions would now take place in the synagogues. These debates helped refine many other aspects of the everyday practice of religion, prayer, and liturgy. The Jews were the first to compile prayer books for congregations and services.

Furthermore, this remarkable Synagogue institution made possible concepts like universal education program, freedom of assembly, self-governance, etc. It would take centuries for other nations to understand, adopt, and practice such concepts. But the Jews had them all even before the Greeks stumbled on dialectics, rhetoric, or stoicism.

Jerusalem became a buzzing seat of learning and intellectual activity. The Jews created a high standard of education and religious practices. Economically too, they improved. As they were almost touching the pinnacle of economic prosperity, history took yet another turn. Jerusalem got entangled in a bloody saga that would last no less than three hundred years. Finally, by the middle of the 1st century CE, the Romans destroyed the Temple of Jerusalem – the monument the Jews had built over the years– and the Jews were thrown out of Jerusalem again. Jerusalem was renamed *Palestina* by the Roman Emperor Hadrian after the Philistines, an ancient tribe of Canaan. With that, the intellectual life of the exhausted and fatigued Jerusalem received a severe setback from which it could never recover completely. Not at least for the next one thousand-odd years. Expelled, the Jews again turned to Babylon. To their chagrin and disappointment, the old Babylon no longer stood there. It had long vanished in the dust. The by-now-exhausted, battered, and penniless Jews were in no position to do anything for Babylon to reclaim the old glory, yet they never lost hope. By dint of their persistence, pursuance, and perseverance, they converted Babylon into a hub and repository of Jewish learning. It remained so, at least, for the next one thousand years.

Chapter – 08

The End Time and Jesus Christ

Cyrus and Alexander

By the 5th century BCE, Greece was politically, culturally, and economically at its zenith. Philosophy, mathematics, astronomy, and rhetoric were flourishing. Greek thought and philosophy were fast making inroads into other cultures and territories through trade routes and caravans. All in all, the proverbial Golden Age of Greece was at hand, except that there was a stone in the Greeks' shoes, hurting and annoying to the extent that leaving it alone was not a sound geopolitical strategy. The proverbial stone in the shoe – the Persian Empire – needed to be attended to, to prevent it from potentially excoriating the heart of the Greek power and civilization. The Persians posed a serious threat to Greek supremacy; lurking in the thickets of the East, they eyed the Greeks' wealth with envy, waiting like a greedy fox for the cover of the night. They didn't miss a beat to mount their attack when the opportunity showed up, confident of squeezing the Greeks into submission.

History is funny. It blatantly disregards linearity and order thrust on it from the outside. It has a habit of carving out an order in its peculiar way, ignoring all external calculations and permutations. Despite all the caprices history respects skills, discipline, and precision. The Persians missed out here. They underestimated the grit and resilience of the Greeks and woefully mismanaged their whole operation. A relatively small contingent of the battle-hardened Greek warriors (Athenians) annihilated their colossal army both on land and sea. That happened in 490 BCE at Marathon, one of the decisive battles of the world. After this humiliating loss at Marathon, Darius, the king of Persia, was preparing another expeditionary force to teach the Greeks a lesson when he died in 486 BCE, leaving the war project to his successor Xerxes.

Xerxes lost no time. He called on all the nations of Asia to contribute warriors to his fleet of soldiers in the name of the Zoroastrian god *Ahura Mazda*. In response, the Greeks called a Pan-Hellenic Congress to consider the threat. The Congress agreed after careful consideration that Greece must be "defended from the north down," "which could be done in the narrow seas and narrow passes," writes Ian Fellowes-Gordon in his essay in *100 great Kings, Queens and Rulers of the World*. To that end, they readied a naval force of 5,000 men under the command of Spartan king Leonidas to hold back an army of 700,000 Persian soldiers at the narrow pass of Thermopylae. But Leonidas was betrayed by one of his fellows, Ephialtes, who defected to the Persian side for gold offered to him as a bribe.

Leonidas was killed in the battle, as the Oracle had allegedly prophesied. Xerxes was upbeat. Pouring libation to the rising sun, he promised his generals that he would destroy the infidel Greece forever. And yet, as the sun rose high, the character of the fight changed. A few hundred remaining Greeks facing certain death "determined to die well; taking ten, fifty, a hundred, each of the enemy [soldiers] with them before they could fight no longer." "They inflicted such shocking casualties on the Persian hordes that, in order to get these into battles, the Persian commanders were forced to drive them on with whips."

Finally, when Themistocles of Athens rushed with his fleet toward the Island of Salamis in the Saronic Gulf, the last defense of the famous Isthmus of Cornith, as the Persians bottled up their ships in that narrow pass, his men smashed them, ripping them to bits. Xerxes received a severe blow at sea. But it was the final defeat in the land battle of Plataea in 479 BCE, from which the Persian empire never really recovered. Emphasizing the significance of Greek victory, Ian Fellowes-Gordon emotionally notes, " But Greece went on, from losing this battle so heroically, to winning the war, and we cannot leave this description of Leonidas and his battle without taking notice of the probable outcome. For if that war had been lost, the whole of Greek civilization would have been lost with it. We might now, in Britain, as all over the continent of Europe, share an Asian culture and speak in Asian tongues. But this was not to be."

For the time being, the Greeks' great anxiety was quite over. The Persians retreated, totally disgraced. The Greeks left the things there, thinking it futile to chase the retreating Persians; instead, they took to celebrating the victory and returning to their favorite past-time – fighting and wrestling.

Only more than a century after their victory over Persia, the idea of conquering the world and exporting the Hellenic culture out of its confines hit the Greek warrior Alexander the Great's mind. Unlike the Athenians, he crushed the Persians decisively there on their native turf and demanded the unconditional surrender of the last king of the Achaemenid Empire, Darius III who ruled Persia from 336 BCE through 330 BCE.

Cyrus the Great had founded the Persian Empire with the care and shrewdness of an astute statesman. He would have never imagined that another "Great" would march from Macedonia two hundred years later, smash his mighty kingdom to smithereens, only to stop at his tomb and pay him tribute. This other fellow was Alexander the Great, son of King Philip of Macedonia. Alexander, this young, bold, and ruthless Macedonian soldier, acknowledged Cyrus's stature as a great statesman and empire builder of the bygone days. Yet unlike him, Alexander the Great used hard power to annex territories for economic benefits and execute his well-thought-out long-term plan of cultural expansion. He used his sword indiscriminately to win the battle of ideas. He was clear in his mind – push through his agenda of Pan-Hellenism and enforce the cultural superiority of Greece. This was the first instance of a well-planned and structured implementation of the nationalist agenda by a government in recorded history.

Alexander's method was simple and effective: he passed orders to his officers and soldiers to intermarry with the native population. Perhaps, he had inferred from Aristotle's thesis that just like cross-breeding was a simple and effective method to manipulate crops and vegetables and domesticate animals, so could intermarriage be used to dilute the ethnic fabric of the conquered territories effectively. The Jews were quick to see through Alexander's intentions. They passed a religious ordinance prohibiting intermarriage with non-Jews. Other communities, not as well-organized as the Jews, failed to resist the bait thrown by the Greek royalty. They jumped on the opportunity to get into matrimonial alliances with the Greeks.

With absolute grit and resolution, Alexander the Great embarked on a difficult task that generally needs years of meticulous implementation. In Asia Minor alone, he founded more than twenty Greek cities in his conquered territories within a decade. He ruthlessly pursued his agenda of Hellenization during his life, but he barely succeeded in his mission in the Middle East. However, this brave, enthusiastic, and ambitious Macedonian king died in 323 BCE, barely 13 years after ascending the throne. Had he lived longer, the history might have been set differently. That was not to happen.

His successors didn't show much enthusiasm for his project of Hellenization. They comfortably ripped Alexander's empire into a couple of pieces of real estate: Greece, Asia Minor, and Palestine. Greece went to Antigonus, Asia Minor to Seleucus, and Palestine, along with Egypt, was grabbed by Ptolemy. All of them more or less subscribed to a "live and let live" policy. In the ancient ruthlessly competitive world order, live and let live was mortal policy. History teaches a simple lesson: if you want to stay in power, use might to make it right. Those who failed to learn this lesson suffered mortally under the cold invisible hand of history. In their lust for luxury, the Greeks, after Alexander, ignored history. They preferred comfort, rhetoric, and dialectic over the might of unity. And history duly punished them. The power went to the Romans.

The first Jihad

The seed that Alexander the Great laid germinated, nevertheless, blooming subsequently into an all-out battle of ideas in the lands of Palestine and Judah. But, before that, the Ptolemies and the Seleucids engaged in a bloody conflict for 125 years over Palestine. Finally, Antiochus the Great drove the Ptolemies out of Palestine. Encouraged by this initial success, Antiochus then took up an expansionist policy pursuing his dream of bringing back the lost glory to the once-mighty empire Alexander had left behind. As his romantic daydreaming took him over to reunify the broken Greek Empire, he foolishly marched into Egypt and was squarely beaten up by the Romans. Afterward, while recuperating from the ignoble setback, the harsh realization that the erstwhile Greek empire was too fragmented to reunite rankled his mind. Finally, the idea hit him: use religion as a political tool. He immediately put the idea into action and started a well-planned, empire-wide religious drive cloaked in nationalism. For the first time in the history of humankind, religious nationalism was formally introduced into politics. Thenceforth, nationalism in its various forms – economic, territorial, and ethnoreligious – became a recurrent theme of politics in the next two thousand years. The seed was laid right here in the Promised Land of Palestine by the Greeks.

The Jews quickly saw through the religious disposition of the Antiochus affair. They refused to obey the Greeks, steadfastly opposing the erecting of statues of Greek Gods. Erecting Greek statues in Palestine wouldn't be allowed - the Jews made it clear to them. Antiochus relented. He did retract his orders, but it turned out later that that was only the beginning of the end for the Jewish control of Palestine. Antiochus's son, Epiphanes, in sharp contrast to his father's hesitancy, favored stern action against Palestine. Viewing Jews' obstinacy as an outrageous affront to Greek suzerainty, he unleashed the Greek soldiers to brutally coerce the Jews into accepting Hellenization as a foundational principle of the polity. The Jews, however, mounted stiff opposition. It cost them hugely.

The situation in the 1st century BCE Palestine turned volatile. Palestine was subjected to unforeseen turmoil and devastation under the Greek sword. The Jews fought a losing battle with fervor and ferocity in the name of religion, which brought unnecessary bloodshed and tragic loss of human life. Yet, the Jews set the weirdest example for posterity by showing that people could fight the mighty not only for economic gains but also for some invisible belief systems deeply engraved in their collective consciousness; and could willingly die for these invisible ideas and perceptions.

The Greeks were baffled by the reaction of the Jews to their seemingly innocuous policy measures. The last thing they expected was the die-hard behavior of the Jews. Why were they so fussy about their Jewishness, the Greeks might have wondered? Little did they know that Jews' anger was fueled by fanatical despisement of the Greek pagan disposition. For centuries, the prophets and the rabbis had steadfastly worked to instill a sense of inner discipline and national integration in the Jewish masses. They encouraged them to bow only to a "High God" in the face of danger. By the time the Greeks insisted on a uniform civil code, the Jews were perfectly programmed into believing that their faith in one God was the only true faith. They were ready to defend their faith at any cost and willingly die for invisible and abstract concepts. It was perplexing to the Greeks how the Jews could believe and worship so fervently a God who could no way be represented in the three-dimensional form.

Antiochus might have wondered where the Jews got this inspiration from. He failed against these impoverished, ill-fed, and unarmed God worshipers in both the battles – the battle for ideas and the battle for territory. It was hard to quell the Jewish rebellion despite using immense brute force. Unleashing a battle of ideas was a strategic mistake committed by Antiochus. It fuelled hatred of the Jews for the Greeks. Although he could slaughter 10,000 Jews in a single show of madness and brute power, this failed to yield the desired results. Instead, it hardened the Jewish stand, stoking woefully vitriolic counterpropaganda of ideas by the Jews. When Rabbi Mattathias was forced to perform a sacrifice to Greek gods, he refused to obey the orders of the Greek official and, in an outburst of rage, slew him. It was the last nail in the coffin.

The whole of Palestine was set ablaze by communal fire. A bitter and bloody war followed – indeed the first religious war or "Jihad" in recorded history – a kind of war that would go on record to set a template for hundreds of other such wars in the next two thousand years of humankind's history. As a result, humanity suffered colossal losses in blood, life, and resources. The Greeks were stunned by how stoically and bravely the Jews died for ideas and not possessions and economic gains. This war changed the landscape of sacred and genuine history for all times to come. This Holy war or Jihad signified a landmark development that had a profound impact on the collective societal psyche of humankind in the centuries ahead.

The End of the Kingdom of Judah

Ideas are powerful. They penetrate the impenetrable, slash the invisible, and can turn out to be harder than the hardest rocks. Although Mattathias and his four sons were killed in the war, his fifth son, Simon, survived to carry on the jihad against the Greeks until a peace treaty was signed in 143 BCE. The impossible was achieved; the Jewish kingdom of Judah was re-established once again. The Jews ripped the self-assurance of the Greeks, leaving a gaping hole in their self-confidence. The jubilant Jews hailed this victory as a landmark step in their struggle to regain their lost glory. Simon became the king. He established the Hasmonean dynasty.

The victory brought responsibilities. It turned out that waging the war of independence was more manageable than maintaining independence. The Jews now had to work on multiple fronts to protect Judah's borders and sovereignty. No sooner had they gotten rid of the Greeks than it became more apparent that they were caught up in a political jungle red in tooth and claw, where nothing but might and unity mattered. There was a dire need for a robust, well-knitted, organized social fabric, and reorganizing their fractured society demanded a high degree of self-discipline from both the ordinary and the elite. Accordingly, the Jewish religious leaders took the lead in handling the challenge at multiple levels and introduced many significant and revolutionary reformations. One of their remarkable achievements was the establishment of *Minyans* or the "social communities or organizations" throughout Judah and other Jewish settlements. The people were encouraged to organize a *Minyan* for every 120 males living within a commutable distance and follow the basic guidelines, rules, and principles stipulated by the Central *Minyan* Authority's document. The *Minyans* settled the disputes in their respective communities through a court system – a precursor of the Sharia court system of Islam – that functioned outside the purview of the state's existing laws, taking care that in the adjudication of disputes, these courts did not conflict with the state laws.

Additionally, the foundation of a network of "charity institutions" was also laid during this period of disruption of Jewish history. The *Minyans* (social communities) were authorized to impose on their members "charity taxes" – a prototype of Christian tithe and Islamic *zakat* – in addition to the taxes they paid to the government of the day. The funds thus collected created a contingency reserve to help out the poor and needy fellow Jews facing a difficult time. The straight consequence of the existence of such a financial system was that the poor and the lower-middle-class Jews then need not ask or pray to the Pagan or the Christian government for financial help. Additionally, this *Minyan* system – the program of social transformation – also stipulated that each community of Jews was religiously duty-bound to establish a school system for universal education.

Change is good. But every change is a motion that unsettles the state of inertia or the comfort zone. That creates resistance to change. It is not always easy to introduce change and reforms in society. The perspective and paradigm of a society determine whether new ideas will be accepted or rejected, no matter whether a particular idea is good or evil. However, what matters is how an idea fits with the mental map of the individuals and society at large. Societies don't tend to be uniform, and neither do they follow a linear pattern in their workings. They are chaotic in character but preserve and maintain a baffling pattern or order even in their chaos. How that "pattern in chaos" emerges is a mystery. A seemingly uniform society folds repeatedly and wraps multiple worlds – physical, mental, and mathematical

– within it with all their constituting diversities and subtleties. In the case of the human world, the mental and the mathematical worlds decide how the physical world will look for humans. The structure of thoughts and memory (the mental world) that creates a particular perspective is unique for each individual. Individual perspectives may intersect or meet, but they are never identical. And, precisely that makes a whole lot of problems. The Jews, despite their notoriety for wit and intellect, couldn't help intergroup and inter-community disaffection and dissent from happening.

Which brings me to the first century CE Judah. The Israelites were now formally known as Jews, and they had already founded a strong and well-knit fabric of an organized religion called Judaism. The centuries of collaborative work had produced an enormous body of literature surrounding their story of faith. Religion, undoubtedly, did play a dominant role in their lives, both at the individual and collective level, but it came with a price. The Jews, in their zeal, forgot that history doesn't bother about finesse, correctness, and syntax of the story's language. They thought they were unique, and their story was the only correct version available, thus marginalizing and isolating themselves from the mainstream geopolitics and the world order of the day. History seldom cares about reason and rationality. It happens.

For three-quarters of a century, the Jews enjoyed self-rule and self-governance in Judah. Although well established and refined by then, the institution of religion couldn't guarantee them "the promised peace" and the "kingdom of heaven" that they'd been yearning for centuries. A lot more remained to be done to hold the Promised Land from slipping under the feet. The religion simply had no solution except to wait for the Messiah who after coming would establish God's kingdom for them (In Islam establishment of the "Kingdom of God" means "Establishment of the Day of Judgement" and the presence of Messiah is theologically mandatory). Ironically, the Jews too were, quite literally, waiting eagerly for him, and so are the Muslims today. To the Jews' chagrin, he was taking too long to arrive. Yet, simultaneously Judah was slipping into more chaos, conflict, and stress. It was facing a potential threat of bondage, servitude, and even annihilation, from all sides.

The Jews were trying to hold Judah literally by the skin of their teeth. They blamed history for being cruel to them, pinning all hopes on the Messiah for deliverance from the hell of wretchedness, chaos, and the overwhelming threat of bondage from all sides. But the promised Messiah was nowhere in sight. Judaism was most evidently failing the Jews yet again at their darkest moment, but they refused to acknowledge the bitter truth that Judaism wasn't enough to tackle the situation. It had done its bit to bind together a fractured Jewish society, but that wasn't very meaningful without the power of the sword.

The preoccupation with scriptural trifles hardly left time for the Jewish elite to consolidate a vibrant polity coupled with a sound economy. The scriptural interpretations and exegesis were a priority agenda for rabbis. It helped them play petty politics. There was no consensus then, as there is none today, as to what was the right and legitimate interpretation of religion and faith. Different textual interpretations gave rise to various socio-political movements and religious streams. In the 1st century CE Judah, as is the case today, religion was a powerful political tool in the hands of a few to create sectarian conflict rather than consensus. The religious factionalism weakened the Hasmonean dynasty and the kingdom of Judah to the extent that the Roman tiger gobbled it up merely 75 years after its second establishment. This time around, the kingdom of Judah was completely emasculated. For the next two thousand years, Jews were not allowed to raise their head again.

The Mass Suicide

With Judah's destruction, one would have expected Judaism to fizzle out. No. It refused to die down. The seed that the Jews had laid, no doubt, remained buried under the dust and debris of history. Yet, it was only a matter of time before it germinated from under the rubble of Judah into an unexpected monster. The monster was much more formidable than Goliath, and no David could kill it. Fighting it would prove far more complicated than expected. The Jews themselves were caught unawares. It would potentially cost the Jews Judaism.

The new monster changed the history of the world most spectacularly. It posed a formidable challenge to all religious and cultural systems, but for the Jews in particular, it proved to be far more dangerous and ruthless than Goliath. The new monster also had a story to tell, except that the story was far more complex and controversial. The story began around an alleged historical figure, Jesus Christ, who was completely transmogrified into a "mythological character." Jesus was cloaked in the divine, and his story metamorphosed into the peculiarly charismatic meta-story – Christianity – that even Jesus would be at a loss to fathom and believe. He would probably get confused about the nature of his person – who exactly is he? A spiritual or a physical being? But that's how stories work. They get stacked and bizarrely warped on one another that an extraordinarily complex tapestry is all that emerges.

Christianity sprang forth from the fertile soil of Judaism. A classical religio-political rift paved the way for Christianity's emergence and guaranteed its establishment as an independent creed in the centuries ahead. The Greeks having been evicted, Judah shifted focus from without to within in search of a new enemy. There was no dearth of enemies there. When the Jews paid attention, they found not one but many of them. As the tension started mounting from within, the pressure built up, blowing the lid finally off. The ugly infighting transmogrified into a dangerous civil war-like situation in Judah.

Jews were set against each other. They bitterly fought each other. In that bizarre drama where each was proclaiming to be a true follower of Judaism, ultimately three prominent sects or parties emerged to the forefront. It is worth mentioning that the sequence of events that shaped 1st-century CE Palestine/Judah's history was by no standards a feature unique to Judaic sacred history. In their days, all sacred histories, particularly of Christianity and Islam, were severely plagued by sectarian conflict, civil wars, and other kinds of turmoil. Historically, civil wars seem to have a characteristic propensity for deeply religious societies.

The three main parties to the dispute in the first century Palestine/Judah were the *Pharisees,* the *Sadducees,* and the *Essenes.* The *Pharisees* thought of themselves as liberals, keen on evolution and reinterpretation of the Mosaic Law. They favored a more elastic and accommodative version of Judaism. Interestingly, the Pharisee line of thought proved to be a pragmatic one, in the sense that the accommodative change as advocated by it proved pivotal to the survival of Judaism during its darkest days ahead. The *Sadducees* also thought of themselves as liberals but only in their political outlook; they behaved more like conservatives in religious matters. They favored the religion of Temple, Priest, and Sacrifice. They opposed the establishment of synagogues and argued for the return to the pre-prophetic form of Judaism. For them, synagogues were irrelevant and blasphemous because they were eating at the importance of the Temple on the Mount. They regarded the

Pharisees as Zealots. The third prominent party in the conflict was the *Essenes.* They were more rigorous, austere, and extremist in religious and political outlook. They were more interested in the theology of "afterlife" and "reincarnation" – not reincarnation as understood in Hindu theology – as life after death or rising from the dead like in Islamic theology.

Of the three sects, the *Essenes* have attracted the greatest attention of historians and religious scholars. The ancient historians Pliny, Josephus, and Philo, have given detailed accounts of the *Essenes,* but their accounts seem to be at variance with the recent evidence gathered from the Dead Sea scrolls found in the caves of Qumran. According to Michael Baigent and Richard Leigh, these scrolls "if properly handled," may provide a better insight into the religio-political landscape of 1st century CE Palestine. Unfortunately, as claimed by Michael Baigent, some Christian researchers have suppressed much of the information contained in these documents. A big scandal surrounding these scrolls surfaced towards the closing years of the twentieth century. Michael Baigent and Richard Leigh, in their expose *The Dead Sea Scrolls Deception* – which created a storm in academic circles – questioned the intentions of the ""Christian" scholars, particularly that of Father De Vaux, who was authorized to handle the scrolls. Other dissenting voices, especially from Chicago University, also joined the chorus to decry the allegedly deliberate suppression of facts by the "Christian" scholars. They accused the international team led by Father De Vaux of releasing only the material that had been tailor-made to fit the prevalent narrative of Christian theological literature. Some critics claim that the Dead Sea scrolls contain so explosive a material that, if exposed, can threaten the very foundations of Christianity. Be that as it may, only time will show whether the Dead Sea scrolls bombshell will explode or not.

The *Essenes,* it seems, were no puritans in the strict sense. Their philosophy was laced with elements of Egyptian and Greek mythology. And some of their practices were quite similar to those of the Pythagoreans. Yet they claimed to draw their inspiration solely from the holy books of the Jewish prophets and practiced purification rituals like baptism (purification by water). However, an essential pillar of the *Essene* faith consisted of the belief in the "End of Time" theology or the apocalypse concept. They sincerely believed that "End time" was nearing and the advent of the Messiah was imminent. They expected the Messiah to come in their lifetime and frankly thought and firmly believed they would witness that event in years ahead. Their belief in the Apocalypse – the end of the world – was so strong and unwavering that they contemplated the world to be annihilated soon. Frankly, their world revolved around Palestine at that time. They believed the Messiah would establish the "Kingdom of God" on Earth after the Apocalypse.

Establishing the kingdom of God, the *Essenes* believed, was the ultimate purpose for which the "world as they understood it" had primarily and precisely been created. They thought they had all the true knowledge and understanding about the world, and that there was nothing more to know. Neither did others need to worry about knowing more, the *Essenes* emphasized. All that the Jews needed, they counseled them, was to listen and follow the *Essene* version of religious wisdom. With all the seriousness, they waited for the Messiah to come, insisting that the time was ripe and more suitable than ever for the End of the world and the establishment of the Kingdom of God – what in the language of Islam is the Day of Judgment. The advent of the Messiah was indeed an accepted knowledge in Palestine, but the *Essenes* insisted on its imminence.

The old popular notion that the *Essenes* were an insignificant party, who lived in small monastic-style communities, and practiced celibacy and nonviolence, was inaccurate. Modern scholars now agree that the *Essenes* and the Zealots are two names of the same sect. The Zealots constituted an extra-radical faction of the *Essenes* fuelled by fanatical hatred against Roman over-lordship. They seemed willing to resort to extreme acts of violence against any group who dared acquiesce to the Roman administration. Furthermore, the account given by the 1st century CE historian Josephus is particularly self-contradictory, as the Dead Sea texts have also revealed. According to these texts, the Essenes were a reasonably robust group with their presence everywhere in Judah/Palestine and were no pacifists.

But as, after the fall of Jerusalem, the Romans systematically wiped out Jewish armed resistance against their suzerainty, the zealot *Essenes* toughened their stand. They captured the fort of Masada and continued their assault on the Roman army from the height of the fort. They proved fierce and resourceful fighters. For more years, they inflicted heavy casualties on the Roman army. Finally, when the Roman army broke their defense line and captured the fort, the zealots preferred mass suicide over surrender. Josephus reports about a speech given by the *Essene* (Zealot) leader exhorting the followers to commit mass suicide rather than surrender before the Roman infidels.

The Messiah

The *Essenes* (the Zealots) differed from the other sects on the question of the Messiah. While they talked about "two types" of Messiahs – one knightly and another priestly – the other sects "thought of Messiah as possessing a combination of both traits," notes Reza Aslan. The Zealots were driven by the aspiration to see the "kingdom of God" established as they firmly believed that the world was coming to an end. They argued it was a great sin to submit to the Roman Yoke when all the signs of the *Apocalypse* were clear. In frustration, they resorted to violence against anybody who didn't or couldn't see things the way they did.

The three crucial characteristics that, in a sense, defined Zealots were religious zeal, violence, and raids. What was peculiar about Zealots was that they looked at violence as an essential component of "religious zeal," feeling no qualms about conducting violent attacks on those who held a different view. For them, "zeal" without accompanying "violence" was incomplete in itself and vice-versa, and violence, according to their theology, was as essential a tenet of religion as the "zeal." They urged the Jews to join them to fulfill their "religious duty" of fighting against Rome. The fight against the infidel Rome was holy. Thus the Jews waged history's first organized "Holy war" or *Jihad* against the occupiers of their land, leaving a dangerous legacy for the later Abrahamic faiths.

Approximately around the same time, a fearsome group of fighters organized themselves under the leadership of one Judas, the Galilean. Judas's father, Hezekiah, had proclaimed to be the Messiah but was killed by the ruler of Galilee, Herod. After Herod died, Judas organized his group to carry forward his father's legacy. Judas, like his father, put out his claim to be the Messiah. His band attacked the Royal Armory and grabbed the weapons and the provisions they could put their hands on. Judas's popularity shot up. As his group gained more sympathizers, he quickly launched a well-organized guerilla war throughout Galilee, plundering, looting, and burning down villages in the name of God and the Holy War. The concept of *Jihad* took root.

In the centuries ahead, Jews no longer remained the sole patent holders of guerilla warfare. Theocracies, secular democracies, and communists used guerilla wars in utter disregard for human blood and life. In the 1st century CE Judah (Palestine), nobody was spared in the heat of chaos. An atmosphere of instability took over there. Only *Yahweh* could now save Judah. The Jews caught up in despair and depression, now eagerly looked up to heaven for the Messiah to descend. He never dropped in Judah. The *End Time* was just at hand, except that it never came. And the "kingdom of God" was about to get established. Yet it never did.

The history of the 1st century CE Judah is complex. Scholars tend to slash history into clear-cut slabs and slices of time as if there were a linear continuity of historical events. History, whether the genuine or the sacred, hardly follows a linear trajectory, yet for simplicity, we look at history as if it were a step-by-step process. Many things get lost in the fog and mist of time only to be replaced by opinions, biases, fiction, and fantasy. It is often impossible to disentangle the complex tapestry that history is in a scheme where the paths of the sacred and genuine histories cross. In Judah, for instance, the Pharisees, the Sadducees, and the Essenes, no doubt, were the major players, but there were other players too – the Romans, the Greeks, the Egyptians, the Egyptians, the Zodakites, etc. – out there also fishing in the troubled waters. According to conservative estimates, there were more than twenty-four religious sects of Jews alone in Judah. Each sect practiced its brand or recipe for salvation. Additionally, many holy men, preachers, and rabbis, some of them fake, were busy teaching the theology of Messiah and End Time.

Despite the minor differences in interpretation and rhetoric, "the advent of Messiah" had become an essential constituent of the religious culture – an article of faith. The holy men (god-men) fervently preached their respective versions of salvation with all seriousness. Among the many itinerant god-men preaching in Judah, there was also one Jesus (Christ) or Iesus (Mashiah), supposed to have been born between years 7 and 4 BCE in Nazareth, when Herod the Great was the ruler of Judah (by then called Judea by the Romans). The Gospels of Luke and Mathew trace the ancestry of Jesus to the house of David through different yet conflicting genealogies.

The Gospel of Barnabas, an apocryphal book, unequivocally claims that Jesus was born of the Virgin Mary. In its first chapter, it records an alleged conversation between the Archangel Gabriel and Mary as follows:

"Fear not, Mary, for thou hast found favor with God, who hath chosen thee to be [the] mother of a prophet, says Gabriel to Mary after saluting her." "The virgin answered, 'Now how shall I bring forth sons, seeing I know not a man?'" Six centuries later, the Quran repeats the exact words about the birth of Jesus almost precisely. The birth of Jesus from a virgin is universally accepted across all the sects of Christianity and Islam. Since there is no record of the birth and childhood years of Jesus in the contemporary history of that period, and the Dead Sea scrolls are also silent about it, the scant (and controversial) account provided in the Gospels and the Quran has become the official narrative of the Christian and the Muslim world respectively. All the thirty or so years that Jesus is supposed to have lived are shrouded in mystery. The Gospels are silent on what Jesus was doing before he suddenly appeared on the scene and disappeared equally suddenly with the crucifixion event. The mystery raises questions about the historical Jesus.

The Gospel of Luke provides only one indirect suggestion in Chapter 2:52; however, the Gospel of Mathew puts forth an ingenious yet curious story to solve the mystery. It says Jesus fled to Egypt to escape Herod's wrath and returned just before he was crucified. Here Mathew agrees with Barnabas, who also mentions that Jesus had fled to Egypt. No other Gospel or historical source reports anything of the kind. Interestingly, in chapter 11 of the Book of Hosea, a prophecy reads: "Out of Egypt I have called my son," meaning that Messiah will come from Egypt. Mathew and Barnabas seemed to have been troubled by this prophecy, and they struggled to corroborate their account of Jesus somehow to fit this prophecy. Since these Gospels were written after the crucifixion, (40 years later, to be precise) the Gospel writers wanted to close all the gaps to uphold the veracity of the Messiahship of Jesus. Hence, they invented the story of Jesus' flight to Egypt.

As per the Gospels, Jesus made the first appearance when he was 28 to 30 years of age (depending on which sources you rely on). Before he took to public life, he was baptized by John the Baptist. John claimed to be a prophet who supposedly taught the *Essene* version of religion. His career was ended by Antipas, the Galilean king, who put him to death, not for political reasons, though, but for his opposition to his (Antipas's) marriage. Jesus, now, took up preaching, taking care not to challenge the accepted Judaic teachings. He invited people to strict observance of the Mosaic laws and emphasized the ethical issues of mercy, tolerance, and compassion for the poor. Yet, he never claimed to be the promised Messiah. So, there was little reason for the Jews to antagonize him. But, as is always the case in a troubled state, he surely was a suspect in the eyes of the Romans. The overall political atmosphere in Jerusalem and the adjoining Middle East was fragile and unstable. The Roman administration was in no mood to tolerate any potential aberration of the law and order situation.

In particular, during the festive seasons, the Roman administration would remain in a state of high alert in Judea (Judah). They would not take the slightest risk that would potentially vitiate the atmosphere in their occupied territory. Accordingly, Jerusalem and the Temple were kept under intense vigil. Jesus had decided to attend the festivities at Jerusalem and perhaps announced his intention to crack down on temple priests, vendors, and money lenders who defiled the Central Temple of Jerusalem, according to the Gospel account. It is unclear whether or not Jesus wanted to announce that he was the Messiah. In any case, Jesus' choice of timing – if the Gospel story is correct – for taking such radical steps was absurd. It turns out he simply couldn't have chosen a worse time.

The Gospels tell us Jesus went ahead with his plan: He reached Jerusalem, entered the Temple, rebuked the priests, and overturned their tables. And then, guess what happened? Pandemonium broke out at the busiest place in the town! The Roman soldiers plunged into action to control law and order. What followed then is, in one word, Christianity – a story shrouded in thick layers of mystery with no exit point. The Romans crucified Jesus like a petty criminal, charging him with inciting disorder. Unitarian Christians (early sect) claimed that Jesus was not crucified, he was raised to heaven, and the Romans mistakenly crucified someone else in his place. Trinitarian Christians (the later sect) claimed that Jesus was indeed crucified, but he rose from the dead. The ghost of Jesus has been hovering over them ever since. Millions of faithful Christians have allegedly met the ghost in the past two thousand years, except nobody has seen Jesus. Yet each believer claims Jesus is omnipresent. Will Christians spot him in flesh and blood at any time in the future? Unlikely.

The End Time

The authors of the New Testament (the Gospels of Mark, Luke, Mathew, and John and twenty-three or so books from "Acts" through "Revelation") make a case for the resurrection of Jesus three days after his death. The "crucifixion and resurrection" of Jesus is the bone and sinew of the whole theological discourse, so painstakingly built up through years of discussion, debate, and deliberation. The theology of crucifixion and resurrection attracted the Romans and the other Pagans into Christianity's fold; otherwise, this new religion would have fizzled out unassumingly before it even started. To put it bluntly, take out crucifixion, and Christianity can't stand it. The curious story – the spiritual Jesus – attracted a vast number of people in subsequent centuries into the fold of Christianity. Nothing of the sort had been told before Christians floated their myth. Nothing of the sort had allegedly happened before it supposedly happened with the person of Jesus. Astounding. It stuck. The story worked like a psychedelic. Listeners hallucinated Jesus' resurrection. As the story caught up, there was no turning back. The unbelievers began to suspect their unbelief. Such is the power of a well-crafted story. The fools and the wise alike hallucinate when the storyline is robust or preposterous. Christianity has both.

The other version of the Jesus story – particularly the so-called Unitarian version – that was in circulation during the formative centuries of the Christian era couldn't help enough tickle the imagination of the Jews. It failed to impress the Jews as well as non-Jews. As a result, early Christianity (Unitarian) remained a fringe religion, a sub-sect of Judaism. Nothing more, nothing less. They faced persecution and prosecution at the hands of the Jews, the Romans, and the Pagans alike. Only by the skin of their teeth, they managed to survive and keep their story alive in certain parts of Syria and Egypt. Finally, by the 3rd and 4th centuries CE, the Unitarians were sidelined and suppressed by Trinitarian Christianity through systematic and deliberate violence. The Gospels like that of Barnabas and Thomas and others which paint a different picture of Jesus' disappearance from the scene of Jerusalem's religious landscape, were banned.

The Gospel of Barnabas, for example, in the 215th verse in its last chapter, reads: "God, seeing the danger of his servant commanded Gabriel, Michael, Rafael, and Uriel to take Jesus out of the world….." and "Judas was so changed in speech and face that he became like Jesus. The Romans mistook Judas for Jesus and crucified him [Judas] in place of Jesus. To the people, it seemed that it was Jesus who was crucified." This version of Jesus' crucifixion survived for a long time in the lands of Syria, Egypt, and other parts of the Middle East. It quietly continued to circulate roughly up until the 7th century CE. The adherents of this Barnabas theology prodigiously upheld the view that Jesus was a prophet and a mortal like us.

Barnabas Christianity, if it may be called Christianity in the strict sense of the word, ultimately lost the ground to the "Trinitarian" Christianity. History has repeatedly shown that story wins in matters of religion or theology. The might and the muscle power tilt toward a more appealing story, and as that happens, nothing stops the story from spreading far and wide. Power pushes the story, and by analogy, a particular religion, down through the society. Logic doesn't always work; the carrot-and-stick method does. The Barnabas theology, though logical, sorely lacked the patronage of the powerful, the stick. The Trinitarians got hold of the stick. They won.

Nevertheless, certain ideas do persist despite all kinds of suppression. They remain hidden and buried somewhere in the deeper crevices of the collective consciousness, only to show up as soon as the landscape of thought is ripe. Barnabas's storyline of Jesus being a prophet and not getting crucified re-emerged in the 7th century CE in the least expected geographical territory – in the far-off deserts of Arabia – renewing the centuries-old battle of ideas. As a result, one of the most attritious confrontations of sacred histories ensued in its aftermath, whose thorns are still butted deep in the flesh of humanity. Ideas die hard, especially when they thrive on compelling storylines.

Which brings us back to the disappearance of Jesus. With Jesus no longer around, his twelve disciples, or the apostles as they're called, had to fend for their lives. The scythe hung on their necks as they were companions of a criminal before the Roman officials. They assumed a low profile, but the stinging discomfiture brought upon them by the crucifixion of their master, who they had claimed was the Messiah, compelled them to bring forth woefully awe-inspiring stories about him. Yet, as pious Jews as they were, they insisted on Jesus' teachings being meant to reform the Jews. Soon, however, that perspective was overridden, as it happens with all ideas, by varied interpretations and viewpoints. In the emerging confluence, the original idea got diluted and almost lost in the jumble of interpretations and opinionated discourses. New narratives overshadowed the older ones.

Jesus' story and teachings got hammered into bits and pieces, attracting intense debate and theological hairsplitting. As a result, a rich plethora of theological literature was birthed. Jesus got transmogrified from a dubious historical personality into an allegedly genuine historical one and then from a human being into a ghost and from a ghost to a spiritual Jesus. The kingdom of God that seemed to be at hand to the Jews never materialized. Yet, the burden of proof was transferred onto the shoulders of the Christian Messiah to return from hiding soon and establish the Kingdom through Armageddon.

The Jews, however, wouldn't budge despite the Romans burning down everything belonging to them and their God. The "Temple of Zion," which housed the symbol of Jewish civilization and religion, the Ark of Covenant, was torched down and burnt to ashes. For the time being, the Kingdom of the "Roman God" was established in place of the Kingdom of the Jewish God. This kingdom persisted through many a storm and turmoil before the "kingdom of another God" chipped away pieces from it. History unfolded bizarrely, and in the tussle of Gods, as it were, the face of the Earth was washed with the blood of innocents.

Curiously, one thing refused to happen – the "End Time." It still refuses to happen despite the wailings and warnings of doomsayers. One day it may show up. It may. But we have to wait long. Not decades, not centuries as the Jewish and other prophets prophesied, but more than four billion years. Four billion years is still a conservative estimate. *End Time* (or the doomsday) seemed to be just at hand to the Jews; it appeared to be just at hand to the Christians, and, not surprisingly, it seemed just at hand to the Muslims. To the Hindus, it has all along been *Kalyuga* – End Time for the world. Strangely for all of them, the End refuses to draw any closer, proving the theologians consistently wrong – notwithstanding their fervently believing, preaching, and shedding the blood of fellow humans. The *End time* stays where it was – in the horizons of imagination! The world didn't stop and won't. The world grew and will flourish further. And history happened. It will happen for billions more years.

Chapter – 09

The Eastern Rome

After the Crucifixion

The Jews are genius. They always were. Diligently working on their creed, they made out of it a supremely systematic and organized religion of the Book, the first of its kind in recorded history. We call it Judaism. Another feat that the Jews accomplished was their firmly establishing the Monotheistic tradition. Furthermore, they created a serious discourse on the *End Time* and the *Messiah*. That debate on the theology of the *End Time* and the advent of the Messiah has kept the world busy for more than 2,000 years now. At present, more than two-thirds of the world population believes in the Messiah's second coming. It has been both a cause of disagreement and a vortex for agreement between the two largest religions of the globe, Christianity, and Islam.

Christianity, as a creed, owes its existence to this Jewish Messianic theme. The early converts tenaciously held on to this theme and succeeded in establishing Jesus as the Messiah. Posthumously. It was hard to do that, given that the Romans had punished Jesus like a petty criminal. The crucifixion of Jesus came as a huge shock to his companions, disciples, and early converts. They did their best to defend Jesus. First, they refused even to acknowledge that Jesus was crucified. He could not be. A great prophet, teacher, and master was crucified unceremoniously. No. They were, in psychology speak, in a typical "denial state." When the acute stage was over and the dust started to settle, it was time to develop an alibi. Barnabas got it the best: It was a look-alike of Jesus, not Jesus, whom the Romans crucified. As Barnabas records, God transformed Judas into a look-alike of Jesus. He spoke like Jesus, walked like Jesus, and became like Jesus. The Romans, those fools, caught hold of this copycat Jesus and put him on the cross.

Where did the original Jesus go? God raised him to heaven, Barnabas records. He was to stay with God. Until the *End Time.* And will come back just hours or days before the *End Time* to establish the Kingdom of God, which he couldn't in his lifetime. The Islamic tradition principally agrees with the account of Barnabas, except that Jesus, it says, will descend just before the Final Judgment Day.

Paul, the apostle, came late, his School even later. Paul had never seen Jesus; witnessed neither his crucifixion nor his sepulcher. He had never seen him rising from the dead. However, he thought and thought. And voila! He got the answer. he came up with a brilliant story. Over time, his story ceased to be a manufactured story. It became a fact. No Barnabas, no Thomas could effectively counter that storyline.

His approach to crucifixion matter was radically different. Whether he suffered hallucinations or was weighed down with contrition, all the same, Paul defended crucifixion as a necessary component of the Messianic theme. He and his school portrayed crucifixion as a sacrifice by Jesus essential for the redemption of the human race. Paul left no scope for the historical flesh and blood Jesus. That Jesus was unnecessary. He created a spiritual Jesus who resurrected, ate the last supper, and will have a second coming. Jesus became Law, Scripture, and Faith, as well as God. Omnipresent, omniscient, and omnipresent. Faith in Jesus replaced faith in God, religion, and Law (Commandments). No Christian is Christian without total faith in Jesus the God and Jesus the son of God, noted Paul. However, Paul did not call Christians, Christians.

These extraordinarily gifted storytellers - Paul and his School - conceived their own incredibly brilliant and abstract theological intricacies like the "resurrection" and redefined "the last supper" and the "second coming" of Messiah on their terms. While the original disciples and early followers of Jesus considered themselves strictly Jewish and forbade proselytizing to non-Jews and Pagans, Paul upended that conservative disposition. He rightly appreciated the futility of debating with the Jews about the Messiahship of Jesus. Jews, he knew, totally rejected the thesis that Jesus was a Messiah. They even denied the premise that any such person as Jesus perhaps existed. Arguing with the Jews was challenging, given the historical context of the happenings in the 1st century CE Jerusalem. As can be recalled from previous chapters, things were unbelievably challenging for the converts to this new religion. Given the stubbornness of the Jews, it was pragmatic to woo the non-Jews and pagans to this new creed. Paul did exactly that. The result? We have all around us Pauline Christianity – the largest organized religion globally.

The early followers and the converts faced a real problem; call it a theological conundrum. The hardnosed Jews prodigiously rejected the Messiahship of Jesus. The truth is Jesus himself never claimed to be the Messiah. At least there is no unequivocal and veracious record to that end. He disappeared from the scene suddenly. His followers and early Christians undertook the job of making the Messiah out of him. Had Jesus not disappeared, things might perhaps have evolved differently. Maybe, there would be no such thing as Christianity.

With the disappearance of Jesus, complex dilemmas emerged for the disciples. They were at a loss to definitively postulate the ascension of their master to heaven and convincingly argue the case of him being the true Messiah. The Jews, very proficient with the intricacies of religious discourse, posed them tough questions. Prophecies. Literature. Theology. The Jews had all of that. They pounded the poor converts full throttle. The incorrigible Jews argued that the true Messiah could not have been arrested and crucified like a petty criminal. He could not have ignominiously gone with the wind. Jesus was no Messiah, and his ministry was fake. Before the Jews, the whole gamut of resurrection was suspect.

It may seem crazy to get into the debate on questions like this, yet for Jews and early converts, it was a life-and-death question. If the resurrection were true, where did the Messiah go after arising from the dead? "why couldn't he establish the 'Kingdom of God,' that he was supposed to?" the Jews questioned. "That Messiah would come to live here and not die at the hands of those he was supposed to overthrow" was the putative Jewish understanding of the scripture. Jesus did not fit in there. That was not at all comforting to either the new converts or Jesus' early followers and adherents.

Despite their failure to tackle these tough questions, the early converts steadfastly held their ground. Commendably the authors of the New Testament put words into Jesus' mouth. Posthumously. That changed everything, but it took quite a while. Eventually, Jesus' depiction as divine, speaking the word of God, proved irresistible to the non-Jews, and they were attracted into the fold of this newfound creed. That was encouraging for the fledgling community of converts. The Jews, however, refused to buy the story. They stuck with their opposition to the Messiah.

Jesus and Saint Paul

Amidst the chaos after the disappearance of Jesus, two leading schools of thought popped up. Both put forward their respective thesis, rationalizing what happened to the supposed Messiah. An extensive theology evolved out of these theses. (The Jews still found serious flaws in it. That is a different matter, though.) The First school comprised the twelve original disciples led by James, the brother of Jesus. Another notable disciple among them was Barnabas. The premise of their thesis revolved around the assertion that their master, Jesus, was neither crucified nor killed. But, God had raised him to the heavens. Period. The Jews countered them with a serious objection: "How could a Messiah be raised by God before his mission – establishing the kingdom of God – even started?" The disciples circumvented this dilemma with an intelligent yet quixotic logic: A "Second coming" of Jesus would follow just before the *End time* heralds the *finish* of this world. The *End time* seemed to them not quite so far away. Just at hand, as they said. The *Pharisees* and the *Sadducees* simply ridiculed this idea of the "Second coming" of Jesus. They didn't want to discuss it further.

All the same, the Second Coming of Jesus was an ingenious idea. The other School of early converts – call them Resurrectionists – quickly picked this idea. This school ultimately overshadowed the first one. For starters, the First school subscribed to texts like the Gospel of Barnabas, Thomas, and certain other now-extinct books. The second school (Resurrectionists) subscribed to what is now called the New Testament (see chapter 8). The Resurrectionists tenaciously held on to the narrative that Jesus was crucified and died on the cross, arose from his dead body in the sepulcher after three days, and would establish the Kingdom of God in his "Second coming." It was a sort of oxymoronic theology. When you have a spiritual Jesus or God who is omnipresent, omniscient, and omnipotent, capable of doing everything for you, why put him back on the Earth in flesh and blood? That is to say, restrict him?

The early scribes battled with all those questions – what happened to Jesus- resurrect, where he went, why people did not see him, the sacred mission he was supposed to carry out, and the like. The concept of " Second

Coming" provided the best escape route out of all this mess of questions and subject matters. Which they readily borrowed from the First school. And it served them right.

The "second coming" concept saved their theology from being run over roughshod. They held on to this narrative, vigorously preaching it to the enthusiasts and swing believers alike. When it comes to fighting the battle of ideas, perseverance matters more than anything. Accordingly, the resurrectionists tenaciously persevered despite all odds. They faced opposition. No doubt. From the James' school and the Jews alike. But, as luck would have it, an influential man who appeared on the scene out of the blue saved their boat amidst the tempest. It was this man who ultimately took this theology from nowhere to everywhere, making it into Christianity proper. A grand revolution was sparked off. History would hardly witness a comparable religious movement for the next six hundred years.

This influential man was a Jew, Saul of Tarsus, who later became Paul–Paul, the real father of Christianity. Paul had never met Jesus in person. And, he was known for his antipathy toward these Messiah believers and persecuted them systematically. During one of his journeys to Damascus, supposedly on a persecution mission, he was blinded for three days by, as it were, a flash of heavenly light. As he regained his sight, he heard Jesus talking to him. That was a turning point for the once-Saul of Tarsus. He returned a different man. A staunch follower of Jesus, with total communion with Jesus the son of God, he now took up spreading the word.

What happened to Saul – Hallucinations post-consumption of some psychedelic nectar? Perhaps. As noted by Brian Muraresku in his best-seller *The Immortality Key*, Paul would claim that he was "caught up to the third heaven" where he heard "things that cannot be told" and had discovered "hidden mysteries" during his communication with Jesus. The audiences, probably themselves in hypnotic trances too, believed in his hallucinations. He became a saint, Saint Paul. His auditory hallucinations aren't difficult to explain given the evidence, unearthed by modern scholars, supporting the consumption of psychedelic substances and wines by the members of religious cults in Judea and other parts of the ancient Middle East.

"The homeland of Jesus," writes Brian Murarseku, "was praised in antiquity for its wine production." The world's oldest wine cellar dating to 1700 BCE, has been unearthed here. The initiates consumed the hallucinogenic liquor to achieve states of trance to gain entry into the mysterious "other world" where they could, depending upon their skill, "secure answers to existential questions from godlike spirits." Tarsus of Asia Minor (modern Turkey), the hometown of Saint Paul, was the famous epicenter of wine mixing and extraction of psychedelic substances from herbs, as documented by one Dioscorides, a contemporary of Saint Paul. Dioscorides was known as the Father of Drugs and studied in Tarsus. It is unlikely that Paul couldn't have come across one or the other form of ancient psychedelic wine, nectar as it was called. What he experienced on the road to Damascus could be nothing but the hallucinatory effect of nectar. That is to say, a drug-induced trance state.

Circumcision and Halakha

Paul threw open the gates of Christianity for the Gentiles, the Pagans, the Romans, and the like. Under his dynamic leadership, early Christianity ceased to be a sub-Jewish religious movement. His gregarious theology endowed it with a cosmopolitan appeal. Paul relaxed the code of conduct, dietary laws, and initiation rules to woo the pagans. Ultimately, this Pauline creed became the dominant sect over time, superseding all other theological streams like the Arian (Unitarian), Manichean, or Nestorian Christianity. The balance tipped in favor of Pauline Christianity partly because the fresh converts were no longer supposed to undergo ritual circumcision and observe *Koshur* or *Kashruth* (dietary laws). It made sense to the pagan mind.

Circumcision is the oldest surgical procedure dating back to 15000 years, says Sir Grafton Smith, physician-anatomist and Egyptologist of the twentieth century. Peter Remondino explains in his book *History of Circumcision* that it began as a form of punishment for a captured enemy, less severe though, to keep him alive to serve as a slave. The ancient Egyptians and the Semites practiced circumcision solely as a medical procedure. Later, it was adopted by the Jews as a religious ritual, followed by the Muslims. The Aztecs and the Mayans also practiced ritual circumcision. In Mesopotamia (modern-day Iraq), the Sumerians, and the Semites practiced it in the 4th millennium BCE. However, the earliest historical record comes from Egypt, dating to 2400-2300 BCE, long before the Patriarch Abraham is supposed to have roamed in Nineveh (modern-day Mosul). What was its significance in ancient Egypt? Perhaps, a mark of distinction for the ruling class. Nobody knows for sure. The Egyptian Sun god *Ra* had circumcised himself, says the *Book of the Dead*, giving credence to the premise that Egyptians too practiced circumcision as a religious ritual.

The Hebrew Bible's Book of Genesis (chapter 17) tells the story of Abraham's and his relatives' and slaves' circumcision. According to the Bible, Abraham had reached his ripe old age when he was circumcised. His progeny were commanded thenceforth to circumcise their sons on the eight-day after birth following Abraham's covenant with God. Circumcision was taken up by the Israelites as a religious mandate, putatively on the Abrahamic story. The Greeks and the Romans abhorred circumcision. They made the life of the circumcised Jews miserable. Yet the Jews radically pushed for circumcision as a fulfillment of Biblical commandments and as an essential and permanent mark of membership in the Jewish faith.

The Gospel of Luke (New Testament book) mentions that Jesus was ritually circumcised. Yet Paul upended this ritual for political reasons. In Islam, by the way, circumcision is considered obligatory. The Quran, too, mentions the story of Abraham. However, unlike the Bible, it doesn't explicitly mention circumcision as an essential ritual.

The Jewish dietary law, *Kashruth,* as can be recalled from the earlier discussion, is expounded mainly in the Biblical books of Leviticus and Deuteronomy (14:1-21). Foods that are permissible for a Jew are called *Koshur* (or Kosher in English). Kosher foods are "fit to eat" as per *Halakha* (Jewish Law), and non-Kosher foods are called *treif* or torn from Halakha. The Torah permits eating the meat, eggs, and milk of only those land animals that chew their cud and have cloven hoofs. Four animals are identified explicitly as non-Kosher and hence strictly forbidden. They are the pig, hare, hyrax, and camel. The pig has cloven hooves but does not chew its cud; the other three chew but lack cloven hooves.

The Torah forbids eating birds of prey, fish-eating birds, and bats. Domesticated fowl like chicken, geese, quail, dove, and turkey can be consumed. Fish with fins and scales are permissible eatables; the rest are non-Kosher, including seafood like oysters, crabs, shrimp, etc. All earth crawlers are non-Kosher. The Book of Exodus prohibits eating meat from animals that the beasts have torn. Anything that has died from natural causes is strictly non-Kosher or treif. All meat must come from animals that have been slaughtered according to *Kashruth* or Halakha guidelines: the animal has to be slaughtered by a single deep cut that severs both carotids, jugulars, and trachea below the larynx. A trained person should perform the slaughter to avoid incomplete or shallow cuts. The slaughterer, called *Shochet,* should be pious, of good character, and an observer of *Shabbat* (day of rest on the seventh day of the week, Friday evening to Saturday night). The knife should be razor-sharp and checked before the cut is made. If the blade has irregularities or the cut is made shallow, the meat is deemed non-Kosher.

Paul, consummate and shrewd, did away with the circumcision ritual and *Kashruth.* Furthermore, he boldly replaced the Torah with Jesus, meaning that only through faith in Jesus could man find the road to heaven. No scripture, no law, no Mosaic commandments could save man, only Jesus. With his consummate eloquence, Paul made Jesus, the savior of humankind. In other words, Jesus became God, a God incarnate.

Three Yeses, One No

Paul did not invent the concept of Savior. Nor did he try to claim authorship of this concept. The notions of Savior, god incarnate, son of god, etc., were already in vogue amongst the Romans and the Greeks. What Paul did was he manufactured his theology out of this confluence of entrenched religious notions thereby custom-fitting the boring, dull, and rigid theology of the James School to a much wider audience. That is to say, Paul carved out of Judaism a new Romanized religion, later called Christianity. All credit goes to him. Yet he never claimed credit for it. He gave credit to Jesus. It is hard to imagine how Jesus would have reacted to Paul's ingenuity if he reappeared suddenly.

With a singular stroke of genius, Paul took the "burden of sin" off the peoples' necks. He put it directly on the person of Jesus: "Jesus sacrificed himself for the whole of humanity, and thus the sins of humankind have been atoned!" A master wordsmith and storyteller, persuasive and consummate, Paul argued that there was no need to offer any sacrifices of living creatures anymore because Jesus had given the "supreme sacrifice" for the whole of humanity and that the last word now belonged to Jesus. Soon in his "second coming," he would take his followers to the Eternal Kingdom. This argument left his audiences spellbound, totally floored. They had heard nothing of the kind. Soon, the pagans and even the Romans began identifying a connection with this theology. The Jews were not impressed. Paul artfully ignored them.

Paul's contribution to Christian theology is unparalleled. Humungous prolific as he was, his Epistles are extensive. They make a significant chunk of the New Testament (the Christian Bible). Yet, it wasn't he who invented the concept of "Trinity." It evolved later. Paul only laid its foundation stone. Unintentionally, perhaps. The Trinitarian concept, when it surfaced, added more air to Pauline theology, creating a mystical and esoteric halo around it. Trinity made Christianity a subject of intense dialogue, discourse, and argument. Christianity was clothed in an intellectually sophisticated abstractionism, which attracted more intellectual discourse and followers. The Unitarian theology (James school and Arian), on the other hand, stubbornly persisted with its woefully inflexible Judaic outlook. Its proselytizing machinery paled before the Trinitarian one. Unitarians could neither convince the Jews, the Romans nor the Greeks – three crucial players in the politics of the then Middle East.

From a theological point of view, what was it that transfixed the Unitarian religion within a limited geographical area, restricting its spread only to some pockets of the then-Middle East? Three Yeses and one No. Which brings us to what in chemistry speak is the "rate-limiting step."

The rate-limiting step determines the success or failure of a chemical reaction. It affects the quality and quantity of the products of a chemical reaction. Now, extrapolating it to Christian theology, there were four theological postulates, call them ingredients, so to say: monotheism, Messiahship, prophethood, and crucifixion. Jesus' Messiahship was the rate-limiting one. How did the Unitarian theology approach it? It firmly said "yes" to Jesus' Messiahship. That is OK. To legitimize the first "yes," it also said "yes" to Judaic monotheism and Jesus' prophethood. Three "Yeses" tipped the balance and trapped Unitarianism in the prison of Judaism.

Following three "Yeses," Unitarianism prudently chose to say "no" to crucifixion; otherwise, three "yeses" didn't make sense. Denying crucifixion was a problematic premise to defend. Take, for example, non-Jews. Messiahship specifically, and monotheism and prophethood generally were alien concepts to them. Add "no crucifixion of Jesus" to these three, and you get a psychological whammy, conjuration, and a suspect thesis implying all those who saw Jesus on the cross were effectively deluded – hard-to-believe conjuration for the 1st century Roman Judeans! That amounted to telling them they didn't see what they saw. The idea didn't sell. The Unitarian chemical reaction slowed down; it almost got jammed. The product it brought forth was unfamiliar to the majority, especially outside the Jewish circle of influence. Even the seasoned Jews found this crucifixion version unpalatable.

On the other hand, the Trinitarians sold their product well, albeit to non-Jews. They stripped their theology of the strict Judaic monotheism and Jesus' prophethood. Accepting Jesus' crucifixion, they clothed this event in an esoteric dimension – resurrection. It clicked. The gullible pagans didn't find it contradictory to their general belief pattern. The Trinitarian theology overshadowed the Unitarian one with time; the latter ultimately collapsing under its weight. Constantine, the Emperor, only wagged his finger at it. Yet, before it entirely evaporated, Unitarian Christianity left a wake that later cast its indelible imprint on Islam and its theology. There it remains alive. Breathing still and refusing to die a silent death.

Deportation Again

The prevailing psychological climate in 1st century Palestine provided Christianity a fertile ground. Whether Jesus was a meek shepherd, king, zealot, or Messiah can all be disputed, yet what is undoubtedly hard to deny is that he was a product of a specific epoch of Jewish history. Jesus, himself, and his contemporaries believed that they lived in the "*End* Time" epoch. Even before Jesus, many had claimed to be Messiahs; some even had been projected as Messiahs. However, by Jesus' time, "Messiahship" had become an almost exquisite and intricate ingredient – or even the hallmark – of the apocalyptic hysteria. Overall, Palestine (Roman Judea) was going through a "watershed phase" of its sacred history – a phase that punctuated an acute "crisis of meaning and purpose" – creating a peculiar climate at Jesus' time. The existing, by then, religious dogmas and theologies were proving dangerously inadequate, almost impotent, in providing a touch of meaning and purpose to life. John, the Baptist, was preaching that doom was imminent to wipe the Judeans off the face of the Earth – the end. To him, it was almost just at hand. Right there. Approaching.

Fear– fear for safety, life, and the world – had wholly overtaken the socio-political and religious climate. The preachers, sages, and holy men incessantly reminded the people of their sins and transgressions of everyday life. Under rabbis' rapid-fire verbal bombardments, the masses felt overwhelmed and overburdened with guilt consciousness. Clouds of despair and depression hovered over Judea. The rabbis and preachers so irascibly accused the people of immorality, corruption, and decadence that they genuinely feared divine wrath and retribution to descend on them soon. The future looked woefully gloomy. Since the Romans – the infidels – were tightening their grip over Palestine with each passing day, the Jews had plausible reasons to fear the apocalyptic prophecies of their holy scripture to come to pass. The frustrated Jews earnestly longed for a genuine spiritual leader to guide them and lead them to salvation and safety

Yet the Jews faced a strange dilemma. How could they reconcile two contradictory perspectives? On one hand, they thought of themselves as the "chosen people" of God and thus lived virtually in the past but, on the other hand, they could not ignore the fact they, as a society and polity, were steeped knee-deep in chaos and ruled by the infidels and polytheists.

The harsh truth was that they had long lost their freedom; they were subjected to shame and humiliation by a foreign power, and their values, culture, religion, and heritage were facing a dangerous threat. The dilemma they struggled with was: Is God really with us? If yes, then how could God in his power allow the defiling of His own Temple by the infidel pagans? How could the Almighty God allow a petty ruler of Rome to run roughshod over his "Chosen people"? These and other questions gnawed at them. In the silence of their hearts, they even looked at their God with suspicion. Yet they knew it was dangerous to think such a thought aloud. To even contemplate such a thought was to commit blasphemy. To say it aloud would be apostasy. Unthinkable. Dangerous. And, unaffordable for a Jew.

But then, what was going on? Was God knowingly and deliberately allowing the misfortune to happen to his chosen lot? Was it that God had abandoned them? If yes, why? These were hard questions for the Jews to answer. Finally, after much introspection and contemplation, they had a three-word answer: They had transgressed. As a result, they had invited upon themselves the wrath of God for their sins. They deserved to be punished. No wonder God was preparing to end their world, the Jews surmised, and create a new and better world for those loyal to him. It didn't take much time for the discourse and the narrative to set the day. An overall sense of guilt and a longing to repent overtook the Jewish psyche. The desire to achieve atonement became the normal collective yearning amidst the dark clouds of despair and fear.

In the turbulent religious-political atmosphere where emotions ran high, the spirits low, and fear was all-pervasive, the Messianic movement nothing but thrived. The majority of the Jews eagerly looked up to saints, leaders, and teachers, expecting the arrival of Messiah. They also looked up to the *Zealots* and the *Essenes* in reverence. There was no abandoning of the hope for an authentic Messiah to come in their midst and rally them against the foreign yoke. The Romans, on their part, genuinely feared that. This fear primarily underpinned the Roman Pilate's decision to get rid of Jesus by crucifying him. The Pilate was fully conscious of the resentment the Jews harbored against the Roman occupation. Finally, nearly three decades after Jesus' crucifixion, the Romans responded brutally when the much-anticipated revolt broke out in Palestine/Judea in 66 CE. The Temple of Zion was destroyed and burnt to ashes; the Jews were wantonly slaughtered, and those left alive were deported. It was one of the worst forms of ethnic cleansing—actual genocide of the Jews. The Jews and their Judaism were reduced to dust. The *End Time* that the Jews talked of for centuries couldn't have been worse. Yet, they rationalized the *End time* has still not come. They looked for the whole world to end, which didn't. And won't soon. To their chagrin, their version of the much-awaited Messiah didn't show up either.

The near-total annihilation couldn't dent the faith of the Jews in *Yahweh*, the omnipotent God. They suffered slaughter, humiliation, and incredible hardships defending their faith, religion, and God. Judaism, no doubt, had evolved after the tremendous reformation, yet its constricting dogmas put the Jews at the receiving end of history for centuries to come. The past haunted them; its imagined glory incapacitated them, and they willingly suffered, incredibly and incessantly, defending it over the centuries. They steadfastly stood by a set of ideas and truisms – abstract ideas and concepts and imagined truth lacking any solid historical basis – with their flesh and blood, and whenever they got the opportunity, they didn't hesitate to spill others' blood. The Jews were not the only people, though, who engaged in irrational behavior. Humankind as a whole quickly falls into the trap of fiction and mythology, thanks to natural selection.

Yet, the Jewish story was far from over. There was more to come.

The Headlines and the Story Proper

The Christians viewed the genocide of the Jews by the Romans as a prophecy fulfilled. For Paul and his associates, pioneers of the idea of a purely spiritual Messiah, the near-annihilation of Judea and Palestine was a "sign." A sure sign. A miracle. It was proof of Jesus being the Messiah. Otherwise, how could they survive the mayhem, these, a bunch of poor and persecuted fakirs, followers of an esoteric cult, Paleo-Christians? It was God who protected them against the mighty. He had promised to protect them. Except, perhaps, that he never had.

In the following centuries, "God's sign" unfurled fully. The followers of Pauline Christianity multiplied, and they were now formally called Christians. The "sign" that Paul had once hallucinated about was erected as the "Cross." However, the early Christians had to pay a heavy price in blood and life for going against the tide of history. Yet it was a matter of a couple of centuries that Christians would get the upper hand. Did they then behave better when they became numerically and politically more potent? No.

The saga that ensued was far more complex, sickening, and vexing. The Christians, like the Jews before them, foolishly poked the Romans. The latter let their hounds and boots loose on them, persecuting and slaughtering them wherever they found them. What did these poor Christians do that particularly enraged the Romans? Like their Jewish predecessors, they refused to accept and participate in the Roman ritual of Sacrifice in the name of the Emperor. However, unlike the Jews, the Christians argued there was no need for any further sacrifice since Jesus had already offered the Grand Sacrifice of his blood and flesh. Why then make any sacrifice that, too, for an infidel king? This Christian talk utterly surprised the Romans. It was an unheard-of nuisance. "Who is 'this bunch' of mad heretics, Christ lovers?" the Romans wondered. Perhaps. And they tightened the noose around these Christ lovers banning their meetings for the communal meal, Eucharist.

Soon gossip picked up. They were called names. New cultists, Christ Lovers, blood drinkers, and much more – who are they? Gossip bred more buzz, and rumors became rife about this new creed. A perfect scandal erupted. A scandal is a scandal, be it today or 2000 years ago. It draws people's attention. The Christians were now incriminated for scandalous and noisome behavior. The common masses turned hostile toward these poor souls, many of whom were from the lower strata of the society.

Circumstances compelled these poor converts to unite immediately. Soon they began running their tiny sort of welfare proto-state in the name of Jesus as their god and savior, which made them truly suspect in the eyes of the people and the Roman state. All kinds of humiliation, torture, and discrimination were meted out to them. They won't budge. They endured all suffering in the name of Christ. Their Saviour. Their God. Their son of God.

By the 3rd century CE, things took an unexpected turn for the Christians. God's sign showed up, as Paul had promised long ago. The Roman Empire was gripped by chaos; the emperors were changing in quick succession; the once-mighty empire quickly became unstable, almost breaking up into pieces. The overtly superstitious Roman emperors became finicky about the gods. New emperors would become indolently preoccupied with searching for a new god powerful enough to help them retain the throne.

When Aurelius, in 274 CE, won the battle in what is now Syria, he attributed his victory to the benevolence of the Syrian Sun god, *Sol-Invictus*. Wanting no cudgels with the Sun god, like a drowning man catching on straw, Aurelius quickly performed sacrifice and worship of *Sol-Invictus*. Emperor Diocletian, in his turn, rejected the Sun god and declared a Persian god, *Mithras*, as the protector of the Roman Empire. Both these were no strong emperors. They were inefficient and too meek to hold that mighty and vast Roman Empire from perilously falling apart under its weight.

In 306 CE, Constantine took over after the death of his father. He planned to march to Rome and capture the city at the first instance, in which he succeeded. Constantine reportedly saw a sign – a "Cross" superimposed on the Sun during his march. He interpreted it as a message from the God of Christians. So goes the legend.

Was what Constantine saw as the sign "Christian God calling him" his hallucination or an expedient imagining? That didn't matter. However, what mattered was that Constantine had found his patron and god in Jesus. That an emperor of the stature of Constantine turned to Jesus was hugely significant for Christianity. It was a heaven-sent gift, especially when this creed was going through its existential crisis. The time for jubilation had come. Christianity's survival and success were now a given. There would be no looking back. It was a matter of time before this religion would bring within its tentacles the whole of the then Middle East, spread to Europe, and ambitiously pursue proselytizing work in other parts of the globe. In the next 1800 years after Constantine's patronage, no religion could match Christianity's sword, pen, and power.

With Rome now legitimately belonging to Christianity, the power equation quickly changed. Almost overnight. Christianity was no more the religion of the humble, meek, and the poor. It became a religion of the powerful. As a state religion, soon it began enjoying the privileges that a mighty empire could offer. The Holy Land of Palestine and Judah came into the limelight after a lull, making the headlines again, except that the Jews were completely out of the picture this time. However, the Jewish ghost would relentlessly haunt the Palestinian religious-political scene for centuries to come. The headlines would be written in ink, but the story proper played out in blood - blood in the name of religion. Yet, religion was only an instrument to play the bloody game. In reality, the rules of the game were set by the economic agenda.

The Bait

Precisely at a time when the Roman world had grown spiritually restless and even skeptical about their Pantheon of gods, Constantine, a consummate politician, shrewdly stepped in. Accurately feeling the pulse of the people, he astutely placed himself on the pedestal of hierarchy which provided the Roman world with a much-needed link between God and Caesar. As a result, he filled the vacuum at the most opportune time throwing in the option of a new religion, and began his preparation for a new Capital city for the Romans. The Romans complied without much fuss. Constantine intuitively knew that the empire's economic stability depended on the consolidation of the East. He surmised that the biggest threat to the Roman Empire – the Goths and the mighty Persians – came from the East.

The Persians were opulently benefitting from the increasing amount of business happening at the confluence of the eastern and western trade routes. The natural crossroads, both on land and water, between the East and the West, was a narrow neck now called the Strait of Bosphorus (modern Turkey). Every boat bringing the merchandise and every caravan carrying the goods would meet here at the important natural harbor – the Golden Horn. A town had thrived here for centuries as the hub of trade and a repository of the wealth of all the nations. Until 330 CE, it was known as Byzantium. Constantine, an astute politician, thoroughgoing administrator, and shrewd economist, couldn't ignore Byzantium. Close by, he inaugurated his capital city, Constantinople, which later became Eastern Rome. His newfound love of Jesus tremendously helped him accomplish the transfer of power from the West to the East smoothly. His decision to declare an eastern religion, Christianity, as the empire's official religion gave a new life to this dying fringe cult. Soon, a sparklingly grand church of God, the Central Cathedral – Santa Sophia – was erected in Byzantium.

Is it fair to say that the Christians got consolidated into a "genuine" community with a firm identity primarily due to Constantine's patronage? Well, yes. As mentioned elsewhere in this book, history has shown that no religion has flourished or even survived long without kings and emperors' patronages. That is to say, political power is essential for Religion's success. Constantine's adoption of Christianity gave a boost to this creed and encouraged the Christians to propagate their narrative vigorously and unimpededly proselytize their theology. The result: Christianity entered everyday life's discourse.

Constantine announced special concessions to the Christians as a matter of policy. Discriminatory, though, at its core, this policy worked as terrific bait, from an economic point of view, to inevitably attract more and more adherents to Christianity. For Constantine, it was a good thing. Numbers matter. When the numbers are acquiescing, monarchy and its deep state are better manageable; and the suck-ups and the sycophants are easier to handle. Constantine, like any ruler, might have strived to keep his capital and dominion free of civil wars and religious conflicts. Theoretically, the more the members belonged to a particular religion, the more harmony and peace would prevail. Perhaps Constantine might have thought along those lines before announcing Christianity as the state religion. That is hard to know for sure, though.

No doubt, religion has the power to create emotional bonds where none exist; the cultures come to revolve around the religious creeds, and religion and culture become so integrated that they become inseparable, yet all that doesn't always translate into societal harmony and peaceful coexistence amongst the followers of a particular religion even in homogenous societies. Utopia can't substitute utility. Religion can't replace good politics. At its core, a theocratic state is a shaky enterprise despite its apparent sheen and luster. In Constantine's case, his strategy paid him short-term dividends, no doubt, but it caused humungous pain and suffering in the long term. His discriminatory theocratic state policy was, to put it mildly, ill-conceived. Unfortunately, modern democracies increasingly tend to turn to such and other failed experiments and painful majoritarian policies despite the evidence to the contrary. Religion blinds people to facts of history.

Initially, Constantine's bait policy delivered encouraging results. In his enthusiasm, he gave a free hand to Christians who used the newfound prestige to create an environment of clientelism and patronage. It didn't take much time for things to turn ugly. Soon the Christians' ax fell on pagans and other non-Christians. By 380 CE, as the non-Christians wantonly suffered harsh penalties for continuing with their pagan traditions, Constantine announced another significant decision: he officially sided with the "Trinitarian Christianity" at the Council of Nicaea. The concept of the Trinity was now formally legitimized and legalized in Christianity. The Arian (Unitarian) Christianity was routed.

Siding with the Trinity was a difficult decision for Constantine to make because the Gospels didn't unequivocally support the concept of the Trinity. He vacillated for some time while each side – the Trinitarian and the Arian – put forth their respective arguments in favor of and against the Trinity. In the end, though, he decided to agree with the Trinitarians. This landmark decision of his was perhaps dictated more by political expediency than by his theological conviction. In the aftermath of his siding with the Trinitarians, things turned ugly. Constantine tried to resolve the ongoing bloody sectarian conflict through debate and discussion, which he succeeded in doing during his lifetime. To some extent, at least. But, after his death, nothing could prevent bloodshed from happening.

The bloody intolerance towards a differing point of view has been a sad part of the history of almost all religions, except that with the three major Abrahamic faiths, in particular, this tragic story played out peculiarly characteristically. The Christians shamefully set out on a wanton sectarian blood hunt (ironically, Muslims did the same when the sacred history of Islam was taking shape), slaughtering their opponents and even burning them alive. The fellow Christians who differed with the majority on theological issues like, for example, the divinity of Jesus, weren't spared either.

Yet, despite sectarian violence and bloodshed that riddled it, Christianity spread its tentacles far and wide, aided partly by trading networks. First, it spread to the East, almost imperceptibly, carried by the Jewish trading communities who had settled in Mesopotamia (present-day Iraq) since their exile from Palestine. The Jewish traders of antiquity served as potential conduits for spreading ideas, religious and otherwise, across the length and breadth of the then-Middle East. As ideas traversed back and forth, they sparked curiosity in peoples' minds and hearts about distant lands and their inhabitants. As mentioned earlier, Byzantium (modern Turkey) occupied a particularly prominent place in the East because it was a converging point of trade routes and communication links. From here, travelers, traders, preachers, storytellers, and even armies could practically crisscross nearly the whole ancient world, carrying ideas and stories to flow in all directions. No wonder Christians could be found all over the Middle East and even in a place that became Afghanistan in 1823 CE.

The *Book of the Laws of Countries*, written in antiquity, has recorded the events in fair detail. Persia, partly because of its proximity to and rivalry with Byzantium, was particularly worried by Christianity which posed a real threat to its Zoroastrian tradition. It was prudent for Persia to act lest Christianity became a nuisance. Accordingly, the state machinery hunted down the Christians persecuted them, and deported them. Bishops, priests, and other high-ranking leaders, who had settled in Persia, were exiled. For example, Demetrius, the first bishop of Gundeshpur, was deported to the South-Western region of Persia. The deportations were a brutal punishment, but they turned out to be a blessing in disguise for Christianity. They helped disseminate the Christians far and wide in the Persian empire and outside it, carrying with them the stories, fables, and myths about Jesus to almost all corners of Asia. These colorful and newly-spun stories raised the "spiritual Jesus" as envisioned by Paul to new heights of divinity.

Furthermore, the deported Christians spread all kinds of stuff about the Persians and their allegedly strange stereotypes. One famous gossip, for instance, that fervently spread far wide in Byzantine towns and Balkans was that the Persians felt no qualms in marrying their mothers, and "those who" then became his (Jesus's) followers "no longer marry their mothers." Such gossip worked in favor of Christianity, and Jesus was introduced to audiences as far off as modern Afghanistan. Every religion has thrived on buzz and story, but Christianity spun out preposterous stuff as part of accepted practice to add power and aura to the supposed miracle-doer –

Jesus – the central figure of Pauline Christianity. The ludicrous gossip and the fatuous stories were willingly hailed and approved by the Church.

Christianity vs. Zoroastrianism

As has always been the case, the competition for resources to feed the royal household, government employees, and the army mandated the adoption of the expansionist policy by the kings and emperors. Wars, battles, and victories and losses happened for economic pursuits, yet bland "profit and loss" alone couldn't sufficiently motivate people and warriors to fight brutal wars and battles. Economics needed to be clothed in sophisticated belief systems to make sense of the brutality, bloodshed, and devastation inflicted on each other. Robust propaganda machines needed to be put in place to disseminate narratives to control the populace's minds deliberately. Inevitably, the institution of clergy (priests, rabbis, fathers, imams) and theologians thrived. Over time, however, the political expediencies unwittingly created room for Clergy to exert its power confidently and aggressively. In Persia, too, as in other empires, the priesthood had proactively extended its role into politics.

The Persian Empire expanded swiftly, and under the clergy's pressure after each military conquest, it erected Zoroastrian temples in the newly annexed territories as a matter of policy. Each conquered territory was supposed to maintain at least five such temples, which made Zoroastrianism come to be seen as suspect. Some conquered peoples took a strong exception to this high-handed Persian promotion of religion in total contradiction to the principles Zoroastrianism supposedly stood for –spiritual salvation. Subsequently, a wave of resentment set off against the Persian religious interference. But, overall, the people were helpless before the priests' power and looked for alternatives. As Christianity was lurking around the corner, it quickly grabbed the opportunity to intensify its propaganda. Many converted to the new faith. The Persians didn't stop them for the time being.

Come Shapur II (309-379 CE), the longest-reigning Sasanian monarch in Persian history. He had long set his eye on the wealth of the Caucasus. In 337 CE, he launched a surprise attack on a vitally strategic outpost for the Byzantines in terms of tribute and border security. Shapur II deposed the local ruler and installed his nominee in his place. Constantine could not simply afford to give a strategic outpost to the Persians on a platter.

He quickly readied his army and assembled his bishops to accompany him on the campaign against Persian belligerence. Christianity was in danger; the infidels had breached the territory of the Holy Empire! Constantine might have fumed. Perhaps.

A replica of the Tabernacle was prepared to be carried along during this war expedition. The carrying of a religious symbol, the Tabernacle, gave a purely religious outlook to Constantine's war with the Persians. To add more fervor to the religious zeal, Constantine decided to get baptized in the River Jordan, as Jesus had in his days. This all left Shapur irritated. But, to the chagrin of Christians, as the war expedition was on its way, Constantine suddenly died. The army fell into disarray. Now, Shapur II, encouraged by the loss of the commander by the Byzantines, threatened the Christians with reprisals. He began the wicked game from home. The Christians were accused of inciting trouble and rebellion in Persia at the behest of the Church of Rome. A crusade of terror and torture was unleashed on them in Persia. In the ensuing blood bath, the Christian Saints, bishops, and learned men were put to the sword at the behest of the Zoroastrian priests. Perhaps.

Constantine, in his wisdom, had moved to the East and adopted the Eastern religion, but he could hardly foresee that his declaration of Christianity as the official religion of the Roman (Byzantine) Empire would put the eastern Christians at the sharp edge of the sword, soon after his death. These so-called eastern Christians were slaughtered like meek sheep by the Persians. A horrible nightmare was set into motion for them, and many were deported and banished. With all his political shrewdness, Constantine might have seen embracing Trinitarian Christianity as one of his historical decisions, but did it serve Christianity well overall? Well, yes, in the short term. Yet, the facts suggest that, in reality, Latin Christianity, post-Constainine, compromised and undermined its future in the East for all times to come!

Conflict and violence have been the hallmark of sacred history all along. That is a paradox because every religion has rhetorically claimed to be the harbinger of peace, hope, and conflict resolution, yet the ground reality has been the opposite. Inter-faith conflicts, violence, and wars have consumed a considerable majority of the human population for centuries, yet intra-faith (in-group) peace and harmony have been uncommon. People have killed, maimed, and tortured their co-religionists throughout history and continue to do so. The inter-faith harmony and cooperation seem like a utopian dream, never to come true, yet intra-faith peace is no less enigmatic. It is hard to identify any period when different religious groups or even the members of the same religion didn't fight against each other on one or the other pretext. Yet there of some instances of cooperation – call them anomalies – between followers of different faiths against a common enemy when economic interests are at stake.

The Hun Nuisance

In the 4th century CE, a horrible nuisance of marauders got the whole of Byzantium, Rome, and Persia shudder to a halt in one fell swoop. The threat of extinction baffled both Byzantium and Persia. For the first time in centuries, Rome and Persia had no time to think of the religious difference. The only thing that could save the hitherto sworn enemies was cooperation. And cooperate they did.

An unprecedented climate change had struck the faraway lands of China, driving out hordes of savage Asian tribes on a killing and looting spree. As they swarmed the Middle East, bringing the Byzantine and Persian empires to the heel, the latter were left with no option but to put religious politics on hold. They shelved their differences, temporarily though, and decided to launch a cooperated effort to repel the merchants of death and destruction. It took them time, however, to organize the defense. By the time it was in place, both empires had grown precariously enfeebled.

Return to Shapur II for a moment. With Constantine gone, Shapur II pursued his expansionist policy unabatedly. By the time he died in 379 CE, the Persian empire had brought major nodal points of trade and communication routes leading to the Mediterranean under its control. As Persia was becoming comfortable, a calamity struck in the Far East that had far-reaching consequences for the rest of the world, especially the Middle East. It happened so, that the Far East was enveloped in one of the worst famines. The perilous climate change converted once-fertile lands of the Far East into barren ones resulting in a considerable fall in grain production. To add to their misery, malaria, and other infections befell China as if the famine wasn't enough. The Chinese kings abandoned their kingdoms. Starvation and death, disease, and despair descended on the East, forcing the tribal hordes from the steppes to ferociously raid the lands spared by famine in search of food and grain. They embarked on wanton looting and killing sprees, just slaughtering the people who came in their way and burning down village after village, creating havoc.

As the villages, towns, and cities capitulated before these swarming hordes of swift horse-riders, they amassed considerable booty and tributes from the fallen populations. By the time they reached the heart of Byzantium, these battle-hardened tribes of the steppes had organized themselves into an army of looters and marauders, pushing the people out of their settlements and inflicting on them unheard-of atrocities, merciless torture, and slaughter. They killed entire populations and burned down entire villages and towns, which instilled fear in people's hearts and minds. Fear of them was one of the keys to their success. People called these fearsome hordes *Xiongnu* or simply the Huns.

The Huns committed atrocities that were beyond the imagination of ordinary folks. They didn't blink an eye while decapitating and burning alive the unarmed civilians. From Bactria up to the Danube, the then border of the Roman (Byzantine) Empire, the whole populace shuddered as the Huns alighted like a tsunami on towns, villages, and settlements, spilling blood where they went. The news that the Huns had driven people inhabiting the coast of the Black Sea off their lands left the Romans and the Persian pissing in their pants. Gathering courage, Eastern Rome mobilized a massive army to counter the advancing Huns, but the latter badly crushed the Romans at Thrace in 378 CE. With that, the empire burst open for these ruthless grunts. The death and destruction delivered by the Huns into its very heart shook the empire to its core.

Persia fared no better, nearly collapsing under the assault. As the towns were burnt down and inhabitants slaughtered, the cities of Mesopotamia, Syria, and Asia Minor provided the invaders with fat booties. In 395 CE, these thriving cities on the banks of Euphrates and Tigris were put to the torch. But Ctesiphon, the capital of the Persian Empire, did not capitulate. It resisted bravely and halted the advance of the Huns. That was, however, not enough to stop the continuous pouring in of these barbarian hordes through the Caucasus. More needed to be done to stop these incessant swarms. Neither Persia nor Byzantium could handle the crisis on their own. The only solution lay in cooperation; otherwise, the Romans and the Persians would be gobbled up by the army of deadly fiends, the Huns. And cooperate they did. For the first time, two empires with opposing religious beliefs put aside their hostility and resolved to fight back a common enemy. Cooperation made history.

The Persians erected a fortification stretching over nearly 125 miles manned by 30,000 troops. Rome agreed to make a regular financial contribution toward maintaining this Persian (Zoroastrian) wall and supply soldiers to guard the fortification. This cooperative effort came a bit late when the damage had already been done to both empires. Rome had become weak, sick, and vulnerable in the aftermath of the Hun invasion. Its borders had become highly porous to other invaders, like, for example, the Visigoths, to pour from the Black Sea belt of the Steppes – another nuisance for the sick Rome. In 410 CE, the Visigoths marched into what is now Italy, then the heart of the Roman Empire, and mercilessly sacked the "city of Rome." That was an unexpected shock to the Romans. Unbelievably the Christians felt that their God had forsaken them just as it had Jesus when four centuries earlier he would bemoan aloud *Eli, Eli, Lama Sabachthani* – God, God, why have you forsaken me? The Christians were helpless. After Rome was brought to th heel, the triumphant Visigoths squelched every sign of resistance. They were about to burn the Holy City down but stopped at the last moment. By a sheer stroke of luck, the City of Rome survived. The Roman Senate heaved a sigh of relief.

It was immaterial whether Rome would be put to the torch or not by then. The empire had already collapsed. A thread now hung its fate. One more pull and it would fall into pieces! The final pull, though, didn't come immediately. Like the dying horse, Rome continued to kick indiscriminately for a few more centuries. What had remained of this mighty empire were a few pieces of real estate like Constantinople, Palestine, Egypt, and some of the provinces of Asia Minor, that were luckily left unscathed by the Huns. After watching his empire crumble literally before his eyes, the Roman Emperor Theodosius II might have been jolted to think: "Nothing can be left to chance; God may not find time to come to our rescue!" He gathered courage and embarked on the mission of fortifying the second Rome – Constantinople – against all odds.

The Huns had been extracting heavy tribute from Constantinople for 15 years. However, now, as luck would have it, the tide turned. A confederation of tribes marched down from the North along the Danube, challenging the supremacy of the Huns. A fierce battle ensued on the Catalonian plains between the Huns and the Confederation. Finally, only a diamond could cut a diamond. As the Huns were decisively beaten, an opportunity opened up for Theodosius to consolidate his position in Eastern Rome. He might have grinned in delight at this heaven-sent opening. He lost no time in seizing the opportunity.

The New Storm

All the same, the Christians' world was collapsing. The sophisticated theology, religion, and prayers seemed not to help them. They had always thought they cultivated a close spiritual relationship with God, Jesus; they were obedient to him. Theirs was the true religion of God, who in his Grace was their protector. Except that he wasn't. "Why does God allow the Barbarians to have the upper hand?" wondered the Christian priests, leaders, writers, and commoners. "Why should enemies rule us and subjugate us?" they questioned. Certainly, something was amiss. But, what exactly? "Could there be anything wrong with God and his true religion, Christianity?" No, that was a sinful thought. How could the Christian God be wrong? It might be that he was punishing his followers for their sins and transgression, just like Yahweh did to Jews. God was beyond fault.

The fact of the matter was that the Romans were not all Christian. There were Pagans and polytheists, too, who actually comprised the majority. How did they look at these events? Did they share the Christian perspective? No. They viewed the situation through their prism of predisposition rooted in nostalgia and despair about Rome abandoning her old faith and turning to Christianity. They sincerely believed Rome herself engineered her demise by invoking the wrath of the Roman gods. "As long as Rome remained sincerely faithful to its Pagan roots and religious practices, she was the master of the world," the Pagan laity and the elite firmly believed. Who was right, and who was wrong? That depends on whom you ask. For the faithful, the "only" existing version of the truth is the version provided by their respective faiths. That is that.

Which brings us back to the Hun invasion. Despite wreaking havoc, the good news for Christianity was that Persia softened its posture. The relations between the two competitors improved to some extent as they both sailed in the same boat. The Huns were inflicting death and fatally severe economic distress on both empires. A brief period of apparent cooperation that followed the two rivals' treaty – dictated, in reality, by economic expediency – was the only period of "inter-religious peace" in the history of that region. In 410 CE, in the aftermath of the treaty, the Shah (the Emperor) of Persia formally allowed the Persian Christian Church to standardize its belief system and Code of Conduct. The Christian population was accorded the liberty to practice their faith.

Ironically, as some semblance of peace and calm had arrived after pushing back the Huns, Christians fell prey to sectarian conflict after a brief period of respite due to the tussle between the two Churches – the Eastern and the Western (Latin). This time the Persians couldn't be blamed. Christians themselves were at fault. As evolution has it, humans are programmed for conflict and violence. Their groups split when the number of members exceeds 150, like in all living species when the number of members in a group crosses a certain threshold. Christianity as a group, like all religious bodies, was bound to split into sects despite the shared stories and belief systems. Different sects meant different dispositions on the same theological issues. Disagreement, discord, and conflict were bound to happen. Violence was inevitable. Period.

In times of relative peace, divergent views and interpretations tend to crop up within the body politic of every religion. The lack of accommodation of opposing viewpoints by competing sects and denominations causes sectoral conflict with the potential to trigger disproportionate violence. In the case of Eastern Christianity, there were already two main rival sects in Persia: *Nasaraye* and *Kristyoxe*. The term *Nasaraye* applied to all the Christians who were non-Persian, that is, immigrants, and the *Kristyoxe* to the indigenous Persian converts. They came at loggerheads, their rivalry reaching its peak, and violence broke out, posing a serious threat to the law and order situation in the Persian Empire. The Shah offered his support for the summoning of a Christian religious Council like that of Nicaea (summoned by Constantine to handle the dispute between Arian and Trinitarian Christianity), hoping that it would have a salutary effect on the situation. In response to Shah's call, the Christian bishops held not one but three councils in the years 410, 420, and 424 CE, respectively. But nothing pragmatic came out of these assemblies. The infighting and the power struggle continued and even intensified. Finally, the Holy Roman Empire recognized the Eastern Church, but the latter continued to remain at daggers drawn with the Church of Rome.

It is not easy to think futuristically because what the mind doesn't know, the eyes don't see. In the 5th century CE, Christians not able to contemplate the future, lost an excellent opportunity for reconciliation. In hindsight, it is easier to judge history, misconstruing it as a cascade of well-defined, strictly succeeding-each-other events, obeying, as it were, a mathematical pattern. Far from that. History happens the way it happens. It shapes itself according to the human perspective, which as we know is never fixed, varying, changing, and evolving as it does at different points in time and space.

In retrospect, whatever came in the way of unification of the two Churches can be debated and is immaterial. Beyond debate, though, is this: Had the two Churches unified, Christianity would have become the most dominant religious force of antiquity. It could have so well penetrated the depths of the societal frame and fabric and wielded such political power that any other religion, Islam included, would have found it hard to displace Christianity in the Middle East in general and Persia in particular. That didn't happen. Instead, bitter sectoral infighting broke out. Either history had different plans, or God had other plans, or maybe both had identical plans in store for Asia.

Each of the two Churches took a stiff and rigid position for economic and political reasons in addition to theological contestations. The Church (and the State) extracted fat revenues from the people and there was no good reason for the Eastern church to relinquish its control over finances to the Roman Church. The two Christian churches became intolerant of each other. Violence erupted—a pandemonium-like situation set in. The emotions ran high on both sides. In their religious zeal, the Christian militants or mujahids from both sides now turned to vandalize religious buildings, churches, and temples. Some Zoroastrian temples were also desecrated and torched. The Persians saw this violence as an attack on their religion and faith. The aristocracy was furious at the behavior of the Christians. "Liberty was not a good idea for the Christians, they should be shown the rod. They deserved it," surmised the Shah. A new wave of persecution got unleashed. The Christians paid a heavy price with their life, blood, and property.

Persecution or not didn't matter for the zealot Christians. They continued with their religious conflict contesting each other's theology. The focus of the nasty debate, five centuries after the disappearance of Jesus, remained anchored in the same contentious issue of the 1st century CE: Was Jesus human or divine? In 451CE, the Council of *Chalcedon* articulated a new definition of Faith henceforth to be strictly followed by the Church and the Clergy. The resolution was laced with a threat of ex-communication for those who didn't deem it fit, for theological reasons, to agree with the *Chalcedon* resolution. The Eastern Church promptly refused to agree with this resolution. It unabashedly criticized its new definition of Faith, calling it heresy.

The Holy Roman emperor and the Church reacted strongly and ordered to close down the School in Edessa in what is now Urfa, south-east Turkey – then the most important place of learning and a strategic propaganda apparatus of the Eastern Church. The schism between Eastern and Latin Christianity deepened after the ban on the Edessan School. After signing the Peace Treaty of 532 CE with Persia, the Byzantine Roman emperor pressured the Shah of Persia to track down and incarcerate the bishops and the priests who opposed the Council of *Chalcedon* resolution. It, too, didn't work. Finally, in exasperation, Emperor Justinian tried to negotiate peace between the two warring Christian factions through the Ecumenical Council held in 553 CE. That too failed. The warring factions won't simply listen to anything. The successive emperors learned a lesson: violence would occur if liberty were given to religion and the clergy. The solution? Forbid the discussion of religious matters altogether in the palace and the empire. Yet that was easier said than done.

The storm in the East refused to settle down completely. Despite being banned, the Eastern school of Christianity continued spreading its tentacles across Asia. Basra, Mosul, and Tikrit became hubs of Christianity. The king of Yemen had also converted to Christianity. In 550 CE, a robust Christian community thrived as far away as Sri Lanka. Samarkand and Bukhara were fast becoming home to thriving Christian communities, while centers like Merv, Gundeshiapur, Kashgar, and others had already become the crucial hotbeds of Christianity. Baghdad had long become home to Christianity. Christianity was rapidly engulfing the future fulcrum of global geopolitics – the heartland of the globe (Eurasia). However, Western Christians hardly ever acknowledge that the expansion of Christianity, at least in Asia, was facilitated by Persia's tolerant and libertarian attitude, especially under the Sasanian king, Khusraw I, who succeeded his father Kavad in 531 CE and reigned till 579 CE. This king was a dedicated lover of literature and philosophy. He extended a warm welcome and respect to the Christian patriarchs and priests. Khusraw I came from being a persecutor to a friend and admirer of the Christians who thrived and continued proselytizing vigorously and fearlessly under his reign.

This religious tolerance during Khusraw I's reign wasn't something unnatural. It was the result of the economic stability of the Persian Empire around that time. The Persians exhibited a growing self-confidence, no more bothered about Byzantine Rome as the latter was busy with crisis management in the Mediterranean. Persia received regular money from Rome for manning the fence to keep away the invaders from the Steppes. Agricultural production was comparatively higher in the 6th century Persian Empire compared to the Byzantines, and a well-paid Persian bureaucracy ensured a smooth administration. The empire's trade flourished with India and China in the East and with the Mediterranean belt in the West. Persia was self-satisfied. It had lost its interest in the proselytizing business. Zoroastrianism was left to exist in name only. Persians were busy enjoying the fruits of politico-economic stability.

Not so with Christianity. It continued traveling along the trade routes. It crossed paths with other faiths and ideas, facing intense competition for spiritual authority. In the ensuing confrontation with other religions, violence invariably followed. For instance, Jews demolished the churches or forcibly turned them into synagogues in their settlements along the Red Sea. In the bloodbath that followed, hundreds of Christians were put to the sword by the Jews, and countless others were maimed and brutalized. For what? For preaching what the Jews did not like to hear. It was a total heresy for them. The virgin birth of Jesus, his resurrection, his sonship of God – all that rang an alarm in the Jewish ear. Hence the Christians, these idolaters, deserved to be mercilessly slaughtered and burnt alive. According to the Jews, the only correct version of faith and religion was theirs since they were the only legitimate People of the Book.

The Jews had a reason to go aggressive whenever they had the opportunity. They harbored scarred souls and psyches. Five centuries ago, they had been mercilessly treated by the Romans and thrown out of their birthplace to wander the globe. Whenever these battered people could get a chance, they would never hesitate to spill out their anger with unimaginable beastly mercilessness on the impoverished Christians they would encounter. All in the name of their religion and their God, *Elohim*.

Weren't the Christians children of the same God? Yes, but their story of faith – the religion – was not the same as that of the Jews.

Christianity didn't have to put up with Judaism alone. Other competitive spiritualities like Zoroastrianism, Buddhism, Hinduism, or Confucianism also had their deeply entrenched spheres of influence. But Christianity managed to steadfastly chip away at these other traditional belief systems and practices. It audaciously penetrated China at a time when at home (Palestine and Eastern Rome), it was being battered to a pulp and managed to grab others' attention, pushing Judaism, Zoroastrianism, and even Buddhism into the corner. By the mid-7th century CE, the writing on the wall seemed to be bold. The religion born in the small village of Galilee in Judea was surely turning out to be the most likely winner in the battle of ideas and religious competition. The progress it had made after the alleged crucifixion of Jesus by Pontius Pilate was a testimony to its appeal. It would now only be a matter of time before Christianity would make a transatlantic voyage to the other side of the globe. This religion was spreading everywhere.

There seemed to be no turning back now. However, little did Christianity know that a revolution was brewing in its immediate wake. A revolution, all set to pose a formidable challenge and inimical threat to its survival in the East and the West. Little did it know that it had to fight back more vigorously than ever to manage its survival. The revolution that threatened Christianity's seat of power arose not from within the Fertile Crescent but from the sands of the desert. History took a unique but significant twist. The tables turned against Christianity as well as Zoroastrianism. A new page was about to be written.

PART 4

The Sands of Arabia – From Caravans to Kingdom

Chapter – 10

The Most Improbable Figure

The Arid Triangle

While the religious-political drama determined the events and set the tone for a checkered "sacred history" in Persia and Eastern Rome, including Syria, Palestine, Egypt, and Abyssinia (Ethiopia), Arabia, despite being situated on the outskirts, was a sort of remote-controlled client state. The two empires (Rome and Persia) supported their respective collaborator, Arab tribes, against one another. Both empires had enough of their headaches, and neither was keen to open one more battlefront in the far, isolated, difficult-to-navigate desert land that Arabia was. Arabia, this innocuous triangle of sparsely inhabited hot and stormy desert trapped between the substantial water bodies – Euphrates and the Persian Gulf on the East, the Red Sea on the West, and the Indian Ocean on the South – hardly drew any strategic attention. Its strange geography, notwithstanding the three big water bodies, one on each side, ensures that this triangle of stone and sand is deprived of any trickle of water and turned arid to the core. The sand on all sides was a formidable barrier against the cavalry movements of the invaders into North Arabia. Southern Arabia (present Yemen), however, did witness a spate of invasions from Ethiopia, Persia, etc.

This hot, stormy, vast sea of sand bereft of trees and vegetation would be terrifying to strangers. It would paint a more horrifying scene than even the terrible steppes of Tartary in the mind's eye of the strangers, for the steppes were comparatively more lush and luxuriant than this harsh and hot desert. In ancient and medieval days, the landscape of sand and dust seemed vast and smooth, barring a few places where some naked and ugly-looking mountains intercepted it. Today, mountains are no longer visible. Huge skyscrapers obscure them from sight. And drip-irrigated farmhouses and air-conditioned greenhouses have turned sands into high-yield agricultural lands. The state-of-the-art network of concrete highways makes it hard to imagine what it would have been like to traverse these deserts on foot and camel-backs for months at a stretch.

Until the recent past, the perpetually receding and reappearing, big and small, hillocks of sand punctuated this vast stretch of the desert here and there. They imparted a peculiar fizzle to the desert surface. And, like the ocean's water, the sand of this desert turned, at times, dangerously aggressive when the gigantic sand waves galloped like demonic dinosaurs to devour anything in their path. Entire caravans and armies of men and beasts of burden have been lost in those whirlwinds of sand and dust.

This triangular desert was and still is, monotonously arid to the naked eye. The rains being scant and the vegetation scarce by a mile – except some hardy shrubs and trees seen sparsely – the wells and the springs were the real "secret treasure" of this desert, attracting people to establish settlements around a green pasture, oasis, or a stream of fresh spring water. As a result, deep within the sand-and-stone landscape of this triangle, Life was thriving around some pivotal points. And, by the 6th century CE, towns and mini-cities had already come up, with trade links established with the heart of Canaan and the Euphrates-Tigris civilization. Whole caravans slugged to and fro, trading goods and luxury items of antiquity. The barter economy of the day, clumsy, though, was still OK to sustain a thriving civilization in Arabia. By the 7th century, a seemingly unassuming religious movement brewed and quickly transmogrified into a formidable religious-political revolution, catching the two dwindling empires – Persia and Byzantium – by surprise. More of that will come in the following two chapters. Here we shall focus on the pre-Islamic socio-political scenario.

Eastern Rome was decaying, and so was Persia, after centuries of confrontation, tussle, and wars over hegemony. By the 7th century, the Middle East witnessed a leadership vacuum and socio-political chaos. Local feudal lords were vying for independence; particularly, the once-great Persian empire was fast breaking into real estate pieces. The Romans had gotten too feeble to gobble up Persia. The borders were practically open for the raiders and petty invaders to enter, grab booty, women, and children, and enslave them. The situation - the breaking empires, turmoil, and above all, the disenchantment of the people with the existing political scenario - was such that an astute invader would have a cakewalk entry into these great empires' remaining dust and debris. For the seventh-century Bedouin

Arabs, it presented a great opportunity on the platter. They marched in, and rightly so, like lightning, burning down, as it were, to ashes the residual rubble of these empires. Soon they built on the ashes of the old, a new realm, thus comfortably wholly transforming the entire sacred history of the region. Over time, this new empire stretched itself far and wide, claiming sovereignty over a significant geographical portion of the world of antiquity. Alongside its temporal power, it expanded its religious influence far and wide, particularly during its formative centuries.

By the time scholars started to compile the history of this triangle of desert and stone, called the Arabian Peninsula, the "sacred history" and the "genuine history" of this region had melded together so thoroughly and intricately that it posed a challenge to tweeze them out from each other. Before the 7th century CE, hardly any written record of the history existed in Arabia proper. Most of our knowledge of the history of the Arabian Peninsula before the 7th century comes from a retrospective account by the later chroniclers who were heavily biased toward the post-seventh century "sacred history." And, there was no way to confirm or refute the authenticity of this narrative until recently when the scientific advances of the first two decades of the 21st century began changing the ball game. Ancient DNA sequencing and fingerprinting, Mitochondrial DNA sequencing, and DNA and Gene editing (CRISPR-R) have made probing into the past easier. It is now possible to solve many mysteries of the deep past. For instance, recent excavations in the Arabian Peninsular region have refuted many myths circulated by the storytellers and duly recorded by Muslim chroniclers.

The Arabs, like the Jews before them, retrojected their religious perspective into the past and manufactured history from scratch. The resulting narrative has become so deeply etched on the collective and individual belief systems that questioning the historicity of this history is fraught with inviting trouble from bubblehead believers who subscribe to the infallibility of this manufactured sacred narrative.

Ad and *Saba* (Sheba)

Geography has separated two different peoples and ways of Life since times immemorial. The Peninsular desert range is divided into Northern and Southern regions. The northern part, which comprises Hejaz and the high lands of Najd, was inhabited by the Bedouins or the nomads who perpetually peregrinated with their tents and make-shift houses in search of pastures. The southern region, also known earlier as Arabia Felix, belonged to the people of Yemen, whose wealth-and-luxury tales find a mention in the stories of King Solomon. These southern people spoke a dialect called *Himyarite*. Much of what we know today about Arabia Felix is a consequence of deciphering the Himyarite script. That, however, doesn't nullify the contribution the Greeks and Romans made to the body of literature. They were, seemingly, more informed than the Arabs about this subdivision of the Arabian Peninsula into Northern and Southern regions. To their credit, they appeared well-acquainted with the cultural subtleties of the different tribes and races inhabiting the southern Peninsula. As mentioned in the Roman records, the *Sabaeans*, for instance, were the inhabitants of Southern Arabia at least before 600 CE.

The later Arab chroniclers didn't do away with this North-South division described first by the Greeks. They followed this schema when they manufactured genealogies. For instance, in an attempt to trace their descent to Noah and Adam, the Arabs arrogated inhabitants of the South – the Himyarites and the Sabaeans – to the descendants of Qahtam (or Yoqtan), and the Northerners – Bedouins – to the descendants of "Adnan" from the line of Ismail (Ishmael), the son of the Patriarch Abraham and Hagar. According to the Old Testament Book of Genesis, Hagar was an enslaved Egyptian, a handmaiden of Sarah, Abraham's wife. Since Sarah was infecund, she gave Hagar to her husband as a concubine. Hagar bore Abraham a son, Ishmael (Ismail). After the birth of Ismail, Abraham the Patriarch was, according to Genesis, commanded by God to travel to Arabia. He took Hagar and Ismail with him, left the mother and son there, and returned to Canaan. Ismail grew up with his mother in the company of strangers. As he reached his age, he was married to one of the women from among the Bedouins. Thence, from Ismail's progeny, the race of the Arabs followed. However, many modern scholars dismiss this Old Testament story, its Muslim version, and the genealogies proposed by the Arab chroniclers as fictitious and biased.

But to return to the Himyarite South: The Abyssinians overthrew the Himyarites in the 6th century CE. With that, the cultural landscape in the South changed, and soon the Himyarite language became dead. The northern Arabian dialect emerged as the dominant language of communication throughout the Peninsula. The old folk tales were recast in a new version, imperceptibly diluting them as usually happens with oral traditions. In the process, only a few legends retained the older storyline well into late antiquity, the majority getting diluted. Over time the north-south distinction became obscure as the common language of communication promoted a cultural fusion. The memories about the past faded, and new memories replaced them - some imagined de novo and some deconstructed old ones. Based on these hybrid oral traditions, the Arab Muslim chroniclers of the 8th century CE began considering some tribes as the original inhabitants of places they didn't historically belong. Modern scholars and historians dismiss these chronicles and stories as pure legendary accounts, inconsistent with the facts established by research.

One such account is that of *Ad* (or Adites) supposedly inhabiting the valley of Hadramawt, adjoining modern-day Yemen. One of their kings – *Shadad,* was credited with constructing the legendary "Paradise on Earth." Before the advent of Islam, the legends describe the Adites, these mighty people who worshipped idols, were sinful. They transgressed and did not hearken to the word that God sent them through Prophet Hud. And God punished them by covering their entire settlement with a "dark cloud" followed by a devastating drought. A roaring whirlpool of wind consumed them, barring a few who had obeyed the prophet Hud. Those who survived multiplied and grew over time to become the "second *Ad*" and inhabited "*Saba*" (Sheba of the Bible), a geographic region of ancient Yemen. Luqman, their king, is supposed to have built the great *Dike of Ma'arib* – the dam regarded by Arab folklore as the most magnificent piece of ancient architecture.

The legendary accounts of the magnificence of the kingdom of Saba are an exercise of sheer exaggeration on the part of storytellers, as usually happens in folklore. Nonetheless, there was a historically genuine reason for the scribes to exaggerate their stories. Saba denoted Arabia Felix (in the Greek and Roman chronicles). This region was comparatively wealthier and more prosperous because of its geographical advantage - ancient trade routes between East Arabia, the Silk Road, and India intersected at Saba. Wealth made the Sabaeans hubristic, and they turned their backs on God. God, then, punished Saba when it was at its zenith - so maintain the Arab chronicles. The story goes that the *Dike of Ma'arib* burst open, inundating Saba so terribly that it vanished without leaving a trace on the face of the earth. Scholars question the veracity of this story of Saba's fall from power.

The historical evidence points to the fact that Saba declined not due to a sudden calamity sent by God but due to a protracted period of disease, depression, and economic hardships that forced the people to abandon the settlement.

The main reason for Saba's economic distress was an abrupt cut-off of the trade routes and traffic in favor of the sea route. Before the sea route, the bulk of trade and business with Syria and the Mediterranean Region happened by land routes passing via *Saba*. The Caravans then traveled North via *Macoraba* (Mecca) to Petra and the Mediterranean. That was till the 8th century BCE when the navigation of the Red Sea proved difficult. After that, transportation technology for long-distance trade underwent a revolutionary change by the standards of the time. The sea routes began to overtake the land routes because marine transportation turned out comparatively cheaper and, thus, more profitable. By the 1st century CE, the land route for trade with India, for instance, was almost entirely replaced by the sea route. Since *Saba* lacked a harbor, the goods, grain, and luxury items were now transported along the coast of Hadramawt, altogether omitting the stopover in Saba.

As Hadramawt overtook Saba as a trade center, the latter's market-dependent economy crumbled. The people fell into poverty. Poverty, a terrible enemy of human civilization, took a heavy toll on the population. Disease and death spread due to hunger, starvation, overcrowding, and inadequate healthcare facilities and treatment options. The Sabaeans' ghettos were a perfect breeding site for pestilences like the plague, cholera, smallpox, etc., to strike with annihilating might. These settlements – an ideal breeding site for infectious agents due to the total disregard for hygiene – caused the epidemics to spread like wildfire, wiping out whole populations in a matter of days and weeks, leaving streets littered with foul-smelling corpses for the dogs and jackals and scavenger birds to devour piled-up rotten corpses. It's nauseating to see with the mind's eye the stench filling up the air, whole armies of flies and insects breeding on the scattered piles of excreta and vomitus - the dreadful scenes of human misery and powerlessness before these pestilences - in turn leading to the more turbulent spread of infectious diseases with resultant wanton death and destruction. Such disasters could seal off the destiny of the defenseless human settlements in a few weeks or months. Saba could be no exception where poverty, hunger, and pestilence forced the people to abandon the once-thriving territory.

The ancient and medieval storytellers saw in the destruction of Saba, the hand of God. How could they not? For them, diseases were sent by God as a form of punishment. They didn't know anything about disease causation, spread, and control. In fact, till the 19th century, Science didn't know much about bacteria and disease-causing microbes. Cholera was thought to spread through bad air caused by witches and ghosts until John Snow, investigating the Cholera outbreak in London in 1854, demonstrated its water-borne mode of spread. Only after Robert Koch identified disease-causing bacteria a scientific revolution ushered in. In the late twentieth century, technology improved to the extent that now microbes, bacteria, and viruses can be identified in the archeological samples, thereby helping correlate the historical finds better with the description of events. In Saba's instance, archeological evidence makes a strong case in favor of the abandonment of the settlement by the inhabitants under economic duress rather than the abrupt annihilation of it by God.

History doesn't mourn for long over the dead. It simply repeats itself. With Saba wiped from the scene, History opened the window for the Himyarites to take the turn. They occupied the territory stretching between the erstwhile Saba and the Arabian Sea and went on to dominate the Peninsula until, as mentioned earlier, the Abyssinians unseated them in the 5th century CE. During that glorious period of Himyarite civilization spanning many centuries, North Arabia remained subdued under their might and muscle. Finally, by the end of the 5th century, the Himyarites lost their conclusive battle with the Northern tribes at Khazaza. This setback broke their back, and they couldn't recuperate from this last and final blow. Though the Abyssinians later used them as a proxy to mount repeated assaults on northern Arabia, the Himyarites couldn't succeed. Failing, they finally quit. Ultimately, they slipped into the hands of the Persians and, by the 6th century CE, altogether ceased to exist as a political entity.

The Arab chroniclers and historians have ignored the Himyarites in their stories and narrations; instead, they have focused more on the Sabaeans. They ascribe the legend of the "Flood of the Dike of Ma'arib" to the *Ad*, toeing in line with the Quranic narrative about Saba (Sheba) in the 34th chapter (Quran 34:15-19). Contrary to the popular Muslim story, scholars like R. A. Nicholson, for instance, draw on numerous authoritative sources and refute the story of the Dike as a legendary account. In his *A Literary History of the Arabs*, Nicholson argues that it was the "Sabaeans II" who, in the first place, constructed the Dike of Ma'arib. Between the mountains of Ma'arib, he writes, a river known as *Adana* made its way. The river bed remained dry during the summer but could become dangerously flooded during the rainy season. The Sabaeans II built a dike of solid masonry to store the water of *Adana*. In the ancient, this dike would well qualify for a feat of civil engineering. However, it couldn't withstand the weathering effects of Nature for long, and like many historical pieces of building craft, it fell into ruin with time. The pre-Islamic Arab legends, too, reckoned the *Dike of Ma'arib* among the wonders of the world. Nicholson dismisses these claims and those made by Muslim historians regarding the architectural grandioseness of the *Dike of Ma'arib* as nothing but sheer exaggeration and pure legend based on pre-Islamic folk tales.

Thamud

The *Thamud* inhabited the area of North Arabia adjoining present-day Hejaz. According to Assyrian and Roman sources, Thamud was the first kingdom of the northern Arabian Peninsula. By the fifth century CE, it had become a client state of the Romans. In the 7th century CE, travelers spotted some remains of sepulchers in an area almost a week's journey from *Yathrib* (Medina). The Arabs ascribed these remains to the *Thamud.* The pre-Islamic and well as Muslim Arab tradition (based on the Quranic narrative) holds that *God destroyed Thamu*d as they had grown hubristic and arrogant. Reuven Firestone, in the entry in *Encyclopedia of the Quran* (vol.5), observes that the Quranic story of the nine wicked men of Thamud is "reminiscent of the Jewish description of the demise of Sodom." Briefly stated the Quran tells us (in the 11th and 27th chapters) *that Thamud* was the *Ad's* successor. These people sinned against God and disobeyed the prophet, Salih. They demanded that Salih show them miracles and portents if he were a true prophet, to which God responded by sending a she-camel out of a rocky mountain. Salih warned them against harming her. Quite in defiance, the *Thamud* hamstrung her, thus inviting upon themselves, according to the Quran, the wrath of God. God sent them a catastrophe and wiped the whole settlement out.

The Muslim sources maintain that the *Thamud* went extinct long ago, perhaps in the deep past. Yet, historians like Pliny the Elder, Ptolemy, and Diodorus Siculus mention the Thamudites as an existing race surviving well into the 5th century CE. Furthermore, *Thamud* (Ta-mu-di) is also mentioned in the Mesopotamian sources. According to Assyrian records dating back to the late 8th century BCE, *Thamud* was the first kingdom of North Arabia. The word "Ta-mu-di," which appears in the Annals of the Assyrian king Sargon II, is construed to mean "*Thamud*." However, the historian Israel Ephal disagrees, questioning the plausibility of Sargon's account. But, in a surviving letter of a Babylonian king, Nabonidus, a mention of "Te-mu da-a" (Thamud) is found, which, the scholars argue, can not be another coincidence.

Additionally, classical sources, for instance, Agatharchides's record *On the Erythrean Sea* (2nd century BCE), tell us the exact geographical location of the Thamud settlement. It says that the Thamud Arabs inhabited a stony and large shore of the Arabian coastline. To cap it all, an inscription in a temple erected in the 2nd century CE for the God *Ih* mentions *Thamud* by name.

Curiously, the *Thamud* per se is infrequently mentioned in earlier Arabian sources. However, the later Muslim chroniclers and historians, in an attempt to reconstruct the history of the Arabian Peninsula, have heavily relied on a confluent mixture of Arab legends and folklore with the stories from the "sacred history" of the Jews. In his *A Literary History of the Arabs*, R A Nicholson refuting the Arab chroniclers' narrative about *Thamud,* observes that the names and figures mentioned in that account do not correlate with research findings. As the Jews retrofitted their history to suit the motif of "Chosen People" by weaving a phantasmagorical story around the imaginary figures, so did the Arabs, in the opinion of scholars, reconstruct their history and genealogies to fit in with the Semitic ancestry.

Mecca, Zamzam and Kaaba

Despite the harsh climate and scarce resources, settlements flourished in the North Arabian Peninsula, especially around natural water sources. A crucially important settlement took root in *Macoraba* (modern Mecca). This desolate place, amidst the barren mountains, attracted desert dwellers because Nature provided a better underground water system here. The well-known water reservoir that Mecca boasted of is known as *Zamzam*. Fed by the sizeable underground spring system, *Zamzam,* this overflowing well of clean water, which never dried up, became a lifeline for travelers, traders, and permanent residents in the hot and arid desert climate. Over time, many legends became associated with the *Zamzam*. Why won't they? The water source in a desert was no less than a miracle from on high. All sorts of tales and stories were woven around this spot, giving it a supernatural significance, as in every culture. The popular Arab narrative about this well has to do much with Ismail (Ishmael), abandoned there by Abraham. The story goes that when Abraham left Hagar with Ismail at the behest of his first wife, Sarah, in the deserts of North Arabia, God made the springs of water flow from beneath the feet of infant Ismail to quench his thirst. Ever since the waters have never ceased to flow, and *Zamzam* has become synonymous with Mecca's lifeline.

Nearby, hardly a few hundred yards from the *Zamzam,* stood the sanctuary that the pagan Arabs called the *Ka'aba* (literally meaning the cube). The pre-Islamic Arabs believed Adam, the first man, founded the sanctuary. The original sanctuary was destroyed during Noah's Great Deluge – more than 3500 years ago (around 2000-1500 BCE) – although many scholars claim that the original *Ka'aba* might have been destroyed even before, around more than six thousand years ago. The Arabs believed that after the deluge, Noah rebuilt the sanctuary. Years later, it again got damaged, but this time remained neglected until Abraham repaired the building during his visit to Mecca with Ismail and Hagar. When Ismail was still of tender age, Abraham had a dream. Acting on his dream, he took out his son Ismail to sacrifice him on the altar of God. When he was about to run his knife to slash Ismail's throat, God sent a ram in Ismail's stead and told Abraham to sacrifice the ram in place of his son. The ritual of sacrifice was established ever since to commemorate Abraham's offering his son in the path of his lord, God. Saved from getting sacrificed, Ismail (Ishmael) then went on to sire a great progeny from whom descended the Arabs of the Northern Peninsula. So goes the popular story.

For scholars and historians, it still poses a tricky riddle to solve as to who built the Ka'aba in the first place. The evidence supporting the involvement of Adam, Noah, or Abraham in its construction is nonexistent or, at the most, scant. However, the fact remains that the Ka'aba has been and is pivotal to both Arab society and the vast Muslim society outside the Arabian Peninsula.

Up until the 7th century CE, the Ka'aba housed the idols. More than 300 of them were cramped inside the cube-shaped structure of the Ka'aba. All the tribes and nationalities had their respective gods, represented in the Ka'aba by their idols. Furthermore, the Syrian God *Habbal*, the Egyptian God *Al-Uzza*, the Nabataean God *Kutba*, and even the icons of Jesus and his mother, Mary, stood here. During festive months, big markets would open in Mecca; the pilgrims would come from all over the Peninsula to pay homage to their gods and perform sacrifices to appease them. All the pilgrims would gather in groups and circumambulate the Ka'aba seven times, pausing to kiss the "Black Stone" installed in one of the corners of the sanctuary. Mecca would be flooded with people to carry out trade during the festive season of pilgrimage. The pilgrimage season very much determined the success or failure of the Meccan economy. It was a season of plenty and abundance, of genuine celebration when cattle and goods would be traded, and haves and have-nots would try their hand at making profitable endeavors. The Bedouins would raise and graze their flocks for a whole year to make their earnings and profit during this pilgrimage season. That is to say, Ka'aba was the nerve center of the economy of this township. No Ka'aba, no pilgrimage, no income.

The Meccans would put in place elaborate arrangements to cater to the physical and emotional needs of the pilgrims. For them, the numerous idols housed in the Kaaba hadn't done much with their faith in a pantheon of gods. Rather this arrangement of things gave them an economic opportunity to benefit from. All the Meccans, irrespective of tribal affiliations, were fiercely proud of Ka'aba, which, by the 7th century CE, had become a famous Holy shrine in pre-Islamic Arabia. The Ka'aba's surrounding area was also held sacred; all kinds of violence were prohibited within three miles of the Ka'aba. So people would carry out trade and business freely and fearlessly within its holy precincts. The Quraysh, the most powerful tribe in Mecca, were the "Keepers" and the guardians of the sacred shrine. Their mercantile predisposition kept them enthusiastically, faithfully, and devotionally involved in the management of Ka'aba.

As pointed out earlier, the Meccans were not polytheists or idolaters in the strict sense. Despite paying homage and respect to minor gods, they tenaciously held on to their age-old tradition – a religious convention revolving around one creator, the all-powerful God they called Allah. He was the supreme God of the Meccans and the Arabs. The gods like *Lat*, *Mannat*, and *Uzza* were simply intercessors between Allah and the people. The Arabs believed that Allah, the supreme God, was inaccessible to ordinary people, and some form of mediation was necessary to approach him. That is not surprising, given the prevalence of such belief patterns in almost all religious denominations. In that sense, the 7th century CE pre-Islamic Arab society wasn't all that paganish.

For centuries, Mecca was only a stopover for the caravans traveling from *Saba* and Yemen to the Mediterranean. Things changed with the fall of Saba and the development of sea routes. By the 6th century CE, pilgrimage and trade had transformed Mecca into a thriving market economy of antique Arabia. Its comparative material affluence now lured the governors and kings of southern Arabia (Yemen). Pilgrims poured in from as far as Syria and Egypt. Trade brought capital and wealth to Meccan society that tickled the rulers of the South (Yemen). They had set their eyes on Meccan wealth. One governor of Yemen - an Abyssinian viceroy - Abraha, began to look for an opportune moment to ride on Mecca. That moment came when an arrogant and hubristic Quraysh tribal headman supposedly committed an act of sacrilege in a church in Sana'a, the main town of Yemen. When Abraha learned about the incident, he became furious and demanded reprisal from the Quraysh—his moment had come. He hastily drew up his plan to invade Mecca. The Church incident served as the much-needed pretext to launch a full-scale attack.

The Army and the Birds

In 570 CE, Abraha began his march toward Mecca with a large contingent of army and elephant artillery. Not facing much resistance from the Arabs, he encamped outside Mecca. The story goes that some negotiations took place between the Quraysh elder men and Abraha's envoys to hammer out a plan for the capitulation of Mecca without a war. The Arab traditions maintain that Abdul Muttalib led the negotiating team from Mecca, but the talks failed, and Abraha announced war. As he began to advance, the traditions say, God, sent hovering flocks of swallows (*Ababil* in Arabic) carrying pellets. The birds dropped the shots from a height over the Abraha's army - the elephants and soldiers - killing them all. In the ensuing confusion, some managed to flee and escape the wrath of God, but Abraha fell, his limbs rotting off. The Meccans were jubilant. Abraha was defeated before the war had even started. This version of the story is also carried in the Quran in a chapter titled "The Elephant."

Abraha's fall has been a topic of fierce debate and investigation for historians and scholars for a long time now. Modern ornithologists tell us that some bird species occasionally vomit out pallets formed of undigested parts of food. Pellets are formed within six to ten hours of a meal in the bird's stomach (gizzard). Hawks, owls, herons, kingfishers, crows, and swallows are known to produce pellets. The pellets may contain unusual items in them. Owl pallets, for example, incorporate the hair, bones, and skin fragments of rodents carrying viable viruses and bacteria. At least two pellet-borne outbreaks of Salmonellosis – a severe diarrheal disease – have been reported recently in schools where the students dissected unsterile pellets.

Some swallow species form large flocks and roost communally. Nigerian barn swallows, for instance, are known to roost in millions. These roosts can be pretty enormous. Most barn swallows feed on flies, beetles, bees, wasps, moths, and flying insects. They also pick up grit, small pebbles, and eggshells which may help swallows digest insects and form pellets. The swallows are also known for picking mud and mixing it with pieces of grass to form pellets for building nests. It is quite possible that Abraha's invasion coincided with the migratory season, and swarms of these birds flew over the area journeying to other brooding places, dropping pellets. The Meccans construed this swarming of these migratory birds as God sending them (*Ababil*) to drop pebbles on the Abraha's army. Since the pellets are unsterile and may contain germs, pellet bombardment might have caused an outbreak of infectious diseases in the army camp. That is one side of the story.

The recent archeological evidence and DNA analysis of the skeletons of that period tell a different story, raising a serious issue with the veracity of the traditional Muslim narrative. According to ancient DNA analysis, it seems more plausible that Abraha's army fell prey to a plague. Some corroborating secular and sacred historical records also support the affliction of Yemen with the plague epidemic during the second half of the 6th century. John S. Marr, in a review article *The Year of the Elephant,* notes, "In 541 [CE], a Bubonic plague emerged in Egypt and spread with such swiftness that in a short while, pathways from Egypt to China and the Island of England began filling with dead bodies. The original culprit was a bacteria [sic] named *Yersinia pestis* which transmits to humans via flea-carrying rats." Between 540 and 750 CE, there were nearly 20 outbreaks of plague, meaning that practically every ten years, there was an outbreak. The epidemic of 570 CE began in Ethiopia and spread via Egypt and Yemen to the Levant (Palestine) and Constantinople. It spared Hejaz. John Marr notes that the sixth-century Syriac accounts called the plague "mawtana rabba." Youhanan (John of Ephesus), who traveled from Egypt to Constantinople in 541 CE, has given a detailed account of this malady spreading and consuming lives mercilessly.

John Marr points out "that the plague had affected Yemen is corroborated by an inscription of Abraha on the Dam of Ma'arib dated to 543 CE, which refers to death and sickness striking the community at Ma'arib." The pre-Islamic poet Hassan ibn Thabit calls this pestilence "the stinging of the jinn." John of Ephesus claimed that God was responsible for this plague, and the Greek priest Zachariah regarded it as the "work of Satan left on a leash by God" to punish people for their sins.

Genomic analysis of the skeletal samples of that period has revealed that *Y. pestis* was the bacterium that unleashed what is known as the "Black Death" from Ethiopia to Egypt, Yemen to Palestine, and Byzantium for decades ahead from 536 CE.

Be that as it may, Abraha's humiliating defeat and death in 570 CE brought huge relief to the Meccans. They reckoned it the most critical event in their history—no wonder a whole chapter is devoted to this story in the Quran.

Abraha and his army's unforeseen annihilations had a profound and lasting influence on the overall psyche of the Northerners. It contrived a sense of patriotism in Hejaz, boosting the northerners' self-esteem and unwavering confidence and belief in the sanctity of the Ka'aba. Suddenly they came to think of themselves as Allah's "chosen people," bestowed with wealth because they were doing His service right. The newfound confidence strengthened the notion that they were the masters of their fate and that all the tribes and families were equal contenders for Mecca's wealth. As a result, the Meccan tribes became more argumentative and arrogant in their dealings with each other and outsiders.

They fought one another over their share of wealth, and in this struggle, some weaker clans, like, for example, *Banu Hashim,* who was left behind, began to nurse a grudge toward others. They felt their very survival was being jeopardized. The situation in parts of Hejaz and Najd other than Mecca was no different. The tribes fiercely competed over Life's basic and mundane necessities. The amenities and resources were sparse. Poverty was rampant. Resources were limited, and the climate was harsh. A piece of bread was a luxury. No wonder people fought each other over a morsel of food.

The convention or *Muruwah*

For us in the twenty-first century, with so much abundance and comfort at our disposal, it is hard to appreciate the primitive, harsh, and merciless life of antiquity overridden with diseases, pestilence, starvation, and high death rates at a comparatively younger age (average life expectancy even in the 1900s was 35 years) due to scarcity of food, absence of clean water and medicines. It is hard to transport ourselves mentally back in time and put ourselves in the shoes of the sixth-century Arab Bedouin. If we did, we would no more be nostalgic for the so-called "good old days!" There was nothing good in that slavery, back-breaking toil, and hunger and incertitude of life.

The records, meager as they are, tell us that tragic story of the past in a fair outline. Life was terrible, harsh, and ruthless for the people of the past than we are used to thinking. They lived and survived by the skin of their teeth. In a matter of days, whole populations could be slaughtered, enslaved, or dispossessed of their belongings by raiders, robbers, or invaders. And if that weren't enough, then plagues and afflictions like tuberculosis, cholera, smallpox, leprosy, etc., would decimate the populations in a tiny period of a few weeks or months. The vibrant and teeming cities and towns would turn into graveyards within days or weeks. People would die in the thousands. Young and old, no bars at all, death swept all. Sixth-century Arabia was a harsh place to live, "harsh" being a mild word. Only God or a Pantheon of gods, depending upon the belief pattern of the society, was the leitmotif of Life. People wailed, cried, and beseeched God for help. He never answered them but sent them plagues and pestilences without asking! Fear of incertitude, destruction with calamity and disease, and fear of God's wrath prevailed everywhere. The prevailing fear psychosis provided a robust opportunity for the seers, sages, and god-men to exploit the people with the fear of God, the unseen, and the reprisal after death. The powerful rampantly oppressed the weak with total impunity. Slavery was the order of the day. Women and young girl children counted for the booty and spoils of war.

An enemy's enemy is a friend in a competitive world. In that ruthless world order, where the rule of thumb was "Might is Right," survival hinged on cooperation between individuals, groups, and tribes. The struggle for survival could even drive the archrivals to collaborate against a common enemy. In Arabia of antiquity, the spirit of collaboration was personified, kind of, in an institution called *Muruwah* – the principle of cooperation based on an ideology very similar to tribal nationalism. *Muruwah,* translated as a convention, worked just like a religious system. A Code of Conduct or a charter, if you will. The participating tribes were dutybound to observe the rules of *Muruwah.* According to it, the tribal chief, or the Sayyid, was to be obeyed by all the tribe members. If an outside tribe committed wrong to a *Muruwah*-abiding tribe, the Sayyid organized a force of men to reprise the offending tribe. In case a tribe member was murdered, the Sayyid was supposed to kill a member of the enemy tribe to exact revenge.

The vendetta or the blood feud was one of the methods to ensure order and security in the tribal Arab society. Usually, the Sayyid would function as an organizer of raids or *Ghazu* (the word *Ghazi*, used as an epithet by some jihadists, is derived from *Ghazu*) and ensure the spoils and booty were equally shared among the members of the tribe. Should the Sayyid fail to retaliate and avenge the enemy, the tribe would naturally feel insecure and even endangered in that order of the day. However, such an order was not typical of Arab society alone. It was prevalent in tribal communities almost everywhere within and outside the Arabian Peninsula. The problem with conventions like *Muruwah* was that some tribes would get engaged in a vicious cycle of violence against each other for decades for petty matters.

Nevertheless, the practice of *Muruwah* served the Arab Bedouin society well for centuries; however, by the 6th century, the changing geopolitical and economic situation of the then-Middle East dented its relevance. By then, a kind of spiritual restlessness had set in, which sparked widespread dissatisfaction among the masses in and around the Arabian Peninsula. The Arabs had genuine reasons to despair. The Persia-Byzantine wars and plague epidemic had severely damaged the caravan trade of Arabs, jeopardizing their economy and livelihood. The two once-mighty empires were trying hard to maintain a facade of grandeur, but from within, they hadn't yet fully recovered from the brutal Hun aggression. Rot infested both, yet the emperors fought each other for hegemony. The burden of war and epidemic ultimately ate into the foundational edifice of these empires.

They were about to crumble and leave a gaping hole for the Arabs to walk in and displace them.

Afterlife vs. *Darh*

Despite the rot, the Byzantine and the Persian Empires were the epitomai of modernity for the tribal Arabs still steeped deep in barbarianism. They looked towards this world – modern for them in all respects – with awe and amazement. The glare and glitter of the Byzantine empire from a distance had long hypnotized them into inertia, immobility, and catalepsy that seemed to freeze them where they were. Back home, fragility overrode their society infested with tribal schism, vendetta, and blood feuds. Yet they cuddled the dream of a united Arab country in their faint imaginings. They couldn't think beyond the possibility of being a client state of the Byzantines, clutching on to straw between the devil and the deep sea. Some bold souls lamented the lack of the will and pragmatism of their compatriots to found an independent kingdom of their own. As Persia gobbled up Southern Arabia, the North Arabian Bedouins felt threatened, intimidated, and insecure.

North Arabians were a trading society at its core. Trading and mobile communities are known for the exchange and diffusion of ideas. Ideas the Arabs brought home by virtue of the caravan trade from the Levant, Byzantine, and Mesopotamia circulated fast in the Hejaz. The Jews lived in the Peninsula since the Romans evicted them from Palestine in the first century CE. Later, Christianity also found its way into the Arab deserts along trade routes and under Byzantine imperial influence. Caravan trade and pilgrimage to Ka'aba increased Arabs' exposure and contact with the outside world, leading to an insidious shift in their religious-political perspective by the 7th century. By then, their inferiority complex before the Semites and their monotheistic religion was causing them deep anguish. And why shouldn't it? They never had a prophet like Abraham, Moses, or Jesus among them. They never had anything remotely resembling a scripture in their language. The Jews and Christians used every opportunity to taunt and jeer them that they had no revelation from God, despite their claimed descent from Ismail. Their taunts and jeers of the arrowed their bosoms.

Deep down in their hearts, though, they acknowledged the Jewish religion was superior to their traditional paganism. They displayed profound respect for the Jews and their faith. At the same time, they were too hubristic to give in to the proselytizing prowess of Byzantium and Persia. Byzantium's use of religion to promote its imperial designs in the region was well known. And the last thing they would accept was any foreign ideology or religious tradition forcibly thrust upon them.

Above all, Judaism was a non-proselytizing religion. With it, though, Arabs had a unique, reciprocal, fine-tuned equation in the context of their claimed common descent from the house of Abraham. As Reza Aslan points out, "The Jews were heavily Arabized, and the Arabs also were significantly influenced by the Jewish beliefs and practices," and "one needs to look no further for evidence of this influence than to Ka'aba itself, whose origin myths indicate that it was a Semitic sanctuary with its roots dug deep in Jewish tradition." Quoting the biblical Book of Genesis (28: 11-19) in support of his research, Aslan observes that the "Black stone" in the Ka'aba "has been originally a stone upon which Jacob [Israel] rested his head during his famous dream of the ladder."

Thanks to the Judaic influence, the doctrine of the "afterlife" made a solid and lasting impression on the collective psyche of the Arab Bedouin society hitherto inclined to a fatalistic belief system - the notion of *Darh* or fate - rather than the "afterlife." The Arabs, no doubt, worshipped at the shrines, but they had not developed any mythology or theological doctrine connecting shrine gods with spiritual Life. Unlike the Hindus, Buddhists, or Christians who created elaborate theology about spirit and spiritual Life, the Arabs, it seemed, were not keen to get into matters of religious philosophy. Neither were they keener on secular philosophical discourses like the Greeks once were. The Arabs were more interested in surviving the adversity and hardships of desert life rather than spiritualism. But by the 7th century CE that was to change.

Hanifism in Mecca

Zoroastrianism, Judaism, and Christianity had penetrated far-off lands. The virulent sands and storms of the North Arabian Peninsula couldn't stop them either; they made their way to the heart of this desert. By the 7th century CE, the three systems of faith melted in this desert crucible and gradually diffused into the traditional paganism of Arabia. The theological confluence ultimately compelled the materialistic Arabs to wake up and ascertain their identity through an innovative discourse on theological matters. Toward the closing decades of the 6th century CE, Mecca was already a pluralistic society, and thus the expression of bold ideas was becoming less risky. Religious experimentation was now hard to stop. Various religious cults popped up everywhere. Some cults embarked on exciting religious experimentation, mostly cropping up in the markets of Mecca, where an atmosphere of intense spiritual restlessness prevailed. One such noteworthy monotheistic movement, underpinned by the spiritual quest, was birthed here, called the *Hanifiyah* religion or simply *Hanifism*. Ibn Hisham, the ninth-century historian from Basra (Iraq), noted in his detailed account of *Hanifism* that it was founded by four prominent men – Waraqa bin Nawfal, Uthman bin Huwairith, Ubayd Bin Jahsh, and Zayd Bin Amr. These four men were eloquent rhetoricians who firmly believed that the Arabs were descendants of Abraham's lineage and should return to Abraham's religion. According to them, Abraham was neither a Jew nor a Christian. He was a *Hanif* – a believer in one God, Allah. The four men were called *Hanifiyahs*, and they and their followers refused to engage in idolatry. Idolatry was an abomination, they emphasized.

Hanifism thrived throughout Hejaz, attracting many followers, especially from its two main towns – Mecca and Yathrib (later Medina). Umayya Bin Abi Salt composed poems praising the *Hanifiyah* religion. In Yathrib (Medina), some influential people like Khalid Bin Sinan joined them. Later he became an influential preacher of Hanifism in Yathrib and earned the famous epithet "a prophet lost by his people." The Hanifiyahs preached that it was not sufficient to abandon idolatry alone; rather, it was imperative to demonstrate an absolute commitment to morality, honesty, and uprightness in everyday dealings with one another. According to them, God was always involved with His creation for good. He didn't need any mediators and lesser gods to convey to him human prayers. He was the compassionate God and the lord the day – "day of reckoning" or "day of Judgment" – when everyone would be called to account for their choices and deeds before Him – the omniscient God, from whom nothing is hidden.

Initially, Hanifism flourished, but then suddenly, three of the four stalwarts left the group at the peak of its success. Their exit severely undermined the movement, dampening their followers' enthusiasm to hold on to and propagate this creed. Waraqa, Uthman, and Ubayd converted to Christianity. Zayd was left alone to defend the *Hanifiyah* faith. It became arduous for him to single-handedly preach, teach, and proselytize. His lone fight ended shortly after when the winds of change created a hitherto unparalleled storm in the sands of Arabia. Little did Zayd know that history had another plan under its sleeve.

The improbable

Barely two and a half decades after Zayd's death (d 605 CE), the once-pagan Bedouins of the Arabian Peninsula metamorphosed into a "conquering people." Within the next hundred years, they became the masters of an empire that stretched from the Mediterranean in the West to the Indian subcontinent in the East, bringing forth a dazzling civilization in the East when the West was still sunken into morass and ignorance. One by one, the lands and territories were falling like domino pieces into the hands of the conquering Arabs. The Persian army, debilitated by centuries of warfare, was quickly decimated by a numerically smaller Arab battalion, bringing this once-formidable Persian empire of antiquity to an end. By 700 CE, big chunks of the Byzantine Empire and North African kingdoms were annexed by the Arabs. It seemed that nothing could stop their blitz into the heart of Europe. Then by a stroke of luck, at Tours in 732 CE, Charles Martel, a Frankish (old French) warrior, effectively stopped them from moving forward. Martel's halting of the Arabs proved to be the most decisive event in the history of both Europe and the Muslim Middle East.

The magnitude of Arab success was nothing but miraculous. All that new history thus created over the rubble of the Roman and the Persian empires resulted from the pioneering labor of one man who, despite lacking formal military training, was a remarkable social, political, military, and spiritual leader. This man was Mohammad (PBUH), the Prophet of Islam, who laid the foundations of a creed that brought within its fold, with magical swiftness, half of the then-known world within barely seventy years. In the words of Max Dimont, "Mohammad is one of history's most improbable figures, an Arab imbued with the fervor of Judaism, proclaiming all the Arabs as the descendants of Abraham, and calling for the Jews and Christians alike to join him in a true brotherhood of man in the name of Allah."

The Jews had arrived in Arabia escaping Roman tyranny in the 1st century CE when Judea was razed, and the Temple of Zion torched. Subsequently, the Jews continued to trickle constantly into the North Arabian Peninsula.

By the 5th and 6th centuries CE, the Jewish immigrants had virtually inundated the Arab lands. Here they lived peacefully and prospered. They introduced handicrafts and art in Arabia; brought with them the Date palm; founded the township of Yathrib, which later became Medina; and helped turn Mecca into a cosmopolitan center of trade, commerce, and religious discourse. They joined hands with the Arabs in defeating the Christian armies, thus helping to keep Christianity- at least for some time - out of the Arabian mainland.

In the Arab lands, Jews flourished. Their rituals, their way of Life, and above all, their Judaism matured here. The Arabs respectfully called them the "people of the Book." The influence of the *Torah* was so profound on the Arab collective consciousness that they began to look back at their own religious identity from a renewed perspective. Out of the confluence of thought streams like Nature worship, the salvation doctrine of the Christians, and the monotheism of the Jews flowed the Arab cultural milieu. By the seventh century, a fertile ground had been readied for a new creed with a solid scriptural authority proclaiming, as Max Dimont puts it, "all the Arabs as the descendants of Abraham, and calling for the Jews and Christians alike to join him in a true brotherhood of man in the name of Allah." The Arab world had longed for it, albeit subconsciously, for centuries. With the Prophet, the Northern Arabian Peninsula got a book, a scripture, and the word of God – all in one, in their own language! It meant a lot to the Arabs, despite their initial resistance to Muhammad and his message. Later events would prove that the Arabs gained immense self-confidence and self-esteem under Prophet's leadership. The Arabs became a political force to reckon with. As a result, barely a decade after the Prophet's death, "the word of God" reached far-off lands outside the boundaries of this desert. A new history was made. A formidable theological edifice was put in place. And with that, the global sacred history changed drastically.

Yet this journey to the pinnacle of history was not smooth. Bumps, hurdles, and impediments showed up, as they usually do, which made the path, despite being backed by lofty spiritual principles, impossible to traverse without spilling human blood in the deserts, lands, and trenches. Islam's "sacred history" was to be written with human blood. The Prophet himself mainly fought the infidels, but immediately after his death, the soil and the sand got soaked in the blood of the faithful, all of whom claimed to be true followers and lovers of Mohammad. The stains of that blood are still fresh; their memory is impossible to erase. But then, history is history. It happens.

Could the bloodshed have been avoided? No, perhaps. Historically, humans have displayed savage, brutal, ruthless, and barbaric behavior toward each other. Violence and wars have consumed a significant chunk of human time and resources. There have been, no doubt, brief periods in the past when peace threatened war, but they can be regarded as anomalies. Normally, the principal equation of Life necessitates the application of violence. Religion - its lofty spiritual principles and rhetoric aside - is simply one of the "means" to secure the "end," i.e., economic gains, mainly. All religions have served that purpose. And Islam, the creed established by Muhammad, as we shall see later, was no exception.

Chapter – 11

The Unanswered Question

Mohammad (PBUH)

In 570 CE, when the Meccan Quraysh were dancing and celebrating their God-sent victory against Abraha, the Abyssinian viceroy of Yemen, who would have thought even for a moment that a boy born the same year to a widow would go on to write a new page in history? The same boy - already an orphan at birth - also lost his mother at the tender age of 6 or 8. He was left under his grandfather's and uncle's guardianship; his grandfather particularly doted on him. As he grew up under the loving care of these two gentlemen, he demonstrated a calm and contemplative demeanor singling himself out from his contemporaries. In his teen years, he sought employment with a wealthy 45-year-old widow to lead her caravans to Syria, Canaan, and other parts of the Byzantine Empire. This young orphan's honesty, integrity, and disciplined behavior impressed the wealthy caravan owner so much that she saw it fit to express her desire to marry this young employee. They got married. The young man now became a merchant in his own right. It was a time when the number of pilgrims to Ka'aba steadily increased, fetching the Meccans fat earnings from the catering business. He earned good profits, and his business expanded to match other affluent and wealthier Quraysh tribesmen. Yet, this young merchant wasn't feeling at home in this comparatively affluent merchant society. Since he had seen adversity and orphanhood in his formative years, he had developed a contemplative mindset early on. He found it hard to feel at peace in the then-Meccan society, where orphans were despised, the poor detested, and enslaved people unjustifiably oppressed and tortured with impunity. The wealthier lot had become hubristic. The poor were getting poorer.

This parvenu merchant possessed a sharp mind. His thinking was clear. He was conscious of what was happening around him and genuinely worried about his society and the people. This worry often drove him to voluntary solitude in the labyrinths of a cave called Gar-i-Hira on a mountain now famous as the *Jabl an-Nur* (Mountain of the Light), to spend days and nights there in contemplation, fasting, and rigorous spiritual practices.

The pagan Arab religious practices did not impress him or arouse his imaginative curiosity. As a merchant, when he traveled with the caravans, he got ample opportunity to meet and interact with people from different cultural backgrounds and religious denominations on foreign soil. As an astute observer of events, he gained from these interactions profoundly; his outlook changed, his passions stirred up, and his intellectual curiosity was fired up. Judaism appealed to him as a simple and relatively straightforward monotheistic religion more than Christianity. Still, it was not an option for him, for there was no scope for people of non-Jewish descent to embrace Judaism – this strictly ethnic, non-proselytizing faith recognizes no conversion. One can be a Jew only by birth.

At a time when the Meccan society was in the grip of spiritual restlessness, some intelligent Arabs were deeply troubled by the fact that none of their professed religions figured significantly in the overall theological discourse of the day. Even a religion like Judaism, egalitarian as it might seem from the outside, had practically closed its doors to Arab pagans. Trinitarian Christianity hadn't much to offer them, given the Arabs' monotheistic predisposition revived by *Hanifism*. The failure of *Hanifism* to sustain was a terrible blow to the indigenous Arab religious discourse that added to the existing religious-spiritual chaos in seventh-century Mecca. Some sensitive minds were quite troubled by this socio-political chaos.

By then, the above merchant, already successful, had been exposed to far-off lands. Gaining a reasonably good knowledge of the culture of different peoples, he had developed quite an interest in the world-shaping events outside the Arabian Peninsula. From his Arab cultural vantage point, he perhaps closely watched and analyzed the events happening at home and outside. The adversity and hardships while growing up as an orphan belonging to a comparatively less affluent sub-tribe of Quraysh (Banu Hashim) had taught him endurance, discipline, and perseverance. An out-of-the-box thinker, he possessed this seed of a leader in him, but he struggled to vent his feelings and thoughts. His time hadn't come yet. Even in his forties, he shied away from taking any bold step. He wasn't ready to traverse the dangerously sharp edge of time. No doubt, turmoil, dissent, and catastrophe had primed society's collective mind for change, but.

The genius of a leader lies in identifying the "time slab" for introducing a novel idea. This ordinary-looking Meccan merchant was undoubtedly an extraordinarily contemplative man with exceptional leadership acumen who had slowly cultivated the audacity and skill of benefiting from adversity. In hindsight, the adversity transformed this orphan from an ordinary resident of the desert into the most successful and, to borrow the phrase from Michael Hart, an influential person in history. His grandfather had given this ordinary-looking extraordinary kid a rare name, Mohammad. This kid grew up to become a successful merchant first and a prophet next, destined to be remembered as the last and final prophet by billions of his followers down history's timeline.

The Christian Jihad

Twenty years before the birth of Mohammad, panic had gripped the Mediterranean region. Death rampaged through the lands like lightning, decimating whole populations. According to contemporary records, entire settlements along the Egyptian border were wiped out; only seven men and a boy survived the onslaught of the plague. Densely populated towns suffered the worst. Estimates were that nearly 10,000 people died daily in Constantinople alone, the capital of the Roman Empire. The disastrous demon of death was exported from the Mediterranean through trade routes to far-flung areas. By the time Mohammad was born, the deadly pestilence had reached the outskirts of North Arabia and annihilated Abraha and his army of elephants. The whole Middle East, except Hejaz, was in the clutches of this bacterial demon – the plague. Not only did this demon cause a colossal loss of human life, but it also brought about a severe economic depression; practically no healthy people were left to cultivate the lands. The resulting severe food shortage led to widespread starvation, further complicating the fragile scenario. Entire fields and open spaces strewn with emaciated, foul-smelling, rotting human corpses filled the air with an intolerable stink. The ultimate culmination of misery and suffering was the famine that struck terribly and mercilessly, culling the remaining already sick and enfeebled population to size as if the plague wasn't enough. Chaos spread everywhere, and if the devastating pestilence spared any pockets and areas, they were raided and plundered by whole bands of raiders and plunderers. The territory controlled by the Roman Empire was the worst hit. These were tough days for the Roman Empire: The Persians were creating trouble on its eastern borders; the Turks were advancing on the other side, leaving the enfeebled Romans woefully overwhelmed with awe and incertitude about their survival. Persia took hold of their strategic towns, taking advantage of the opportunity. That broke the Roman Empire's back. Soon after, Justinian II, the Emperor, died of a nervous breakdown in 574 CE.

It took some time for the Romans to gather courage and resources to put up resistance against the Persians. As the hostilities between the two empires reopened formally, the Middle East and the Mediterranean entered a tumultuous period of history. The terrible warfare that followed for decades between these hostile neighbors, already battered by the Black Death, hollowed both to the core. To a 21st-century observer, it may seem nonsensical and ill-conceived that the two enfeebled Empires were fighting, killing, and displacing each other's populations. But that was it. They inflicted horrible pain, poverty, starvation, and death on each other's populace to grab land and territory. But in the 6th-century agricultural society with meager resources and marginal yield from even the most fertile lands, the surer way for the empires to survive lay in territorial expansion to ensure grabbing the possessions, belongings, and agricultural produce of entire villages through organized raids, loot, and plunder. How else could the empires increase their tax base and revenue to sustain their economy and the Empire's administrative network if not by territorial expansion?

As the hostilities continued between the Romans and the Persians, fatigue set in on both sides. The soldiers lost enthusiasm, preferring to settle for the booty that came their way. Their morale dipped. Recruiting fresh warriors was becoming increasingly difficult. Both sides were compelled to use religion to manipulate the people - manufacturing consent - drive their passions, and get them to participate in "holy war." Extremely vicious religious propaganda was unleashed by both sides to win over their respective populaces and keep the soldiers upbeat. Both sides spent resources on client tribes in places as far removed from the battlefield as the Arabian Peninsula. Accordingly, the Christians persuaded the Meccans to take their side, and the Persians wooed the Yathribites (Medina). The power equation was fast changing.

In 580 CE, a Persian general, who had grown popular during the war, overthrew the Shah of Iran, Khusraw II. The Shah fled and paradoxically sought asylum with his enemy, the emperor in Constantinople. The Roman emperor delightfully obliged, providing him asylum for 11 years. When Khusraw II wanted to return to reclaim his throne, Persia had already grown weaker, with its fault lines wholly exposed to the Romans. Khusraw II had to concede many important territories to the Romans during the negotiations to pave his return to the throne.

Soon, i.e., within a decade, the Roman Empire saw internal revolts and rebellions, and the Emperor busied himself with dealing with the disorder. Khusraw II sensing the opportunity reneged on his treaty with the Roman Emperor and began reconsolidating his position. He captured town after town and knocked out a vital point of the Roman defense system in Mesopotamia (present-day Iraq). Once again, the Persians were pushing ahead. In the autumn of 613 CE, Damascus, a vital financial center for the Roman Empire, capitulated to the Persians – an insult that the Romans won't take easily. The angry mobs revolted against their emperor, murdered him, and paraded his dismembered body through the streets of Constantinople. And Heraclius was made the emperor. He proved no more effective than his predecessors against the Persians, who had now set their eyes on the Holy City of Christendom, Jerusalem. Capturing Jerusalem would mean the triumph of Zoroastrianism over Christianity – the victory of Persian cultural and religious supremacy over the West.

The Persians put Jerusalem under siege in May 614 CE, sending shivers through the entire Christian world, including the Arabian Peninsula. Christians outrightly blamed Jews for this, who, according to them, hatched a conspiracy with the Persians against the creed of Christianity to occupy their sacred city and destroy their holy temple of Jerusalem. They accused them of scheming to slaughter the innocent Christians in Jerusalem with the Persians' help to exact reprisals from the Romans. The latter, they knew, had evicted them from their homeland and banned them from entering Jerusalem. The Christians, convulsing in anger against the Persians and the Jews, had no option but to defend Jerusalem with blood. Holy war was announced. The faithful who would die in this "Holy war" or Christian Jihad would be honored and dignified as "martyrs" in the name of Christ. The war cry - Christianity was in danger of annihilation at the hands of Persian infidels; nothing short of dying for Christ could save Christianity - was raised throughout the Roman Empire, intensifying religious propaganda.

Simultaneously, the Persians began closing in on the seat of power of the Roman Empire, Constantinople. It was an absolute disaster. After the fall of Constantinople, Jerusalem, the Persians had calculated, would automatically capitulate. As the Christians imagined the whole picture playing in front of them, a feeling of doom and gloom gripped them.

"Why?" they perhaps asked in despair, "Why has God allowed the infields to overpower and overthrow our kings? Why has God forsaken us?"

The desperate Christians – the clergy and the ordinary folks – wailed and beseeched their God, but strangely, the Christian God seemed to not hear them leaving his "Chosen people" all to themselves. The Zoroastrian infidels were trampling town after town under their feet. They seemed undaunted. The end of Rome was nearing. The Christians desperately looked up to the Cross, knowing the odds didn't favor them. In Mecca, the pagan Arabs, historically sympathetic toward the Jews because of trade ties, were jubilant over the Persian victory. But history plays no favorites. It respects power, patience, and strategy.

As the Persians began their last and final assault, history revealed the plans it had up its sleeve. It took an unexpected turn. The fragile balance tipped over to the other side. As always, it is incredible twists that make history. The Turks descended on the Caucasus, and Khusraw II hurriedly decided to defend his Balkan border as the frontier was left unattended for a long. Had he waited, the Turkish advance wouldn't have turned out as damaging as he imagined. He shifted his priorities in a rush of madness, hoping that time would wait for him. He was wrong. Turks posed no severe threat to the survival of his Empire, as the later events showed. Caught between the devil and the deep sea, he committed a strategic blunder, and history punished him duly. Reckoning he wouldn't be able to handle two simultaneous war fronts – clearly his inimical miscalculation and political immaturity – he called off the plans to capture Constantinople, albeit temporarily, and withdraw troops to consolidate his defense at the Balkan borders. As he suddenly abandoned the strategically critical war front in favor of the Balkan frontier, shrugging off and grossly underestimating Heraclius and his political cunning, the Romans sighed in relief. Jesus had hearkened to their wails. It was a moment of celebration.

Heraclius didn't miss a beat. He made a risky yet strategic move for which history will never forget him. While his soldiers pursued the retreating Persian army, driving them like cattle, he quickly arranged for a pact with the Turks. He didn't hesitate to offer the Turk leader, Khalgan, his stunningly beautiful daughter Eudokia in marriage. With the Turk's help, Heraclius mounted an offensive on the Persians at Nineveh. The town fell quickly. The Persians became panicky, and the armed men rebelled against the Shah. In hysteria, the rebels assassinated Khusraw. In the din, his son, Kavad, somehow managed to ascend the throne, but the chaos refused to settle. There were more surprises to follow.

With Khusraw's assassination, dangerous fault lines appeared within the rank and file of the Persian armed forces and Royal palace. The revolts and the power struggle brought the Empire to the tipping point of instability. One more nudge and the Empire would crumble. Heraclius intensified his intelligence operation against the Persian Shah. He covertly backed the Persian generals against the Shah to bring down the Empire, cunningly and shrewdly using the Persians against each other. The Romans succeeded in stoking factionalism in Persia, which the Persians failed to see through. Back home, Heraclius rallied the masses using his tremendous demagogic genius. He "played heavily on religion to build the support and stiffen the peoples' resolve during his empire's dark hours," writes Tom Holland, making his domestic policy resonate with the Christians' religious aspirations with remarkable precision. The people fell into his trap. They fought valiantly in the holy war, essentially fulfilling Heraclius's political ambition rather than serving their God.

The Persian-Roman war was history's second well-organized and meticulously planned *Jihad* of Christianity against Zoroastrianism. The Jews carried out the first - they actually invented the concept of Jihad or "Holy war" in the first place - against the Greeks and Romans over the possession of Jerusalem. Christians and later Muslims picked up the thread where the Jews left it. In the Christian Jihad, too, Jerusalem was at center stage. After beating the Persians to a pulp, the upbeat Christians felt vindicated that they genuinely enjoyed God's blessings. Heraclius marched triumphantly into Jerusalem and restored the "True Cross" to the Church of the Holy Sepulcher. The leftover Jews in Jerusalem's precincts who survived the carnage were forcibly converted. All the other Jews residing outside were banned from coming within 3 miles of Jerusalem.

Eastern Orthodox Christianity was officially declared a heresy. All the other Christian sects living within the Roman Empire were coerced into accepting the teachings of the Latin Church (Roman Trinitarian Christianity). The writ of Latin (Roman) Christianity now ran supreme; God was with this religion and had made it triumphant. What other proof the people needed?

Edessa, the seat of the Eastern Christian School of thought, was wholly taken over by the Roman Church, and the latter issued orders to drive out all the Eastern Orthodox Christians from Byzantium. As the plague had struck Shah Kavad, and Zoroastrianism was fast losing its appeal due to the discontent of its followers, Heraclius decided to convert Persia into Western Christian territory. He boasted, "Christianity was the true faith; the hand of God was directing and guiding its followers."

Heraclius didn't know he was wrong. The needle of history had already begun to tick in a different direction. True, Persia, with its Zoroastrianism, would be swept over, but not by Heraclius or his Christianity. God had other plans.

The Prophet

While the Christian Holy war was in progress in the Fertile Crescent and its adjoining lands in Hejaz, Mohammad, this successful and contemplative merchant, announced that he was a Prophet of Allah. In 610 CE, according to Islamic tradition, he received his first revelations. For some time, he kept quiet about it. Finally, in 612 CE, he came out in the open, according to him, on the insistence of God, announcing what God revealed to him from time to time through the archangel Gabriel (Jibreel in Arabic). As he drew the attention of the people, not all went smoothly. A few, though, paid heed to him, mainly the poor, despondent, and oppressed section of the society, including slaves. The affluent mercantile class was primarily uninterested in his revelatory proclamations. At least initially.

Hadhrat Mohammad laid great emphasis on justice, morality, honesty, and mercy and condemned oppression and exploitation of the poor, orphans, and slaves. Like the *Hanifs* before him, he insisted on worshiping one God. To that extent, the elite and the Quraysh leaders tolerated him. But, when he started criticizing the Meccans for patronizing idolatry in the precincts of Ka'aba, he poked at the sore spot. The Quraysh, the Keepers of the Ka'aba, now became suspicious and apprehensive about his preaching activities. They construed Mohammad's activity as a direct assault on their livelihood. For them, Ka'aba was of paramount economic significance. It attracted pilgrims from all over, who, irrespective of their faith and beliefs, filled the streets of Mecca. The Meccan economy was largely dependent on the pilgrimage season. When the idols were to be removed from the sanctuary of Ka'aba, the Quraysh leaders were afraid there was nothing left for the pilgrims to come to Mecca. "What message does Mohammad want to go out? Was he serious about closing the doors of Ka'aba to pilgrims by denigrating their gods and idols?" the bemused Meccans asked. Now, they had no misgivings about Mohammad. His preaching imperiled their economic interests.

The pilgrims, the Quraysh knew, came to Mecca to pray and worship their respective gods. Here was a man who proclaimed to be a prophet of God and condemned idolatry as an abomination and sin, warning them if they didn't abandon this practice, God would *punish* them as He had, the *Ad*, *Thamud*, and others in the past. In that case, they asked why people should choose Ka'aba for pilgrimage. Mohammad responded by affirming that he was saying nothing but what God revealed to him through his angel. All this came at a time when the Meccan economy began to contract due to the war in Syria. The caravans were persistently being raided and looted on their way. Mohammad was treading a dangerous path. He urged taking a drastic step – abandoning patronizing the gods of Ka'aba. People from far-off places visited here to pay respect to those gods. They spent their earnings, traded, and exchanged goods, thus, sustaining the livelihood of the Meccans, especially when the caravan trade was getting tough. The Quraysh sternly questioned the logic behind Mohammad's call against idolatry.

Not willing to jeopardize the pilgrimage custom, the mercantile society of Mecca refused to listen to Mohammad's call to one God (Allah). In their wisdom, Mohammad was propagating a dangerous idea – an idea opposed diametrically to the cultural diversity, religious tolerance, and, most importantly, economic stability of the Meccan society. They decided to fight him systematically to nip the whole idea in the bud. And the trouble started. Amar bin Hisham (later Abu Jahal), Mohammad's uncle and a firebrand leader of the Quraysh, was severely annoyed by his stubbornness. He resolved to excommunicate him. Accordingly, the Quraysh imposed a strict social boycott on Mohammad and his band of followers, ushering in harsh and challenging times for the new converts.

There were other reasons for the Meccans to turn down Mohammad. He wasn't the only person to preach monotheism. There were plenty of these "copycat prophets" who rose to prominence during the years of the Persian-Roman war. Like him, they also claimed to receive revelations through the agency of Gabriel, reciting, as it were, their respective scriptures in support of their claims. The competition between prophets was fierce in this region. To verify Mohammad's authenticity, the Quraysh elders sought counsel from some learned Christians of Yathrib, a town 300 miles from Mecca. These learned men suggested the Meccans ask Mohammad three questions: How many sleepers were in the Cave; Who was the traveler who reached both ends of the Earth, and what is the Soul (the Spirit)? If he answered correctly, they added, he was an authentic prophet.

It was an excellent opportunity for Mohammad to prove his credentials. The Quraysh also were serious about settling the matter with Mohammad; otherwise, why would they depute representatives to undertake a journey of six hundred miles (to and fro) to seek counsel in Yathrib? When Mohammad was posed with the three questions, he promised to report back with answers the next day. The day went by; he didn't show up. Two weeks went by; he didn't bring them the answers. The Quraysh elders made the air turn blue. He was a fake. Nothing could convince them to believe him. They intensified their opposition to him, notifying him against creating a fuss. Finally, when Mohammad came up with the answer, it was late. The delay had already jeopardized his position. The Quraysh would have none of his revelation things. They began to doubt his claim to prophethood seriously. He was to face unimaginable hardships and trouble at the hands of his co-tribesmen. The story of the Seven Sleepers, outlined in the Quran in the chapter *The People of the Cave* (18: 9-26), won't cut ice with them.

The "Seven Sleepers" was a story circulated by a sect of 5th-century Christians, mainly Trinitarians. According to the legend, in Ephesus, a town under Roman occupation, the Romans persecuted a group of young converts to Christianity under the orders of Emperor Decius. They fled and hid in a cave. As they were tired, they fell asleep. Christian sources said they slept there for nearly two hundred years (from 252 until 448 CE). In 447 CE, as it were, a landowner opened the mouth of the cave, which woke the Sleepers. By then, it was the emperor Theodosius's reign. The sleepers felt they had slept hardly a day and sent one of their colleagues to the market to buy food, warning him to be careful. When he arrived at the market, he almost lost his mind. He saw churches and buildings with Crosses everywhere. It didn't dawn on him immediately that he had been sleeping for 200 years. How could it? In those two hundred years, as it were, the Seven Sleepers had overslept, the Romans themselves had converted, and Christianity had become the state religion of the Roman Empire. Ephesus was transformed from a pagan city into the city of God, Jesus.

When the Sleeper took out the coins, the people in the market, according to the legend, were surprised to see that the coins belonged to the Decius era. They called on the bishop to investigate the matter. The Seven Sleepers were summoned to recount their story. It turned out they lived during Emperor Decius's reign. After they finished the story and learned that they had been sleeping for 196 years, they died. So goes the story. This story was widely circulated throughout Christendom. A frantic search for the Cave of the Seven Sleepers began, and several sites have been identified so far, each claiming to be the original site. But none has been archaeologically confirmed so far as the Seven Sleepers' cave.

The first version of the Seven Sleepers story was put out by a Syrian bishop, Jacob of Serugh (450-521 CE). Gregory of Torus (538-594 CE) used Jacob's version to outline the story in detail. The Syriac accounts say they were eight in number; some maintain they were three brothers. There is no consensus as to their exact number. Likewise, there is no consensus regarding the duration of their sleep. The alleged Sleepers' event had been arrogated to a time when in Ephesus, the Romans under the emperor Decius persecuted Christians for their refusal to bow to Roman idols, i.e., around 250 CE. In his book *Millennium: The End of the World and the Forging of Christianity*, Tom Holland, after eloquently and pithily contesting the historical authenticity of this story based on available historical records and data, leaves no doubt in the fictitious nature of the story. He concludes, with cold logic, that the Christians spread Seven Sleepers and other tall tales of miracles when Latin (Roman) Christianity was actively engaged in proselytizing across the length and breadth of Iranshaher (Persia).

When Mohammad finally came up with the revelation, it didn't alleviate the suspicion of the Quraysh. The revelation (Quran 18:9-26) doesn't give the exact number of the sleepers either but asks us not to "engage in disputation about the number of sleepers." It says the sleepers included a dog (verse 18), and they all slept for 300 years and nine, meaning 309 years. The Quran also affirmed that these sleepers (allegedly Trinitarian Christian converts) were righteous believers in God. Furthermore, a little later, in verse 23, it gives the reason behind the delay in revelation: "and never say of anything, 'Indeed, I will do that tomorrow.'" Since Mohammad had not uttered the phrase *Inshaallah* "God willing" (when he promised the Quraysh that he would answer their queries the next day), God, according to the Quran, intentionally delayed revealing to Mohammad the answers to the question posed to him by the Quraysh. The justification didn't convince the Quraysh elders.

The Quraysh became harsher in their attitude and more atrocious toward Mohammad. The social boycott imposed on him, his family, and his followers' families made their lives miserable. Khadija, the prophet's first wife, originally from a wealthy background, became so sick and frail after weeks of starvation that she succumbed to death. The Prophet endured hardships with courage, patience, and determination. It was a watershed period for his career. The adversity compelled him to think, contemplate, and seek "out of the box" solutions. In a society governed by *Muruwah* rules, the Prophet had no choice but to save his clan, Banu Hashim, and his followers or get annihilated himself. Circumstances were fragile. His group was numerically small. A head-on confrontation would be perilous. He carefully considered all facets. After consultation with his followers and well-wishers, he devised a plan to leave Mecca for Yathrib.

It was a painful decision, but the vicissitudes of life had left few options for this small community of followers of the Prophet. As the first contingent of emigrants was evacuated, enemies were alerted. The Quraysh sent a gang of armed men to raid the Prophet's house at night to finish him off. But he gave them the slip and escaped under cover of the night, aided by his cousin and confidante, Ali bin Abi Talib. The next day, the Prophet, accompanied by his close friend and follower Abu Bakr Sidiq, fled to Yathrib on his she-camel, traveling cautiously along a longer but less risky route. This voluntary exile from Mecca, known as *Hijrah*, marked a turning point in the career of Mohammad. History was about to change permanently; the *Hijrah* was the first landmark step of his unexpected journey full of twists and turns. Soon Yathrib would transform, and so would the whole Arabian Peninsula.

Abu Jahal (a nickname given to Amar bin Hisham by the early converts to Islam) and his contemporary Quraysh elite failed to see the future unfolding before their eyes. Given their narrow doctrinaire utilitarianism, it was hard for them, like any mortal, to foresee the events and think pragmatically and futuristically. Blinded by their unfounded fear of losing business, they steadfastly, and paradoxically too, opposed an idea that turned out to be enormously beneficial economically to the Arabs for generations to come. When the time came for Mohammad's vision to take root, in the decades ahead, Mecca would be flooded with pilgrims as never before. Every year the number of pilgrims increased, and it continued to do so till today. How would Abu Jahal have reacted if he had witnessed Mecca's bustling markets under Mohammad's leadership? (Abu Jahal was killed in the battle of Badr long before Mecca capitulated to the Prophet's forces).

Conversely, had Abu Jahal, say, acted pragmatically and lent his support to the Prophet, would Islam's sacred history have followed a different course? Perhaps, in that case, the Arabs' history wouldn't be fascinating at all. Or, maybe Islam would have been just another *Hanifiyah*-like sect confined to the Meccan society. Perhaps the sacred history wouldn't have been sprinkled with the blood of innocent Muslims and non-Muslims. All this is debatable. One thing is sure, though. You wouldn't be reading this book.

The Undisputed Chief

Yathrib was an agricultural settlement where Jews and Christians lived alongside Arab Bedouins. Not peacefully, though. They were hostile to each other. The Jews engaged in trade with the Meccans and were comparatively more prosperous. As the Yathrib's Arab community welcomed Mohammad and his companions, the Jews and Christians felt uneasy. To top all that, Mohammad's proselytizing made these people of the Book peevish. Communal harmony became a challenging task. Yet, with the support of the Yathribites, called Ansars, the Prophet became a Sayyid, or chief, to arbitrate disputes among the communities and interested groups. Initially, Mohammad was excited and confident of the support of the Jews, and accordingly, he adopted a conciliatory approach towards their religion and scripture. He announced the revelation, addressing them, "Indeed, the believers, Jews, Christians, and the Sabaeans – whoever truly believes in God and the Last day and does the good, will have their reward with their Lord. And there will be no fear for them, nor will they grieve (Quran 2:62,

5:69)." The Muslims were directed to pray facing east towards Jerusalem as their Qibla (the direction for prayers). Such conciliatory gestures, however, didn't fully assuage the Jews' doubt about Mohammad and his preaching. Finally, Mohammad turned his back on them in disappointment, deeply troubled by their attitude of intransigence, obstinacy, and suspicion about him.

Some smaller Jewish clans cooperated with Mohammad on everyday matters yet disagreed with him on religion. By 624 CE, he finally understood that the Jews would not budge, notwithstanding their severe and irreconcilable theological differences from the Christians. Though he regarded both as the "people of the book," each denomination vehemently defended the authenticity of its respective lines of theology against Mohammad's creed. Sensing the futility of wooing them and disillusioned by their stubbornness, Mohammad announced a change in the direction of the Qibla in January 624 CE. Henceforth, the newly organized community of Muslims would offer prayers facing Ka'aba rather than Jerusalem. This day marked when Mohammad formally launched Islam as an independent religion and defined it as the original and pure faith that Adam, Noah, Abraham, and all other earlier prophets had professed and taught. Announcing Ka'aba as the Qibla had a resounding impact on the psyche of the fledgling community of immigrant Muslims. It boosted their spiritual bond with their fatherland and the sanctuary of the Ka'aba.

With the formal entry of Islam into the competitive religious arena, Mohammad and his small community of followers faced new challenges. During the preceding two years, none of the migrants had secured a means of earning a livelihood in that alien territory, Yathrib. The migrant community comprised traders and merchants who had left their businesses in Mecca; Yathrib was primarily an agriculturist settlement. The immigrants were not well-versed in farming, and toiling in the fields was the last thing they could do. Their joblessness and inability to toil in the fields had become a problematic and pressing issue needing immediate attention lest the Ansars might stop feeding them. The immigrant community was compelled to resort to other means of earning a livelihood, such as caravan raids (*Ghazu*). With that, the trouble started.

Mubarakpuri notes in *The Sealed Nectar* that Mohammad sent his cousin, Hamza bin Muttalib, to lead the first raid barely nine months after the immigration when the Amar bin Hisham (Abu Jahal) was camping with his caravan at a place called al-Is. According to Ibn Ishaq, Mohammad duly permitted to conduct raids on the enemy caravans to seize the booty. Following this, the Ghazu expeditions set a chain reaction in motion, culminating in the bloody conflict of the Badr, the Uhud, and the battle of the Trenches. Most exegetes of the Quran, dissecting the sequence of events that led to these bloody conflicts, have omitted to comment on economic expediencies in the causation of these battles. That leaves a pivotal period in the life of Mohammad poorly understood and ignores the context of the passages of the Quran that describe these battles.

In the 7th century CE, Yathribites, primarily a hard-working farming community, earned bread by the sweat of their brow. In contrast, for immigrant merchants and traders, farming under the Sun was not their cup of tea. They had never cultivated the land, barring a few who engaged in shepherding. Even shepherding wasn't easy because it was a full-time job demanding a peripatetic lifestyle, with the disadvantage of leaving a shepherd out of touch with the immigrant community and the politico-religious upheavals in Yathrib. Initially, the Yathribites, in a demonstration of generosity and hospitality, received the immigrants in their homes, for which they were lovingly called the *Ansars* (helpers) by the Prophet. But the Ansars' altruism couldn't be relied on indefinitely. Going about life without a source of income was impossible. How long could they afford to feed these immigrants and their families who were practically no good as farming apprentices? More so, after the change in the Qibla, the immigrants became the "other." A simmering restlessness set in, exposing the cracks and fault lines in the relationship between the Jewish and Christian Yathribite tribes and the fledgling community of immigrants. The immigrants sensed the mood.

After prolonged deliberations, the Prophet gave a green signal to *Ghazu* – the practice of raiding the caravans, capturing the booty, and distributing it equally among all. Making a two-time meal by raiding was easier than toiling on the lands under the desert sun. In the Arabian deserts, the bands of people who carried out *Ghazu* (called *Ghazis)* were supposed to follow specified rules. They would only attack the rear end of the caravans and capture whatever they could put their hand on, taking care to avoid killing the caravan men. Under the convention of *Muruwah* prevalent in 7th century Arabia, murder called for reprisal, unleashing a chain reaction of vendettas and counter-vendettas. Considering everything, the immigrants decided to carry out *Ghazu* on the Meccan caravans. They ambushed and raided them. This entire affair irritated the Quraysh, but they ignored it until the immigrants drew up the plan to attack the caravan of Abu Sufyan, the most prosperous Quraysh merchant, and son-in-law of the tribal chief Amar bin Hisham, returning from Syria. His caravan was expected to cross the outskirts of Yathrib, near a valley called *Badr*. The immigrants decided to ambush it there. As the news leaked to the Meccans, they became furious. "How come this bunch of ill-fed and poverty-stricken homeless exiles were plotting to plunder our caravan?" thundered Amar bin Hisham. "They sure haven't learned the lesson yet," roared others, each arguing to take the bull by the horns to end this raiding menace once and for all.

In Yathrib, the Muslims began preparations to attack Sufyan's caravan, hoping to fetch fat booty. It was too audacious and reckless for a handful of immigrant renegades to attack the caravan of the son-in-law of a Meccan tribal chief. It put the Meccans' blood on a boil. They sent a message to Abu Sufyan to change the route immediately. At the same time, Amar bin Hisham (Abu Jahal) and his fellow tribesmen assembled to embark on Yathrib to tackle these renegades. As they reached the valley of Badr, they saw Mohammad and his companions, all 300 in total, already camped there. The plan changed on both sides. None had envisioned a face-to-face encounter taking place. The fight ensued, first, one-to-one, as was the rule. As the passion peaked, the Muslims suddenly stormed into the rank and file of the Quraysh elders. In the ensuing pandemonium, many Meccans were slaughtered, notably the chief – Amar bin Hisham. The ones who survived retreated hastily, leaving behind all their belongings and stocks of food - handsome booty and spoils for the Muslims. The unexpectedly beaten Meccans had never imagined that they would be so grossly humiliated at the hands of an orphan who had once fled for life under cover of the night. Mohammad achieved his first victory on the battlefield. Thus began a new history on the sands of the Arabian Desert written in human blood. It changed the Yathrib's religious landscape. Permanently.

The beating and thrashing that Meccans received at Badr did not go well with their sense of pride. They were shattered. The only thing they now sought was revenge. With Amar bin Hisham gone, the leadership responsibility fell on Abu Sufyan's shoulders. His wife, Amar bin Hisham's rakehell daughter Hind, burning with hatred for her father's killers, would not let her guard loose for even a moment. Her obsession with revenge was, at times, even annoying to Sufyan and others. She could not forget the scene when Hamza bin Muttalib killed her father in the battle. She insisted the Meccans exact a lethal reprisal from the Muslims. So, at her insistence, an elaborate plan was given formal shape to eliminate Prophet Mohammad from the stage and squarely decimate the immigrants. When the preparations were completed, the Meccans launched the offensive. The two sides met at a place called Uhud. A fierce battle ensued; the Muslims got a thorough beating, shaking their morale. The Prophet was also severely wounded. Some of his companions surrounded him and carried him out of the battlefield to a safer place. As the Meccans could no longer see the Prophet on the battlefield, they mistook him as dead. That was enough to call off the fight and trumpet the victory. On the way back to Mecca, their celebrations were cut short by the news that the Prophet was only wounded and had survived, meaning their victory was not yet definitive. Though Hind had succeeded in getting Hamza bin Muttalib, her father's killer, the Meccans had missed the primary target. They bitterly resented their impatience. No hand-wringing and cursing would help them now, for they had lost the opportunity: the first and the last.

After a short period of lull, the hostilities renewed. To undo their colossal blunder of Uhud, the Meccans prepared to launch another assault on the Muslims. In 627 CE, barely two years after the battle of Uhud, they again struck, grossly underestimating their opponent. This third battle, the Uhud II, or the Battle of the Trench, turned out to be the beginning of their end. The Prophet had gathered reliable intelligence inputs that the Meccans were preparing for another war to eliminate him. So, he meticulously laid the trap. He got a deep trench dug around the settlement of Yathrib and covered it with a false ceiling of straw and dust. As the Meccans advanced, galloping atop the trench roof, they fell into the Trench. In the resulting stampede, the Muslims trampled over them with a lightning-like swiftness. In utter confusion, the Meccans beat a hasty retreat, ceding defeat. The Muslims chased them for a distance and returned to celebrate the victory. The trumpets blew, and the word quickly spread. The Muslims became a force to reckon with. The Prophet became the undisputed Sayyid or chief of Yathrib. Soon, Yathrib would go on to become Madina, the city of the Prophet.

The Yathrib Confederacy

Power doesn't come on a platter. It asks for a price. The Prophet paid that price. He had seen adversity, trouble, and hardships. One would expect, after the victory, the woes would be over, with no threats to his life and his companions. Now that he was the acknowledged Sayyid, one expected life to become easier for him. No. Not for him. For a leader destined to change the course of history, life never ceases to be life. Great leaders walk on the edge. They don't have time to celebrate and relax. The leader's genius lies in their readiness to make harsh decisions in the most demanding times. And great leaders set their sights on the horizons of change. For them, an opportunity missed is an opportunity lost forever. So they create opportunities where there are none. They are seldom afraid of change. They thrive on it.

By 625 CE (the time of Uhud I), Prophet Mohammad had already attained a transparent thought process, extraordinary contemplative, and remarkable leadership capacity. The winds were changing. The God of the Muslims was proving much more reliable. The proof lay in the victories at Badr and Uhud II, where the Muslims frontally took on the numerically superior enemy. The Prophet recited the revelations to his followers about how Allah helped them overpower their enemies (The Quran chap. 3&4). As the word spread, many tribes solicited allegiance to the Prophet Mohammad. The Prophet now built a Confederacy of tribes, laying down the charter that stipulated member tribes desist from supporting each other's enemies. Some Meccan tribes, too, began to support the Confederacy of Yathrib. It was, by now, becoming evident to the Meccans that their gods were failing them.

The Yathrib Confederacy was not a homogeneous, attrition-less coalition. Individual tribes had agendas, interests, and goals that clashed with other tribes' claims. Naturally, fault lines were bound to appear. The three Jewish tribes – Qanuqah, Nadir, and Qurayzah – were particularly unhappy with the arrangement as they didn't want to jeopardize their business relations with the Meccan mercantile class. For them, joining the Yathrib Confederacy underscored heavy economic losses, especially at a time when Yathrib hadn't yet developed a market. Mecca was still the center of trade, especially during the pilgrimage season when its streets flooded with traders, merchants, and livestock holders. Understandably, the Jewish tribes of Qanuqah, Nadir, and Qurayzah were reluctant to sever the trade links with their Meccan contacts and partners. They were serious businessmen and maintained their private armies to care for their caravans. Thus, the Muslims perceived them as a potential threat to the newly formed coalition.

The Qanuqah tribe rebelled against the Prophet in 625 CE. He put down that rebellion with an iron hand and exiled the whole tribe from Yathrib. It was followed by the Nadir tribe that ended up in exile to Khaybar as they were accused of plotting the assassination of the Prophet. In Khaybar, the Nadir joined hands with Abu Sufyan, thus proving more dangerous, in the long run, than they were in Yathrib. The prophet viewed the decision to exile Nadir to Khaybar as his strategic blunder. The Qurayzah had sided with the Meccans at the Battle of the Trench (Uhud II), breaking the Confederacy Charter. Subsequently, the Prophet dealt with them much more harshly than the previous recalcitrant Jews. Qurayzah was besieged; the men were slaughtered, and their women and children were taken as slaves.

By the end of 627 CE, the Muslims had eliminated all the potentially inimical forces. The Muslim historians unanimously agree that the Jews, especially Qurayzah, were punished harshly as per the law provided in the Jewish scripture. Modern scholars, however, contest the Muslim version of the story, especially the Qurayzah massacre. Interestingly, some scholars call the Muslim narrative an outrightly fabricated and inaccurate rendering of history. Modern scholars observe that the Qurayzah massacre never actually took place.

In his book *In the Shadow of Swords*, Tom Holland outrightly rejects the story of the Qurayzah massacre, calling it nothing but fiction. He points out severe flaws in the historicity of the claims made by the Muslims about the punishment meted out to the Jewish tribes by the Prophet. He notes, "It is not simply that the three Jewish clans mentioned by the historians do not feature anywhere in the 'Constitution of Madina,' there is another, and familiar, problem: that our sources for the annihilation of these Jews are suspiciously late." Tom Holland affirms that the Prophet's infliction of punishment on Jews is simply a fabrication inserted by the later-day Muslim chroniclers to serve some potentially vested interests.

Be that as it may, the situation in seventh-century Arabia was precariously dangerous for the newly formed community of believers in Islam – the Muslims. In an environment of sectarian conflict, with a convention like *Muruwah* being the law, the chief of a tribe or community was not expected to show mercy toward the traitors, as the stakes were high. Survival itself was endangered. Compassion was a sign of weakness. As Karen Armstrong, justifying the Qurayzah massacre, alludes to in her book *Mohammad, A Prophet For Our Time,* Mohammad had practically only two options: either put himself and his handful of community in danger of extinction or respond with an iron hand. The execution of the Qurayzah might have sent a strong message to other tribes of Yathrib - the Prophet would not hesitate to use force with impunity against the conspirators. Such measures might have been intended to bring the hostilities to a halt. Naturally, also, it might have sent a strong message to the Meccan Quraysh and their allies. Temporarily though, but still.

A significant social change was taking place. Islam was fast shaping itself into a new and independent religion. Yathrib transformed into Medina. Never mind, the sands, though, had been mantled red with human blood... the bloodshed has nearly always been a collateral of all religious transformations. Sadly.

The Victory of Mecca

To a large extent, Prophet Mohammad successfully handled the volatile situation in Yathrib. Now, he wanted peace in Yathrib to build its economy, which the tribal wars and conflicts had severely derailed. As Sayyid, the community's economic welfare was one of his top priorities. Any prolongation of a civil war-like situation would adversely affect his plan because the Muslims were already drained and exhausted. Bearing that in mind, he intelligently defused the prospect of yet another severe confrontation with the Meccans by entering into a pact with them under the famous *Treaty of Hudaybiah.* This treaty helped achieve a truce with the Meccans. In retrospect, it proved a "masterstroke" strategy giving the Muslims an unhindered opportunity to engage in *Ghazu* (raids) to consolidate their position economically and numerically.

In 628 CE, the Prophet and his companions proceeded on a pilgrimage to Ka'aba. The Quraysh stopped him from entering the city. The situation grew tense, but finally, one Suhayl bin Amar, the emissary of the Quraysh, began the negotiations with the Muslims. As the peace talks proceeded and the treaty document was being hammered out, some companions of the Prophet, particularly Omar bin Khattab, objected to it because the document addressed the Prophet as "Mohammad bin Abdullah," omitting the mention of the word "Prophet." The fiery Omar bin Khattab took it as an affront that Mohammad had agreed to not mention "the Prophet" in his name. The treaty also stipulated that if any of the Meccans switched sides with Mohammad without the permission of their guardians, the Muslims would return them to the Quraysh, while if any of the Muslims slipped to the Meccan side, the Quraysh were not obliged to return him to Mohammad. This clause infuriated Omar even further, and he protested. But another senior colleague of the Prophet, Abu Bakr Sidiq, pacified him. All the companions, including Omar bin Khattab, then swore fealty to the Prophet. With that, Ali bin Abi Talib finalized the document. The Muslims returned without performing pilgrimage as the 10-year truce was agreed on that condition. Later, Mohammad recited to his companions the revelation (Quran 48: 18-20), "Indeed, Allah was pleased with the believers when they gave the pledge to you under the tree. He knew what was in their hearts, and He sent down tranquility upon them, and He rewarded them with a near victory."

To some extent, peace returned. The Meccans concentrated on improving their business to cover the losses incurred during the conflict. The Prophet diverted his attention to consolidating his base and proselytizing to other regions of the Arabian Peninsula and foreign kingdoms. In his book, *Life of Mohammad*, Haykal observes: "History has proved that the Treaty of *Hudaybiah* laid down a very important foundation for Islam's political career as well as for its spread throughout the world." He sent letters to Heraclius and Khusraw asking them to accept Islam or face the consequences. After the Battle of Khaybar, he expelled all the Jews from Yathrib (now Medina).

Executing the treaty is one thing, but honoring the treaty is another. One day, a Quraysh woman, Umm Kulthum, fled from her husband. Her two brothers soon found out that the Prophet Mohammad had given her refuge. When they approached him to seek her release, the Prophet, Ibn Ishaq, points out, refused to hand her over to them, judging by the revelation (Quran 60;10), "O ye, who believe, when the female believers come to you as fugitives, examine them. Allah is best aware of their faith. Then, if you know them as believers, send them not back to the disbelievers. These women are not lawful for them….." In doing so, according to Ibn Ishaq, Mohammad broke the treaty. The Quraysh protested, but they had grown too weak to take any punitive action against the Prophet. Later, when he learned from his sources that the Meccans were no longer a united lot interested in fighting battles, he began to accept men who defected from the ranks of the Quraysh. That strained the relations between the two sides further.

In 630 CE, when the Meccan Quraysh violated the treaty, the Prophet announced war on them, marching upon Mecca with a whole army of his followers. The Meccans capitulated without putting up resistance. Mohammad entered Mecca victorious without firing an arrow. No bloodshed. No violence. It was a smooth takeover as the Meccans preferred surrendering to warring. The prophet and his army then smashed the idols of the Ka'aba and rededicated it to one God, Allah. The pagan Arab ritual of pilgrimage was given Islamic significance and retained as Hajj, constituting one of the five pillars of the new religion. The Prophet's final remarkable yet bloodless victory convinced the people of Mecca and their chief, Abu Sufyan, that their old religion had failed before this new religion. It was pretty reasonable for them to swear allegiance to Mohammad. Accordingly, they did. When Abu Sufyan, the bitter enemy of the Prophet and the leader of the Quraysh, was brought in, the Prophet said, "Woe to you, Abu Sufyan. Isn't it time that you recognize that I am God's apostle?" When Abu Sufyan expressed his doubt about that, one Abbas counseled him, "Submit and testify that there is no God but Allah and that Muhammad is the apostle of God before you lose your head." Abu Sufyan, a wealthy merchant, quickly understood the futility of being obstinate. He complied. The rest is history. Mecca was subdued.

Mecca's fall was a significant victory, but it didn't complete the Prophet's mission. For him to be the undisputed Master of Arabia, one more thorn had to be removed from the path: Malik bin Awf controlled Ta'if, a settlement whose inhabitants had woefully rejected the Prophet years ago. They were pretty disdainful of the Quraysh for their capitulation before the Muslims. So, the Prophet challenged Malik at a place called Hunayn. In that battle, Malik bin Awf was routed. Ta'if, now fallen, Prophet showed some favor to a few recent Quraysh converts while distributing the booty. When one Muslim asked him about this favoritism, the Prophet replied, "If justice is not to be found with me, then where will you find it," hinting thereby, the Quraysh, after all, need to be applauded and comforted for their accepting Islam and joining the fight against their once-friendly Ta'ifites. The prophet was careful to take no credit himself for the victory over Ta'if. He announced that he received a revelation explaining that the Muslims won because God helped them (Quran 9: 25-27).

After consolidating Mecca and Ta'if, Mohammad, now an undisputed Master of Arabia, returned to Medina. After years of fighting and bloodshed, a sense of peace prevailed over the two towns.

Now, it was time to put into effect the "Constitution of Medina," with a clear mandate. This famous document spelled out the authority that rested in the hands of Mohammad to arbitrate disputes in Medina. Muslim historians celebrated it as the world's "first written constitution." Calling this document the "first written constitution" may be a bit of an exaggeration, as written or inscribed edicts were issued by kings in ancient, too. Be that as it may, Mohammad was now unequivocally recognized as the Messenger of God and the "Sayyid" of Madina. To the believers, he was the one who spoke with authority from God, and he had come to establish a just socio-religious order backed by the law of God. The revelations he received from God were systematically memorized by his followers and written on barks, bones, leather sheets, parchment, and primitive paper. These manuscripts were later sorted and compiled in book form following the injunctions of the Prophet. We call that book the Quran.

The Quran

The Quran is a compilation of revelations that Mohammad received over twenty-three years from 610 to 632 CE. It comprises 114 chapters; some are exceptionally long, especially the first few chapters, and some consist of a few short verses. The chapters, however, are not set in chronological order. For instance, the first verses received by the Prophet figure in the 96th chapter of the Quran. Broadly the chapters are classified as Meccan (86 in number), and Medinite (28), depending on whether they were recited by the Prophet to his followers before Hijra or after.

As for the foundational themes of the Quran - the oneness of God, the Creation Story, and the "End Time" - they are identical to those of the Hebrew Bible. The Early Meccan chapters (7:54, 32:4) say that God created the universe (the sky, the Earth, and the stars) in six days. However, in a later Meccan chapter (41:9-12), it turns out, that the Quran says the universe with its Seven Skies (41:12) was created in eight days. It is not surprising that the Quran mentions Seven Skies. Till the 16th century, the accepted folk wisdom was that there are seven skies or heavens above us. It was based on an intellectual conception that originated in Greece and was promoted by Aristotle and Ptolemy. Following the same lead, De Dondi, as noted by Jacob Bronowski in his book *The Ascent of Man*, even built a clock in AD 150 with seven dials representing seven heavens. Interestingly, 41:9-12 is not the only passage of the Quran that falls in line with the popular folk wisdom and common sense of the time. And, about common sense, you know what they say in Science! There are many other verses and passages (7:54, 13:2, 14:33, 31:29, 35:13, 36:38-40, 39:5, 55:5) in the Quran which align with the same cultural milieu that upheld common sense conclusions as incontrovertible fact. In these verses, the Quran talks of the creation of the day and night from the vantage point of the motion of the Sun and the moon along definite paths in the sky. That is to say, the Quran takes a Geocentric view of the Universe - originally a Greek concept based on observational common sense or logic - and stresses at multiple places that God created the Earth and the skies in six days. In Chapter 35:41 it says, "Indeed, Allah holds the skies and the Earth (stationary) lest they could move, and if they move none other than Him can hold them back (in place)." In other words, the Quran maintains that the Earth is the center of the universe and is unmoving, in line with the accepted folk wisdom of the seventh-century world upheld by Greek science of the day. In the earlier mentioned passage (41: 9-12), the days spent by God in creating the world add up to eight instead of six in other verses. Abdullah Yusuf Ali, in his Commentary of the Holy Quran, acknowledges that 41:9-12 is "a difficult passage" of the Quran "describing the primal creation of our physical earth and the physical heaven around us." But clarifies that "the Commentators understand the 'four days' in verse 10 [of the above passage] to include the two days in verse 9 so that the total for the universe comes to six Days [sic]."

The Jews and Christians sincerely believed that the "End Time" was nearing. Some pious believers even expected the day to come in their lifetime. The Hebrew Bible and the New Testament have devoted many passages to the End Time theme. The Quran is no different. It unambiguously affirms in chapter Saba (34:30), "say, the term (mi' ad) for you is of One day, which you cannot put back an hour, nor put forward." The translators and exegetes of the Quran render the word "mi 'ad" in the 34:30 as "appointment" or "promise," however, Shams Naveed Usmani disagrees, and rightly so. According to Usmani, "mi 'ad" means a term or period, and then, as per the definition of the Quran (32:5), he says, one day equals a thousand years. In that sense, Usmani emphasizes, that the "End Time" or the doomsday, as explained to the infidels of Mecca by the Quran, was to happen one thousand years after the revelation of the Quran. That is to say, the Quran, in essence, upholds the Judeo-Christian concept that doomsday is not very far in the future, and living in fear of the End Time is perfectly genuine.

For Muslims, the Quran is a miracle sent upon Mohammad to preach to society that was highly proficient in the art of poetry and wordsmithery. It outperformed and outshone all the poetic literature and prose of the time. Its innovative and exemplary style set the trend for future Arab literature. The themes in the Quran are overtly overlapping, at times incoherent and discreet. There are no neat paragraphs, no logical beginnings, and no endpoints. The textual style of the Quran is unique in the sense that no scripture has adopted this style, except maybe, the biblical Book of Isaiah, the book of Prophecies. In the literary history of the Arabs, the Quran became a foundational text.

The Quran, the Prophet said, was a complete book of revelation, word by word, from the one God, and it was a book of guidance for all the generations to come. In the Quran, the answers to all the questions were laid down directly from God, said the Prophet. Mohammad himself followed the teachings of the Quran in letter and spirit, demonstrating to the people and his immediate companions that he was a living embodiment of the teachings of the Quran. He implemented rules and laws according to what was revealed to him from time to time: Alcohol was discredited, usury was banned, *Zakat* (tithe) was implemented for the poor and the needy, and distribution of wealth, inheritance laws, and women's rights was spelled out, and punishments were codified. All aspects of individual and social life were touched in the Quran, and the Prophet routinely emphasized and implored the followers to abide by what had been revealed therein.

Though the Prophet reiterated endlessly that the Quran was revealed to him, word by word, from Allah, the critics maintain that the Quran, like other scriptures, is simply a recapitulation of the circulating stories and folk tales of the day. The Quran, they argue, doesn't contradict the existing popular knowledge of the 7th-century world; rather it invokes the existing stories to put the point across to its audience of the day. For instance, the book upholds the geocentric concept of the world, the creation of the world in six days, the creation of Adam from clay, the existence of seven skies, equating shooting stars to devils, the creation of human offspring from the seed of men (sperm) without any role of the female ovum (egg). The Manusmriti (first century AD Hindu scripture), for example, also maintains that women are like a field in which men sow their seed and so the production of the field is man's. Compare this with Quran 2:223 "Your women are tillage for you, so go into your tilth from where you wish, and plan for the future of yourself." Usmani in his Tafsir explains this verse as follows: "that the women are just like the tillage in which the sperm drop is the seed and the children are just like the products." According to Manusmriti women possess inferior intellect and are unreliable as a witness. The Quran says in Chapter 4 that two women witnesses equal one man witness.

The Quran doesn't condemn slavery or abolish it the way it abolished interest-based transactions in one stroke. That is not surprising. Slavery was an established institution since and before the Greeks. The entire economy and socio-political fabric depended on slavery. The Quran did also not touch the subject. Nobody could have. In the 7th century world who could have imagined in their wildest dreams that in the next thousand years human thought process would progress to an extent that the human rights issue would be a hot topic for discourse in the Christian West and slavery would be abolished officially in 1860 CE. The believers of the Quran followed suit despite no Quranic injunctions to do so.

The Messenger of God tackled the religious and spiritual aspects as brilliantly as he tackled the social and political issues confronting his handful of followers. His genius lay in consolidating the economic position of this community of penniless and helpless immigrants, and in ultimately opening up for them the corridor to the outside world. Soon after tackling the opposition in Medina and other North Arabian subsidiary towns, he resumed *Ghazu* activities and set his gaze out of the peninsula to benefit from the opportunities opening up due to the emerging power vacuum in the aftermath of the Persian-Roman war.

Mohammad's timing was calculated and precise. Take, for example, his Persian expedition. After Persia's debacle in 629 CE, the Empire, gripped by rebellion and revolt, gave way to anarchy. The individual kings, warlords, and tribal heads claimed independence, leaving the Empire teetering on extinction. Mohammad saw the opportunity and, without much dithering, sent out his expeditionary forces to the southern frontier of Persia to test the waters. The newly formed independent kingdoms there, already battered by long years of war and plague, and hollow to the core, were ill-equipped to counter yet another assault. Seeing the Arab *Ghazis* advancing on them, they quickly capitulated. The senior Persian commanders willingly agreed to pay tribute to the Arabs to save their lives. With that, the beginning of the end of the old Persian cultural era commenced. The good days for Muslims, after so many years of struggle and stress, had finally come. More tributes would follow, and more wealth would flow into Medina. Soon the Muslims would become affluent. The economic success lured more and more followers into their ranks.

Mohammad knew quite well that it was not the spiritual rewards alone that won the people over to a new religion; economics was an equally important key to religious success. The evangelical zeal coupled with economic benefits played a vital role in the success of Islam. The financial well-being sustained the religious enthusiasm of the later converts tremendously.

The booty and spoils were profuse. The Prophet declared that goods and booty seized from the non-believers were to be distributed only among the Muslim community. This decision boosted the confidence and self-esteem of the Muslims and smoothly aligned economics with the religion. Furthermore, he created a system of *Diwan* in 630 CE. The *Diwan* was established as an institution tasked with overseeing the fair distribution of booty per the principle of hierarchy. The Prophet himself kept 20% of the booty, spoils, and captives, the rest was distributed among the participants and supporters of the Ghazu. Those who had converted early, the senior believers, were to get a proportionately greater share. As more Muslims enjoyed the spoils and booty, more pagans began to convert and join the ranks of the Muslims. The *Diwan* system proved a highly efficient mechanism, working like bait to drive the expansion of the Muslim community and the conquest of other peoples.

The Prophet now commanded Muslims to take on Christians and Jews until they accepted Islam; in case, they persist with their respective religions, impose *Jizya* (Poll tax) on them, the Prophet conveyed, so they would feel belittled and constantly reminded of their inferior status (Quran 9:29). In 631 CE, he ordered *Ghazu* on Tabuk, a garrison of the Byzantine Empire. As the Muslims advanced toward the Byzantines, the latter fled their post, preferring not to engage with Muslim warriors. Soon after this success, the Prophet decided to evict the Jews and Christians from Arabia. According to Sahih al Bukhari, he reportedly said, "I will expel the Jews and the Christians from Arabia and will not leave any but Muslims." By that time, nearly all the Arabian tribal lords and petty rulers had submitted to the Prophet and accepted to pay tribute to Medina. The remaining few, for example, the Al Harith tribe, who resisted, were subdued later by Khalid bin Walid, the fearsome lieutenant of the Prophet.

The expansionist strategy with its attendant economic benefits adopted by the Prophet turned Yathrib into a thriving city – Medina. Economic prosperity, however, brought with it its trail of challenges. Priorities changed and new problems emerged. As long as the Prophet was alive, it was easy to settle the differences of opinion. His word was final. The revelations that the Prophet received, collected, and compiled as the Quran, provided the guidelines incumbent on followers to adhere to. The believers found answers to all the issues within the pages of this book up until the Prophet fell ill. As he left the world, one crucial question remained unanswered. It remains so to this day.

The prophet did not answer it directly; neither did the Quran provide an unambiguous answer. The unanswered question created a nightmare that left the rank and file of Muslims disgruntled for all generations to come. As soon as one group tried to offer a solution, others disagreed. Even after the believers shed each others' blood on the sands of the Peninsula, the enigma persisted. It was a delicate matter, and the Prophet either deliberately did not propose a clear answer or waited for an opportune moment to spell it out. Or maybe such a thought simply never came to his mind. No one knows for sure what the reason is that a delicate question on which the political fate of the Umma hinged, as we shall see later, remains unanswered in the Quran or the lifetime of the Prophet.

Two years after the *Diwan* system was implemented by the Prophet, an unexpected event happened. The Prophet unexpectedly died in the summer of 632 CE. What followed in the aftermath of that fateful event made the sacred history of Islam increasingly murkier with each passing decade. It seems that history was fated to be written in blood. It got written. Could the history of Islam have taken a different, or better, course had the Quran not left a simple question unanswered? Maybe. What was the question, after all?

It was not extraordinary. "Who will lead the newly formed community of believers – the *Umma* – after the death of the Prophet?" This seemingly simple question proved to be a formidable knot in the proverbial chain of the sacred history of Islam. Not even the thick blood of believers could loosen this knot! History has its caprices. It doesn't listen to logic and rationale.

Chapter – 12

A Flood of Blood

The sudden Leave

Mohammad (PBUH) never missed a chance to remind his followers about the transient nature of worldly life and the certitude of the Day of Judgment. He never arrogated any supernatural power to himself and went to lengths to stress he was a mere mortal except that he was a prophet of God, assigned with a job to carry God's message to the people. And one day he would die just like the prophets before him did. All that was fine. But, no one suspected that he would depart soon after his last Hajj, although, he hinted at that possibility, it is said, in his last Hajj sermon. Barely three months after his last pilgrimage to the Ka'aba, he suffered a febrile illness from which he never recovered. His death after a brief illness came as a shock to the entire community of Muslims. The Muslims were yet to establish a fully structured Islamic State and his guiding hand was no more there. Who would lead their community after the Prophet?

There were no clear-cut instructions in this regard. Neither did the Quran touch this topic directly nor did the Prophet unambiguously clarify the matter during his lifetime or the days of his terminal illness immediately before he was gone. Some scholars, including Lesley Hazleton, conjecture that the problem probably wouldn't have even arisen if Mohammad had left a son behind him. Unlikely. Hereditary succession was an uncommon practice in that Arab egalitarian society. Without instruction from the Quran and the Prophet himself, the issue of succession was bound to become controversial whether or not the Prophet left a male offspring behind. It strikes as strange - and touch confusing - that a matter that was to determine the socio-political fate of the House of Islam didn't merit a mention in the Quran. The chilling ambiguity surrounding this significant issue in the word of God has exacted a huge cost in terms of the life and blood of Muslims. In contrast, God seems to be more interested in denying inheritance rights to adopted sons - which in any case has never been an issue with extraordinary implications in any existing culture, never mind Islam - and marriage of the Prophet to the divorced wife of his adopted son, a former slave. The Quran devotes a full passage to this matter whereas it leaves a significantly tricky matter that had disastrous socio-political consequences untouched. The latter dispute has not only led to bloodshed and social unrest but has kept the different factions busy refuting each other's reading of the sacred records for the best part of the fifteen hundred years of the existence of Islam.

Arabia was destined to witness a profound social transition and political transformation in the 7th century C. After two decades of agony and tribulation, the community of Muslims (*Umma*) finally witnessed success after success under the undisputed leadership of the Prophet. In campaign after campaign, he led his followers to victory, particularly during the last two years of his life, collecting lots of booty and spoils of war, and men, women, and children as slaves - vital assets for building a state. Without captive labor and a supply of women slaves, it was difficult for any early State to survive back then. Long before the Romans and Muslims set out on building a State, Aristotle had claimed, with all seriousness, that an enslaved person was a domestic animal as an ox might be. That this Aristotelian mindset prevailed through and through up until modern times is a well-documented, undeniable fact universally accepted by modern scholars. French political philosopher Alexis de Tocqueville, for instance, in his critical examination of Europe's success observes thus: "We should almost say that the European is to other races what man himself is to the lower animals; he makes them subservient to his use, and when he cannot subdue, he destroys."

In wars for booty and captives, all early states strongly preferred women of reproductive age and children. Such a policy wasn't unique to the Roman and Muslim war expeditions alone. James Scott elaborating on early state morbidity in *Against the Grain – A Deep History of the Earliest States* notes, "In wars for captives, the strong preference for women of reproductive age reflects an interest as much in their reproductive services as in their labor. It would be instructive to know the importance of slave women's reproduction to the demographic stability and growth of the state." The Quran, for example, lays down a set of instructions regarding women in its fourth chapter "*An-Nisa*" (The Women). This chapter has two parts. The first part deals with orphans, free and slave women, and their matters of inheritance, marriage, and family. In his Commentary of the Quran, Abdullah Yusuf Ali observes that the first verses (2,3) deal with the issues of the orphans left behind by the Muslims killed in expeditions and battles (Uhud). The third verse is explicit: "If you fear that you shall not be able to deal justly with the orphan girls, then marry women [with orphaned girls (Maududi)] of your choice, two, three, or four; but if you fear that you shall not be able to deal justly, then (marry) only one, or (a captive[s] and slaves) that your right hand possesses (that you own). That will prevent you from doing injustice." Maududi explains, "This expression [what your right hand possesses] denotes 'slave girls' i.e. female captives of war who are distributed by the state among individuals when no exchange of prisoners of war takes place."

In Tafsir Al Jalalayn (Exegesis), the commentary on this verse goes, "restrict yourself to what your right hand own of slave girls since these do not have the same rights as wives, in case it is not possible to marry one among the free orphan women." Tafsir Ibn Kathir, Razi, and other influential ones concur with Al-Jalalayn's explanation. Women of reproductive age, whether free or enslaved, were an asset for the early States from a demographic point of view. Exposure to devastating epidemics due to crowded habitation along with livestock rearing routinely threatened early state populations, as James Scott explains "germs and parasites move with people and animals." in such circumstances, women, especially young captive and enslaved girls, compensated for the high infant mortality by increasing the number of births. No wonder, then, the chieftains, kings, and emperors, including Muslims under the leadership of the Prophet and the Caliphs engaged in wars and *Ghazu*-like expeditions to capture women and children as a part of the booty.

The enslaved people captured through raids and wars performed the drudgery of plowing, canal digging, mining, quarrying, road building, and other menial tasks. In polities like India, where agriculture was the sole and primary industry, the *Varna* (Caste) system substituted slavery, and the menial drudgery fell on the shoulders of the lower caste population. Scott points out that free men shunned that sort of heavy work. And it was dangerous for the States to compel their free population to undertake drudgery and menial work lest they may rebel or desert. He observes, "Over and above the drudgery of plough[sic] agriculture, the military, ceremonial, and the urban needs of the new state centers required forms of labor in terms of kind and scale that had no precedent." The captive and enslaved population was the cheapest workforce (proletariat) available to perform hazardous labor. Since Medina under the Prophet was an upcoming urban center, probably the existence of a fair demand for the war captives and enslaved population to build the state infrastructure at the lowest possible cost to the free people can't be ignored. Additionally, selling and buying slaves was at least as profitable, if not more, an enterprise of the day as any other trade, say, cattle and goods trade. No wonder there is not a single passage or verse in the Quran that unambiguously bans slavery or promulgates the institution of slavery as unlawful before God. That is to say, slavery is lawful before God. In the Qur'an, there is no attempt to abolish it, as can be seen concerning the practice of usury (la ta'kulu riba - Eat not riba (usury) doubled and multiplied Qur'an 3:130). Instead, Muslims are enjoined to follow rules while distributing and trading slaves.

As Medina's Muslim community became economically well off by dint of *Ghazus* and booty wars, the quality of life and the living standard improved. Medina became a center of trade, and although its magnitude of business was still petite than Mecca, yet it was a great achievement of the Muslim community under the Prophet's leadership. As Muslims' success stories circulated and they began consolidating the State of Medina, all of a sudden, the Prophet died. It left them all to themselves at a critical juncture of history when Mohammad's political genius and administrative prowess were needed the most. At this brittle moment of history, the Prophet even didn't formally name a leader of the *Umma*.

The Prophet's illness started with a mild headache and fever that became severe and incapacitating over a week, and on 8th June, 632 CE, he breathed his last in the chamber of his beloved wife, Aisha. The unexpected had happened at an unusual time taking Medina by storm. Unrest, disarray, and chaos spread in the rank and file of believers. The Prophet himself would probably have never wished that his death were followed by tremendous grief and utter confusion. People were wailing and weeping, arguing loudly, shouting, and stampeding each other. There was no leader in the community to handle the situation. And soon, the fault lines began to appear in that community that was completely united just hours ago. In a leaderless climate, where everybody had an opinion and perspective, mob control became an exacting task to handle. In that din, it was difficult to smoothly prepare the funeral prayers and organize the last rites on the Prophet's body. Moreover, the million-dollar question that surfaced was who would lead the funeral prayer? Of course, a leader, but.

The Prophet had left no instructions about his funeral. Yet everyone claimed insight and understanding, making inferences from what the Prophet had alluded to now and then. However, as soon as one person would come up with a suggestion, others differed with him. Everyone was sure about their conclusion but, to borrow from Lesley Hazleton, "certainty was a matter of faith rather than fact." The community, despite seeming united like brothers in religion, faced a dilemma about who would lead them at that moment and in the future and failed to resolve this dilemma to the satisfaction of all parties. The failure to settle the issue amicably and smoothly continued to haunt the sacred history of Islam creating irreconcilable schism in that once seemingly united community of the Faithful.

History leaves records – oral, written, inscribed, etc. – and archeological evidence, yet records seldom tell the whole story. Some details get lost in the fog of time. More often than not, historians build edifices of literature out of the leftover shreds, driblets, and streaks of evidence. Their narrative as always is riddled with a perspective bias (or cognitive bias). Often, they tend to present the "history of the past" through the prism of the "present." It is hard to blame them, for the human brain lacks an appropriate mental mechanism for perfect information processing. Cognitive bias may lead to perceptual distortion, inaccurate judgment, or illogical interpretation, with the result that people create their own " subjective social reality" based on individual perceptions and paradigms. That is to say, people's view of the world dictates their behavior. The innate (or subconscious) tendencies and preferences are difficult, if not impossible, to overcome.

The Muslim chroniclers tried to customize the historical narrative per the prevailing directions of the winds – not always, though – yet whenever the situation demanded. Events on their own are neutral. When viewed through the prism of a belief, they attain a color, transforming them into leitmotifs of an opinionated and polarized narrative. The facts become fiction, and the fiction becomes fact. As the beliefs and perspectives mold the course of sacred history, objectivity becomes a casualty in the hands of the narrative. It becomes challenging, then, to excoriate truth from the tapestry of opinionated logic and rationalizations. However, in the tapestry of narrative, the chroniclers did leave scope for the dissection of certain events that occupy a central or pivotal place in shaping the circumstances, contemporary and otherwise. These events help to understand the context of the socio-political history of Islam during its formative years.

Western scholars look at the sacred history of Islam from the vantage point of their own religious and sociocultural paradigms. That is fine. But back home, the Sunni Muslim scholars dismiss certain events as trivial that the Shia Muslim scholars see as crucial to their side of the narrative and vice-versa. Who is right and who is wrong? That is hard to decide. Yet, much rests on which of the two sides wield more power. Fortunately, not all information yields to censorship and suppression by the powerful. Some sources do, directly or indirectly, help trace crucial events.

The Necklace Episode

One of the pivotal episodes that had a tremendous effect on the relationship of family members of the house of the Prophet and also the subsequent cascade of events was the *Necklace episode*. The Quran gives it a fair space precisely as it became a hot topic in Medina. The gossip surrounding it sowed seeds of discord within the immediate family of Prophet Mohammad. Over time the seed germinated into a full-blown conflict whose reverberations haunt the minds of the faithful to this day. The strange tempest that arose after the infamous *Necklace episode* left the ship of Islam severely battered. Ali bin Abi Talib, the cousin and son-in-law of the Prophet, and Aisha bint Abi Bakr, the third and the youngest wife of the Prophet, never spoke a civil word to each other after the Necklace Episode neither in the presence of the Prophet nor when he was no more. Nearly two and a half decades later (656 CE) the feud between Ali bin Abi Talib and Aisha culminated in a full-blown war, which claimed thousands of Muslims' lives. Ironically, each side claimed to be the representative of true Islam. Developments like this and others set the stage for a permanent schism and an unbridgeable chasm in Islam.

Syeda Aisha, the youngest of the nine wives of Prophet Mohammad, would often accompany him on his *Ghazu* expeditions. While returning from one such trip, she stepped down from her howdah to attend to the call of nature. There, in the bushes, her *necklace* broke. By the time she gathered it and returned, the caravan had left. She had no option but to sit back and wait, hoping the caravan people would soon find out she was missing. To her fortune, good or bad, Safaan, a young man who lagged from the caravan's main body, was riding back home alone. When he saw Aisha, he offered her the camel ride to Medina. She agreed. In Medina, as the caravaners were anxiously looking for her, she was spotted arriving with the young man. That was all that the gossip mongers needed for a headline. Soon a character assassination campaign against Aisha blazed up. By all definitions, a scandal erupted.

A scandal is a scandal, even by today's standards, but in the 7th century Medina, this scandal made perfect fodder for the street singers and bards. The story spread like wildfire. The Prophet initially dismissed the scandal as a baseless trifle. But, as it turned out, that was his misreading of the public mood in Medina. Soon the streets were becoming increasingly bustled with lampooners, and the gossip spilled from Medina over into the markets of Mecca. It was then that the Prophet began to seriously worry about the turn events had taken. As the distress became palpable in the Prophet's house Aisha felt compelled to leave. She returned to her father's house with a heavy heart. With Aisha gone and the increasing intensity of gossip on the streets, the Prophet found himself on the back foot. The whole thing taxed his mind. He could no longer afford to ignore the scandal. But, the dilemma he faced was this: if he divorced Aisha, that would prove her guilty; if he took her back, that would lead people to suspect he was too doting on a young girl. Both edges of the sword were sharp.

Should the Prophet ask Ali bin Abi Talib for counsel? Indeed. Ali bin Talib was his cousin and son-in-law. In matters of religion, he was among his first followers. It was but natural for the Prophet to turn to Ali for discussion and counsel on matters of importance. He was a philosopher, orator, and spiritually mature member of the Prophet's family. Yet, in the present case, Ali was straightforward and blunt: "There are many women like her. She [Aisha] can be easily replaced," Ali allegedly told the Prophet. The Prophet mulled over the options. After three weeks of indecision, he went to Abu Bakr, his friend, companion, and father-in-law's house. There, he declared having received a revelation that Aisha was innocent, following which Aisha returned. Immediately, the Prophet announced punishment for those who would indulge in further gossip. The storm in Medina began to settle. The streets fell silent. However, the storm in Aisha's heart refused to die down. She never forgot, and she never forgave Ali and his family for the counsel he gave to the Prophet.

As the rumors were silenced and the accusers and gossip mongers were punished by flogging, the bards immediately changed the track and started singing ballads praising Aisha. In that eerie calm prevailing in Medina, Aisha's heart reportedly continued to harness the smoldering fire of revenge. As the later events showed, even the blood of the faithful couldn't douse that fire. But that is merely a subjective qualification of the events. In her heart of hearts, Aisha knew that she was childless, and as such, there was no room for her under the proverbial "cloak of Mohammad" or "*Ahl-al-Bayt*." The place was reserved for Ali and his wife Fatima Zahra, the daughter of the Prophet from his first wife, Khadija-u-Kubra.

Another dimension of the Necklace episode was no less consequential than the Aisha-Ali one: The Prophet's father-in-law and his senior-most companion, Abu Bakr Siddiq, also took a strong exception to Ali's blunt proposition. Another father-in-law and no less influential companion of the Prophet, Omar bin Khattab equaled Ali's comment to a slur on the family of Abu Bakr. "Ali should have restrained himself," Omar bin Khattab is said to have bemoaned.

Prophet on Deathbed

During the last days of his illness, the Prophet lay on a couch in Aisha's chamber in the courtyard of the mosque of Medina. As his condition deteriorated, the situation in Medina grew tense. Panic gripped the town. Outside Aisha's chamber, the crowd swelled in the yard; the people jostled each other, shouting and yelling as they tried to make their way through to glimpse the Prophet. On the hot summer day, as the temperature was soaring and the Prophet's fever and headache worsening, naturally the constant noise became intolerable for him. As the panicked visitors stampeded into the chamber, he gestured for the crowd to vacate and leave him alone with Ali and Aisha beside him. Interestingly, Ali and Aisha had not seen eye to eye ever since the Necklace episode. And here, they both were supposed to cooperate in tending to the Prophet. The two were caught in an awkward situation. Perhaps they could hardly steal their glances.

By the ninth day of illness - just before his death the next day - the Prophet's condition briefly improved, unexpectedly. Some modern scholars are inclined to think the Prophet might have slipped into what is called in medical terminology the "lucid interval" – a transitory improvement in symptoms after which the condition quickly deteriorates. That is speculation at best. However, it doesn't matter to us here. During this state of apparent improvement, the Prophet asked for a "pen and parchment" (paper or writing material). "What did he intend to do with the pen and parchment? Did he want to scribble something? Maybe he intended to dictate his will? Did he want to write down the name of the leader of the Umma?" – the crowd present there wondered. The request for pen and paper set off a chain of argument and debate among those present there, for it was a strange request on his part. The Quran repeatedly emphasized that the Prophet was unlettered.

What should they do? Should they hand over the pen and the paper? They couldn't decide. It was hard to question and suspect the good intentions of his followers present there. All of them wanted to safeguard the religion, yet at the same time, each person perhaps wanted to take care of their personal interests too. For the *Umma*, the personal and the communal interests overlapped – all were convinced that the two things were the same - as their devotion to the cause of Islam was unquestionable. Yet, as it usually happens in politics, everyone wanted the Prophet to spell out his choice of the leader after him (successor), but no one wanted to ask him outrightly; each of them wanted to know his will, but no one wanted to hear it clearly from the Prophet's mouth. As a result, amidst the heat of the arguments and debate, the Prophet was denied the pen and parchment.

As the Prophet's condition deteriorated, the followers began shouting and yelling at each other attempting to implore all to maintain silence. In doing so they made more noise, increasingly causing distress to the sick Prophet. As they shouted at each other to stop arguing, the resulting noise was making the Prophet's headache unbearable. He sorely wanted to be left alone. Finally, he ordered everyone to leave the chamber. Omar bin Khattab pacified the confused crowd by reassuring them, "The Quran is sufficient for us." The people immediately obeyed and left the room to wait outside in the mosque's courtyard. Ali bin Abi Talib and his uncle stayed back and settled the dying Prophet on the bed, and only after that they, too, left the room.

Ali's uncle sensed that the Prophet was dying. He reportedly cajoled Ali to clear the matter of leadership one last time with the Prophet, but the latter refused to ask the dying Prophet a direct question. Even Ali, it seems, was not ready for clarification of the leadership question. He was a man of patience, piety, and compassion, and believed firmly in destiny. He reportedly explained to his uncle that if the authority were to be given to them (Banu Hashim tribe), no one would take it away from them after the death of the Prophet other than God.

So far, it seemed that succession was not an important matter after all. But, politics is politics. Everywhere. In 7th century Arabia, it was no different. The Quran says that the Prophet was unlettered. It was unlikely that he would have written anything on the paper or parchment. There was no good reason to disobey the Prophet when he asked for the pen and paper. But still, the pen and the paper weren't handed over to him. What if Ali turned out to be the Prophet's choice? Would anyone want that in writing? Probably not. Some Shia traditions (see later) insist that the Prophet indeed had written Ali bin Abi Talib's name as the leader of the *Umma*. The piece of the paper was lost in the din following the death of the Prophet. The Sunnis disagree.

As soon as Ali came out of the chamber, Mohammad breathed his last. Immediately, Aisha broke into a wail. The other wives of the Prophet soon joined in. It was terrible news for all –back-breaking news for the companions and other Muslims. Omar bin Khattab, the firebrand companion of the Prophet, refused even to acknowledge that the Prophet could die. All hell broke loose. By then, Abu-Bakr Sidiq had managed to reach Medina back from his business trip. He went in and covered the face of the Prophet with a sheet and pacified the crowd. Ali went inside and set about to prepare the body of the Prophet – his uncle, father-in-law, and beloved mentor – for the grave.

Then came the real twist to the story. Barely hours after the death, a sordid tussle unfolded that never ended. Even to this day. It assumed such ignominious a proportion over the years that its wounds refuse to heal even after fifteen hundred years.

The tribal chiefs of Medina assembled to deliberate on selecting a chief or Sayyid of the Medinite Muslim community in Sa'ad bin Obada's courtyard. There were two main groups of Muslims in Medina: the *Ansars,* the indigenous inhabitants of Medina, and the *Immigrants.* Sa'ad bin Obada was the senior-most among the *Ansars.* It was he who had invited Mohammad to immigrate to Medina a decade ago and had vowed to extend his unconditional cooperation to him to save him from the Meccans' tyranny. As the news of the Prophet's demise spread, the Ansars assembled in Sa'ad's courtyard to discuss the issue of selecting a leader for Medina's Muslim community. Simultaneously, the immigrants had also called an assembly in the house of the seniormost immigrant, Abu Bakr Sidiq to discuss the same matter. Soon the word reached the immigrants that the *Ansars* were laying claim to the leadership of the Muslims.

The immigrants rushed to Sa'ad's house to cross-check the facts. They were surprised - even stunned - when they heard the old and frail Sa'ad urging the *Ansars* to choose a leader from among them. Sa'ad affirmed, "The Medinites have trusted Mohammad as he was one of their kinsmen." Mohammad's grandmother was from Medina, and "that bond had kept them connected with Mohammad; the immigrants who followed him during and after the *Hijra* (migration) were but a different matter," Sa'ad exhorted. It was true that the Medinites tolerated the immigrants, but they never accepted them as kin. No doubt, they were brothers in religion, but they were the "others," nevertheless.

The Tussle of Succession

As soon as the Prophet left the scene, suddenly, a sense of leadership vacuum began to prevail. Before his death, he hadn't fully consolidated his victories, and neither had he created a well-structured Muslim state. As his time was abruptly cut short, the fledgling Muslim community was fated to face chaos and confusion. As they say, old habits die hard, and so did the tribal and kinship politics spring up again to the forefront. In Sa'ad's courtyard where the deliberations were going on among the *Ansars,* politics was in full swing. The Meccans (immigrants) - startled as they were by the show of solidarity by the *Ansars* - quickly threw in their weight to scuttle the Ansars' plan. As the politics over the leadership issue intensified, the Meccans put their foot down. The debate turned vitriolic; heated arguments were exchanged between the Meccans and the Ansars. It was a total deadlock. No consensus could be reached. The Ansars led by Sa'ad were adamant about having their way - their right to retain power. However, unbeknownst to them, the Meccans had decided to not hand over to them that luxury on a platter. There were senior immigrant companions of the Prophet among the Meccans and the leader would naturally be one among their lot, they surmised. Furthermore, as per the *Diwan* system, the seniors figured first in the list when booty and spoils of war were distributed during the Prophet's time. So it was but natural, they reckoned, that the leadership should go to one among their lot. The Ansars differed.

The quarrel in Sa'ad's courtyard exposed dangerous fault lines in the Muslim rank and file, the beginning of a serious conflict that would show up its sinister head decades later causing irreparable damage to the reputation of the House of Islam. For now, to break the deadlock, the Ansars, at some point, proposed a compromise formula of two Caliphs, one from the Ansars and the other from the Meccans that would lead their respective communities. The immigrants rejected this power-splitting formula, vociferously emphasizing their status as the *earliest* believers and thus seniors, implying thereby the right to leadership should rest with them. The tussle intensified, notwithstanding, that all Muslims intuitively recognized in the heart of their hearts that Religious unity should be maintained at all costs, yet in that hour of crisis it seemed singularly impossible to reach a consensus. Heated arguments dragged on throughout the night into the next day. At times, the participants came to blows and fistfights. That is fine. Amiable debate and discussion couldn't have been expected in a tribal society faced with disagreement on a critical issue. Both parties remained adamant about their stated positions.

When the fatigue set in, Omar bin Khattab bluntly announced that since the Prophet came from the tribe of the Quraysh, only the members of that tribe could rightfully succeed him. The Ansars didn't give in. The war of words continued. The Sun was about to set on yet another day, but there was no agreement between the two sides. Convinced of the unity of the *Ansars*, the seasoned and witty stalwart negotiator Abu-Bakr Sidiq then deliberately broached the subject of Ansars' history. He took a calculated risk as he was now tired, irritated, and disappointed. Without mincing words, he pointedly reminded the two tribes of the Ansars (the *Khazraj* and the *Aws)* present there of their pre-*Hijra* animosity toward each other. As he recounted how the Prophet united them under the banner of Islam, he posed them a question: How would you, two tribes, decide about a consensus candidate suited to both of you, given your history? Immediately a ripple was palpable in the assembly. That was it. Abu Bakr had dropped a bombshell!

This seemingly simple poser proved no less than a masterstroke. It changed the direction of the whole debate by catching the two major Ansar tribes in a state of heightened awareness about each other. They shifted the discussion entirely to their side. Soon, the Ansars were arguing, yelling, and booing at each other - all their unity began to crumble. Sensing the opportunity, Abu Bakr Sidiq quickly and suddenly proposed the name of Omar bin Khattab as the leader of the Muslims, amidst chaos and confusion. Abu Bakr's proposal at this fragile moment led to an all-out cacophony and disorder. Amidst the uproar, Omar bin Khattab reached for the sword with one hand, and with the other, he locked hands with Abu Bakr Sidiq and loudly declared him the leader. All hell broke loose.

In that pandemonium, Omar bin Khattab, the left-handed firebrand companion of the Prophet, known for his impulsive uprightness and temperament, yelled, "Kill Sa'ad!" At this moment, Sa'ad, the grand old man, grabbed Omar bin Khattab by his beard and pulled him down. It was only when Abu Bakr intervened that Omar left Sa'ad alone. But in the din this old man was stampeded and trampled upon, leaving him half dead. With difficulty, he slugged to safety, his body half-broken. The Ansars lost the day. Abu Bakr Sidiq became the leader or *Caliph*.

While all these quarrels, fist-fights, and brawls took place for two days in Sa'ad bin Obada's courtyard, one man was conspicuously absent from the scene. This man, Ali bin Abi Talib, stayed with the dead body of the Prophet, all along waiting to initiate its burial. He received the news there that he was not to be the Caliph; instead, it was the Prophet's widow, Aisha's father, who had become the one.

More than one and a half days (two days and one night, according to some reports) had passed since Mohammad had breathed his last. In a month like June, the delay with burial was a serious issue. The custom was to bury the dead as soon as possible, preferably within hours. But the problem in the Prophet's case was that even after 24 hours, there was no agreement on who would be his successor. By the fall of the second night, as Abu Bakr Sidiq had scarcely managed to become the leader, he banked on the opportunity to lead funeral prayers. Prophet Mohammad's funeral was a significant event and the most opportune moment for Abu Bakr Sidiq, to declare his authority as the Caliph and ask for the allegiance of all the Medinites and Meccans. That would put the stamp of legitimacy on his leadership of the *Umma*. Since it was getting late, the Prophet's burial was postponed till dawn.

That was not to happen. Ali and his relatives wouldn't wait any further. They dug a grave there, in the chamber of Aisha, during the same night, as two days had already passed since the Prophet's dead body was lying there. They buried it before dawn. None of the wives present, no immigrant, and none of the Ansars around, Ali managed to put the body of his beloved uncle, the Prophet, in the lap of the Earth without a formal funeral. In perfect silence. Haykal notes in *The Life of Mohammad*, "Aisha said, 'We did not learn of the burial of the Prophet of God until midnight or later,' and so did Fatima report [the same]."

All the biographers of the Prophet, including Safi-ur-Rhman, and Haykal, concur that his body was washed the same evening as Abu Bakr was announced the Imam (Caliph) and shrouded in three white Yemeni cotton blankets. The funeral prayer was neither led by an Imam nor was there any procession to carry the body of the Prophet to any burial site. In *The Life of Mohammad*, Haykal points out, "Throughout the Muslims' disputing of the question of succession at the courtyard of Banu Sa'idah[sic] and in the mosque, the Prophet's remains were lying on his bed surrounded by his next of kin." He adds, "After the election of Abu Bakr, there was a disagreement as to where the Prophet was to be buried." Safi-ur-Rahman agrees with Haykal. In his book *The Sealed Nectar,* he concurs, "A sort of disagreement arose concerning the burial place. Abu Bakr said 'a prophet is buried where he dies.'" Clearly, there was no funeral procession nor a collective funeral prayer (Jinaza) for the Prophet. Instead, as the biographers say, people entered the room where the Prophet's body lay and offered prayers one by one. Which raises the question: when Abu Bakr Sidiq was already the chosen Imam at that time, why didn't he lead the funeral prayer? It turned out that Abu Bakr had overlooked - as the later events showed - one last yet formidable obstacle to authority besides the Ansars. He had forgotten about Ali bin Abi Talib. Ali and his kin denied Abu Bakr the luxury of leading the funeral prayers and burial of the Prophet.

The first Caliph and War of Apostasy

Aisha's chamber now housed the grave of the Prophet. Years before, the founder of Islam had evaded death by slipping to safety under the cover of night. Ali stood by his side then. Now, he went into the lap of the grave, this time again, under cover of the night. Once again, Ali stood by his side. Strange coincidence! On both occasions, Mohammad was almost alone, except that a decade back he was a fugitive. But now, he was an undisputed leader with devoted followers in thousands. As fate would have it, all were busy at the time of his death. Nobody was free to arrange a formal funeral for this remarkable man - in the words of Michael Hart, the most influential man in history. He deserved a grand see-off, no doubt. It is a pity that history denied him precisely that what he would never deny any departing soul. He would always organize and lead others' funeral prayers himself. But then, politics is unpredictable by nature. It mocks its own rules. And religion - in itself, an expression of politics and power - dons strange facades under its cloak.

Abu Bakr Sidiq became the Imam (leader) and the first Caliph. He adopted the title of "Viceroy of the Prophet" (Khalif-at-AlRasul). Both the Ansars and immigrants accepted the verdict in the mosque before the Prophet was buried by his cousin and son-in-law, Ali. He and his clan, Banu Hashim, seemed to resent the whole affair. They had been conspicuously absent during the selection dispute, as it were, in the courtyard of Sa'ad. Consequently, Ali and his family refused to pay allegiance to the new Caliph. He reportedly also discussed the matter with the Ansars. Even though the Ansars supported Ali, at the same time, they did not want to prolong the conflict either. So Ali did not agitate openly but returned to his wife Fatima's house, adamantly refusing to pay allegiance to Abu Bakr. Omar bin Khattab and his men besieged the house, but Ali won't come out to face him. As Omar, reportedly barged in, the door hit Fatima, felling her down. She was pregnant at the time. She suffered an abortion following the trauma.

Failing to secure allegiance from Ali, even after Omar bin Khattab's belligerent intervention, the Caliph ordered ostracism or boycott against him. In a closely-knit society, a boycott is a dangerous weapon. It can break the opponent's determination easily. Years ago Ali had experienced the power of boycott firsthand meted out to them by the Meccan Quraysh. But that was then. Now he faced a boycott from his brothers-in-religion in Medina. Even, in the mosque, Ali would pray alone. It would have been quite distressing and depressing for this remarkably pious nephew, son-in-law, and companion of the Prophet whom the latter unquestionably loved and respected.

At this point the stalemate would have ended should Ali reconcile. But no. So, Abu Bakr Siddiq passed the orders to disinherit Ali's wife, Fatima, of her estate– the garden of Fadak and the Oasis of Khaybar – bequeathed to her by her doting father, the Prophet. Abu Bakr justified his order by stating that the property of the Prophet belongs to all, not to Fatima alone - an opinion he clarified by sending the message "the whole community of the *Umma* (Muslim fraternity) is the family of the Prophet," to Fatima in response to the complaint she had lodged with him. Yet it would be wrong to presume that Abu Bakr was alone in subscribing to such a viewpoint. The overall mood of the public during those days was that *Ahl-al-Bayt* or the House of Mohammad did not mean only the kith and kin of the Prophet. The Caliph, sensing the public's mood, lost no time to push the orders to disinherit Fatima. He awarded a good portion of the property to the widows of the Prophet. Aisha, too, got a good share – the garden of Fadak. For Fatima, it came as a shock. She couldn't openly oppose the decision of the Caliph, although she reportedly complained to him about this decision. The Caliph refused to budge. From that day on till her death, it is said, that the heartbroken Fatima never again spoke a word with Abu Bakr Sidiq.

Barely three months had passed since the Prophet was gone; Fatima, now heartbroken, sick, frail, and anemic after the abortion, died. Her husband, Ali bin Abi Talib, clandestinely managed her burial. Reportedly, Fatima had confided her will in Ali months before her death that Abu Bakr Sidiq should not lead her funeral prayer. After her death, Ali continued to dispute the legitimacy of Abu Bakr as Caliph. Ali's defiance was becoming a matter of grave concern for the Muslim community, especially at a time when the fledgling Muslim community was going through a fragile period of transition. Amidst other challenges and conflicts, like those of the secessionist tribes from Northern and Central Arabia threatening to stop paying tribute and tax to Medina, disunity and discord within the rank and file of leadership would prove inimical to the future of the *Umma*. Solidarity and unity were the need of the hour.

Ali came under pressure. This was not the time to settle the scores. The expediency demanded presenting a unified Muslim front. Ali's defection, sort of, could prove inimical. After deep contemplation and counsel, Ali finally came to terms with the situation and agreed to extend his hand of allegiance to Abu Bakr Sidiq in the interest of Islam and the *Umma*. He was undoubtedly a devout Muslim and didn't want to be seen as a troublemaker when many tribes in Northern and Central Arabia threatened to break away and stop paying their tribute to Medina on the pretext that after the Prophet's death, they were no longer obliged to remain as vassal territories of Medina.

As Central Arabian tribal units proclaimed their autonomy, some other prophets like Masalma bin Habib and his wife in eastern Arabia, Aswad bin Ansi in Yemen, and Tulayhah bin Khalid in north-central Arabia, were encouraged to demand allegiance from the Muslims.

Abu Bakr Sidiq was infuriated. He could ill afford to ignore these prophets and let them have their way to subvert what had been achieved by the Muslims after a decade of sacrifices. For Ali bin Abi Talib, this was a test, a higher call on his loyalty. He chose to take a higher ground for religion and *Umma*. As Ali buried the grudges, Abu Bakr, the Caliph, eagerly welcomed his support. He now declared an all-out war on the rebel tribes and prophets. The Caliph ordained that tribute belonged to Islam and not to the Quraysh, and hence the refusal to pay the tribute by the renegade tribes was an act of apostasy. Such tribes were to be considered enemies of Islam and deserved to be killed. Abu Bakr supported his decision to order the killing of apostates with the Prophet's saying: anyone who left the religion (apostate) should be killed. The Quran, however, broaches the subject of apostasy in the chapter titled "*Mohammad*" (47: 25-27), and enumerates punishments for apostates. Killing is not one of them.

All the same, the Caliph deputed Khalid bin Walid with explicit instructions to eradicate the apostates. Al Tabari reports that the Caliph instructed him to raid and "kill or burn them in case they [Khalid and his army] didn't hear a people make *Adhan* (call to prayer)." It was a difficult assignment for Khalid bin Walid, but he succeeded in quelling the rebellion. He killed apostates sparing only those who re-professed faith in Islam. Except for that one tribal chief, Malik bin Nuwayrah, was beheaded after he reportedly re-professed faith in Islam, and Khalid took his wife for himself. When Omar bin Khattab, now second in command after the Caliph, learned about the incident, he harshly chastised Khalid - a hero now - on his return from the expedition for this action of his. But Abu Bakr intervened, "O Omar, I will not sheathe a sword that God has drawn against the unbelievers," and pardoned Khalid for killing Malik and taking his wife.

In the meantime, Masalma bin Habib (Musaylima), the prophet, began his advance on Medina. Again, Khalid was sent to take on him. He defeated him, and with that, this rebellion finally collapsed by March 633 CE. The Caliph ordered to put to death all the adult men of the tribe of Banu Hanifah on charges of supporting Musaylima as a prophet. After waging the Wars of Apostasy (*Ridda* wars) ruthlessly for a year, the Caliph managed to crush almost all the resistance.

The Second Caliph (Amir-al-Mu'mineen)

By August 634 CE, after completing two years as Caliph, Abu Bakr's health began to fail him. Now it was time for the *Umma* to elect his successor, if one goes by the argument made by the Sunni school that Abu Bakr Sidiq had become the Caliph through a process of debate and discussion by a "body of elder men" called "*Shura*." That didn't happen. Instead, Abu Bakr directly appointed Omar bin Khattab as his successor shutting the door to any discussion, debate, or election. It strikes as strange that the Caliph found good reasons to distrust the process of "*Shura*." Why didn't he want to leave the selection of his successor to a *Shura*? It seems the answer is simple. Despite the Sunni school's insistence, what transpired in the courtyard of Sa'ad immediately after the Prophet's death was anything but remotely resembling a convention of elders or *Shura* discussion. For Abu Bakr, Omar bin Khattab was the natural choice given the rapport the two enjoyed over the years. Possibly, the idea of a *Shura* might simply not have crossed the former's mind. Who knows? It is hard to speculate the intention behind Abu Bakr's decision. Be that as it were, clearly it left many, particularly Ali's supporters, the *Shiat-e-Ali*, disgruntled. They reckoned the Meccan elite again outmaneuvered Ali bin Abi Talib, yet Ali prevailed upon them to maintain peace. A funeral was organized for Abu Bakr, and he was buried alongside the Prophet's grave.

The left-handed, fiery companion of the Prophet, Omar bin Khattab, known for his short temper, outspokenness, and disciplinarian attitude, became the Caliph in 634 CE. He dropped the title of "Viceroy of the Prophet" (*Khalif-at-AlRasul*) that Abu Bakr had adopted and instead assumed the title of the "Commander of the Faithful" or *Amir-al-Mumineen*. Ali prudently reconciled with the changing scenario. As a gesture of goodwill and conciliation, he married Abu Bakr's widow, Asma, reportedly to prove that "he meant what he said," believing sincerely to strive for the *unity* of the *Umma* at any cost. Going a step further, he gave his daughter (also the granddaughter of the Prophet) to Caliph Omar bin Khattab in marriage. This gesture of Ali bin Abi Talib was unprecedented for he was 13 years younger than Omar bin Khattab, and yet he became his father-in-law – a travesty of fate, as it were.

On the face of it, an atmosphere of conciliation seemed to prevail. But then, power and politics are tricky things. Politics doesn't care much about the alliances unless expediency demands so. Did the matrimonial alliance with the *Amir-al-Mumineen* lend any political mileage to Ali bin Abi Talib in the coming years? No. It didn't matter except that the *Amir* settled a part of the Prophet's estates on Ali – the ones that Fatima had been denied in her lifetime by Abu Bakr. Now, Omar bin Khattab had a double relationship with the late Prophet. He had been the father-in-law of the Prophet, and now, after marrying Fatima's daughter (the granddaughter of the Prophet), he became the son-in-law of Ali and grandson-in-law of the Prophet. This relationship made both Omar bin Khattab and Ali's positions secure. Ali came closer to Amir. He was appointed an advisor to the Caliph. In the caliph's absence, Ali would be in charge of the affairs of the state. The signs were clear that Omar bin Khattab might nominate Ali as his successor. Only signs.

Under Abu Bakr's Caliphate, the *Ridda* wars (Apostasy wars) had been quite successful. Handsome booty and spoils of war and enslaved captives were poured into Medina in great numbers. The living standard of the Muslims was boosted. However, sans the Ridda wars, sans the booty and spoils, and comparatively lower quantity of tribute from the subdued tribes and kingdoms of Arabia, Medina's income base was negatively affected. That was bound to happen for as per the injunctions of the Prophet and the Quran when the rebelling settlements accept the overlordship of the Muslims and convert to Islam, they automatically qualify for exemption from paying the tribute. Such a convention, good, though, for the spread of Islam in Arabia, created a severe hurdle in sustaining the economy of the Muslim Medina. In the Prophet's time, Medina had become an essentially "mosque economy" with the *Diwan* system in place for distributing booty, spoils of war, and slaves among the Muslims. Accordingly, the *Amir*, Omar bin Khattab, was compelled to adopt a forward-looking expansionist policy that eventually shaped Medina like ancient Ur III of Mesopotamia – a centralized, regimented, and militarized - "command and control" economy. Omar took the *Ridda* war to the next logical level. His was a perfectly expedient approach in a world order constrained by meager economic resources. Only a coordinated and systematized territorial expansion was the best and the most profitable enterprise to ensure a relatively steadier flow of tax, tribute, and booty and a constant supply of enslaved women, children, and young men for a rapidly expanding community.

Ever since the appearance of humankind, power, politics, and religion have gone side by side, complementing each other. The time when *Amir-al-Mumineen* lived was no different. Religion without power is a blind tunnel, good to roam in but leading nowhere. In an age of urbanization, Medina like any other upcoming city required resources and power to develop and feed its citizens. The responsibility of feeding the populace lay on the shoulders of the leader, in this case, Amir. The Amir understood as well as his predecessor and the Prophet that power doesn't come on a platter. It has to be sought. And, without power, the emerging Muslim Arab polity was going to evaporate as the Hanifiyah movement did before it. The most important way to support a city was by transporting enough food from the surrounding area to feed a large urban population that was stuck in place unable to switch back to a nomadic lifestyle. So in the past, urbanism relied on growing food. But that wasn't enough. Food must be stored to preserve it for long periods and to provide - beyond immediate needs - safety against pests, droughts, and famines. Martin Puchner, agreeing with James Scott's research (mentioned a few pages earlier in this book), points out in his book *Culture*, "Those who controlled the storage of grain gained immense power, which created hierarchical social structures, making it possible for individuals or groups of people to own wealth that was limited only by the size of storage and the ability to control it by force." We have seen that happen in Egypt and Mesopotamia culminating in the rise of the centralized palace and temple economy states respectively. Medina was an upcoming state with a "mosque" economy during the Prophet's and Abu Bakr's time, which survived on Ghazu and tribute. There was no formal expansionist policy in place yet. Medina couldn't grow enough food on its own and it could also not import or buy food grains from other states for the citizens. There were no diplomatic ties or trade relations in place with Persia and Byzantium. Omar bin Khattab understood, as the later events showed, that religion was good, but spirituality alone wasn't enough to feed the population. In the 7th CE world order, as before, the stark reality was that either you gobble up as much as you could or else get gobbled up by mightier fish. Successful expansionism was the option for Medina to survive as an urban center of power for Islam.

Persia and Byzantium were both economically and militarily overstretched and enfeebled by the wars and plague epidemic. History had presented a window of opportunity that no Arab leader could afford to miss. As luck had it the leader was Omar bin Khattab. He ordered his men to swiftly advance into the heart of these once giants of empires. It was hard for these empires - particularly Persia, as it had broken into self-governing satrapies and kingdoms - to put up significant resistance against the Arabs, for they were already collapsing under their weight. In 637 CE, when Amir's men advanced on them, the Persians quickly capitulated. As the domino effect spread, the heart of the Christian Byzantium – the prized city of Jerusalem – fell in the hands of Arabs practically without a fight. Omar bin Khattab triumphantly entered the "City of Faiths" and offered his prayer, both as a show of power and his gratitude to the God of Islam, Allah. This triumph was uniquely significant for the political future of the house of Islam. It vindicated the Muslims' faith that Allah had bestowed his grace and blessings upon them. Remember, two decades ago the Persians had tried hard to capture the "City of Faiths," but *Ahura Mazda*, the Zoroastrian God, had failed them - at least the Christians thought so. The latter had jubilantly celebrated, then, the victory of their God, Jesus, who, in their opinion, had protected their sacred city from the infidels. Now, to the Christians' utter dismay, the tables turned. Allah was the Almighty, and his Islam was invincible. The Christian god was no match for Allah.

The successful expedition brought enormous wealth and booty into Muslims' possession. A handful of warriors from north Arabia that they were, they wouldn't have imagined in their wildest dreams that they would become the masters of vast stretches of Byzantine and Persian territories. Yet, here they were – the Masters of land and grain and livestock and people. They were now in control of practically the whole of the famed Fertile Crescent. They had put their hands on an unimaginable treasure trove. Suddenly, they found a flood of tribute and protection money, *Jizya*, dangling at their feet. As a rule, big wealth leads to big problems, especially for parvenus. As the Arab Muslims' wealth suddenly multiplied, their heads began to swell. The Prophet, though, had established the system of *Diwan* for equal distribution of booty and spoils, but it proved inefficient to handle the enormous amounts of tribute, slaves, and captives that poured in from all sides.

Omar bin Khattab was a genius administrator and disciplinarian, his impulsiveness and short temperament, notwithstanding. He quickly introduced important administrative reforms. Borrowing from the Byzantine and Persian systems, he introduced four important organizational pillars of his caliphate: the Treasury, the State Records, the Revenue Ministry, and an Army of paid and full-time soldiers. Despite his advisor Ali bin Abi Talib's protests that the Quran and the religion did not determine these practices, Amir went ahead with implementing his plan. He laid much emphasis on seniority, lineage, and tribal affiliation instead of merit in distributing spoils and booty, basing his premise on simple logic: those Muslims who initially fought against Mohammad and converted after the victory of Mecca couldn't be equal in status to those who fought alongside the Prophet right from the initial days of Islam. That was that.

The *Amir-al-Mumineen* had no particularly bad intentions. He simply wanted to reward the earliest converts generously in recognition of the sacrifices they rendered for Islam during its most fragile days. The fattest and largest stipends, thus, were allotted to the earliest converts. The fact that the Amir never increased his (personal) salary despite repeated suggestions from his companions to do so was a testimony to the fact that took higher ground, above personal interests, for the welfare of the Muslim state. Yet his intentions, howsoever noble, couldn't stop politics from happening the way it happens. In matters of politics and statecraft, the temporal aspects take precedence over the spiritual ones. It is hard to guess whether he had even the faintest clue about the unwanted implications of his well-intended decision. It was precisely his system of wealth distribution that institutionalized discrimination and corruption in the Muslim state, later on.

Under Amir's *Diwan* system, the Arabs placed themselves superior in rank to non-Arabs, the Meccan got preference over the Medinites, and the free men became supernal to enslaved. Similarly, among the Medinites, the tribe of *Aws* surpassed the *Khazraj*. The non-Arab Muslims were designated as clients or *Mawali*. The Mawali status was perceived by many non-Arabs, especially the Persians, as an affront and slur meted out to them by the Arabs. Many influential converts from non-Arab lands crazily adopted surnames like *Qureshi, Hashmi, Abbasi, Ansari,* etc. to hide their Mawali epithet. Others prefixed their names with epithets like *Syed* ostensibly to claim direct lineage from the Prophet and his tribe, although *Syed* never happened to be the Prophet's surname. "Syed," meaning "Chief of a tribe" in pre-Islamic Arabia, connoted nothing but a title with no relation to lineage or surname. Contrary to what the *Amir-al-Mumineen* had intended, a competitive environment of discrimination on racial and tribal grounds was wheeled into motion in the cumulative Islamic cultural landscape. The crazy pursuit of non-existent surnames was just one of the many practical consequences of Amir's discriminative *Diwan* system.

During Omar's caliphate, the Arabs, no doubt, penetrated the heart of Asia. However, they deliberately avoided imposing a systematic policy of conversion on the conquered populations, not because the Arabs were naive or unenthusiastic about the propagation of Islam but rather because the policy of conversion was economically unprofitable for the state of Islam - the obligatory conversion of non-Arabs would inimically cut the revenue of the Caliphate from tribute, spoils, booty, slaves (men and women) and captives. No doubt, the spread of Islam was a top priority for all the Caliphs and their successors, but as per the Quran, conversion to Islam would render the conquered non-Arabs nontaxable with *Jaziya*, which could potentially stifle the revenue base of the empire that was still in making.

The Amir was astute enough to let Islam be perceived as an "Arab creed" and the conquered people as Mawali or clients. The arithmetic was simple: the fewer the number of stakeholders, the larger each individual's share of wealth under *Diwan,* i.e., the better fed would be the army and the administrative bureaucracy, and as a consequence the more efficient the "command and control" economy under the Caliph. Yet, the last thing that the Persians could reconcile with was this label of Mawali. They perceived it as a demeaning insult to their history, culture, and self-esteem. As a result, during Omar bin Khattab's reign, they desisted from converting to Islam. Only after his death, the Persians embraced Islam in large numbers, that too when the circumstances were somewhat different.

Despite all the above the critics of the *Amir* acknowledge that he always displayed uprightness even in constrained situations and demonstrated brilliant decision-making prowess as a leader and statesman. He seldom shied away from implementing drastic measures when the interests of the evolving empire were jeopardized. As an honest, upright, and stern administrator, the *Amir* swiftly disposed of matters brought to his notice and seldom hesitated to take risks whenever quick deliverance of justice was needed. He introduced some specific laws and amendments to the existing conventions and diligently put in place an organized justice system. For instance, he introduced "death by stoning" as punishment for adultery, although the Quran didn't prescribe this form of punishment; and abolished the custom of temporary marriage called *Muta'a* despite the protest from some sections of the population.

Omar bin Khattab was undoubtedly the most successful of the four Caliphs when judged in terms of administration, delivery of justice, and military campaigns. Yet he couldn't successfully eliminate the mutual distrust, suspicion, and attritive conflict between the various clans, tribes, and factions within the community of Muslims (*Umma*). It may not be out of place to point out that his *Diwan* system (wealth distribution system) helped deepen further the discord within the *Umma* rather than alleviate it. The resulting unhealthy competition turned out to be far more malignant in the long run than the Justinian plague that crippled the Byzantine Empire during its heyday. Which needs a bit more elaboration.

The Amir-al-Mumineen had approved this system of *Diwan* - in essence following a pattern of hierarchy - to distribute tributes, booty, and spoils of war, including enslaved men, children, and women. Over time this system led to uneven distribution of power and privilege resulting in the concentration of political and economic power in fewer and fewer hands. Other serious shortcomings of this system came to the fore when, for instance, piety, merit, and faith, though subjective and hard to ascertain, got to be ignored. Furthermore, by presenting Islam as an Arab creed, a clear ethnic supremacy was projected that couldn't later on be prevented from becoming institutionalized. During the first few years of his reign, the Amir failed to see it through - a slip he later regretted according to the Abbasid era historian Al Yaqubi. In *Tarikh ibn Wadih,* Yaqubi reports that toward the 10th year of his reign, the *Amir* recognized the damage done by his hierarchy system of finance and seriously thought of abolishing the institution of *Diwan*. He sorely regretted, Yaqubi says, his decision to put in place the hierarchical wealth distribution that bred a sort of casteism and racism in an already hypersensitive society. Now as the Amir was seriously thinking of somersaulting, time was no more on his side. He was assassinated.

Khalif-at-Allah (Viceroy of God)

As he was scrambled up on the bed, soon to bleed to death, the *Amir-al-Mumineen* decided to name his successor. Ali bin Abi Talib was confident about his nomination. And, the Amir did indeed name Ali but with a rider attached: he named five more people in addition to Ali and left them the task of choosing the leader. As mentioned a couple of pages earlier, the first Caliph (Abu Bakr Sidiq) had set a precedent for successive caliphs to nominate their successors and it was expected that the Amir would follow Abu Bakr's convention. But no. Instead the Amir set the precedent aside and nominated six people to convene a *Shura* (council of elders). Ali's supporters were left jaw-dropping. Ali bin Abi Talib's chances of becoming the Caliph were starkly diminished according to his supporters. Indeed, after three days of discussions, Othman bin Afan, a companion, and another son-in-law of the Prophet, was selected over Ali.

The proceedings of the Council were far from smooth. Ali's supporters inferred that the framing of the Council itself was a trap to co-opt Ali into accepting Othman bin Afan (an Ummayad candidate) as the leader. They tried to prevail upon Ali to outrightly abstain from joining the council nominated by the dying Amir. Ali bin Abi Talib didn't listen. He went ahead and joined the debate and heated arguments ensued. The Umayyads (the supporters of Othman) disapproving of the conduct of Ali's supporters (the Hashemites) also took to the streets, resulting in noisy scenes followed by cudgels and minor skirmishes between the two. The mood on the streets naturally reflected the proceedings of the council. The council was vertically split and the two sides adamantly stuck to their stated positions, refusing to budge.

As the arguings the council were about to turn volatile, one member, Abdal Rahman bin Afan, vested with the authority to mediate broke the stalemate when he posed his final question: Who will follow the example of Abu Bakr and Omar bin Khattab in addition to the Quran and the Prophet? Othman bin Afan immediately affirmed he would unflinchingly abide by that convention. Ali disagreed, arguing that there was no need to follow Abu Bakr and Omar bin Khattab's convention when there was the Quran. Abdal Rahman bin Afan got the answer. He approved Othman bin Afan for the post of Caliph.

Ali lost the race. His supporters complained that Ali chose not to be as assertive and insisting as he could be. Ali, after all, was Ali, the noble and pious cousin, companion, and son-in-law of the Prophet. It didn't behoove him to press for leadership any further after Abdal Rahman had given the verdict in favor of Othman bin Afan. He refused to come under the pressure of his protesting supporters. Othman bin Afan a ripe old man to become the Caliph was much older than Ali. The latter willingly pledged allegiance to the elected leader. Ali's gesture, however, didn't prevent two parties – *Shiat-e-*Othman (the party of Othman) and *Shiat-e-*Ali (the party of Ali) – from emerging officially in Medina, the city of the Prophet. The lid on the volcano simmering since the day of the quarrel in Sa'ad's courtyard was finally blown off. Soon the lava would put on fire the House of Islam that was diligently built by the Prophet over 23 years. No external forces were involved here. No conspiracy theories explain the unfolding of the subsequent events. The rot came from within the rank and file of the *Umma.*

Othman bin Afan became the Caliph in 645 CE. He adopted the title *Khalif-at-Allah* (Viceroy of Allah) rather than Khalif-at-al-Rasul (the caliph of the Prophet). Abu Bakr was the only companion who assumed the title of the "Caliph of Prophet." Othman bin Afan, the *Khalif-at-Allah,* continued the expansionist policy of his predecessor. The Arabs reached the Aegean, the North African coast, and the frontiers of India. Tremendous amounts of tribute, spoils, and captive men and women poured in from these new territories. Success after success adorned the Arabs. The annexed territories, unlike previously, were now administered by Governors deputed by the Caliph. Medina became the center of power of Islam both military and economically.

During Othman bin Afan's reign, the compilation of the Quran was also completed, and the authorized text, pronunciation, phonetics, and sequence of the sections and paragraphs of the Holy Book were duly commissioned. Henceforth, the Quran will always be written and recited in the Quraysh or Meccan dialect. The above achievements, no doubt, were a feather in the cap of the Caliph, but unfortunately, his overall administrative inefficiency overshadowed his achievements, unlike his predecessor.

The Umayyads, once completely subdued by the Prophet himself after the victory of Mecca a decade ago, grabbed the opportunity to reassert themselves. They had perhaps been waiting for the right moment. With one of their kin, Othman bin Afan, in power now, they used their connections to project themselves as the "men of entitlement" giving the notion that the Caliph, a pious and honest person, was unable to rein them in effectively. The critics saw it as a well-planned and well-orchestrated "Umayyad conspiracy" and complained about Othman bin Afan for feigning ignorance about the indiscipline taking place under his watch. The critics accused the Caliph of yielding to the pressure of kinship politics with an utter disregard for merit, righteousness, and the principles of religion in the dispensation of administration and justice. Indeed, the top and lucrative posts like the governor's office went to the Umayyad family.

Nobody doubted the Caliph's devotion to Islam, but at the same time, everybody suspected him to be mindful of the family ties too. When he insisted on being called the deputy of God, *Khalif-at-Allah*, the Medinites, and the Hashemites strongly and openly resented him.

Soon, the complaints about the misconduct and misbehavior of his Governors began to pour in, making the atmosphere politically charged. The reports suggested that the Governor of Kufa, and half-brother of the Caliph, Walid had presented himself in the mosque in a drunken state. When the matter was brought to the notice of the Caliph, he mulled over it for sometimes perhaps asking for more investigation to satisfy himself. The people got impatient. As the bar was lowered, the companions of the Prophet protested with the Caliph. He didn't dismiss Walid, though.

The eerie calm that prevailed in Medina was finally broken when the five men (*Shura*) who had selected the Caliph came out in the open to criticize him. They were joined by other surviving companions of the Prophet like Abu Dhar Gaffari and Amar bin Yasir. The Caliph was left with no option but to take cognizance of the matter. Paradoxically, though, he didn't recall and punish the Governor of Kufa. Instead, he took action against the protesters. Abu Dhar Gaffari was exiled to Syria. The Caliph's action encouraged the Umayyads, who took the law into their hands and beat Amar bin Yasir to death for his protest against the *viceroy of God*. The balance was tipped against the Caliph.

Ali bin Abi Talib now joined in the protest. Aisha, the Prophet's widow, also was incensed. She won't wait. She came out openly and heavily against the Caliph. For the first and probably the last time in her life, Aisha found herself on the same side as Ali, criticizing the Caliph for his reluctance to punish his half-brother Walid, the Governor of Kufa. But Othman bin Afan underestimated the prowess and popularity of Aisha. Perhaps. At the morning prayer time one Friday, she stood up brandishing a sandal of the Prophet and yelled at the Caliph in that shrieking voice of hers. Suddenly, the whole mosque erupted in her support and condemnation of the Caliph. Under pressure, Othman bin Afan had to recall Walid from Kufa, but he was still reluctant to pass the orders to publicly flog him. That infuriated Aisha. Now, she won't listen. She launched an all-out blistering attack.

Aisha called on all the Muslims from all the provinces to defend Islam against injustice and corruption and wrote letters to all prominent persons in the name of the "Mothers of the faithful" (the epithet given to the wives of the Prophet). The response to her summons was surprising and brisk. The warriors arrived in large numbers from Kufa, Basra, and Egypt to show solidarity with Aisha. The situation in Medina became tense. The attack on the palace of the Caliph was all too imminent.

Sensing the danger, Ali bin Abi Talib jumped in as a mediator to avert the potential mayhem. Unfortunately, the Caliph's cousin and advisor, Marwan undercut Ali's efforts at negotiations - the same Marwan, later an Ummayad Caliph, whose father Al-Hakam was exiled by the Prophet; and neither Abu Bakr nor Omar bin Khattab had revoked his ban on entry into Medina. Othman bin Afan repealed Al-Hakam's prohibition and allowed him to return to Medina, and also inducted his son, Marwan to head his Public Relations team.

Ali bin Abi Talib tried hard to persuade the Caliph to punish Walid, but the latter seemed not convinced. Tension in Medina soared with each passing day, reaching its peak on Friday, the day of congregational prayer in Islam when it was time for the Caliph to ascend the pulpit to lead the prayers. In a frenzy, the crowd hurled stones and pebbles at him. One stone hit the aging Caliph, and he fell. He was immediately removed from the scene and escorted to his palace. The episode in the mosque of the Prophet left him shaken, but he steadfastly refused to use force against the rebels as he was recovering from the trauma. Finally, on Ali's insistence, he agreed to dismiss both the Governors of Kufa and Egypt (also the caliph's brother-in-law) against whom also there were complaints of misconduct. The Governor of Egypt was to be replaced by Mohammad bin Abu Bakr, Aisha's brother, as the new Governor. The crisis abated. But it was too early yet to celebrate peace in Medina engulfed by chaos for two full weeks.

The rebels having achieved their goal set out on their return journey. On their way, they intercepted a person carrying a message allegedly from the office of the Caliph to the erstwhile deposed Egyptian Governor. The contents of the letter were unbelievable. It asked the erstwhile Egyptian Governor to behead the returning rebels as soon as they reached Egypt. For the rebels, the letter was a breach of trust on the part of the Caliph's office. Their heads now hot and blood on the boil, they returned to settle the matter with the sword. They won't listen to anybody now. As they stormed Medina, they gave the ultimatum to the Caliph to immediately abdicate the office and besieged the Caliph's palace. Period. As Othman bin Afan refused to abdicate, denying any knowledge of the letter, the rebels under the leadership of Abu Bakr's son barged into his heavily guarded palace.

Surprisingly at that very crucial time, Aisha decided to go ahead with her plans to leave for Mecca. Marwan, the Chief public relations officer of the Caliph, rushed to stop her from leaving at that critical juncture. He wanted her intervention to defuse the situation. She refused. She went ahead with her plan. Marwan tried to impress upon her that she was the one who ignited the fire of revolt in the first place, and she couldn't quietly leave Medina. He pleaded with her that her intervention was the only thing that could save the Caliph, briefing her about the danger lurking all around. She won't listen to his pleadings.

Meanwhile, the rebels broke the lines of defense and entered the room where the Viceroy of God (*Khalif-at-Allah)* was seated reciting the Quran, seemingly undeterred by all that was happening outside his palace. In a fit of anger, one of the rebels slashed a dagger across the old Caliph's head. Others fell on in, their knives striking the Caliph again and again. Blood spilled and splashed onto the floor and spluttered the walls. Naila, the Syrian wife of the Caliph, tried to fling over her husband's body. A knife slashed down and cut off her right hand. She couldn't save her husband. The Caliph was dead. A pool of blood surrounded him.

The Triangular Front

As the news of the Caliph's assassination spread, Medina was engulfed by chaos and turmoil. A dark hour descended on the house of Islam. The *Khalif-at-Allah* (the Viceroy of God), the senior-most companion of the Prophet, was murdered not by infidels but by his co-believers in Allah, the Prophet, and the Quran. How would Medina respond to this heinous crime committed by the faithful? How would the believers reconcile with this dark hour in the history of Islam? Such and other difficult questions had no immediate answers. The murder of the Caliph was a bolt from the blue particularly for the Umayyah tribe (to which the Caliph belonged). The Caliph's body was buried, but his blood-stained shirt was exported to Syria. It would be displayed by Muawiyah, the Governor, to the Muslim crowds in Syria during the Friday sermons. His message was vivid and clear: "The blood of a devout Muslim was shed in Medina by a bunch of misguided and crazy rebels. The Ummayads will exact the revenge." The beginning of the end of Muslim unity was already visible. A protracted bloody conflict followed. The sacred history of Islam would now be written with the blood of Muslims. The ugly power play used religion as a mere garb under which the horrendous drama was played out.

Which brings us to Ali bin Abi Talib. At last, in 656 CE, the moment for which he and his supporters had waited for twenty-four years finally arrived. Little did Ali know that all his wait and patience for years would culminate in his presiding over and getting consumed by a full-fledged civil war. Two and a half decades ago when he buried the Prophet, it was in June. Now as he became the leader of the Prophet's followers, again the month was June. A strange coincidence. The Medinites quietly pledged their allegiance to him in the mosque compound. The oath ceremony of the new Caliph gave the impression that the masses supported him. Yet that was merely a perception. Beneath the surface, the trouble and turbulence were insidiously gaining woeful momentum. The Umayyads, naturally, were seething with anger and visibly upset to see Ali as the new Caliph. The Quraysh joined them, expressing their reluctance to support Ali.

The Quraysh themselves eyed the post of the Caliph. They supported Talha and Zubair. In addition, the Umayyads and some other Meccans also supported the two men. But that wasn't all there was to it. The converts from Kufa, Basra, and Egypt also had become politically aspirational by now and wanted to have a say in the king-making process. They declared their support for Ali. With their support, the number game turned in his favor. Talha and Zubair came under duress to pledge their allegiance to Ali to avoid an all-out clash at a critical moment in history. Ali's supporters had made clear that it was an "All or None" game – either Ali or a Civil war.

Aisha was never comfortable with Ali, and the last thing she could agree on was Ali's selection as the Caliph. She was still a tremendously influential figure in Meccan politics. At the time of Ali's appointment, Aisha still in

Mecca immediately raised a war cry, and demanded immediate punishment for Othman bin Afan's killers. Her fiery speeches left her audiences spellbound. The trouble erupted, and the firebrand Aisha was seen heading the rebellion. Talha and Zubair defected to her side, kick-starting a terrible campaign against the Caliph, Ali ibn Abi Talib.

Ali, the noble, pious, and devoted believer, and companion of the Prophet didn't seem to be much concerned about the storm brewing right underneath his nose. A firm believer in Allah, he was unmoved and dismissive of the politics happening in Mecca. His firm belief that if Allah has willed that Caliphate shall go to him, no one can snatch it from him, made him a touch complacent. Rather than setting the tone of politics of the day in his favor and building alliances, he preoccupied himself with undoing what he saw as the damage done to the cause of Islam during his predecessors' reigns. Accordingly, as he set his agenda for running the administration, he outlined a couple of top priority policies: 1) running the affairs following the Quranic precepts as he understood them, and 2) making necessary administrative appointments based strictly on merit and righteousness. In theory, Ali's policy was commendable. In practice, it turned out a fatal political miscalculation on his part.

No doubt, Ali was a great warrior of Islam, admired and adored by all and sundry for his courage, honesty, and impeccable character, and held in high esteem for his sacrifice for the unity of *Umma* (Community of Muslims), but all this was no substitute for understanding the ground reality. He badly missed the point that politics had already undermined religion. Ignoring the bold writing on the wall, he proceeded against the tide trying, in his zeal, to make politics subservient to religion. He should have known better. It was religion that history always put subservient to politics and not vice versa. Anytime politics was made subservient to religion, it failed and led to the downfall and demise of the kingdoms, empires, and states. Akhenaten did so and lost. Ashoka did so and buried the Mauryan empire. There are many examples in history.

Yet it is hard to blame Ali bin Abi Talib for his political brashness. He was not the only one who carried the smoldering fire of faith in his bosom. Allah, his word, and the Prophet were supreme. The Caliphate should run strictly according to the Book of God. In his zeal to defend the basic precepts of Islam, as a devout follower of Islam, Ali didn't bother to gauge the pulse of the populace. A philosopher-scholar, well versed with religion and a superbly eloquent orator that he was could have served him well, yet the impulsiveness with which he oftentimes brushed aside the counsel of his advisors put him in a precarious situation. In that sense, he behaved like his predecessor, Othman bin Afan, yet tried to fix the wrongs with the same political mindset that had primarily brought about the latter's downfall. Ali flagrantly overlooked, to his peril, the cracks and the fault lines that were appearing in his home turf, Medina and Mecca. Noble at heart and a sincere believer in Islam, he refused to fathom that it takes a cold-blooded genius to look at the political math objectively. He lacked precisely the cold-blooded calculation and insight that politics and leadership demand. No wonder he made strategic blunders both politically and militarily.

In hindsight, it strikes as strange and paradoxical that, as one of the first students of Prophet Mohammad, Ali should have glossed over the trouble so evidently brewing under his nose. Even more perplexing is that he unwisely opened up new fronts in far-off lands without consolidating his position in Mecca and Medina. Not that he was not counseled by his well-wishers and advisors against it. He was. Yet he insisted on militarily deposing the governors of Kufa and Damascus, gravely underestimating the power of the tribal political arithmetic. He left Medina at a most inopportune time from a political standpoint.

Take, for example, the Prophet. When he was recognized as the *Syed* (Chief), he took particular care to consolidate his position by first taking the tribal chiefs of Medina into confidence. Then he established a Confederacy of tribes, giving each of them a fair share in power and politics, and only then confronted the Meccans - first on his turf, embarking on Mecca only when he had consolidated power in Medina. Ali badly missed the point. He underestimated Talha and Zubair and unnecessarily alienated them by not giving them a good share of power. Later on, though, he did offer them governorship, as a damage-control strategy, but that was far below their expectations.

Talha ad Zubair annoyed, Ali opened the war front against the governors of Kufa and Damascus – both powerful Umayyads – leaving him with practically no time to devote to the administrative affairs in Medina. Finally, when he left Medina and headed to depose these governors, the Meccan Umayyads – by then uncomfortable with the austerity measures that Ali had imposed – opened a formidable front on the home turf spearheaded by Aisha along with Talha and Zubair. Aisha, the fiery orator and mobilizer of the masses, announced war on Ali, on the pretext that the latter didn't bring the murderers of Othman to book. She and her two confidantes – Talha and Zubair – proceeded to Basra (present-day Iraq) with their followers to fight Ali. In Basra, more people joined her camp. However, Ali managed to capture the fort of Basra, and many fighters from Aisha's camp then defected to his side.

As the two, Aisha and Ali, came face to face with their armies, Ali, as a last resort, tried to negotiate peace with Zubair and Talha. The talks took place outside the boundary of the battlefield for three days but eventually failed. The battle was announced. Aisha, riding on her camel, led the front. As the fight picked up the tempo, both Zubair and Talha were killed. Aisha, now the lone leader of her battalion, continued to push on. As thousands of Muslims were slaughtered on both sides, Ali bin Abi Talib, now visibly distraught and in desperation, asked his arrow men to target Aisha's camel. It was only after her camel succumbed that Aisha capitulated and accepted defeat. In this unnecessary clash of egos, some ten thousand lives were lost, all Muslims, believers in Allah, and followers of the Prophet. Some estimates put the number of dead at more than ten thousand. That doesn't matter. What matters is that it was the Muslims who killed each other, both believing they were on the right path and the right religion.

After Ali decisively defeated Aisha on the outskirts of Basra, he grabbed the opportunity to take noble revenge on her, knowing perhaps full well that she hadn't forgiven him for his role during the "Necklace episode." Ali acted piously and nobly. He arranged for Aisha to be sent back to Medina with a full escort, despite her reservations. Be that as it may, Ali's chivalrous conduct toward Aisha was no compensation for the dent that the "Battle of the Camel" caused to the integrity and credibility of the *Umma*. It was a tragic event in the sacred history of Islam where two sides fought in the name of the same God and religion, each one genuinely believing in the authenticity of their respective version of the narrative. Each party sincerely believed they were fighting to defend true Islam. In defiance of the proclaimed spirit of Islam, Muslims slaughtered each other, spilling blood on the sands; each party precisely understood what they understood, and each party called their dead warriors martyrs in the path of Islam. That was that. The travesty of history.

After the Battle of the Camel, the epicenter of Arab political power permanently shifted out of Medina. Damascus and Mecca intensified their efforts to grab their share of the pie. As a result, the power tussle was played in a triangular contest in which Damascus, the Umayyad hub, was steadily emerging as the victor. With each passing day, the equation of power was changing. Ali's terrible diplomatic mistakes cost him dearly. He was losing control over Medina as well as Mecca. As the balance was tilting towards Damascus - an erstwhile Byzantine city - Ali was increasingly pushed against the wall. Frustrated at the ominous atmosphere of rebellion that was in the making, he took yet another unprecedented ill-thought step: He shifted his capital to Kufa, leaving Medina and Mecca completely unattended. It proved a gigantic policy blunder of Ali that spelled a death knell to the future of the Arabs State of Medina.

In Kufa, Ali fought the Ummayad governor and deposed him. Encouraged by this small success, he aspired to settle the scores with another but powerful Umayyad governor - the astute statesman and a strongman, Muawiyah, a relative of Othman bin Afan - who controlled Damascus. Again Ali completely underestimated the opponent's prowess. Muawiyah was a hard nut to crack. He had openly defied Ali and adamantly refused to pledge allegiance to him. Ali knew that Muawiyah aspired for the coveted post of the Caliph. He would bluntly argue that Ali bin Abi Talib didn't qualify for the post of the Caliph, audaciously reckoning himself a perfect leader to rule the *Umma*. After the murder of Othman bin Afan, he had been relentlessly rallying the Syrians against Medina demanding revenge for his death. As can be recalled, Naila, the Syrian wife of Othman, had managed to send her severed fingertips and the blood-stained shirt of her husband to Muawiyah. The shrewd Muawiyah would display the shirt regularly on the Friday sermons and vow to revenge the Caliph's murder. His steadfast propaganda had many takers in Syria. Ali bin Abi Talib was painted as one of the co-conspirators of Othman bin Afan's assassination. Ali's government was to be brought down. That was that.

Irritated by Muawiyah's stubbornness, Ali advanced on Damascus. The battle ensued. Ali's troops launched a frontal attack and were just close to having the day. Muawiyah, an astute politician, military strategist, and schemer, sensed the imminent danger. He came up with an ingenious trick. Suddenly a contingent of his soldiers rode to the battlefield mounting copies of the Quran on spears. As they displayed the Holy Book, they shouted, "Let the Book of God be the judge between us!" What was going on? Muawiyah's guile was unprecedented. Ali was stunned. His troops were confused.

They began to scatter and leave their positions after seeing the Holy Book mounted on spears. Ali tried hard to persuade his men not to fall into the trap Muawiyah had laid. However, despite Ali's exhortations, the Basran regiment of his army hesitated to continue the fight fearing the desecration of the Holy Book. They decided to disobey the Caliph, and Ali's line defense began to wilt away. That was what Muawiyah wanted. Without wasting time he dealt his masterstroke: he suddenly sent the emissaries to Ali proposing negotiation. Many of Ali's men were delighted at the suggestion. Ali had no option but to yield as these men now totally refused to fight. As Ali agreed, Muawiyah put another rider demanding to take the Quran as the sole guide for negotiations. Though Ali saw through the whole game of Muawiyah, he couldn't help but agree.

The behavior of his troops defogged Ali's mind. Hadn't he nearly won the battle, yet he lost the war? For the first time, the Quran was used as an overt political weapon to win the war. It became clear to him that the countdown had begun. His days in the seat of power were limited. The tables had turned almost completely against Ali. In Kufa, his capital, the masses booed and jeered at him. In Basra also a rebellion quickly gained momentum. The rebels outrightly condemned Ali for his decision to accept Muawiyah's proposal for negotiations. Negotiations for what? Negotiations for who is the Caliph? Really!

The rebels openly castigated Ali for casting doubt on his leadership of *Umma*. For Ali to accept to negotiate with Muawiyah for viceroyship was preposterous before them. These rebels, later called *Khariji* (Kharijites), didn't want to listen to any explanation from Ali. They adamantly accused him of betraying the Muslims and the Prophet by not fighting Muawiyah till the end and defeating him. The Kharijite leader, Abdal Wahab, openly derided Ali in the mosque, scorning him: "You have now completely forfeited the divine right to succession to the Prophet because you accepted Muawiyah's proposal to arbitrate on the issue of *Khilafat* (succession)." With their war cry, "Judgment belongs to God alone," the Kharijites turned to violence. Ali found himself thrust against the wall, completely helpless, with nowhere to go. Each passing day brought in more frustration taking a heavy toll on his nerves. He reportedly acknowledged his helplessness when he confided with his cousin, "Things are now getting against me."

Ali had a reason to be upset and depressed. He had spent nearly twenty-five years standing in line patiently only to prevent *fitna* (civil war) from happening. Now, that he had become the Caliph, he had gotten knee-deep in an all-out civil war. He had to resort to the bloodshed of his coreligionists to secure his rivals' allegiance. That thought sickened him. Perhaps.

The Division

The arbitration with Muawiyah took almost a year. In 658 CE, the two sides agreed on the division of the caliphate - Damascus went to Caliph Muawiyah and Kufa went to Caliph Ali. Interestingly, after the death of the Prophet, the Medinites under the leadership of Sa'ad bin Obada, as mentioned earlier, had proposed a two-Caliph arrangement. His bones were then broken by the Meccans. Twenty-six years later the Meccan Umayyads pushed for a two-Caliph system. The old man, Sa'ad, was proven right. The Muslims would have been better off with two Caliphs right from day one. Perhaps.

Ali bin Abi Talib reconciled with the division of the Muslim state. What he didn't reconcile with was the politics of money and power. He pushed on with the policy of equal distribution of the revenues of the Caliphate among all the people. He emphasized piety and equality before God; he insisted that all Muslims were brethren – the basic principles laid down in Islam long before Ali reiterated them – which surprisingly did not go well with the elite, bureaucracy, and the deep state. The elite had tasted the wealth and favor in the previous regimes, and here their wings were being clipped by the caliph. They became his dedicated opponents.

Ali thus created new enemies by alienating influential people through his austerity measures. He ignored the fact that all early Muslims including himself had suffered from poverty and hardships for a long and only of late had begun to see some good life, wealth, and plenty of slaves at their disposal. Ali bin Abi Talib urged them to rely on the rewards in the afterlife in line with God's word. On the contrary, Muawiyah provided his loyalists with wealth and luxury here in this world. Ali was trying to use politics within the confines of religion, but Muawiyah was using religion for politics. Muawiyah won the day.

After settling the scores with Ali in Damascus, Muawiya turned his attention to Egypt. The Egyptian governor, who was Ali's man, was captured and burnt alive after being stuffed into a donkey's carcass. This horrible incident was a humiliation for Ali bin Abi Talib. He had already grown too weak militarily to take any befitting action against Ummayads.

Emboldened, the Umayyads now mounted ruthless attacks elsewhere in Ali's territory. He was now totally caught up in a trap. Back home in Basra, the *Kharijites* attracted more and more followers to their side with each passing day. The rebellion spread. Ali was losing control over his administration. Simultaneously, the Umayyad forces acting on their intelligence inputs began a series of well-planned organized raids with lightning-fast speed into his territory, ousting his governors and crushing his soldiers. Muawiyah now, in a show of his strength, sent troops to Medina and Mecca, and Yemen, slaughtering thousands of Ali bin Abi Talib's supporters like meek sheep.

At this crucial juncture in history, Ali could not mobilize his army. How could he? He was facing a financial crunch due to his bad handling of the economy of the State. Frustrated, he turned his verbal gunfire toward his soldiers, berating them, quite unwisely, in his eloquently stinging speeches, invoked on them the wrath of God. But it was too late to mobilize the Kufans. Ali's eloquent oratory fell on deaf ears. Soon, he became convinced that the Kufans were dead like stones, not interested in heaven and paradise.

He could chide and berate the Kufans as much as he wanted. They hardly paid attention to his preaching. They saw pretty clearly that he was failing as Caliph. The politics of purity and piety; and spirituality didn't impress them much. What they wanted, first and foremost, was to feed their families, and enjoy a good and prosperous life like the Syrians did under Muawiyah. Yet Ali bin Abi Talib remained impervious to their material aspirations. The Kufans, like all humans, saw religion as a means to temporal ends and faith in Islam to secure their personal and collective lives with blessings, abundance, and grace from God. Even though it is argued that religion is needed solely for achieving spiritual ends, the fact remains that people turn to spirituality primarily to satisfy their basic material needs. Ali bin Abi Talib stubbornly relied on the spiritual aspects to govern his subjects, ignoring the material needs of the soldiers, state officials, and commoners. The people didn't buy his arguments. His treasury was empty, and he couldn't generate funds to finance the wars. An organized army can't be maintained without adequate finances. Ali, it seemed, lived in world of metaphysics far removed from practical politics. The masses saw through this all. They had begun to lose faith in his leadership long before he woke up to reality.

Ali bin Abi Talib became discouraged and depressed with each passing day. A low-intensity civil war had gripped his part of the Caliphate. He was no more in control; the rebellion could flare up at any time and put an end to his tenure. Only a trigger was required. The rebels won't wait for the trigger to mount a coup. They assassinated Ali in the wee hours of dawn on his way to the mosque for prayers. That was in January 661 CE. Before he breathed his last, he made a will asking his sons (Hassan and Hussein) to put his body on a camel and let her loose. His body should be buried at the spot where the camel stops. Accordingly, after washing their father's body and shrouding it in robes, his sons acted on his will. The camel stopped at Najaf, six miles away from Kufa. It was a barren hillock, then. There, he was buried – the man who would thereafter be known as the "First Imam of the Shias." Twenty years later, his younger son, Imam Hussein, returned to the place where his father was killed. He, too, met his death here at a place seventy miles from Najaf.

Muawiyah quickly consolidated his power and established his dynasty. Before becoming the undisputed Caliph, Muawiyah had to remove one last thorn from the path - the elder son of Ali bin Abi Talib, Imam Hassan - that could (possibly) claim his right to Ali's part of the Caliphate. Understandably, Muawiyah was quite apprehensive about Imam Hassan donning the mantle of leadership, so he sent his emissaries offering him a handsome pension to persuade him to return to Medina. Hassan agreed. He quietly abandoned his political aspirations in exchange for the financial support provided by Muawiyah's government and returned to Medina, where he later died under mysterious circumstances. There are claims that his Syrian wife poisoned him at the behest of Muawiyah.

The other surviving son of Ali, Imam Hussein, temperamentally different from his elder brother, nurtured his father's zeal to establish "Piety over Power" and "Religion over Politics." It seemed he paid no attention to history that played out before his eyes. He and his father should have known better, that when the Prophet was building up his follower base, he never ignored the economic aspect of the religious polity. He organized *Ghazus* and raiding expeditions to capture as much of booty, spoils, and captives - men, women, and children - as possible. He kept two parts of the spoils with him and distributed the remaining eight parts among his follower companions. The surplus that he kept with him would usually be spent on the poor, orphans, and the destitute in the Muslim community. The Prophet had a perfect grasp of the economic expediencies required in state-building. He was very outgoing when he built alliances during his initial days in Medina. Ali ignored that and failed. Unfortunately, Hussein, too, had not learned the lesson. He, like his father, was unable to see the writing on the wall: "Might is Right." Might *comes* with Money. Spirituality, philosophy, and rhetoric don't fill your stomach.

Imam Hussein firmly believed that politics should be subjugated to faith and religion – a decent premise indeed from an ideological standpoint. Unfortunately, the world he lived in – and we live in – was far from ideal and perfect. Politics requires adjustments, fine-tuning, and compromises. It requires the leader to make calculated moves, guided by expediencies. Like his late father, Hussein believed that faith and religion had to be put above politics simply because the "Word of God" was supreme. Unfortunately, he hadn't learned – not even from the mistakes of his father – that faith and religion were, in fact, two distinct entities, even though people perceived them as interchangeable and synonymous concepts. Religion is a story of faith, and this story is influenced by society's prevailing political, social, and cultural milieu. Politics is easily done on religion, yet it is hard to do religion on politics. Keeping religion above politics opens the gateway to political failure, sooner or later. Ali did the same and failed. Now Hussein wanted to tread the same path; it was perilous, yet he decided to go ahead with it. The Kufan experience of his father should have been alive in his heart and mind. But he couldn't help it. His passion and zeal for Islam put a blinker on his eyes. He couldn't see the treacherous danger lurking around him. As he jumped into the fray, he put faith above fortitude, ready to set sail in dangerous waters.

The Battle of Karbala

Muawiyah, the Caliph, possessed an army, wealth, and power. With that came luxury. He grew obese and unfit. As he neared his last days, he nominated his son, Yazid, as his successor to run the affairs of the Caliphate. Hussein couldn't digest it. He fervently expressed his intent to bring back the Caliphate to where it belonged – the house of the Prophet, according to him. However, the odds were against him. Yazid may have been an alcoholic, but he had proved himself a successful administrator and a capable commander in the field - indeed as Muawiyah had envisioned his son to be. Hussein dismissed Yazid's military experience and administrative skills as superfluous.

Since Hussein had received a barrage of letters of support from the Kufans, he reckoned that he was in better touch with the people on the ground than Yazid was. By that metric - call it the popularity index - Hussein presumed he had a rightful claim to be the Caliph. It was true that Hussein was a man of the people, but it is also true that ordinary folks don't fight wars. Soldiers fight wars. And he had none. He hastily planned his expedition against Yazid's forces, counting on the promised support from the Kufans. His cousin reportedly counseled him against that dangerous expedition, but Hussein refused to listen. "Whatever is fated is fated!" Hussein retorted back to him. And proceeded.

With a band of seventy-two followers, including his household members, Hussein began his ill-fated journey to Kufa. Yazid's generals and governors had already taken drastic measures in Kufa, imposed martial law, and silenced the popular rebellion through indiscriminate use of force. When Hussein reached the Kufan boundary, some messengers were sent to him by Yazid's commanders to persuade him against entering Kufa. He refused and refused. With each passing day, Hussein became more and more adamant and obstinate. How could he go back? What was Yazid worth with all his power before the power of Allah? Wasn't Allah with the believers? And didn't Allah make a handful of the believers victorious against their enemies in the Battle of Badr? Surely, thoughts like that might naturally have popped up in Hussein's mind. He dismissed any idea of backing out.

Yet, Hussein perhaps missed out on one important incident – the event of Hudaybiah. He had probably forgotten that his grandfather had secured a Treaty when faced with the potential of bloodshed against the numerically superior belligerent Meccans and returned without performing the pilgrimage. The senior companions of his grandfather had expressed their reservations then about that so-called humiliating-for-them treaty of Hudaybiah. But that didn't deter the Prophet from carrying out what was expedient at that hour of crisis. He secured the treaty with the Meccans and returned to Medina. Hussein should have known better.

He refused to back out. Instead, he put everything at stake! What transpired next was one of the most horrendous events in the sacred history of Islam. The infamous ten days of torture that the Prophet's grandson, Hussein, and his family and followers had to endure at the hands of the co-believers were the most ignominious, cruel, and sordid. The history of Islam hasn't recorded anything with so much depth and detail (mixing fact and faith) as the event of *Karbala* (Present-day Iraq). Long story short, Hussein's camp was sieged, and their water and food supply were cut off to compel him to capitulate. As he refused to budge, the fight ensued. By the 10th day of the siege, the Yazid's army under the command of Shimr killed him and all his male family members, along with infants. His head was put on a lance and paraded through the streets of Kufa, and other dead bodies were left for the wolves to devour. The women and the children were taken captives.

On reaching the Kufan governor's palace, the commander, Shimr, tossed the prized trophy, the head of Hussein, onto the floor before the governor, Ubaydallah. The latter grinned with satisfaction, poked the head, and sent it rolling on the floor. One of the people present there strongly objected to Ubaydallah's action. He was dragged out of the door.

In the aftermath of the Karbala massacre, one Ibn Zubair rebelled, proclaiming himself the Caliph of Mecca. Yazid immediately sent his forces to deal with him. As the battle progressed, Ibn Zubair and his men took shelter in the Ka'aba. The Umayyad forces pursued them and attacked Ka'aba, burning it down. Ibn Zubair was decimated. Mecca fell to the Ummayads. However, as the confrontation was still on, Yazid suddenly died in 683 CE. The hostilities were put to a halt and the army was recalled to Damascus. Yazid's son Muawiyah II was proclaimed the Caliph. With his ascension to the throne, the office of the Caliph was transformed permanently into a hereditary monarchy.

Muawiyah II was shortly deposed by another Ummayad, Marwan (the same Marwan who was Caliph Othman's PRO), in a battle in 684 CE. That ended the Sufyanid Ummayad dynasty. Marwan became the Caliph and established the Marwanid Ummayad dynasty. Marwan himself ruled for less than a year. But his dynasty went on to rule uninterruptedly for ninety years. Marwanid dynasty successfully undertook the policy of territorial expansion – a policy successfully introduced first by Omar bin Khattab (the second Caliph). The domination of the Arabs over the non-Arabs was now firmly institutionalized. The ninety years of Arab rule saw many successes; however, it was also riddled with wars, turmoil, intrigue, and murders for the most part.

The Umayyads were finally overthrown by the Banu Hashim tribe of Mecca. They were the descendants of Abbas, the uncle of Prophet Mohammad. The revolt that culminated in the fall of the Marwanid

Umayyads began in Khurasan (Iran) in 719 CE. By 747 CE, it gained the requisite strength, resilience, and momentum to launch the final and decisive assault on the Marwanids. In 750 CE, the Abbasids finally defeated them in a battle fought in Iraq.

Abu-al-Abbas became the Caliph. He ordered every member of the Umayyad clan to be caught and killed. The new Abbasid Caliph's order was carried out dedicatedly by his men, and almost all Umayyads were slaughtered one by one. The royal family fled and hid but was hotly pursued by the Abbasids and caught and killed. All except one, Abd-al-Rahman. He escaped to Spain.

Baghdad, Mutazila, and Ibn Sina

Damascus was left in tatters. The Abbasids shifted the Caliphate's capital to Iraq. On the banks of the Tigris, a new town emerged called Baghdad, which soon became a dazzling city. After a century of wait and suffering, Banu Hashim had finally put their hands on the buttons of power. It was they who established, in the true sense, what is called the Arab (Islamic) civilization and empire. The Islamic empire reached its zenith here in Baghdad, the new epicenter of trade, business, literature, art, and luxury. The Arab civilization came to be reckoned now at par with other world civilizations. Wealth flowed in from all sides. A scintillating society emerged here on the dust and debris of long-forgotten Babylonia. In a sense, Baghdad represented a medieval renaissance of ancient Babylonia. That Abbasid Baghdad still fascinates the imagination of Muslims and non-Muslims alike is a testimony to its grandeur.

The second Abbasid Caliph, al-Mansur, who built Baghdad in 762 CE, was an efficient administrator, good economist, and lover of art. He built Baghdad keeping in mind the principles of Euclidean geometry i.e., the city was built as a perfect circle, symbolizing, as Martin Puchner puts it, the rising power of Arabia in a single center. It was an ambitious project designed to make the circular city a world center of knowledge. Libraries were established that would amass texts and manuscripts from different cultures across the rapidly expanding realm. A new genre, *summa,* or summation of knowledge was meticulously given shape here in Baghdad and Aristotle was placed on a high pedestal as a philosopher. Like the Assyrian king Ashurbanipal's famous library at Nineveh, Al-Mansur's palace also housed a huge palace library that preserved the written record of the past. It was a Storehouse of Wisdom. It stored Persian writings like *Kalila wa Dimna,* Mesopotamian manuscripts, and Indian works on astronomy including *Surya Siddhanta* translated into Arabic. Baghdad also housed an institute of astronomy, a testimony to the extent to which Abbasid rulers wanted to gather knowledge. Euclid's geometry was the first Greek text translated into Arabic. Soon others followed. Almost all the extant works of Aristotle were later procured and translated. Aristotle became known as a philosopher courtesy of these translations. The Jews played a significant role in accomplishing the arduous task of translating the texts from Greek and Persian into Arabic and vice versa. Art, literature, philosophy, and astronomy flourished. It was these Arabic texts that later caught the eye of the West spreading Greek philosophy far and wide.

Despite his love of letters, Al-Mansur was wise enough to keep his empire under strict supervision. He introduced the world's first Postal System. During his and his successors' reigns, the intellectual curiosities of the people were allowed to expand. Al-Khwarizmi, the father of Algebra, adopted the works of the Indian, Greek, and Persian mathematicians (e.g., Fazari) into his famous treatise on astronomy. Baghdad became the center of the study of Theology giving rise to various theological schools of thought. Islamic Religious Jurisprudence as an independent branch of theology was also born in the circular city of Baghdad. Between 760 and 900 CE, the period saw the evolution of the Muslim theological discourse, the compilation of traditions of the Prophet or *Hadith*, and the edification of the *Sharia* law or Islamic Jurisprudence.

Harun al-Rashid, a famous Caliph, brought much prestige to the Abbasid dynasty and made Baghdad a splendid city and center of trade, culture, and literature. Greek philosophy was curiously studied here, and the Greek influence became conspicuously visible in the Muslim scholars' writings and discourses. During his reign, the city's markets were bursting with goods and wealth. Baghdad traded with China, India, Sri Lanka, and some Far East and African countries. Art and architecture received significant attention. Building and sculpting flourished.

The slave trade was at its zenith. Russian (Kievan Ru's in the 8th century) and Caucasian boys were traded at the highest prices. Overall, the city had become cosmopolitan, and the society was comparatively tolerant. Probably for the first time after the advent of Islam, people with different sexual orientations, eunuchs, and captives who were forcibly castrated, were tolerated in that society of Baghdad without much discrimination – a contravention of the Quranic injunctions in the context of Lot's story (Sodom and Gomorrah).

After the death of Harun Al-Rashid, a fierce war of succession ensued in which Al-Mamun succeeded in ascending the throne. In Al-Mamun's time, the Greek influence on the Middle Eastern and Arab discourse and thought process was unequivocally evident. Nevertheless, the balance still leaned more toward Persian and non-Arab non-Greek philosophy and rhetoric. In these circumstances, the *Mutazila* (rationalist) theological movement gained acceptance, and Caliph Al-Mamun himself took a keen interest in such socio-intellectual development. The *Mutazila* movement originally began in Basra. It was kick-started by a debate that ensued over a strange yet straightforward question: if a believer in Islam commits a grave sin, should they be regarded as merely a sinner or excommunicated from Islam? One influential theologian and philosopher, Wasil bin Ata argued that as long as the person accepts the unity of God and the Prophet, he is a Muslim and not an infidel. Others differed. The debate continued for years. It attracted a lot of attention from religious scholars and common folks. Eventually, a movement called *Mutazila* emerged which gained quite a following. In 849 CE, *Mutazila* became an independent School of Thought.

Adherents of this school argued that human beings should use their wisdom and rational thinking instead of blind faith to determine whether God exists or not. They urged the people to do introspection, stressing that if a Muslim believes that God created this universe, he must also ask himself what God wants from him as a human being. The *Mutazili* were lucky to be patronized by a Caliph like Al-Mamun, who was a man of words and tolerant of innovation in Islamic theology. During his reign, the *Mutazila* school flourished. However, the royal patronage swelled the Mutazili's heads. They became pushy and arrogant in their argumentation and proselytizing agenda, ever ready to resort to extremism and violence to silence the voices of critics and opponents. These benign-looking *Mutazilis* began a systematic campaign of persecution against traditionalist scholars and men of religion. They were now perceived as fundamentalists by the people. As the opposition to them began to grow fast. With the death of Caliph Al-Mamun, the good days for the *Mutazilis* were over. Absent royal patronage, the tables turned, and suddenly, they were at the receiving end, unscrupulously persecuted, attacked, and suppressed by those whom they once persecuted. As the 9th century CE came to a close, the *Mutazila* movement was almost extinguished. Their numbers came down to a handful of adherents confined to some isolated pockets of Basra.

In 980 CE in northeast Persia (today's Uzbekistan) a boy was born to a merchant family that grew up to become Ibn Sina (Avicenna in the West). He was a typical product of the Baghdad project. By the age of ten Ibn Sina was proficient in the recitation of the Quran. An Indian merchant introduced him to arithmetic and when he was a teenager a tutor taught him *falsafa (Philosophia* in Greek). Falsafa was a difficult-to-absorb tradition and Aristotles's metaphysics of cause and effect left him intrigued forever. One day he procured Al-Farabi's treatise on falfasa, which explained Aristotle in Arabic and that changed his whole perspective. Seeing Ibn Sina's interest in falsafa and medicine, a wealthy merchant commissioned him to write a treatise explaining falsafa in simple and easy-to-understand language. That was a lucky break for the young scholar. He managed to get access to the Sultan's library and immersed himself in the translations of the Greek texts. No sooner had he completed his manuscript that Bukhara, his native place, was caught up in political trouble. Ibn Sina had to flee to save his life. He would spend the rest of his life without a permanent home, fleeing from one province to another avoiding imprisonment for writing on subjects on logic, mathematics, physics, and metaphysics. But his peripatetic life didn't deter him from writing on medicine, ethics, human behavior, politics, and economics. In doing so he came up with a system of science that elaborated on Aristotle's system. He concluded, Puchner points out, that all humans are uniquely endowed with the capacity for rational thought, which can be elaborated by the rules of logic, what Aristotle had called the rational soul. That wasn't enough. Ibn Sina needed to address the question of how his system relates to Islam and its conception of a creator. He juxtaposed Aristotle's cause-and-effect concept with Islamic theology proposing God as the ultimate cause of all causes - in a way substituting Aristotle's prime mover with the God of Islam. Ibn Sina argued that rules of logic apply to the causes but God, the cause of all causes, is not bound by logic.

When Ibn Sina reached the age of fifty he was struck by a debilitating disease and could no more write by himself. His students, notably Al-Juzjani, took on to take dictation from his master and put them in writing. Ibn Sina's thought survived to posterity thanks to the Baghdad translation project and became the model for what the West would call *summa*, the sum of knowledge. As he became famous his works were read and consulted by prominent thinkers and theologians of the day. An intellectual awakening dawned on the then-Middle East. Science, mathematics, astronomy, medicine, and philosophy began to progress by leaps and bounds until an extremely influential theologian, Al Gazali, issued a fatwa against philosophy and mathematics. For the next eight hundred years Muslim astronomy didn't move beyond updating calendars, calculating the direction of Qibla, and sighting the crescent of Ramadan.

The Kingdom of God

By the 10th century, the Abbasid Empire was 150 years old. Its time had come to depart from the political scene. As the rebellions broke out almost everywhere, the sick and weakened empire began to crumble under its weight. The trade shrunk, and the wealth stopped pouring in as it used to. The economy deteriorated primarily because of political instability and incertitude. The state revenues sharply fell as the territorial expansion and annexation of new lands became impossible. The booty, the spoils, captives, and slaves that sustained the empire could no longer be fetched in adequate numbers. With no fresh captives and slaves, the state infrastructure and economy suffered severely. The activities like quarrying, mining, road building, logging, canal digging, and other dangerous yet essential tasks halted as the proletariat of captives and slaves shrank.

It wasn't easy, as we know, to carry out efficient trade in antiquity with no network of good roads and efficient means of transportation. The assets of these primitive agrarian states were captives, slaves, and convicts. Wars were fought precisely to maintain a constant supply of these assets in addition to tributes from the defeated populations. Any empire that couldn't carry out efficient war was doomed to fail. The Abbasid Empire had reached a point where it couldn't muster enough strength to wage expansionist expeditions. It was bound to crumble like the empires before. It had reached an age of senility.

The early agrarian societies engaged primarily in the barter trade of food grains, slaves, cattle, and items of medieval luxury like perfumes, art pieces, or jewelry. Food was perpetually in shortage. The lack of know-how and technology to introduce high-yield seeds and handle pests and crop infestations put a formidable brake on agricultural produce and thus revenues. This inefficient and primitive agricultural economy was as dangerous as precarious, an unreliable guarantee for an empire to sustain for long.

As the Abbasid empire began to crumble, the populace became restless. The tribal leaders actively sought independence from the Abbasid overlordship sparking off a climate of anarchy and chaos. The Caliph was helpless, unable to finance the army to control the deteriorating law and order situation. The royal house was in shambles. The bureaucracy was preoccupied with intrigues of power politics. By the end of the 10th century CE, Baghdad was no longer the Baghdad of Al- Al-Mansur and Harun Al-Rashid. All dazzle as lost. The empire had fallen apart into pieces. What remained behind was only the nostalgia for the Arabian Nights.

The Abbasids predicated their legitimacy to rule on their descent from the house of the Prophet. The lineage, they argued, vested them with a divine right to hold the crown of the Islamic kingdom in their possession. They held, according to them,. a unique social position. God had bestowed them with the right to rule. He had answered their prayers. Did God bother about them? Really? Even if he did, did history pay any heed to their sentiments? History certainly didn't allow them to retain leadership any longer than the Umayyads, whom they regarded as illegitimate usurpers of power. It is history that holds the final brief. The Umayyads, too, in their heyday, had reckoned themselves as the sole and rightful owners of the crown. They claimed to be totally devoted to the cause of Islam and dedicated to the welfare and well-being of *Umma*. Who among the two dynasties was the rightful owner of the crown of Islam? Who was the legitimate owner of the caliphate of God? Did God even want anyone to possess the crown of a Caliph at all? Or, did God even touch the subject of the Caliphate anywhere in the Holy Book of Islam, the Quran? No, no, and no.

Had the Abbasids been correct in their claim, they should have retained the crown longer than others. They couldn't.

A dazzling empire that had emerged from the desolate sands of the Arabian Desert gave a sense of satisfaction to the caravan traders of the desert that Allah was all too bountiful and benevolent to them. As the Arabs subdued the *Fertile Crescent* (Modern Iraq and the Middle East), other peoples and kingdoms on the outskirts watched with awe that the God of Trinity, God of Zion, God of Persian Fire, and the gods like Laat, Mannat, and Uzza were no match to the God of Islam. The Arab imperial grunts were trampling under their boots whatever came their way, and it seemed to all that there was no going back. The grandmasters of the political chess game silently yet keenly watched the history unfold in the Fertile Crescent. There was nothing they could do.

Earlier in his day, three centuries ago, the Prophet of Islam, Mohammad, also had keenly observed the *Fertile Crescent* from his vantage point in Mecca and Madina. As soon as the opportunity presented to him, he tried his hand to fill in the vacuum left by the warring Christian and Zoroastrian powers. He had Allah helping, empowering, and sustaining him, as he claimed. Time refused to be on his side, though.

There couldn't be another Mohammad now. Who could fill the political vacuum, as history was repeating itself – except that now it was the turf of Islam disintegrating? Would the followers of Allah and Mohammad hold on to the sparkle of political power? Or would the God of the Trinity take the turn to show His power? After all, his followers had been beseeching him for more than three centuries - since the fall of Jerusalem.

"*La taku'un'u Talatah* – Don't say, Trinity," the Quran had rebuked and admonished the Christians in the seventh century. They didn't mind it then. They won't mind it now, either. The Prophet lovers or Saracens, as the Arabs were called, incessantly irritated the Christ-lovers for four centuries. All those years they patiently waited for the empire of Islam to crumble, busy organizing their decisive punch against the Saracens. The tipping point was about to arrive. The power of the Trinity in the flesh and blood of his faithful followers was about to sweep the Saracens. The Trinitarians embarked on a Crusade – the Christian Holy War or *Jihad* – against the Abbasids, the allegedly rightful owners of the "Caliphate of Allah." The holy warriors of Jesus - the Chosen people of God of Christianity - reckoned the "rightful owners of the Kingdom of Allah" as infidels deserving to be trampled to so that the Kingdom of Their God and Jesus on the Earth be established. With passion, zeal, and devotion, the army of Jesus devotees marched off to deal a death knell to the Abbasid Caliphate. In 1099 CE, the believers in Allah and Mohammad were slaughtered like meek sheep in the name of Jesus in the Holy Land of Jerusalem in an all-out wholesale massacre. The Jesus devotees saw the hand of God, Jesus, in their victory against the Saracens.

Forty thousand inhabitants of Jerusalem were put to the sword. The Christian chroniclers boasted that blood flowed like a flood and their horses would go knee-deep in that flood of blood. The Saracens and Jews were cut to pieces, for the scavagers to devour. Piles of corpses were left to rot. For Christians, it signaled the triumph of the Triune God over the God of Islam, finally after a wait of more than four centuries. Yet it was too early for them to celebrate; the Christian God hardly had a complete victory yet. The Abbasid Empire had only crumbled and disintegrated, not vanished. The pockets that remained here and there would give enough headaches to Christians for another eight to nine hundred years. The costs in terms of human life and blood were enormous. But then, that has been the order of history, as always, ruthless. Unfortunately.

Final thoughts

History has had its compulsions to happen the way it happened. It is hard to blame one race, one tribe, one religion, or any one people. The human species has been collectively responsible for all the mayhem that it unleashed on itself and other species. But that is because we humans were able to establish control and supremacy over the food chain and the environment. Could there have been a different way to handle human affairs? Probably not. Life on this planet has hinged on violence. Throughout history, the animal world has sustained itself on violence, and so have humans, the only difference being that animals "commit violence to eat," but humans "eat to commit violence." As a result, history has been replete with cruelty, mercilessness, and savagery. History can't be changed now. However, the wisdom that allowed the human species to build history on violence can also open up an opportunity to handle the history of today and tomorrow through less violent means. Standing on the shoulders of History, looking into the horizons of the future, and not repeating the mistakes committed in the past is the way forward for us. "Today" is simply the future of yesterday and the past of tomorrow. We must keep in mind that history is not merely a story of the past; it is a science like Biology that can teach us to create a better future for humankind and the rest of the living species.

The human species will evolve further, and together with it, every aspect of human life and interaction including science, religion, thought and discourse will change. With the rapid progress of science and technology religion will face a tough challenge. It remains to be seen how far it can evolve in the post-human world as the twenty-first century unfurls fully.

Or, will the twenty-first century witness a New Religion? Well, that remains to be seen! As Adam Rutherford points out in *The Book of Humans,* "We have created gods, we can tuck them away," but what should bother us more than anything else is how much more violence "tucking gods away" can bring along.

As we come to the end of this book, I will leave you with a question to ponder: Was the bloodshed that religion and sacred history brought about *really* necessary?

Bibliography

1. Arnold, TW. The Caliphate. Delhi. Adam Publishers. 2013
2. Asbridge, Thomas. The Crusades: The War for the Holy Land. London. Simon & Schuster. 2012.
3. Ali, K. A Study of Islamic History. Delhi. Adam Publishers.
4. Akbarabadi, S. Islamic History: The Rise and Fall of Muslims. Delhi. Adam Publishers 2001.
5. Akbar, MJ. The Shade of Swords: Jihad and the Conflict Between Islam & Christianity. Delhi. Lotus collection. 2002.
6. Aquil, Raziuddin.The Muslim Question. Penguin Random House India, 2009.
7. Armstrong, Karen. A history of God. London. Vintage, 1999.
8. Armstrong, Karen. Islam, A Short History. Pheonix, 2001.
9. Armstrong, Karen. Holy War – the Crusades, and their impact on today's world. Anchor Books, 2001.
10. 10. Armstrong, Karen. Islam - A Short History. London. Phoenix Paperback. 2001
11. Armstrong, Karen. Jerusalem: One City, Three Faiths. London. Ballentine Books 2005.
12. Armstrong, Karen. Fields of Blood – Religion and the History of Violence. London. The Bodley Head. 2014.
13. Armstrong, Karen. The Great Transformation. London. Atlantic Books. 2007.
14. Armstrong, Karen. The Bible – The Biography. New Delhi. Manjul House. 2009.
15. Arendt, Hannah. The Origins of Totalitarianism. Penguin Classics. 2017.

16. Aslahi, Mohammad Yusuf. Fiq-al-ISlami. Delhi. Markazi Maktaba Islami Publication.2020.
17. Aristotle. The Politics. (Translated from Greek by AM William Ellis) Fingerprint Classics.2020
18. Aslan, Reza. No God but God. Arrow Books 2011.
19. Aslan, Reza. God – a human history. Transworld Publishers (Penguin Randon House) 2017.
20. Aslan, Reza. Zealot: The life and times of Jesus of Nazareth. Harper Collins Publishers 2016.
21. Atkins, Peter. Conjuring the Universe. Oxford University Press. 2020.
22. Ahmad, Ziauddin. Al-Quran: Divine Book of Eternal Value. Delhi. Royal Publishers. 1990.
23. Azad, Abul Kalam. The Tarjuman Al-Quran (3 vol). Edited and Translated into English by Syed Abdul Latif. Delhi. Kitab Bhavan. 1990.
24. Aziz-us- Samad, Ulfat. A comparative Study of Christianity and Islam. New Delhi. Adam Publishers. 2004.
25. Ajijola, AD. The Hijacking of Christianity. New Delhi. Adam Publishers. 2001.
26. Ahmad, Tauseef. Why Karbala? (2nd Edition) Srinagar. Jammu Kashmir Imamia Foundation 2019
27. Ali, Amir. A Short History of Saracenes. Delhi. Adam Publishers. 2015
28. Asai, Haider. Muslim Understanding of Other Religions. Delhi. Adam Publishers.
29. Akbar Shah Najeebabadi. The History of Islam (3 vol.), Darussalam 2001.
30. Max I Dimont. Jews, God and History. 2nd edition. Penguin Books Ltd, 2004.
31. Daniel Gordis. Israel– A Concise History of a Nation Reborn. Harper Collins Publishers, 2016.
32. Shashi Tharoor. Why I Am A Hindu. NewDelhi. Aleph Book Company, 2018.
33. Christophe Jaffrelot & Laurence Louer. The Islamic Connection South Asia & The Gulf. Penguin Random House, 2017.
34. Yuval Noah Harari. Sapiens - A Brief History of Humankind. London. Penguin Random House, 2011.
35. Bamber Gascoigne. A Brief History of Christianity. London Robinson, 2003.

36. Lesley Hazleton. After the Prophet - the Epic Story of the Shia-Sunni split. Anchor Books. 2010.
37. Tarek Fatah. The Tragic illusion of an Islamic state. Kautilya, 2015.
38. Tom Holland. Millennium,, Abacus, 2009.
39. Bertrand Rusell. Human Society in Ethics and Politics. Routledge Classics, 2010.
40. Arthur Herman. How the Scots Invented the Modern World. Crown Publishers, 2001.
41. Michael Baigent. Racing Toward Armageddon. HarperCollins paper bag edition, 2010.
42. Robert Wright. The Evolution of God. Abacus, 2010.
43. Francis Fukuyama. The Origins of Political Order, from Prehuman Times to the French Revolution. Profile Books Ltd, 2012.
44. Daron Acemoglu & James A. Robinson. Why Nations Fail. Profile books, 2012.
45. Stephen Prothero. God is not One. Harper One, 2011.
46. Edward W. Said. Covering Islam - How the media and the experts determine how we see the rest of the world. Vintage 1997.
47. Ludden, David. Making India Hindu: Religion, Community, and the Politics of Democracy in India. Oxford University Press. Second Edition,1996.
48. R. H. Tawney. Religion and the Rise of Capitalism. Aakar Books, 1926.
49. Thomas Piketty. Capital in the Twenty-first Century. Belknap Harvard, 2014.
50. V.S. Naipaul. Among the Believers. Picador 2010.
51. James Wasserman. The Templars and the Assassins: The Militia of Heaven. Inner Traditions Rochester, Vermont 2001.
52. Martin Puchna. The Written World: How Literature Shaped History. Granta Publications 2017.
53. Walter K. Anderson and Shridhar Damle. The RSS – A view to the inside. Penguin Random House India 2018.
54. Bernard Lewis. The Middle East, 2000 years of History from the Rise of Christianity to the present day. Pheonix Press 2000.
55. Nicolas Wade. A Troublesome Inheritance: Genes, Race and Human History. Penguin Books 2015.
56. Maurice Dobb. Studies in the Development of Capitalism. Rutledge paperback 1963.

57. Francis When. Marx's Das Kapital. New York. Grove Press, 2006.
58. David Reich. Who Are We and How We Got Here? Oxford University Press 2018.
59. Noam Chomsky. Hegemony or Survival. Penguin Books 2003
60. Noam Chomsky Power and Terror – conflict, hegemony, and the rule of Force. Pluto Press 2011.
61. Archie Brown. The Rise and Fall of Communism. Vintage Books 2010.
62. Peter Frankopan. The Silk Roads – A New History of the World. Bloomsbury Paperbacks 2015.
63. Tom Holland. In the Shadow of the Sword- The Birth of Islam and the Rise of the Global Arab Empire. Anchor Books 2012.
64. Robert Wright. The Moral Animal – Why we are the way we are. Vintage Books 1995.
65. Jack Lewis. The Science of Sin – Why we do the things we know we shouldn't. London. Bloomsbury Sigma 2018.
66. Rajiv Malhotra. Being Different – An Indian challenge to Western Universalism. Harper Collins Publishers, 2013.
67. Ed Hussain. The House of Islam - A Global History. London. Bloomsbury Publishing 2018.
68. Slavoj Zizek. The Year of Dreaming Dangerously. London. Verso 2012.
69. Slavoj Zizek. Interrogating the Real. Bloomsbury Academic 2006.
70. Slavoj Zizek. Agitating the Frame. New Delhi. Navayana. 2014.
71. Slavoj Zizek. Antigone. London, Bloomsbury Academic 2017.
72. John Canning. 100 Great Kings, Queens, and Rulers of the World. New Delhi. Rupa Paperbacks 1991.
73. Niccolo Machiavelli. The Prince. Fingerprint Classics 2018.
74. S. Irfan Habib. Jihad or Ijtihad. New Delhi. Harper Collins Publishers 2011.
75. Eugene Rogan. The Fall of the Ottomans. Penguin Books 2015.
76. Plato. The Republic. Maple Press. 2013.
77. Jack Lewis. The Science of Sin. Bloomsbury Sigma 2018.
78. Arun Shourie. The World of Fatwas. Rupa Paperback 2002.
79. Sriya Iyer. Economics of Religion in India., Harvard University Press 2018.
80. Upinder Singh. Political Violence in Ancient India. Harvard University Press. 2017.

81. Christophe Jaffrelot and Laurence Louer. (Editors). The Islamic Connection: South Asia and the Gulf. New Delhi. Penguin Viking 2017.
82. Neil Macgregor. Living with the Gods. Penguin Random House UK 2018.
83. Michael Scott. Ancient Worlds – An epic history of East and West. Penguin Random House UK 2016.
84. Romila Thapar. History and Beyond., Oxford University Press 2004.
85. Jyotimaya Sharma. Hindutva: Exploring the Idea of Hindu Nationalism. Penguin Books India 2015.
86. Bertrand Russel. Why I am not a Christian. Routledge Classics 2004.
87. Jonathan Haidt. The Righteous Mind – Why Good People are Divided by Politics and Religion. Penguin Books 2013.
88. Joseph Ratzinger Pope Benedict XVI. Jesus of Nazareth –Bloomsbury Paperback 2008.
89. S.A.A Maududi. Towards Understanding the Quran (Tafhim al-Quran). MMI Publishers 2006.
90. Mohammad Marmaduke Pickthal (Translation). The Holy Quran (Revised Edition). Delhi. Adam Publishers and Distributors 2005.
91. Ashraf Ali Thanawi. Quran-e-Majeed (Translation-Urdu) Islamic Book Service.
92. Tafsir Ibn-e-Kathir. The Holy Quran. (Urdu) 5 vol. Aetiqad Publishing House, New Delhi.
93. Maulana Badee-U-Zaman. (Translation). Edited by Aetiqad Husain Siddiqi. Jamah Tirmidhi (2 Vol) Arabic to Urdu. Aetiqad Publishers. 1983.
94. Allama Shabir Ahmad Usmani.The Noble Quran (Tafseer). (3 vols.) Islamic Book Service, New Delhi.
95. Dr. Mohammad Tahir-ul-Qadri. Tafseer Minhaj-ul-Quran. (vol 1). Jilani Book Depot 2010.
96. Maulana Mohammad Yousuf Shah. Bayan-ul-Furqan. (2 Vol. in Kashmiri). Srinagar. Ali Mohd and Sons.
97. Abdullah Yousuf Ali. The Holy Quran – Translation and Commentary. Good Word Books Pvt. Ltd; India 2003.
98. Imam Abu Zubaidi. (Compilation). Dr. Muhammad Muhsin Khan (Translation Arabic-English.). Sahih Al-Bukhari (Summarized), Maktaba Dar-us-Sala, Riyadh 1994.

99. Sir Syed Ahmad Khan (in Sir Syed Ahmad Khan aur Unka Aihad (Urdu) by Surraiya Hassan). Tafseer-al-Quran. Aligarh. Educational Book House 2015
100. Bill Bryson. A Short History of Nearly Everything. Transworld Publishers, Penguin Random House UK. Blackswan Edition 2004.
101. Jared Diamond. Collapse: How Societies choose to fail or survive. London, Penguin Books 2011.
102. SMA Sayeed. The Myth of Authenticity – A Story in Islamic Fundamentalism. New Delhi. Kitab Bhavan 1999.
103. RG Collingwood. The Idea of History. Oxford University Press 1994.
104. Noam Chomsky. Understanding Power., Edited by Peter R Mitchel, John Schoeffel. New Delhi. PRH India Penguin Books 2003.
105. Noam Chomsky. On Language. New Delhi. Penguin Random House 2003.
106. Kaushal Goyal. Alexander the Great – A Biography. Delhi. Pigeon Book 2015.
107. Paul Kriwaczek. Babylon – Mesopotamia and the Birth of Civilization. London. Atlantic Books 2012.
108. Brain Cox, Andrew Cohen. Human Universe. London. William Collins 2014.
109. Christopher Hitchens. God is not Great. London. Atlantic Books, 2018.
110. Robert Greene. The Laws of Human Nature. London. Profile Books 2018.
111. David R. Hawkins. Transcending the Levels of Consciousness. New York. Veritas Publishing 2006.
112. Stanislas Dehaene. Consciousness and the Brain – Deciphering how the Brain codes our thoughts. New York. Penguin Books 2014.
113. David R. Hawkins. (Edited by Scott Jeffrey). Dissolving the Ego, Realizing the Self. New Delhi. Hay House 2011.
114. Guy Deutscher. The Unfolding of Language – The Evolution of Mankind's Greatest Invention. London. Arrow Books 2006.
115. Steven Pinker. How Mind Works. London. Penguin Books 1999.
116. Simon Schama. The Story of the Jews: Finding the Words. London. Vintage Books, 2014.
117. Charles Darwin. The Origin of Species. Delhi. Goyal Publishers 1992.
118. Kathleen Kenyon. Archeology in the Holy Land. India. Routledge 2016

119. Amit Goswami. God is not Dead. Mumbai. Jaico House 2013.
120. Roger Penrose. Shadows of the Mind: A search for the missing Science of Consciousness. London. Vintage 1995.
121. Jim Al Khalili, Johajoe MC Fadden. Life on the Edge. London. Transworld Publishers 2015.
122. Duncan Greenlees. The Gospel of Islam. World Gospel Series. Chennai. The Theosophical Publishing House 1948.
123. Joseph Smith, Jun. (Translation). The Book of Mormon. Utah, USA. The Church of Jesus Christ of Later day Saints. 1920.
124. Swarupanada. Srimad Bhagavad Gita. Translation, Comments, and Index. Kolkata, Adaita Ashrama 2004.
125. Paul Davies. The Mind of God: Science and the Search of ultimate meaning. London, Penguin Books.
126. The New Testament. New International version. New York. Bible Society International 1973.
127. Holy Bible. Authorized King James Version. The USA. Authentic Books.
128. Ahmed Deedat. Christ in Islam. New Delhi. Adam Publishers 2007.
129. Ahmed Deedat. Was Jesus crucified? New Delhi. Adam Publishers 2006.
130. Michael Baigent, Richard Leigh. The Dead Sea Scrolls Deception: The explosive contents of the Dead Sea Scrolls and how the Church Conspired to Conceal them. London. Arrow Books 2006.
131. Michael Baigent, Richard Leigh, and Henry Lincoln.The Messianic Legacy. London. Arrow Books 2006.
132. The Holy Blood and the Holy Grail. Michael Baigent, Richard Leigh, and Henry Lincoln. London. Arrow Books 1996.
133. M. Scott Peck. The Road Less Travelled. London. Arrow Books 2006.
134. Baungardener and Crothers. Positive Psychology. India. Dorling Kindersley. 2015.
135. Swami Harshanada. Hindu Gods and Goddesses. Madras. Sri Ramakrishna Math 2007.
136. Swami Nityanand. Symbolism in Hinduism (compilation). Bombay. Central Chinmaya Mission Trust. 1983.
137. Roy Shiv Mohan Lal Mathur. Qadeem Hindi Falsafa (Urdu). New Delhi. National Council for Urdu. 1980.

138. Jo Durden Smith. The Essence of Buddhism. London. Arcturus Publishing 2006.
139. Lonsdale, Laura Ragg. The Gospel of Barnabas. New Delhi. Islamic Book Service 2001.
140. Sir Mohammad Iqbal. The Reconstruction of Religious Thought in Islam. Srinagar. Gulshan Publishers. 2003.
141. Ibn-e-Arabi. Wisdom of the Prophets. New Delhi. Idara Ishaat-e-Dinyat. 1999.
142. Sayyid Abu Ala Maududi. West versus Islam. New Delhi. Markazi Maktaba Islami Publishers 2010.
143. Maurice Bucaille. The Bible, the Quran & Science. New Delhi. Adam Publishers 2007.
144. Robert Thurman. Infinite life: seven virtues for living well. New Delhi. Hay House Publishers 2012.
145. Sam Harris. Waking Up: A guide to spirituality without religion. London. Transworld Publishers. 2015.
146. Sam Harris. The Moral Landscape. Free Press 2011
147. Imam Al-Ghazzali. Ihya Ullum-Din. Translated in English by Maulana Fazlul Karim. New Delhi. Islamic Book Service 2005.
148. A.H. Vidyarthi. Mohammad in World Scriptures. New Delhi. Adam Publishers and Distributors. 2005.
149. Swami Madavananda. The Brhadaranyaka Upanishad. Kolkata. Advaita Ashrama. 2008.
150. Edward Gibbon. The History of the Decline and Fall of the Roman Empire. Vol. III. London. Penguin Books (Classics) 1995.
151. Ramanuj Prasad. Know the Puranas. New Delhi. Pustak Mahal 2005.
152. S. Radhakrishnan. The Bhagavad Gita. New Delhi. Harper Publishers. 2009.
153. Swami Gambhiranada. Svatasvatara Upanisad. Kolkata. Advaita Ashram. 1986.
154. Swami Vireswarananda. Brahma Sutras (according to) Sri Ramanuja. Kolkata. 2008.
155. Swami Gambhirananda. Chandogya Upauisad. Kolkata. Advaita Ashram 2006.
156. Swami Gambhirananda. Eight Upanishads (2 vols). Kolkata. Advaita Ashram 1989.

157. Richard Dawkins. The God Delusion. London. Transworld Publishers 2007.
158. Abdu'L-Ahad Dawud. Mohammad in the Bible. New Delhi. Adam Publishers 2007.
159. Karl Marx. Das Capital. Moscow. Progress Publishers 1963.
160. Georgi Plekhanov. Selected Philosophical Works. Moscow. Progress Publishers. Vol. II. 1976.
161. R.A. Nicholson. A Literary History of the Arabs. New Delhi. Adam Publishers.2006.
162. Babaji Larwi. Asrar-e-Kabiri. Srinagar. JK Cultural Academy 2005.
163. Mohammad Tahir-ul-Qadri. Haqiqat-e-Tasawuf. New Delhi. Maktaba Rizwiya 2006.
164. Mohi-ud-Din Ibn-Arabi. Fatuhaat-e-Makiyah (3 vol.) Translated by Naem Chisti. New Delhi. Aetiqad Publishrs1994.
165. Research and Publication Department (Government of Jammu and Kashmir.) Kashmiri Shaivaism. Srinagar 1962.
166. Hafiz Jalandhari. Shahnama-e-Islam. Delhi. Farid Book Depot.
167. Mohammad Imran. Idol worship v/s God worship. New Delhi. Islamic Book Service 1997.
168. Maryam Jameela. Islam versus Ahli-al-Kitab. New Delhi. Taj Company. 2002.
169. Mohammad Qutb. Islam and the Modern Materialistic Thought. Delhi. New Crescent Publishing Co. 1999.
170. MA Enan. Ibn Khaldun: His life and works. New Delhi. Kitab Bhavan. 2000.
171. Sigmund Freud. The interpretation of Dreams. Delhi. KRJ Book International.
172. Abbe J.A. Dubois. Hindu Manners, Customs and Ceremonies. New Delhi. Rupa Publishers 2009.
173. Som Dev. Katha Sarit Sagar. Translated into Kashmiri by Amar Malhami. Srinagar. JK Academy of Art and Culture. 1996.
174. Shamas Naveed Usmani. Agar Ab Bhi Na Jaagey To (Urdu). New Delhi. Fareed Book Depot 1989.
175. Jalaluddin a's Suyuti. History of the Caliphs. Translation HS Jarret. New Delhi. Kitab Bhavan 2017
176. Masudul Hassan. History of Islam. New Delhi. Adam Publishers. New Delhi 2011

177. Mohammad Suhail. Administrative and Cultural History of Islam. New Delhi. Adam Publishers.
178. Moinuddin Nadvi. Tareekh-i-Islam.(2 vol). Lahore. Idaara Islam.
179. Ghulam Nabi. Khilafat in Theory and Practice. New Delhi. Adam Publishers.
180. M Sharif. History of Muslim Philosophy. (2Vol.). New Delhi. Adam Publishers.
181. M Enan. Decisive Moments in the History of Islam. New Delhi. Adam Publishers 2001
182. R A Nicolson. Kashf Al Mahjub (English translation) New Delhi. Adam Publishers.
183. A H Siddiqui. The Caliphate and the Muslim Sultanate in Medieval Persia. New Delhi. Adam Publishers.
184. Safdar Hosein. The Early History of Islam. New Delhi. Adam Publishers.
185. Khuda Baksh. The Orient under Caliphs. New Delhi. Adam Publishers.
186. S Wolfgang Fuchs. In a Pure Muslim Land. New Delhi. Speaking Tiger Books 2019
187. Will Durant. The Story of Philosophy. New York. Pocket Books 1961
188. Bernard Lewis. The Middle East: 2000 years of History. London. Phoenix Paperback 1995
189. James Wasserman. The Templars and the Assasins. New York. Inner Traditions International 2001
190. VS Naipaul. Among the Believers. London. Picador 2010
191. Mirza Tahir Ahmad. Revelation, Rationality, Knowledge, and Truth. Gurdaspur. Nazarat Nashru Islam. 2009
192. S Suhrawardi. The Awarif ul Ma' Arif. Tran. HW Clarke. New Delhi. Taj Company.2000
193. Ibni Arabi. Fasus ul Hikm. Urdu Translation by Qadir Sidiqui. New Delhi. Aetiqad Publishers.
194. Holger Kersten. Jesus Lived in India. Gurgaon. Penguin Random House 2001
195. Javed Ghamidi. Islam: A comprehensive introduction. New Delhi. Al Mawrid Foundation 2019
196. Edward Said. Culture and Imperialism. London. Vintage 1993.
197. Edward Said. Orientalism. London. Vintage Books.

198. Trevor Curnow. Wisdom: A World History. New Delhi. Speaking Tiger Publication 2015
199. Fritjof Capra. The Tao of Physics. London. Flamingo 1991
200. Henry Kissinger. World Order. London. Penguin Books 2015
201. Hasan Ali Nadvi. Islam and The World (Urdu). Lucknow. Academy of Islamic Research.
202. G W Bowersock. The Crucible of Islam. Harvard University Press 2017
203. Brain Cox & Andrew Cohen. Forces Of Nature. William Collins 2017.
204. Peter Heather. The Fall Of The Roman Empire: A New History. Pen Publication 2006.
205. Stephen Kershaw. A Brief History Of The Roman Empire. Robinson Publication 2013.
206. Eric Brown. Ancient Rome. Guy Saloniki Publication 2019.
207. Michael Scott. Ancient Worlds: A Epic Story Of East & West. Random House UK 2017.
208. Andrew Knoll. A Brief History Of Earth. Mariner Books 2020.
209. Umar Ahmad Usmani. Fiqh Al Quran. (Urdu) New Delhi Taj Company 2012.
210. Muhammad Yousuf Aslahi. Fiqh Al Islami. Delhi. Markazi Maktabe Islami Publishers 2018.
211. Muhammad Bin Ishaaq. Seerat Ibn Ishaaq (Urdu). New Delhi. Milli Publications 2020.
212. Kermit Pattison. Fossil Men. Harper Collins 2020.
213. Sam Harris. The Moral Landscape. Free Press 2011.
214. Carl Zimmer. Life's Edge. Dalton Publications 2021.
215. Thomas Higham. The World Before Us. How Science Is Revealing a New Story Of Our Human Origins. Viking Publications 2021.
216. Vybarr Cregan-Reid. Primate Change. How The World We Made is Remaking Us. Octopus Publishing 2018.
217. Henry Gee. A Very Short History of Life On Earth. Picador Publishing 2021.
218. Roger Penrose. Fashion Faith & Fantasy in The New Physics of Universe. Princeton University Press 2018.
219. Robert Wright. The Evolution Of God. The Origin Of Our Beliefs. Abacus 2009.
220. Albert Einstein. Relativity. Fingerprint Classics 2022.
221. H. G Wells. A Short History Of The World. Fingerprint Classics 2021.

222. J. M Roberts. & Odd Arne Westad. The Penguin History Of The World. 6th Edition. Penguin Books 2014.
223. Robin Dunbar. Human Evolution. Pelican Books 2014.
224. Tim Lewens. The Meaning Of Science. Pelican Books 2015.
225. Simon L Lewis. & Mark A. Maslin. The Human Planet. Pelican Books 2018.
226. Jonathan Holslag. A Political History Of The World. Pelican Books 2018.
227. Gregg Braden. The Mystery Of 2012 & a New World Age. Hay House Publishers 2010.
228. Muhammad Innaytullah Asad Subhani. Jihad Aur Rooh-i-Jihad (Urdu). New Delhi Hidayat Publisher 2017.
229. Hirsi Ali. Why Islam Needs a Reformation Now. Harper Collins 2015.
230. Aristotle. The Politics. (Translated from Greek by A. M Williams Ellis. Fingerprint Classics 2020.
231. Graham Hancock. Magicians Of The Gods. Coronet 2016.
232. Graham Hancock. The Sign and the Seal. AQuest for the Lost Arc of The Covenant. Arrow Books 1993.
233. Peter Atkins. Conjuring The Universe. Oxford University Press 2020.
234. Sean Carroll. Something Deeply Hidden. One World Publication 2019.
235. Brian Clegg. Dark Matter and Dark Energy. Icon Books 2019.
236. Robert Spencer. The History Of Jihad. Bombardier Books 2019.
237. Hermann Hesse. Siddhartha. Fingerprint Classics 2022.
238. Jack Lewis. The Science of Sin. Bloomsbury 2018.
239. Brian Muraresku. The Immortality Key. St. Martin's Press 2020.
240. Peter Wohlleben. The Inner Life Of Animals. Bodley Head 2017.
241. Shibli Nomani. Al-Farooq. The Life Of Omar The Great. Idara Impex 2019.
242. Ali Muhammad As-Sallabi (Trans. Nasir Khattab). The Biography Of Uthman Ibn Affan. Dhun Noorayn. Riyadh Maktaba Darussalam. 2007.
243. Ali Muhammad As Sallabi. The Biography Of Abu Baker As-Sideeq. Darussalam. Riyadh 2007.
244. Imam Bukhari. Al-Adam Al-Mufrad (English). Idara Impex 2021.
245. Asghar Ali Engineer. Islam Women And Gender Justice. New Delhi. Gyan Publishing House 2001.

246. Ibn-Qayyim Al-Jawziyya. (Al-Tib Nabvi) Healing With The Medicine Of The Prophet (English). Riyadh Darussalam 2003.
247. Ibn Khathir. (Qasus Al-Anmbia) Stories of The Prophets (English). Riyadh. Darussalam 2003.
248. Rutger Bregman. Human Kind: A Hopeful History. Bloomsbury Publishing. 2020.
249. Eric Weiner. The Socrates Express. New York. Avid Reader Press 2020.
250. David Graeber, David Wengrow. The Dawn Of Everything. Allen Lane 2021.
251. Homer: The Iliad & The Odyssey. Translated by Samuel Butler. Fingerprint Classics 2021.
252. Plato. The Republic. Maple Press 2013.
253. Kalidasa. Raghuvamsa. A.N.D Haksar. Penguin Books 2016
254. Kautilya Arthashastra. Chanakya. Fingerprint Classics 2022.
255. Shakespeare. Julius Caesar. Fingerprint Classics 2021.
256. Linda Yueh. The Great Economists: How Their Ideas Can Help Us Today. Penguin Books 2019.
257. Adam Smith. The Wealth Of Nations. Fingerprint Classics 2018.
258. Edith Hamilton. Mythology: Timeless Tales Of Gods And Heroes. Grand Central Publishing 2011.
259. Jennifer Dounda, Samuel H Stenberg. A Crack In Creation: Gene Editing and the Unthinkable Power to Control Evolution. Vintage 2018.
260. Niall Ferguson. The Ascent of Money: A Financial History Of The World. Penguin Books 2019.
261. Jared Diamond. Guns, Germs and Steel. Vintage 2011.
262. Kenneth Clark. Civilization. John Murray Publishers 2017.
263. Justin Marozzi. Islamic Empires. Penguin Books 2021.
264. Simon Wolfgang Fuchs. In a Pure Muslim Land. New Delhi. Speaking Tiger Books 2019.
265. Vaclav Smil. How The World Really Works. London Viking 2022.
266. Jacob Bronowski. The Ascent of Man. BBC Books 2011.
267. Richard Dawkins. The Selfish Gene. Oxford University Press 2006.
268. Richard Dawkins. Science in The Soul. Blackswan Edition 2018.
269. Graham Lawton, Stephen Hawking, Jennifer Daniel. The Origin of Almost Everything. John Murray Press 2019.

270. Stephen Hawking. Brief Answers Big Questions. John Murray Publishers 2018.
271. Irfan Habib. Religion in Indian History. New Delhi. Tulika Books.
272. Bibek Debroy, Dipavali Debroy. The Holy Vedas. B.R Publishing Corporation 2018.
273. Eric Hobsbawm. On History. UK Abacus 1998.
274. Isaac Newton. The Principia: Mathematical Principles of Natural Philosophy. Snowbell Publishing 2010.
275. Ahmad Raza Khan (Barelvi). Kanz-Ul-Iman. (Translation Of The Quran. New Delhi. Hafeez Book Depot.
276. Abdul Rahman Kailani. Tayasur Al Quran. New Delhi. Farid Book Depot 2008.
277. Muhammad Muhsin Khan, Taqi-Ud-Din. Interpretation Of The Meanings Of The Noble Quran. New Delhi. Darussalam Publication.
278. Imam Muslim. Sahih Muslim (English). 4 Volumes. New Delhi. Islamic Book Service 2012.
279. Muhammad Idrees Kandhalvi. Maarif-Ul-Quran (8 Volumes) Urdu. Farid Book Depot 2012.
280. Imam Jalal-Ud-Din Shafi, Jalal-Ud-Din Suyuti. Tafsir-al-Jalalayn, Urdu (7 Volumes). New Delhi. Farooqia Book Depot 2014.
281. Salahuddin Yousuf. Tafsir Ahsanul Bayan, Urdu. New Delhi. Islamic Book Service 2002.
282. Richard N Haass. The World: A Brief Introduction. New York. Penguin 2020.
283. Adam Rutherford. The Book of Humans: A Brief History of Culture, Sex, War and the Evolution of Us. UK Weidenfeld & Nicolson 2018.

www.ingramcontent.com/pod-product-compliance
Lightning Source LLC
LaVergne TN
LVHW091247150826
845673LV00006B/1348